GRAND HOTELS

GRAND HOTELS

REALITY & ILLUSION

An Architectural and Social History

Elaine Denby

REAKTION BOOKS

In affectionate memory of my parents,
who opened the first grand hotel door
for me at an early age.

Published by Reaktion Books Ltd
11 Rathbone Place, London W1P 1DE, UK

First published 1998

Designed by Ray Carpenter
Photoset by Tom Knott
Printed and bound in The Netherlands by
Waanders, Zwolle

British Library Cataloguing in Publication Data:
Denby, Elaine
    Grand hotels : reality and illusion : an architectural and
    social history
    1. Hotels – History 2. Hotels – Design and construction –
    History
    I. Title
    728.5'09

ISBN 1 86189 010 9

ILLUSTRATION ON PAGE SIX: Santiago de Compostela, Hotel de
los Reyes Católicos, founded by Queen Isabella and King Ferdinand
as a hostel for pilgrims in 1499, designed by Enrique de Egas.

PHOTOGRAPHIC ACKNOWLEDGEMENTS In a substantial majority
of cases, picture material and/or permission to reproduce it has been
provided by individual hotels or hotel chains, for which generous
assistance both author and publishers are most grateful. It would be
unduly repetitive to credit individually each hotel or chain, as earlier
acknowledgements made at the beginning of the book include these
contributions, which form such an integral and indispensable part of
the whole.

Clarke Andreae p. 39; the author pp. 20, 27, 28 bottom, 31, 51 lower left,
61 bottom, 74 bottom, 75 top, 79, 89 top, 117, 120 bottom, 146 bottom left,
150 top right, 245, 246 bottom, 247 top right, 263, 275 top, 280 bottom
left; Pascal Boissel p. 80; Carl Bomers p. 17 middle- and bottom-left;
City of Bristol Museum & Art Gallery p. 47, left; Oliver Carter Collec-
tion pp. 46, 47 right, 51 top right, 53, 63, 65, 69, 70 bottom, 71; Thomas
Cook p. 185 top; Andrew Dow Collection p. 56, left; Florida State
Archives, Tallahassee pp. 228 top, 229; Halpern Partnership p. 61 top;
Hastings Museum & Art Gallery p. 28 top; Hillsborough Public Library,
Tampa, Florida p. 228 bottom; Robert Holmes p. 230 top left; Peter
McCormack p. 70 top; National Archives Singapore p. 205 top left;
Norfolk County Council Library p.19 top; Gordon Patterson pp. 10, 15,
246 top right, 247 top left and bottom right; Philipson Studios p. 71;
Raffles Hotel Collection p. 205 middle left and right; Royal Commission
on the Historical Monuments of England (National Monuments Record
Office) pp. 50, 52, 57, 66 bottom left, 73, 78, 146 top, 146 bottom, 155 top,
240 top right, 243 bottom; Comune di Salsomaggiore Terme pp. 271, 272;
Société des Bains de Mer/Coiron pp. 90 top, 91 top; SBM/Lacroix
pp. 90 bottom, 156 top, 157; SBM/Loli pp. 91 bottom, 156 bottom;
Science and Society Picture Library p. 244 top; Ritz Hotels p. 237;
Azar Soheil Jokilehto p. 13, Donald Southern pp. 55, 89 bottom, 155
bottom right; University of Melbourne p. 173 top left; and Bertil Wöllner
p. 106.

CONTENTS

HOTEL

HOSTAL
DE LOS
REYES CATOLICOS

In gathering information and illustrative material from a wide field I have received help from too many sources to be listed fully here, but my personal thanks have, I trust, reached most of those whose time and interest have been involved. Public reference libraries have upheld their best traditions, with the Royal Borough of Kensington and Chelsea heading the list. Others whose care and patience have helped to lighten tasks which sometimes seemed fruitless were those in Brighton, Cheltenham, Cleveland and Norwich. The Museums and Art Galleries in Bristol and Hastings must be added, together with more specialized institutions – the Royal Commission on the Historical Monuments of England, the British Architectural Library at the RIBA, and the Science Museum's Science and Society Picture Library. Overseas help came from Tampa-Hillsborough County Public Library, Florida State Archive, Saratoga Historical Society, the Office de Tourisme in Aix-les-Bains, France, and the tourist office of Salsomaggiore Terme, Italy.

Organizations linked directly with the hotel and travel industry provided not only many illustrations but also information and publications of historical value. Hotels Alexandre de Almeida, Thomas Cook and Sons Ltd, Concorde Hotels, Forte Hotels, Inter-Continental Hotels, ITT Sheraton (including CIGA), Société des Bains de Mer, Monte Carlo, the Oberoi Group, Steigenberger Hotels and The Taj Group of Hotels all supplied very useful material, and special thanks go to Lisa Bovio, Jackie Butcher, Jacques Courivaud, Genevieve Frieh, Gabriella Gonzaga, Tamara Jenewein, Jill Lomer, Riichi Matsumoto, Sudha Narayan, Giuliano Saccani, Bernadette Tosello and Christine Tronstad.

In the hotel management world, the short list of special mentions starts in Switzerland with Michel Rey of the Baur au Lac and the management of the Dolder Grand, both these hotels being in Zürich. Helen Jacob showed me the Suvretta House, St Moritz, in great detail, from attics down to the solid rock in which the cellars are formed. France is represented by Michel Palmer, manager of the Negresco, Nice, and in Paris by Pascal Boissel, distinguished hotel historian who introduced me to the Second Empire *Salle des Fêtes* in the Grand Hotel Inter-Continental.

R. J. Pearce at the Adelphi, Liverpool; Brian Shanahan and Giles Shaw at the Queen's, Cheltenham; Mr and Mrs F. Cridlan at the Regent, Leamington Spa, all recounted or provided histories of their long-lived English hotels. Giuseppe Spinelli at the Hotel and Villa Serbelloni, Bellagio, and Gianni Boccardo and Livia Bartolini of the Royal, Sanremo, Italy, embody the essence of hospitable management. In two Madrid hotels I was conducted on thorough and memorable inspections backed up by excellent information from Mariola de Calderón at the Ritz and Juan J. Bergés at the Palace.

Hotels reaching grand old ages of 75–100 years published commemorative histories of their evolution, almost all concentrating on their social functions and some adding studies of their design and building. From such volumes, generously given, I have benefited greatly. These include the following: the Balmoral and Caledonian Hotels, Edinburgh; the Langham and Savoy, London; the Metropole, Brussels; the Palace Hotels in Madrid and St Moritz; the Alfonso XIII, Seville; the Gellért, Budapest; the Grandhotel Pupp, Karlovy Vary; and the Bristol, Warsaw. From a greater distance the book list includes Reid's, Madeira; the Grand, Calcutta; the Bela Vista, Macau; the Imperial, Tokyo (the FLW building); the Mount Nelson, Cape Town; the Windsor, Melbourne; and the Greenbrier, West Virginia.

Across the Atlantic, acknowledgement is due to Barbara Heimlich at the Banff Springs Hotel, Alberta, Canada; to JoAnn K. Bongiorno at the Drake, Chicago; and to Ann McCracken at the Willard, Washington, D.C. As historians, David de Giustino for the Grand, Mackinac Island, Michigan, and Art Bagley at the Kelce Library, University of Tampa, Florida, for details of the Moorish building which started life as the Tampa Bay Hotel, both deserve thanks. Sian Griffiths at the Peninsula, Hong Kong, supplied me with many illustrations and thanks are due to Gretchen Liu, Curator of the Raffles Hotel Collection and author of a comprehensive book on the Raffles Hotel, Singapore, which I have found to be an exemplary study and was delighted to receive.

Friends and colleagues have helped and encouraged me over the past few years and their enthusiasm has often strengthened mine. Thanks go to Roy Johnston, Gordon Thomson of the Halpern Partnership and Oliver Carter, railway hotel historian and architect, who has been very generous in contributions from his own picture collection. Donald and Honor Southern not only lent me accommodation at Menton-Garavan during my early researches, but Donald took photographs for me and Honor later pursued some Mentonnais history; Robin and Priscilla Gamble kindly offered hospitality in Madrid as, nearer home, did Elisabeth Fletcher. Mavis Bimson provided the Hôtel de Paris *vignette* from America's Rocky Mountains at Georgetown, Colorado, and Clarke Andreae found in New England and liberally gave me out-of-print books and illustrations I would not otherwise have discovered. For detailed biographies of Frederick Hervey, Bishop of Derry and Earl of Bristol, I am grateful to David Erskine. Arthur and Helen Grogan, Themy Hamilton, Evelyn Paczosa, Rutty Wadia and Doris Wasserman variously lent me books not easily obtained, recalled background scenes and improved some of my translations. Patrick Denby, my brother, gave particular help in more lengthy translations from the Spanish and I am very much indebted to Liz Sutherland, who has turned the captions, acknowledgements, bibliography and index into presentable form. On several European holidays, Gordon Patterson nobly forfeited leisure in favour of seeking and photographing particular hotels which I surreptitiously added to some of our itineraries. Throughout the book's long period of preparation, Derek Linstrum has made valuable contributions, giving me access to his extensive library and reading my script as it proceeded. His corrections and comments and our resulting valuable discussions have undoubtedly improved the finished work.

The first taste I had of a grand hotel was an overnight London stop on the way from the North of England to Mallorca by rail and sea, and it was at the Midland St Pancras Hotel. My recollections are of a vast cathedral-like building and of a bathroom where the white-tiled bath seemed to be nearer to swimming-pool than domestic size. These memories stuck, to be augmented by further ones of the Caledonian Hotel, Edinburgh, and the Hôtel de France et Choiseul, Paris. My attraction towards hotel culture was stimulated by Max Beerbohm's essay 'Ichabod' in his book *Yet Again*, which to me seemed to be a tragic tale about the collection of hotel and travel labels he had so carefully acquired on his leather hatbox, only to receive it back from the repairer stripped clean of them with 'it's glory … departed'. The loud lament was fortunately short-lived, as Beerbohm realized that he could then look forward to another ten years of hotel visiting to replace his first collection.

My own interest in visiting hotels persisted, even when I had to pay the bills myself, and has matured into this book. *Grand Hotels* endeavours to show how the evolution of a new building type depended on advances not only in building technology but also in the road and railway engineering that could deliver consumers to the point of sale. The period 1830–1930 represents the approximate life-span of the grand hotel and its particular culture. *Grande hôtellerie*, a term that is difficult to translate, has always been a precarious trade, relying heavily on individuals and dynasties whose lives were dedicated to the constant refinement of their product.

Starting with the basic requirements for early travellers, we look briefly at the caravanserais and ancient lodgings from which primitive inns and post-houses developed. A bed, clean or dirty, and a meal, good or bad, were offered in the latter, which catered primarily for transient customers. Over a long period there emerged from these categories the hotels at which people began to expect comfort and service. Once the idea of a hotel as a resting place was accepted, new technology and the awareness of the infinitely higher standards

that were attainable led to new and larger buildings able to exploit such possibilities. In this way, and with the palatial examples in front of them that the powerful and rich had created for themselves, 'grand' or 'palace' hotels came into being.

To describe the rise and fall of this special type of building I have chosen a relevant time-span from *c.* 1830, when rail transport was evolving, to *c.* 1930, when the profound social changes following the Great War of 1914–18 had reduced the demand and left many of the grand hotel buildings falling into decay. Fortunately, hotel culture continued to attract interest to an extent that has, in the post-Second World War climate of building conservation, saved many of its buildings for a new lease of life. In style, neo-classicism had been their architectural inspiration throughout almost the whole period. Many variations can be seen in the form of structural and decorative elements, but the arrangement of columns with bases and capitals, plinths, entablatures, architraves, friezes, cornices and pediments in accordance with the classical Orders of Architecture dominated most types of substantial buildings in the period. A few neo-Gothic hotels were built in England, some Scottish Baronial north of the Border, with counterparts in other countries, for example Canada and Switzerland. Much Art Nouveau design was used for interiors and exterior ornamentation for about ten years around 1900, widely flung from Moscow and Warsaw hotels to others in Palermo, Paris and Brussels. The Modern Movement is marginally represented, but versions of 'modernity' are characteristic more of the skyscraper hotels in Shanghai, New York and Canada rather than of the few in Europe.

The magic of grandeur and luxury, essence of our subject, required two basic components: architectural design on the one hand and practical but sensitive management on the other. Deployment of theatrical qualities was necessary in both these fields for the grand hotel to attract and maintain successfully a starry – and wealthy – clientèle to act on its stage. Appreciation of the chief participants in its turn required an audience to support each day's parade. The Theatre proper has always dealt essentially in convincing illusion as its first commodity, whereas to *hôtellerie*, the realities of comfort, food, drink and personal service took precedence. In a world both real and unreal the hotel culture of the nineteenth century evolved its own patterns of behaviour. In America these were rigidly administered from the early days of the Astor House in New York until, at the beginning of the twentieth century, intransigent ladies of impeccable social standing selected Louis Sherry's restaurant for the breaking of taboos. They achieved this in ways that the management considered scandalous but found difficult to prevent. Unaccompanied females (unaccompanied, that is, by men) – women who smoked in public and respectable ladies whose dress revealed even a modest degree of *décolletage* – all broke the approved codes, but the time for these freedoms was ripe and hotel culture quickly recognized the need for their acceptance. The public background that the grand hotels provided was thus a paradoxical element, giving opportunity for changes leading ultimately towards decline in formality and splendour.

Smooth continuity is not manifest in the history of grand hotels, which, as servants to many capricious influences, defy straightforward classification. Sometimes the siting of an individual hotel could offer a monopoly of particular amenities or panoramic views as relatively permanent sources of delight. More frequently, during boom years, a change of fashion in society or of transport systems could soon reduce the popularity of any but the most zealously run establishments. Apparently irrelevant happenings in the form of historic commemorations or international exhibitions could prompt development for a single occasion but might leave in its wake a great asset in the form of a fine hotel for the capital or other city. Vienna, with the Imperial at the time of the International Exhibition of 1873, gained welcome accommodation; Athens at the revival of the ancient Olympic Games in 1896 substantially increased its prestige as a capital with the Grande Bretagne and Seville, where, with the King as its patron, the Alfonso XIII was proudly opened in 1928 by him for the Ibero-American Exhibition. All these benefited their communities and countries culturally and commercially, as they continue to do.

Hotel visiting can be an addictive occupation and, once enchanted by its spells, the victim will not easily escape, and life without grand hotels will seem dull. I have tried to put together a representative picture of a many-sided subject and to evoke something of past glories and enjoyments, making a great deal of pleasure for myself in the process. For others, I hope that the information and anecdotes in the following pages will inform the student and enthusiast, inspire interest in the hesitant, and gratify many hoteliers.

I.
ORIGINS

Trade and Travel

Rapid movement over great distances is taken so much for granted as part of present-day life that it is as well to remind ourselves just how recently this has come about and for how long the conception of a day's journey was tied to direct physical propulsion by man or animal. Short sketches of transport, trade and travel in their early evolution are therefore intended to give historical perspective, however episodic, as a backdrop for our subject. The story is full of contrasts and similarities between the centuries and takes its momentum from world history, characterized by numerous stops and starts, periods of regression and ages of discovery.

Early civilization arising in about the third millennium BC in the Middle East gradually became able to produce a food surplus from irrigated fields in the flood plains of the great river valleys of the Tigris and Euphrates. The very nature of this agriculture had required communal efforts and organization beyond the individual, laying foundations for social systems that had commodities to spare and could devise tax structures to support the growth of cities. Cultivation and yield could be extended by the development of the plough and the emergence of metal-working techniques, resulting in larger surpluses which could be traded for raw materials and exotic products. Ancient Mesopotamia for a time used barley grain as a trading currency, to be superseded by silver bars. By 1800–1700 BC cuneiform writing was in use and recorded on durable clay tablets the remarkably advanced systems of law and business used in Babylon at that time. The Sumerians and Akkadians had already shaped mathematics and astronomy as well as measuring the seasons to provide a calendar. Against this background of growing knowledge, wars were fought, dynasties, boundaries and rulers changed,

but the need to maintain and protect the routes which had gradually been established for the exchange or purchase of goods persisted.

Caravanserais and the Ancient World

These trade routes in the ancient world gave rise to the earliest regular needs of accommodation for travellers. Pack and saddle animals were the means of transport, and caravans, usually camels in western Asia and the arid zones where human societies were coming to birth, were formed for safety in carrying goods for long distances. Babylonian law provided for the needs of merchants in this respect and, in addition, exempted them from military service. Armies, in the ensuing ascendancies of Assyrians and Persians, often cooperated with the merchants in providing protection against robbery and in maintaining a road system suitable for wheeled vehicles which accelerated transport of goods at the same time as it produced military and policing advantage for enforcement of the imperial power. Cities flourished under a remarkable degree of self-government although local authorities were required to subscribe to central government funds.

Provision of caravanserais was made in both urban and rural situations to lodge goods and travellers safely for rest and refreshment and to function as customs posts on the transit of merchandise. The building of these establishments and the necessary catering operations for the long-distance travellers were frequently entered into as a pious duty. Few early examples have survived in spite of the long history of the great Silk Road and other Asian trade routes where methods of transport remained largely unchanged for centuries. A day's travel would be fifteen to twenty miles, necessitating many stopping places at suitable intervals. For these, mud brick would be the main building material and was subject to weather erosion even in desert conditions, but enough

Ludlow, the Feathers, a Shropshire coaching inn built in 1603, and today one of the best-known urban examples of the region's 'black and white' style.

evidence remains for us to see that consistent needs gave rise to a recognizable building type. Shelter and security were the most important requirements and were met by a square enclosure of considerable height and strength entered through a central gatehouse. The outer wall contained few apertures, but it is reasonable to suppose that the raised gatehouse provided lookout posts for security and normal observation purposes. Ranges of rooms, stores, stabling and other offices usually backed on to each external wall and were reached by way of a continuous quadrangular colonnade which was also useful in giving shade from the sun. In the central courtyard a well or cistern was a basic need although water sources were very variable in quantity and quality. In winter, altitude and cold desert nights made provision of fireplaces desirable in some areas for general heating as well as cooking. Food was not invariably supplied but must always have been prepared, either by resident personnel or by the travellers themselves, in designated spaces within the compound.

In towns or cities, caravanserais were often located near to the main gates and were manned as tax gathering points as well as for accommodation. Large caravans might take several weeks to clear these formalities and created a need for additional nearby lodgings and warehouses where trade could be pursued during these waiting periods. Standards were far from uniform and purposes of individual buildings varied with local demands. The needs of military defence and the billeting of standing armies were not always distinct from mercantile uses and royal or governmental progresses made further calls on the available lodgings.

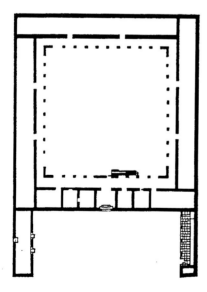

Plan of *khan* or caravanserai at Qaṣr al-Ḥayr al-Gharbī, AD 727, near Palmyra, perhaps the earliest dated example of this type of accommodation.

Ribāṭ-i Sharaf, a staging post in the time of Seljuk Sanjar, built *c.* 1124 and restored in 1154 with carved stone decoration.

An exact date can be deduced for a *khān* or caravanserai at Qaṣr al-Ḥayr al-Gharbī, 37 miles west of Palmyra, of AD 727, making this the probable earliest dated example of such a structure. The plan represents a typical courtyard layout within walls of mud brick on a stone base, with two additional wings projecting at right-angles to the entrance wall, one to the south containing a *mihrāb*, or prayer niche, and one to the north, a water-trough. The rooms surrounding the courtyard were vaulted and evidently covered by a flat roof reached from ground level by a permanent staircase. The remains of fixings in a stone lintel indicate that the Umayyad Caliph Hishām was in power at the time. Later, in eastern Persia under the Seljuk Sanjar, a staging post, Ribāṭ-i Sharaf, between Merv and Nishapur was built on a grander scale comprising outer and inner courtyards, the latter containing a mosque and accommodation suited to royal use but also likely to have been available at other times for government officers, well-known merchants and envoys on whom depended much of the country's organization and economy. While the inner courtyard also contained a central water cistern, a large chamber with finely-detailed stucco decoration, and ranges of other apartments, the outer area provided stabling and simpler facilities served by an independent water cistern. Defence was not a first consideration in these instances although space would have allowed for a sizeable military presence in emergency. Ribāṭ-i Sharaf was restored in 1154, according to a royal inscription, and was probably built 30 years or so before this. Its quality of decoration indicates unusually high standards, and undoubtedly, when furnished with rugs, cushions and hangings, it fulfilled more than adequately the role of temporary palace for the ruler Sanjar on his journeys.

Isfahan, Abbâssi Hotel courtyard, a recent photograph of this hotel which was originally a caravanserai from the early eighteenth century.

Subsequent Mongolian conquests diminished the importance of this particular route but other 'Sultan Hans' of a high standard were built further west in central Anatolia in the first half of the thirteenth century. These were characterized by large vaulted halls suggesting audience chambers, again decorated with fine carving, all built in stone and with the central building complex being surrounded by an outer walled courtyard. The Karatay Han and the Aksaray Han represent royal caravanserais in this category but less elaborate intermediate staging posts would have served the bulk of the regular traffic. The Karatay Han, known as the Emir's caravanserai and first described in AD 1276–7, was a charitable foundation providing free supply of food, bath facilities, medical aid and blacksmithing except when the sultan was in residence. The caravanserai attached to the Madrassa Madir-I-Shah, Isfahan, in recent times became part of the Shah Abbâssi Hotel.

Looking eastwards in the last decade of the century, we find Marco Polo at the court of Kublai, the Great Khan of all the Tartars, in Khan-balik (Beijing) as a trusted messenger and representative of the Khan. His many journeys in this capacity and his lively observation produced an excellent picture of the state of communications and the amenities which

Isfahan, Abbâssi Hotel, the courtyard, dome and minaret are part of the Madrasseh of Châhâr-Bâgh (Madar-e Shâh, the Shah's Mother) which still has its original function. The hotel is a recent construction incorporating the eighteenth-century caravanserai.

the Khan's envoys might expect, though perhaps some allowance should be made for exaggeration:

Many roads lead out of Khan-balik towards different provinces; each road bears the name of the province to which it goes. Kublai Khan has seen to it that his envoys are supplied with everything they need when they ride along these roads.

This particular service is organized in the most amazing fashion. Every twenty-five miles there is a beautiful, palatial post house where the messengers can stay in magnificent beds with silk sheets and every other luxury suitable for a king. There are always 400 well-kept horses ready, which are supplied and fed by nearby towns. There are more than 10,000 such palaces, all beautifully furnished, and more than 200,000 horses in all. It is hard to imagine so grandiose an organization – the only one of its kind.

Travellers can even find post houses in the wilder parts of the empire, for Kublai Khan has had them built there and has himself supplied them with horses and harness. However, there may be as many as forty miles between them. The Great Khan sends people to cultivate the land around these post houses and as a result villages develop. In this way Kublai Khan's messengers can travel in any direction, always finding lodgings and a change of horse.[1]

The Khan also had a system of unmounted couriers, wearing belts hung with bells to announce their approach, and each running three miles at great speed before passing on their messages to the next relay. An even faster system of relay horsemen was created for emergency news-bearing, allegedly able to cover 200 to 250 miles a day at full gallop.

Merchants from all over the world travelled to Beijing for the silks, cloth of gold, spices, pearls and jewels, and were housed in the outskirts of the city, each nationality having its own lodging-house, and Lombards, Germans and French being specifically mentioned. Trading ships as well as overland caravans plied the various alternative eastern routes with exotic products as cargo. Those who owned or organized the entrepots levied tax at every opportunity, and there is little wonder that, at their final destination, the goods had become precious luxuries.

Europe meanwhile had already from 500 BC onwards reached high levels of civilization, first under Greek influence, subsequently in a modified and widely diffused Hellenistic form and later still to be superseded in the early centuries of the Christian era by the Roman empire. These changes had had only limited effect on patterns of travel in the Middle East and beyond, but began a great transformation westwards around the shores of the Mediterranean and north to Britain and the Danube basin. The extraordinary practical efficiency and powers of organization in which the Romans excelled enabled them to leave imprints, still existing, in the form of public buildings, private dwellings, temples, aqueducts, bridges and road systems.

Standards of living for well-to-do Romans provided a degree of sophisticated comfort which, after the final decline of their empire on the death of Justinian in AD 565, was not again recovered for many centuries.

In spite of this, there is unexpectedly little in the way of staging-post accommodation to compare with the caravanserais of Asia, but the milder climate and more frequent settlements made such provision less vital. Roads were superbly built to serve the Roman empire, which needed the best possible lines of communication, but efficiency rather than comfort was paramount and much of the traffic was official and military, with the bulk of trade within Europe limited to necessities rather than luxuries. Accommodation for travellers engaged in trade and commerce seems to have been at basic level, *tabernae* being frequently of one room only, with access directly from the street. They were not well-considered in the social scale, and inns where refreshment could be obtained also seemed suspect as likely centres of political discontent. Roman urban development incorporated very mixed uses, with baths, barracks, theatres and civic buildings being interspersed with large and small houses, tenement buildings, shops and workshops. Remains at Pompeii indicate about twenty hotels or *hospitiae* near the city gates and at Ostia there seem to have been two hotels and fourteen taverns. In Britain, Silchester, Chelmsford and Wall, on Watling Street, possessed unattributed courtyard buildings, some with groups of three rooms together, which suggest possible use as inns.

The needs of populations were, through the Dark Ages of barbarian invasion and into medieval times, of relatively straightforward character which could generally be satisfied by the farming and manufacturing systems of the area without much recourse to the old extended trade routes, although as we have seen, these did remain in use, stimulated by the rise of Islam after the death of the prophet Mohammed in AD 632.

Medieval Pilgrimages

From a short survey of early travels in the pursuit of trade, when the protection of groups of merchants made an absolute necessity of the caravanserais as secure stopping places, we take a brief look at the pilgrimages which, from the foundations of almost all religious beliefs, had become regular observances by faithful followers.

These journeys too, generated the construction of buildings for accommodation, but as motives were religious, provision was simple even if the shrines to be visited became elaborate. Islamic practice made the *hajj* to Mecca obligatory for every adult Muslim of sound mind and body to perform once in his lifetime, and many of the *hāns* mentioned above could have been put to this use. Other Muslim holy places include the Dome of the Rock in Jerusalem, mosques and mausolea at Kūfa, Mashhad, Ardebil and Samarkand.

Crusades from the west to protect the Christian holy places in the eleventh and twelfth centuries were largely military ventures into hostile lands needing highly fortified castles rather than civilian staging-posts on pilgrim routes. Jerusalem, as a focus of Christianity, Judaism and Islam, holds pride of place among centres of pilgrimage. These different religions each provided for their own communities to a considerable extent, but biblical references indicate the existence of secular inns. The spread of Christianity via Rome and the discovery of sacred relics, real or mythical, in many parts of medieval Europe led to the creation of pilgrim ways and celebratory buildings around which much of the cultural life of the times began to flourish. Santiago de Compostela in north-west Spain is perhaps the greatest of these pilgrimage centres, based according to legend on the discovery of the tomb of the Apostle St James after a vision by the hermit Pelayo in AD 813. The development of the 'Way of St James' across the north of the Iberian peninsula from the Pyrenees to Galicia formed a channel along which Christian influence flowed and came to supersede, in the *Reconquista*, Islamic rule in southern Spain. Pilgrims on this route sought security in numbers and were provided for in hostels, hospices and inns at frequent intervals. Heat, snow and rain, wolves and robbers all played their part in the experience of cleansing the soul while undoubtedly mortifying the body and religious indulgences at the end of the long, arduous journey were well-earned.

Most of the Spanish hostels or hospices of early dates have disappeared, although the Codex of Calixtus, written in the first half of the twelfth century and detailing the thirteen stages of the *camino francés* from Roncevaux to Compostela, describes this route in some detail. Rest and recuperation between stages was obviously needed and catered for in these variously named buildings spaced at irregular intervals along the route. Terminology ranges from inns to hostels, hostelries, hospitals, hospices and even hotels, all variants connoting slightly different degrees of care but a common provision of food and much-needed shelter. One of these, between Somport and Puente la Reina, the Santa Cristina Hospital, was considered by Aimérique Picaud who wrote the Codex, to be one of the three most important in the world. Other early foundations were at Leyre, where the monks still run an inn, Roncevaux itself, a much altered building, ruins at Pamplona and at Navarete, Santo Domingo de la Calzada rebuilt in the fourteenth century and now again adapted as a *parador*. Next come Villafranca de Montes de Oca and its hospital of La Reina, San Juan de

Ortega where the monastery remains as a pilgrims' staging-point and so westwards along the *camino* through Leon and then Astorga, which is recorded as having 22 hospitals in medieval times. One of the oldest hostelries, founded by Alfonso VII in the twelfth century, Santa Maria de Arbás, is off the main route on the way to Oviedo, where the shrine of San Salvador was venerated. As the Way reaches its climax in the centre of Santiago, one of the world's great architectural achievements is revealed. The medieval scene is transformed by the superimposition of Renaissance and Baroque additions to the cathedral and other major buildings. Among this amazing and magnificent collection of churches, palaces, monasteries and colleges of all periods which surround the great cathedral, the earliest Renaissance façades belong to a most important landmark in our study of travellers' accommodation. Placed close to the Gelmirez Palace at the north-west corner of the cathedral and facing south across La Plaza del Obradoiro, this is the Hotel de los Reyes Católicos. Designed by Enrique de Egas, of Flemish descent and probably the most successful early sixteenth-century architect working in Spain at the time, the building was started in 1501 and took ten years to complete. It had been founded in 1499 to

Courtyards with varied arcading and well-heads or fountains provide much-needed shade: Hotel de los Reyes Católicos.

house pilgrims on arrival at their destination and to take care of the infirm. From the start, it was destined to be a building out of the general run of pilgrim lodgings because of the royal patronage by Isabella and Ferdinand and the dramatic opportunities of the site. In form it is a large rectangle containing four courtyards and centred on a Gothic chapel. The external severity of line and strong horizontality of the main façade is expressed in the cornice and the long bracketed balconies, interrupted by the entrance portal in Plateresque style as a central vertical punctuation. In spite of the elaboration of figures set in tiered niches that terminate in a forest of pinnacles, the decorative elements are restrained between Italianate pilasters and do not destroy the balance of the elevation. The solidity of the walls, in a rich golden-coloured stone, is offset within the colonnaded courtyards by the fountains, often enhanced by the decorated ogee arches that frame interior vistas. Following the Santiago pilgrimages to this splendid culmination has carried us out of the Gothic age and into the Renaissance, and we have to leave aside numerous other shrines that drew their own devotees, few of whom would be lodged quite as handsomely.

In England, Glastonbury and Canterbury were perhaps the foremost sites that attracted pious travellers. Glastonbury retains many legends, going back to the arrival of Joseph of Arimathea in AD 60 bearing, some say, the Holy Grail which he buried, and also the Holy Thorn as his staff, which blossoms at Christmas. St Patrick and King Arthur are linked with the Abbey, which was founded *c.* AD 700. Many pilgrims found their way there over the centuries and the surviving pilgrims' hostelry dates from 1475, when its rebuilding by Abbot John de Selwood was completed. It is now known as the George and Pilgrims and is a substantial three-storey building, stone-fronted in Perpendicular style with an off-centred arched entrance gateway and a full height splayed bay window to the lefthand side. The main rooms are on the first floor, reached by a stone newel staircase, and original internal wood panelling still exists. Its association with the Abbey obviously stood it in good stead and enabled it to offer a very comfortable standard of accommodation.

Canterbury pilgrims, enshrined in English literature by Geoffrey Chaucer writing at the end of the fourteenth century, are brought miraculously to life for us by his pen. In the spring, we learn, 'people long to go on pilgrimages / And pilgrims wish to seek the strange places / Of far-off saints, hallowed in sundry lands'. His own fictional group prepare for their journey from London to Canterbury from the Tabard in Southwark, where 'The rooms and stables of the inn were wide / They made us easy, all was of the best'. Co-erced by the hospitable innkeeper, each undertook to tell tales to shorten the long hours on horseback. From one character in particular there seemed every likelihood of entertainment – the Wife of Bath:

She had thrice been to Jerusalem
Seen many strange rivers and passed over them
She'd been to Rome and also to Boulogne
In Galicia at St James, and Cologne.

Quite a tourist!

Chaucer himself was familiar with the problems of travel, having held responsibility for maintaining walls, ditches, sewers and bridges in the Greenwich area, and subsequently having visited Genoa in 1372 and Milan in 1378. The visit to Genoa was undertaken just 74 years after Marco Polo – when in prison there – had dictated the story of the travels in Asia he claimed to have made.

Discoveries and Social Change

Whereas there was relative integration of cultural style in western Europe during the thirteenth and early part of the fourteenth century, and commercial enterprise increased with the benefit of comparatively low-cost coastal and inland waterway trade, the political scene was complex and subject to changing philosophical thought and values. Feudal society was breaking up in England, and greater freedom of movement became possible when working people were no longer tied to the land. In spite of wars in France and battles between the houses of York and Lancaster at home in England, education spread beyond the religious foundations through new-founded grammar and 'public' schools, boosted by Caxton's printing activities, enabling knowledge and ideas to reach more and more individuals.

Overseas, the great European voyages of oceanic exploration began to set out from Portugal and Genoa, the Italian Renaissance reached its apogee in Leonardo da Vinci, and Luther, in Germany, set in train the great debate of the Reformation. These historic events conveniently pivot about the half-millennium of 1500 and mark one of the major steps in the development of Western civilization, but no accompanying transformation of the means of overland travel occurred. Roads for foot and horse traffic were little better than they had been for the previous one thousand years, although there were more of them and the urge to travel had received stimulus from pilgrims' tales. Vehicles were being built with some improved comfort and weather protection, but the rough roads and bad weather could easily damage both vehicles and horses, not to mention passengers,

Grantham, the Angel (now called the Angel and Royal); a fine medieval inn on the Great North Road claims to be the oldest in England, once housing Richard III.

Grantham, the Angel, with ribbed ornamental stonework of unusual quality for a fifteenth-century inn.

and highway robbery was an ever-present hazard. In England, the advent of the Tudors did bring a greater degree of order to the country at large, and trade with northern Europe and the Mediterranean countries was expanded. Woollen cloth from London reached the markets of Venice and Pisa and enriched merchants in East Anglia, the Cotswolds and other centres where its manufacture sustained the local economies.

Inns and Innkeeping

The stone-built Angel and Royal (originally the Angel) at Grantham on the old Great North Road lays claim to being England's oldest inn. It had certainly been distinguished enough at the end of the fifteenth century for Richard III to sign and seal the Duke of Buckingham's death warrant there in preference to the castle. Dating from this period is the near-symmetrical two-storey façade with a carriage arch flanked on each side by stepped buttresses and full height bay-window features. It is built in ashlar, of local oolithic stone, and decorated with well-cut hood moulds over the windows terminating in carved animal-head corbels. An oriel window surmounts the central archway, splayed to match the flanking bays but, unlike them, supported on a curved corbelled sill above the central figure of a carved angel. This was formerly gilded and skilfully integrates the carriage arch with the remainder of the rectangular composition.

Internally, the first-floor solar that housed the King in 1483 occupied the whole of the frontage. Stone twin-panel vaulting to the ceilings of the projecting bays are another rare survival in this exceptional building where we can discern

Norton St Philip, the George, once owned by a Carthusian order. The timber framing surmounts a medieval stone ground floor, rebuilt after a fire to house bales of wool.

a foretaste of almost classical feeling, entirely absent from the contemporary Glastonbury example, the George and Pilgrims, and to which the title of 'Maison du Roi' can truly be applied.

At Norton St Philip, Somerset, another unusual three-storey medieval building, the George Inn, remains. Ground floor and flank wall are in stone, again with more or less central arched entrance and, to the left, two stone bays with Perpendicular cusped windows. The main upper floors were originally also stone-built, but as a result of fire damage were rebuilt in the fifteenth century or early sixteenth and are now timber framed, the first floor oversailing to the extent of the lower bays and with three timber bracketed oriel windows that give distinctive character to the whole. Above the hostelry accommodation on the first floor there are no corresponding windows in the front of the building, only timber framing and plain panels to the second floor, which was used as a wool warehouse. The Carthusian Priory of Hinton owned the inn and manor and was closely involved in local affairs to the extent of accommodating not only the annual wool fair but also the weekly markets from the days of Edward I. Until the fall of Cardinal Wolsey and the Dissolution of the Monasteries in the 1530s, strong Church influence permeated travel and lodging. Although there were increasingly well-furnished rooms in the larger Church-owned inns and guest-houses for prestigious visitors, rush-strewn flea-infested floors on which straw pallets might still be laid had often to suffice for the lower grades of traveller. With luck the pallet might be made with a raised edge to keep out draughts, and a straw bolster offered instead of a primitive wooden log as pillow.

Oundle, Northamptonshire, the Talbot, typical of the stylish stone-built Tudor coaching inns, a number of which are still in use.

To replace monastic traditions, a system of local road surveyors was set up under the 1555 Highways Act, but this did not work either fairly or satisfactorily and the state not only of roads and bridges but also of guest-houses and hospices was deteriorating. Fortunately, the growth of a more sophisticated commerce helped to arrest the decline, and there was a demand for a better type of accommodation towards the end of the century. Matters again improved and travellers could hope, on the main highways, for food and lodging in well-found inns. The landlord, 'mine host', would often dine with his guests in the main parlour while his wife and family prepared food in the screened-off kitchen at the rear, with beer, wine and spirits being kept in vaulted cellars below. Separate large rooms were available in a number of the bigger inns, and the uses to which they were put varied from hearings by the justices and military recruitment to bear-dancing or cock-fighting. Fires burned in large open hearths and, at some additional cost, in bedchambers. Logs would be the usual fuel, but in London and towns accessible from east coast ports, sea-coal shipped south from Newcastle was in use. Town inns might have two galleried bedroom wings at the back of the building, reached through the main carriage arch and providing an ideal courtyard setting for the travelling entertainments of the time. Probably there would also be a second rear courtyard containing stabling, coach housing and other offices. Many of the old City of London galleried inns organized a one-way system for the wagons or coaches by providing some sort of service road at the back of the stables. County towns needed similar coaching facilities, and the New Inn, Gloucester, fulfilled all such needs, although when first built c. 1457 it had predated the real coach traffic.

The seventeenth century was a time when, under the Stuarts, social change was slow in England, though overseas enterprises in North America laid the foundations for the subsequent opening up of the New World. Inheriting the older pattern, the early part of the century at its best is represented by three excellent examples of the well-developed coaching inn, sited on main roads when they were built and still taking their places as fine stone buildings: the Lygon Arms at Broadway, the Haycock at Wansford and the Bell at Stilton, bearing a certain resemblance to each other by virtue of the Cotswold and related freestone of which they were all built. In a different idiom and from the mid-century is a no less impressive brick-built structure, the White Hart at Scole in Norfolk, built in 1655 by John Peck, a Norwich merchant. Its present row of five steep Dutch gables alternately crowned with triangular and segmental pediments is striking enough, but the effect must have been startling when

THE WHITE HART INN AT SCOALE NORFOLK.

Scole, Norfolk, the White Hart Inn, built in 1655, when the elaborate carved oak sign spanned the road. Made by John Fairchild, a village carpenter, the figures of Diana and Actæon crowned the lintel and it was described by a Norwich doctor of the time as the 'Noblest Sighnepost in England'. It disappeared in the mid-eighteenth century, but the inn remains substantially unchanged.

prefaced by a fantastically carved timber sign spanning the road and depicting, among a welter of scrolls, figures, pendant pilasters and cornice, the tale of Diana and Actæon.

Civil war, plague and conflagrations were not conducive to building development except where, as in London, following the Great Fire of 1666, rebuilding after the extensive damage did take place. Legislation in the form of Building Acts in 1707 and 1709 controlled in London various aspects of materials and design with the aim of reducing future fire risk. Timber cornices under the eaves were prohibited and stone, brick or, later, stucco were to be substituted, to be surmounted by a solid parapet wall of similar material so that

Ludlow, the Feathers, a timber construction dating from the early 1600s contrasts with the greater restraint of contemporary stone façades, but is similar in scale and basic disposition of rooms. Jacobean plasterwork using strapwork, vines, thistles and roses ornaments the interior.

potential spread of flame could be checked. Sash windows were to be recessed from the face of the external walls for the same reason. Here already was a recipe for the typical Georgian brick façade that was adopted in all parts of the country except where local building stone was more easily available. New inns followed the fashion and many old ones were refaced to bring them up to date for the increasing number of travellers making frequent use of the main coaching routes. Design was simpler than it had been, relieved perhaps by traditional bay windows and by classical doorways or pediments. The White Horse at Eaton Socon, Cambridgeshire, is a well-known example, which may have been the original for the description by Tobias Smollett in his novel *Sir Launcelot Greaves* (1760–62) of an inn kitchen of the time:

paved with red bricks, remarkably clean, furnished with three or four Windsor chairs, adorned with shining plates of pewter, and copper saucepans nicely scoured that even dazzled the eyes of the beholder; while a cheerful fire of sea-coal blazed in the chimney.

This was further mentioned as being the only room for entertainment in the house.

By contrast, the much-quoted comments of the Hon. John Byng, later 5th Viscount Torrington, let fly at the state of the inns in England between 1781 and 1794:

The imposition in travelling is abominable; the innkeepers are insolent, the hostlers are sulky, the chambermaids are pert, and the waiters are impertinent; the meat is tough, the wine is foul, the beer is hard, the sheets are wet, the linen is dirty and the knives are never cleaned!!

Byng elaborates in the same vein, but he does manage to find at the White Hart in Broadway a 'delicious loyn of veal … and had then a superabundant temptation by an apricot tart'.[2]

Mobility, Comfort and the Grand Tour

Towards the end of the eighteenth century there were extremes of comment on the joys and trials of travel and innkeeping in England. A great number of favourite stopping places housed behind good stone or brick fronts could be found, such as the George at Grantham, the Rutland Arms, Newmarket, the George, West Wycombe, and elsewhere along the length of the main roads whether in hamlet or high street. Travel by coach had by this time been long established in the rest of western Europe and conditions in northern countries could compare favourably in many respects with France and England. Until the end of the sixteenth century,

Shrewsbury, the Lion, dating from the late 1770s. It seems to have adopted the name hotel at an early date. Its amenities included a library and this first-floor ballroom with an apsidal end and some elegant Adam-style plaster decoration on the walls, ceiling and small central dome.

the French and English had tended to consider it manly to ride on horseback rather than in the uncomfortable carriages or coaches then available. Elizabeth I suffered badly from bruising and discomfort in her own coach, and as a result, we assume, she was still choosing to ride a horse when she visited Norwich in 1578. Development of more comfortable vehicles was then long overdue and the solution lay in devising satisfactory springing systems. Privately-owned carriages came into wider use during the seventeenth century, and in 1668 Samuel Pepys, after long consideration, ordered a coach of which he took delivery at his office 'to my great content, it being mighty pretty'. This was sufficiently unusual an item, even for a man in Pepys's established position, to provoke the envy and jealousy of others. Coaches and carriages were status symbols everywhere, and their use was steadily spreading through the various social levels in major cities from Warsaw and Copenhagen to London and Paris. From a total of 320 public and private carriages on the streets of Paris in 1658 the figure had increased by 1763 to more than 14,000. The French aristocracy made immediate use of the greater comfort available, and Madame de Sévigné, travelling from Orléans to Les Rochers in Brittany, took her carriage by boat for part of the journey down the Loire, using it as a small private cabin. From Blois she wrote to her daughter on 9 May 1680 from the 'hôtellerie La Galère', where they had both previously stayed together, close to the river bank and where a 'thousand nightingales' could be heard.

For those using public vehicles, posting houses, stages and fresh horses – still usually six in number – could be expected on all main highways, which seem in France at this time to have been rather better maintained than those in England. Calais was the main port of entry to France for travellers from Britain, and Dessin's Hotel was well-known as the Hôtel de l'Angleterre, probably one of the largest inns in the world. Coaches could be bought there and, in 1797, Dessin's contained its own 'squares, alleys, gardens … and innumerable offices'. Contemporary with this, other foreign visitors to Paris were finding adequate accommodation for their needs. Laurence Sterne used the Hôtel de Modène in Paris and the Hôtel Cordon Bleu at Versailles and Thomas Jefferson found two different 'Hôtels d'Orléans' in Paris. Nantes, where Madame de Sévigné had earlier used hotel accommodation, provided Arthur Young with lodging at the Hôtel de Henri Quatre, of which he wrote with great enthusiasm in the 1780s. It comprised 60 bedrooms, some additional apartments and stabling for 25 horses, and Young was 'in doubt whether the Hôtel de Henri Quatre is not the finest inn in Europe'.

German states benefited from increased commerce and prosperity and inns of the seventeenth century became the hotels of succeeding years, much as in England, and the architectural historian Nikolaus Pevsner mentions some of the better-known.[3] One is the Rotes Haus in Frankfurt which had already in 1635–40 been built to an exuberantly attractive design with ground and four upper floors in a nineteen-bay façade of pedimented windows. The top two floors were contained behind three Dutch-type gables between which smaller individual dormers were interposed. In this building the coronation celebrations of the future Joseph I as Roman Emperor took place, but in 1767 it was replaced by a neo-classical building by H.J.A. Liebhart, with pedimented wings extending at the back to enclose a large courtyard garden. From a contemporary print it appears correct but unexciting, with a five-bay pediment and central balcony to the street frontage. It continued to attract royal Prussian visitors in 1716 and 1792, and after a transformation into the main post office in 1837 survived until demolition in 1900. Another vanished town hotel, the Drei Mohren at Augsburg, started as a medieval inn and was rebuilt in 1722 for the coaching trade by Ignaz Gunezrainer. Rococo in character, with fluted Corinthian pilasters and decorative window surrounds, it was planned around two courtyards and included its own chapel, a *Rittersaal* and ballroom on the main upper floor. The entrance hall and staircase were seemingly laid out on the grand scale and although kitchen and dining-rooms appear rather small by our standards, for a purpose-built hotel the accommodation would have been advanced for its time and it, too, was long-lived, existing to an age when it was able to be photographed bearing a sign 'Palast Hotel'.

Augsburg, Hotel Drei Mohren, 1722, by Ignaz Gunezrainer. Fronted by a Rococo façade, it was built around a courtyard behind which was a garden and stabling. Earlier inns on the site dated back to the fourteenth century.

Frankfurt, Rotes Haus, c. 1635–40. An early version from the seventeenth century. Subsequent rebuilding in neo-classical style followed after 1767.

Italian cities were well accustomed to catering for commerce and its attendant travel, much of it being linked to trade from overseas, including the Far East. The Venetian Republic functioned as a great entrepôt, and colonies of different nationalities were established to include inns and lodgings among the warehouses of the city. Shared rooms or dormitories were commonplace, but better accommodation for rich merchants, nobility and gentry was usually available at a price. People of importance travelled with elaborate retinues in earlier times, even with furniture and their own cooking resources. A great deal more forethought in preparing the commissariat was needed when large parties of travellers and servants were on the move and sources of supply were likely to be unreliable. Centres of pilgrimage in Italy were experienced in dealing with large-scale demands, and in Padua, the Bull (Hospitium Bovis) is recorded in 1440 as being the best inn in Italy, with large ornate stables for 200 horses and with innumerable rooms. In Rome the very large number of 1,022 inns is quoted in the fifteenth century, but one would expect that many of these were modest in size and in their standard of accommodation.

Grand Tours of the principal cities and sights of Europe were embarked on from early in the eighteenth century by young men of position as an accepted means of completing a proper education. They were accompanied by suitable tutors, many of whom, as employed by the wealthier families, carried much scholarship and distinction. Among these 'bear-leaders' were Thomas Hobbes, Joseph Addison and John Locke, who gave their fortunate young charges unrivalled opportunities to improve their minds and manners. The term 'grand tour' was originally in use as a French form, first appearing in 1748, but it soon became anglicized as the enthusiasm for travel never lay far below the surface and the conception of an extended journey of years rather than months was quickly adopted as an exercise rich in all sorts of rewards for those with the interest and means to indulge it. Many of the English and Scottish aristocracy pursued the fashion and increasingly took with them their expectations of proper travelling amenities wherever they went. Writers, architects, geologists, antiquaries and art connoisseurs accompanied their noble patrons or travelled on their own account, finding hospitality or paying for their lodgings according to their opportunities and resources. Many complaints were recorded about the quality of the so-called service, the beds, the bugs, the fleas, the cold, the dirt, the food and the people. With experience, travellers adjusted to habits which were viewed as merely un-English and they became selective in finding and encouraging inns where comfort and civility could be found. Sometimes the reported noisy and aggressive behaviour of the travellers would have given rise to offence in the reverse direction, but there was obviously a network of acceptable stopping places where good relations and hospitable welcomes awaited and where familiar visitors reappeared. At all social levels it was not uncommon for furnished houses or apartments to be taken when medium or longer-term stays were contemplated. These arrangements varied according to the visitors' retinue of staff and the amount of service the owner or landlord wished to offer. The great benefits were the degrees of freedom and privacy that could be enjoyed and the possible control over catering and housekeeping matters. In 1714 the young Richard Boyle, 3rd Earl of Burlington, took with him not only a tutor but also an accountant, three other gentlemen, an artist to draw selected buildings and finally five or six servants. The historian Edward Gibbon was told towards the end of the century that, including the servants they brought, there were 40,000 English living or travelling on the Continent of Europe.

Italy was being scoured for objects of *vertu* to enhance the classical Georgian mansions being erected in most parts of the British Isles. Pictures and sculptures both antique and new were sought after and agents were appointed in Venice, Rome and other centres for advice and to procure suitable items. To fulfil all these demands a real tourist industry developed, and with few exceptions the general level was high. The taste of the collectors was discriminating and the contents of the numberless fine houses of the time were assembled with a great deal of percipience and skill. The English country house digested all these contributions and became in itself an unparalleled work of art, having created a vast heritage of excellence and produced a way of life on which succeeding generations have endeavoured to model their own backgrounds. The influence of the country house way of life was to be felt not only in the private houses of the affluent but as a very recognizable ingredient in the development of the grand hotels.

While many Britons spent long periods living and travelling in Italy, Austria, Germany and France, few acquired such reputation as Frederick Hervey, Bishop of Derry and 4th Earl of Bristol, who, in spite of his family, his bishopric in Ireland and his Irish estates of Downhill and Ballyscullion as well as Ickworth in Suffolk, managed to spend an aggregate of more than twenty years indulging an incurable lust for travel.[4] Between 1765 and 1803 he made six extended journeys, ranging from the first which was less than a year in length to the last eleven and a half years of his life, which came to an end with his sudden death while returning from Albano to Rome. He was taken ill with an old stomach complaint and expired in 'the out-house of a cottage in consequence of the unwillingness of the peasants to admit a heretic prelate to die under their roof' in the words of Lord Cloncurry. His eccentricities of dress and behaviour had made him a well-known figure on the repeatedly trodden routes of grand tourism, and the aim of many of his travels was to collect and commission works of art for his two Irish houses and for Ickworth, which was not completed until after his death. He was a rarity as an Earl-Bishop and, with an insistence on wearing his own flamboyant interpretation of a Protestant Bishop's garb, attracted notice wherever he went, though particularly in Rome where he acquired the popular titles *Milordo Hervey* or *Milor il Vescovo*. On many of his journeys he spent some time at Bad Pyrmont, a small spa near Hanover, and also with or near Sir William and Lady Hamilton in Naples. His habit was often to send his cooks ahead with supplies 'of mutton and geese' among other things, to prepare the next inn for his reception. The Stella d'Oro, Padua, he described in 1766 as 'of the "bad but best" order' with the next day's stop at the Due Torri, Verona, ranking as a 'good inn'. La Corona, Roveredo, and L'Europa, Trento, both pass without comment on subsequent nights of his journey to Switzerland from Venice, where he had patronized L'Écu de France, favoured by distinguished visitors, including the Prince of Brunswick. In 1777 his wife was writing to their daughter Mary, Lady Erne, who herself had been staying at the Armes de France in Spa during the previous month, that they had expected to find convenience and comfort in Verona

but the innkeeper had changed for the worse and there was 'no other tolerable Hotel in the Town … Our present apartment is over ye stables, & Louisa is confin'd all day in ye stink, besides what we suffer ourselves from it'. Reminders of Lord Bristol's obsessive travelling are still present in the numerous hotels named 'Bristol' after him in various parts of Europe. Whether this eccentric man had actually stayed in them or not, the title was – and still is – taken to convey a recommendation of good quality.

Another comment on the problems of eighteenth-century travel comes in 1791 from Georgiana, Duchess of Devonshire, in Lyon and on her travels with Lady Elizabeth Foster, a daughter of the Bristols. The Duchess writes to her children in England: 'It is a very good Hotel we are in, but as a Nasty Man will not give up his room, Bess & I are oblig'd to go along an open Balcony evr'y night, & sometimes in the Rain.'[5]

Spas and Cures

Before pursuing the changing character of travel into the nineteenth century, when the single most powerful catalyst in its development, steam locomotion, was about to appear, we need to look back at a less dramatic but far older influence. This was the perpetual search for preserving health which set people on the road and materialized eventually in the spas. Although the name *spa*, after a town near Liège in Belgium, did not come into use until the middle of the sixteenth century, the quest for mineral springs which were thought to have curative properties goes back to far earlier times. Sources of water were closely observed by communities dependent on them, and even in pre-scientific days local wisdom attributed, often with reasonable accuracy, specific powers to the waters bearing elements and minerals in various strengths, combinations and temperatures. By reason of their seeming reversal of the natural order, hot springs have been noted from earliest records, occurring in all parts of the world and generally associated with volcanic activity. In pre-Roman Italy south of Siena, the Etruscans channelled hot springs that are still flowing, having apparently been in continual use for the relief of rheumatic ailments ever since their discovery. The Romans exploited medicinal waters throughout their empire, from Rome, Pompeii and Merano to Pannonia, Aix-les-Bains, Baden-Baden and Bath. Bath houses, *hammams*, were part of Middle Eastern cultures, and other suitable types of building were evolved to cater for users of the hot springs that are found in Japan, China, North America and elsewhere.

Discovery of an accessible spring or springs needed endorsement either by popular trial and error or by some kind of approved medical practitioner before it would attract visitors with faith in its powers. After this, entrepreneurial efforts were required to enable treatment to be taken and suitable lodging to be provided. Finally, if the sources came up to expectation, patients and others needed varied entertainment that would no doubt help to convince many of them that they were feeling a great deal better. Across the whole spectrum of spa culture there has obviously been great variation, but the fundamental appeal of health-seeking, sometimes with religious connotations, was able to generate consistent interest and patronage over long periods. Changes came with the growth of medical knowledge, the technical inventions affecting transport and the inevitable movements of fashion in what had become a flourishing industry.

North of the Alps the Roman town of Civitas Aurelia Aquensis (Baden) was one of the earliest spa towns and grew up around the focus of its natural hot wells. Emperor Caracalla (AD 211–17) came to sample these as a cure for his rheumatism as, at 154°F, they are probably the hottest in Europe. Caracalla, whose vast *Thermae* in Rome used heated water for bathing, evidently had a personal hand in the design of the Baden Aquæ Aureliæ also. At the highest level on the site was the imperial bath, with other separate baths at successive lower levels being provided for officers and then legionaries, as may be seen today in the preserved Römische Badruinen. The weakening of Rome resulted in barbarian destruction of the town in the Dark Ages, but from the twelfth century it became the seat of the Margraves of Baden, and by 1541 Paracelsus had become physician to the then Margrave and was propounding the God-given virtues of the 'Badin' waters, which he believed to have more strength than learned prescriptions and so to be 'more perfect than anything else'. Further destruction by Louis XIV's armies intervened, but the town was again back on the map in the eighteenth century and early nineteenth when extensive redevelopment of the Kurhaus took place. The earlier building of 1765 was superseded by a fine neo-classical design by Friedrich Weinbrenner (1766–1826). In addition to other civic buildings, several grand hotels came into existence during the same period, and building continued as Baden's popularity grew from the years of the Grand Tour through to the Belle Epoque. Some of this growth will be looked at in chapter Three, which deals in more detail with the Badischer-Hof (1807–9) and the period when Baden (the name was not doubled up until after the Great War of 1914–18) gained its reputation as the summer capital of Europe.

Another German spa that was conceived as a more in-

tegrated layout was Wiesbaden. Centred axially on the columned and pedimented Kurhaus, it grew in the years 1816–39 to designs by the architect J. Christian Zaïs (1770–1820), with the Theaterplatz to one side and several hotels balancing the composition. Zaïs was a pupil of Weinbrenner at the celebrated school of architecture maintained in the Weinbrenner house in Karlsruhe, now demolished. He was closely engaged in the Wiesbaden enterprise of the Hotel Vierjähreszeiten in 1817–18, designing the building and also providing finance and patronizing it when complete. It was known as the foremost hotel in the spa, with 140–150 bedrooms, 44 bathrooms and a memorable columned banqueting hall to seat 124 people. It was remodelled in 1881 to create a palatial background for the wealthy spa visitors but was largely destroyed in the Second World War.

Not only was Zaïs involved in the overall town-planning for the centre of Wiesbaden and in the Hotel Vierjähreszeiten, but he, together with Johann Freinsheim, acquired a suitable site on which Freinsheim built a small inn and bar in 1813. Freinsheim died six years later and his inn, which was first called the Nassauer Hof at about this time, was sold to Frederick Goetz for 20,005 guilders, soon being passed on to his nephew Karl Goetz. Accommodation was available for permanent tenants and for lodging only of more transient visitors, whose food and drink had to be brought in from other hotels or restaurants. The town's population in 1815 was 5,000, with visitors to the spa reaching a further 10,000 and causing food and shelter to be scarce. At the Kurhaus, a week's notice was often needed for booking weekend meals. In spite of this, it was not until 1830 that the Nassauer Hof was licensed to supply the necessary sustenance.

In Britain the most important Roman resort followed an early history not unlike that of Baden. This was Bath or Aquæ Sulis, which declined after the Romans left in the fifth century. The hot baths were, however, restored to use under monastic care in the twelfth century. Bath did not suffer at that stage any destruction by war, but neglect and decline did occur when religious houses were disinherited, and a drawing of 1675 by Thomas Johnson depicts the resulting state of affairs. Bathers of both sexes, some naked and some clad, are shown disporting themselves in the baths open to the sky, surrounded by spectators. The scene appears far from attractive to a potential visitor, and according to John Evelyn there was only limited organized entertainment to be had and the overpriced inns were less than adequate. Bath had to wait until the early eighteenth century for Richard 'Beau' Nash to take the Master of Ceremonies role and clean up not only the streets and bathing places but also society and its manners. The majority of visitors took lodgings, but by the end of the century two neo-classical hotels were built. The Grosvenor Hotel in Grosvenor Place by John Eveleigh (1801) was sold in an unfinished state and came into use when completed as Grosvenor College. A four-storey heavily corniced street front of stone with giant six-bay Ionic order and rusticated plinth, it originally gave carriage access to the pleasure gardens beyond, which were advertised as 'near 14 acres'. The Sydney Hotel was built in 1796 by the architect C. Harcourt Masters, probably making use of an earlier design by the City Surveyor, Thomas Baldwin. It is an admirable compact three-storey pavilion design with rusticated ground storey and five-bay pedimented entrance elevation. With attic alterations by Sir Reginald Blomfield in 1920, it is now in excellent use as the Holburne of Menstrie Museum. This hotel, too, was designed to give access to large pleasure gardens, although in neither case did the proposed comprehensive development succeed according to the promoters' expectations.

Aix-les-Bains in French Savoie is again a spa founded by the Romans as a result of the hot springs but neglected over long periods, although royal visits by Charlemagne and Henri IV are recorded. In the late eighteenth century there was a revival of interest and some building took place but it was not until after the Revolution that its real success began. Napoleon's sister Pauline came to live there in the Villa Chevalley, and subsequently the ex-Empress Joséphine did likewise. Fashionable scandals seem to have been the order of the day, masked by the avowed aim of taking the waters, and the Bonaparte family played no small part in these intrigues. The main period of hotel development in Aix did not occur until after the opening of a casino in 1849.

Brighton had to some extent emulated Bath at the end of the eighteenth century as a fashionable resort. Although it had not the advantage of hot springs, there was the sea for bathing in at a time when royalty had already, in the person of George III, taken to salt water at Weymouth. Royal connections there continued for some time, and Gloucester Lodge was built for the Duke of Gloucester's private use before being adapted as an hotel. It was built soon after 1780 in red brick in the late Georgian style, and unusually for the period was sited directly on the sea front. In Brighton itself, the Prince of Wales, later to become the Prince Regent and finally George IV, celebrated his coming-of-age by making his first visit to the resort in 1783, a journey which he repeated frequently, year in and year out for the rest of his life.

Dr Johnson, the Thrales and Fanny Burney had been regular visitors to Brighton from the mid-1780s, by which time the famous Dr Richard Russell's 'sea-water cure' was well-established, and in 1782 the brave Fanny and Mrs Thrale

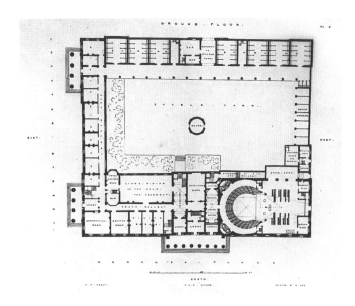

Plymouth, the Royal Hotel, Assembly Rooms and Athenaeum. Ground and first floor plans of John Foulston's 1811 competition-winning design, which was completed in 1819 (*see illustration overleaf*). The social activities of both town and hotel visitors were catered for by the provision of a theatre, a ballroom and spaces for meetings, dining, a bar and recreation.

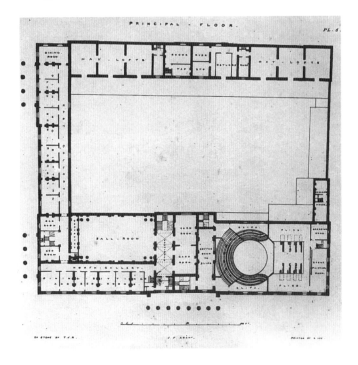

immersed themselves in the November seas for the good of their health. As Brighton's popularity increased, more accommodation was necessary and the Castle Inn (1817), the Royal York (1819), the Royal Albion (1826), the Clarence (1820–30) and the Bedford (1829) all augmented the supply. The last of these was designed by Thomas Cooper and was often known as Brighton's best hotel. With its classical

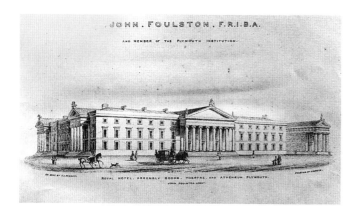

Plymouth, the Royal. The perspective displays capable neo-classical treatment, its three Ionic porticos offset by the separate Doric Athenaeum building to the right. Neither of these buildings survives.

ordered façades and impressive entrance hall, it came fully within the 'hotel' category and reminds us to take stock of the preceding 50 years of improvement in travel and lodging facilities that had received impetus from the Grand Tour participants and was bringing the coaching age towards its close.

Evolution of Hotels

Once the idea of travelling for pleasure had arrived, the differentiation between roadside inn and residential hotel began to mark the change and to be catered for accordingly. (The English use of the term 'hotel', a French contraction of 'hostel', dates from 1765 and denotes 'an inn, especially one of a superior kind'.[6]) Coaching inns and post houses, with their extensive stabling and needs for warmth and refreshment to be speedily available, posed a different set of problems from the demands of longer-stay parties or families. Hotels had no special need of early morning starts for the noisy bustling stagecoach traffic, nor did cold, thirsty and hungry passengers invade the dining-rooms and monopolize the large fires after the trials of a long day on the road. Private sitting-rooms and residents' coffee-rooms could now be expected in the hotel category, with probably a second dining-room and, where the prospects of the local social life seemed likely to be favourable, an imposing Assembly Room which it was hoped would make the fortunes of the hotel as a centre of the town's entertainments. The Lion in Shrewsbury provides one of the best and earliest examples in England of this 'county hotel' type, possessing a fine late eighteenth-century ballroom in an Adam style with saucer dome and elegant plasterwork. The Royal Clarence Hotel in Exeter was known

as 'The Hotel' when founded in 1768 by William Praed but was altered and updated in 1827. An important development in Plymouth no longer exists but, as the Royal Hotel, Theatre and Athenaeum, this was an impressive building complex, a leisure centre of its day, designed by John Foulston, a pupil of Thomas Hardwick. Foulston won the architectural competition in 1811 and building was completed in 1819. It was built around a large courtyard, some 200 × 100 feet in extent, with colonnaded stables and coach houses forming two sides of the rectangle. The main range of building for public functions was entered under a large Ionic portico on the north side, giving access to the theatre on the right and the 'Large Dining Room or Room for Assembly' together with the Commercial Room, Coffee Room and smaller dining-rooms on the left. Two smaller porticoes balanced the façade on the east side and served the hotel accommodation of 50 bedrooms, each *en suite* with dining- and sitting-rooms, on two upper floors. Regency stucco formed a background to the Greek Ionic orders of the porticoes on the main building and on the separate Doric 'Athenaeum' to the west.

Revolution in France had its effect on the hotel world, causing many refugees to flee across the English Channel from persecution, bringing their skills of catering for aristocratic tastes to augment Britain's traditional cookery and services. French influence took firm root and caused its own revolution, with French restaurants appearing and the French language being so widely used in the new hotels that it became a hallmark of stylish establishments, many terms and phrases being totally assimilated into the English vocabulary.

In the naming of English hotels, royalty featured largely, and in the period of the Regency in 1811 until the railway revolution in the 1840s, a representative list of 30 new hotels contains not only well over half with royal associations but twelve with the actual use of 'Royal' in the title, such as 'Royal Exeter' and 'Royal Bath', Bournemouth, Royals in Great Yarmouth and Ross on Wye and 'Copp's Royal' in Leamington Spa. Princess Victoria was later to become a much-travelled sovereign addicted to British and foreign hotels, and her debut in this respect was made at the age of eleven in 1831, when the first occasion of her sleeping in a public building was at the Regent in Leamington Spa, which had already been noticed by and renamed in honour of the Prince Regent twelve years before. Owing its existence in the first place to the Spa, this hotel survives in continued use, another handsome stucco building with Doric portico, built as 'The Williams' Hotel' in 1819 to the design of C. S. Smith. He had been a pupil of Jeffry Wyatt (later Wyatville), and would

Leamington Spa, the Regent, built in 1819 to the design of architect C. S. Smith. A pleasing façade with Doric-columned portico in simple neo-classical style with stuccoed finish, ornamented only by the Prince Regent's arms and crest.

therefore have been familiar with Wyatt's classical country house style, which the new hotel followed. Its accommodation, built around three sides of a courtyard, provides the usual coffee-room, sitting-rooms, bar and bar parlour and waiters' room. The original kitchen was across the open courtyard from the dining-room, and food had to be carried from one to the other in all weathers. This difficulty was overcome by a later alteration occupying the courtyard and so simplifying service. Laundry facilities were provided, with a wash-house or brew-house, probably of Victorian date, in a wing at the back of the hotel where a drying ground backed onto the mews. The two most important rooms – dining-room and drawing-room – overlooked a garden with a fountain, and were of plain but elegant design in harmony with the main divided staircase leading to the upper floors of bedrooms, originally 60 in number.

In the period before the young Princess Victoria succeeded to the throne and the railway age became a reality,

two transitional English hotels from the years 1828–9 and 1838 were leaving behind the Georgian era and adopting the greater levels of comfort available by way of new manufacturing products. The first of these was a forward-looking enterprise on the south coast, a comprehensive seaside development on the western edge of Hastings in Sussex by the Burton family of London builders. James Burton (1761–1837), a Scotsman, had built on the Foundling and Bedford Estates in London's Bloomsbury before cooperating with John Nash in the building of Waterloo Place, Regent Street and the Regent's Park terraces. His next ambition was to create a 'Regent's Park by the Sea', and with the aid of his tenth son Decimus, whom Nash had helped in his architectural career, a Regency-style 'Burton's St Leonards' was designed. This was to front the sea for well over half a mile, and at the centre St Leonard's Hotel provided a fine pedimented focal point with double arched entrances and two tiers of giant Corinthian order. A gala opening in 1829 with fireworks and a great bonfire of blazing tar-tubs was preceded by a banquet where 'two hundred of the great men of the district and their ladies sat down'.[7] Social success continued as the small resort took shape, and the Duchess of Kent with her fifteen-year-old daughter, Princess Victoria, came to stay in 1834, setting a precedent for other royalties. After Victoria's accession to the throne the hotel became, with permission, the Royal Victoria Hotel. Interior remodelling was carried out in 1903 and a Grade II listing more recently has encouraged careful restoration in the 1980s. Inconsequentially, near to the site of the gala bonfire there is now a large flat-topped stone bearing on a plaque the following cryptic words:

Tradition says that William the Conqueror landed at Bulverhythe and dined on this stone.

The other transitional building that survives as part of the street scene and is also unusually widely documented by local archives is in Cheltenham. Its history down to the present day gives a good perspective of the way in which an early grand hotel could, with skill, care and some good fortune, be usefully preserved. The town may not have acquired the title 'Royal' as did Leamington Spa, although George III and his family paid it a visit in 1788, increasing its popularity by his presence. There was none the less a lasting benefit as the need was underlined for more comfortable accommodation. Private visits to friends with country estates could not answer the demand, nor could the available lodging houses. The new conception of the hotel as a respectable alternative took some time to mature while Georgian building was creating an elegant urban scene among the springs and spas. A large house in Crescent Place was used as the Clarence Hotel,

Burton's St Leonard's, Royal Victoria, 1829, formed part of an ambitious urban development facing the sea near Hastings. David Roberts's watercolour conveys well the neo-classical conception enjoyed by Princess Victoria in 1834.

James and Decimus Burton's original designs for their hotel suffered various additions, but the essential character has not been destroyed.

named after a stay by the Duchess of Clarence (the future Queen Adelaide), until becoming the police station in 1859. Local enterprise had in the meantime been at work, announcing in 1834 that a new hotel would be built at the south end of the Promenade. This would necessitate the dismantling of the Imperial Pump Room then occupying the site and its subsequent rebuilding lower down the Promenade where Royscot House now stands. Preliminary negotiations and the formation of a joint stock company to raise capital took two or three years during which the short reign of William IV came to an end and Princess Victoria became Queen. The new hotel was named for Queen Victoria, and no other hotel in the early Victorian years was to be more of a landmark in showing the style and improved standards which could be achieved. It was heralded locally in the *Cheltenham Looker-On* for the opening day as

One of the noblest buildings of its kind in Europe ... Situated at the end of one of the finest carriage drives in this or, perhaps, in any other country ... commanding consequently the most

Cheltenham, Queen's Hotel, 1838. With this handsome building the concept of the hotel as comfortable lodging acquired its first overlay of grandeur and provided an example for large hotels to come. This work of Robert William Jearrad and his brother Charles became a landmark in Cheltenham's architectural scene.

extensive picturesque views – in the immediate vicinity of the principal Spas, and in the very centre of gaiety and fashionable attraction.[8]

The date was 21 July 1838, and press coverage both then and in the following years bears further quotation, showing contemporary attitudes towards Cheltenham's new asset, which was leading the way in grand hotel development.

The architects were Charles and Robert William Jearrad, referred to as 'from London' although the brothers made many contributions to the town's architecture, as a press cutting of 10 May 1830 shows:

The whole of the Montpellier property belonging to P. Thompson Esq. has been let to the Messrs Jearrad, gentlemen of great opulence, and well known in the metropolis; and will henceforth be conducted under their superintendence.

Much of the Lansdown estate, Christ Church in Malvern Road and a fine Literary and Philosophic Institution with excellent Doric portico (now demolished) were all to their credit. In the design of the new Queen's Hotel, Pevsner divined similarity with the classicism of St Petersburg. Bryan Little found kinship with Palladian models – by Leoni or John Wood the elder of Bath. Wherever the Jearrads might have looked for their inspiration, a distinguished pedimented façade with full Corinthian dress, five engaged columns on each side of the projecting hexastyle portico, could be envied by any proud city or hotel owner. The *Looker-On* for 21 July 1838 celebrated

R. W. Jearrad Esq., a gentleman who has contributed more to the architectural adornment of Cheltenham town than any other person, living or dead, and who, by this recent effort of

his creative genius, has added greatly to his reputation, and entitled himself to the best thanks of all who wish well the prosperity and fair fame of the place.

A lengthy description of the interior indicates that no basic alterations have occurred in the public rooms apart from some changed usage. One can see the Lounge and Bar to the left of the main entrance, the Coffee Room (or restaurant) to the right and the central Foyer, Lounge and Staircase occupying the remainder of the main block on the ground floor. A further rear section to the west, facing the road to Montpellier Spa, was known as the Boarding House and Table d'Hôte. It was arranged to be entered separately from the main section of the hotel as a quieter area away from the public rooms, although it did have ladies' and gentlemen's dining- and sitting-rooms with apartments capable of use individually or as suites.

On the main first floor, the large northwest corner room with carved marble fireplaces and gilt looking-glasses was well-suited to important occasions, and further adaptability of other sitting-rooms could accommodate varying degrees of grandeur:

By a simple contrivance, the six sitting and two other bed rooms, constituting the eastern portion of the series, may be completely separated from communication with the other parts of the hotel, having the rooms of this suite opening into one another, or into a passage admissible only to the members of the particular family

Cheltenham, Queen's Hotel. The elegant staircase is supported by slender ironwork that was probably added at an early stage.

that may be in occupation of the group, and thus enjoying at the same time the quiet and retirement of a private dwelling with all the superior advantages and accommodations of a first-rate hotel.

The simple contrivance referred to was no doubt the same as used for

four other handsome sitting rooms, which may be thrown into display, or effectively separated by the introduction of moveable blank doors which being inserted into the framework of the real ones, completely disconnect one room from another.

Thus from the very start provision was made for a suite of royal standard which could be conjured up with little or no disturbance.

Furnishings in the middle of the century, probably inspired by the Great Exhibition of 1851, included Turkey carpets, crimson damask moreen curtains and carefully described wallpaper, 'the finest specimen in its class ever executed in England', for the drawing-room, with 'an entire length of all upon the rooms and passages of nearly 50 miles'.

References in Harper's *History of Cheltenham* (1853) tell us that the hotel was built

at a cost of upwards of £40,000, and comprises on the principal and upper floors, 70 best bed chambers, 30 servants' sleeping apartments, 16 elegant sitting rooms, richly embellished, and 2 excellent suites of apartments ... In the kitchen is a gigantic steam-boiler by Marshall, which not only supplies water for domestic uses in any part of the vast building, but also, at five minutes notice, fills a bath in any room where required, however elevated.

Carrying hot water for baths must have persisted for many years, unspecified 'lavatory and bath rooms' being advertised as an attraction in the *Cheltenham Annuaire* at the late date of 1893. Other first appearances in the same annual include room for bicycles (1900), heated corridors, electric light and motor garage (1907), lift and first-class chef (1911). The stables, of which little remains, were to the east of the hotel with gardens between. These at a later stage were encroached on for tennis courts. The main view from the hotel had been down the Promenade and over Imperial Square, which at that time was occupied by Mr Hodges' Nursery, but is now a formal garden with well-grown trees.

The fortunes of the Queen's were erratic and, after a spectacular illumination of the façade for Queen Victoria's wedding in 1840 and a grand public dinner in honour of Sir Charles Napier in 1848, it was soon put up for sale. Napier was a local resident and the town wished to mark his de-

parture on his last military campaign in India. The management of the hotel seems after this to have lost its way in attracting custom, and the noble building on which £47,000 had been spent had to be bought in at £18,000, finally selling at auction in 1852 for a mere £8,400. At this bargain price the purchaser, W. S. Davis, was able to undertake a comprehensive programme of repairs, alterations and improvements. Among the latter appeared two cannon taken at Sebastopol in the Crimean War, ceremonially received and set up on raised plinths in front of the portico, where they remained until devoured for 'recycling' in the Second World War. Only one of the plinths remains. The hotel's revived status during Davis's ownership began to attract social celebrities – a Russian Grand-Duchess, Maria, a Bonaparte, Prince Charles, and the second Duke of Wellington. The 1880s began with Prince Louis Jerome Napoleon, and the right sort of interest had been regenerated to bring in the famous and talented. Singers, composers and musicians were particularly well represented by Butt, Patti, Melba, Kubelik, Sarasate and Paderewski, with Elgar eminent among them. In 1897 Edward, Prince of Wales, added the Queen's to his long list of hotel experiences when he lunched there on the occasion of his reviewing the Royal Gloucestershire Hussars.

Adaptation to the twentieth century and its two World Wars came slowly, with corporate ownerships looking more widely for custom. The Music and Literature Festivals have supplemented horse-racing since 1945 and all regard the Queen's as probably the first truly grand hotel in Britain and a grand survivor too in the architectural field, one of Cheltenham's most precious possessions. The cultural gain of such a building is slowly being recognized as an irreplaceable asset in urban life, to be valued for far more than its price as a potential development site.

These two hotels, progressive for their time, in St Leonard's and Cheltenham had moved towards greater sophistication in the provision of rooms, food and general standards of service, and they maintained in outward appearance their loyalty to the neo-classical language of Regency or comparable architectural styles. The means of travel had not altered in kind but had undergone much improvement in quality in respect of both public and private coaches and carriages. This was true particularly of British-built vehicles, which were much in demand for their comfort and performance, but the same could not be said for British and other road systems that were failing to keep pace with traffic requirements. Slowly in Britain, turnpike and toll-road enterprises had been launched with legislative backing and at long last new road-building techniques, developed by Thomas

Bedford, the Swan Hotel, 1794, by Henry Holland.

Telford and John Macadam, produced solidly based hard-wearing surfaces that could not only stand up to the wear of heavy loads but immediately resulted in fewer travelling accidents and an increase of average speed.

Alongside the improved roads and carriages, the patenting of James Watt's first workable steam engine took place in 1769. This was a fixed piston-driven machine that was soon adapted to achieve mechanization of textile mills, and it made an initial vitally important step in the Industrial Revolution that steadily engulfed and transformed the western world. Britain retained the lead in technical invention, and the crucial steps in converting a stationary source of power into a moving vehicle strong enough to tow a number of wagons were first taken by the Cornishman Richard Trevithick and second by George Stephenson, whose steam locomotives *Locomotion I* and *The Rocket* brought into existence the earliest railway trains. The availability of steam power was indeed revolutionary and presented many social problems in usurping hand craftwork and in displacing great numbers of highly skilled craftsmen. At the same time it created the means of enlarging the scale of all kinds of enterprises and services. Manufacture and transport both accelerated dramatically, but obsolete laws and the need to legislate for greatly altered business and social circumstances slowed the pace of change to some extent and gave people a little time to absorb at least some of the implications of the new inventions. For the first time on dry land, movement about the earth's surface was freed from the limitations of the horse as a universal source of power. Steam was also beginning to take over on sea as well as land, and long-distance ocean transport, initiated by Isambard Kingdom Brunel's achievements, was making the transatlantic routes accessible to greatly increased numbers of emigrants from Europe to North America.

2.

SIZE AND GRANDEUR IN THE UNITED STATES

The Napoleonic War had ended at Waterloo in 1815, and for many the pioneering opportunities offered in a young energetic country across the Atlantic were far more attractive than life under the established hierarchies in western Europe. New World ideas and needs developed in different time scales from their European counterparts and with differing priorities. One cannot therefore make close comparisons in such matters as hotel building, although the characteristics of the 'grand hotel' as it was maturing in the nineteenth century could easily be recognized in their provision for new ways of life.

In the new United States, hotel history began at the end of the eighteenth century with an almost immediate emphasis on size and a willingness to incorporate the latest technology as it became available. When the conception of housing large numbers of people away from their own homes or their usual lodgings was established, the old idea of the inn needed transformation into a new type of building. The fresh demands led to many changes in detailed requirements, but America was moving forward as an independent nation hampered by little in the way of historical baggage and ready to tackle the problems from straightforward first principles.

Provision of bedrooms came first, followed by some form of sitting-rooms, private and public. A communal dining-room with kitchens and food storage facilities was essential and then the ancillary circulation spaces, coffee-rooms, lounges, library, ladies' sitting-room, billiard-room and ball-room were considered all according to individual circumstances. Initially, sanitation seemed to be very low on the list. All the basic needs were common to both America and Europe but with economic and political systems differing widely, relative progress varied too. Generally, long corridors and rows of rooms were stacked up floor by floor to a maxi-

mum of six or seven storeys until the advent of lifts and elevators. Public rooms occupied the entrance level, the kitchen territories were down below and rooms for additional social activities spread to the first upper floor or to unused areas of the basement if appropriate. This arrangement constituted the accepted building formula in the transitional period between recognition of the demand for better travelling accommodation and the supply of such comfort and luxury as would later be held as essential for the grand hotel.

Pevsner mentions the City Hotel (1794–6) as being the first of its kind in New York, with 73 rooms on five floors but described as 'really no more than two houses'. In Boston, the Exchange Coffee House (1806–9) by Asher Benjamin ran to seven storeys surrounding a domed atrium in which the commercial Exchange was reputed to have been housed. Access to the various rooms was from classical pillared galleries and the 200 hotel apartments occupied the top two floors. At the lower levels a dining-room over 70 feet long and a grand ball-room with three domes and twelve Corinthian columns, reached by a curving staircase, presented an impression of some grandeur at a relatively early date and had moved far forward in developing the hotel idea as distinct from previous conceptions of the inn. As with so many hotels, gas lit and sometimes heated by open fires, it came to a fiery end, being burned down in 1818. One reflects on the high fire risks that tended to increase until control of building standards to provide greater safety was enforced by relevant authorities. Developers themselves became aware that visitors sought a degree of protection against fire and began to advertise fire-fighting equipment and fire alarms as among the benefits of their hotels.

American hotels answered the universal demand in large cities for comfort and service and gradually shed their original endeavours to pack in as many beds as possible. The custom of living permanently in hotels did not have a true parallel in Europe, where availability of alternative residential buildings was generally greater and denser social fabrics

OPPOSITE West Virginia, the Greenbrier in 1913, one of the foremost resorts in the United States. It was founded as a simple spa hotel in the eighteenth century.

existed where a choice of lodgings, clubs, apartments and houses in town or country could be offered on lease or for sale. Of the earlier hotels which were used by well-to-do travellers as well as being home to a number of 'boarders', we gain a fair impression and picturesque detail from Charles Dickens's *American Notes*. He wrote these in 1842 on his first visit to America, travelling with his wife Catherine, her maid, and his secretary for the trip, the Bostonian George Putnam, on a circuit that took in Boston, New York, Philadelphia, Washington, Baltimore, Pittsburgh, Cincinnati, St Louis, Niagara and Montreal. They used railroads where possible but carried out most of the journeys in steamboats and a selection of stage-coaches and carriages, of which these last seem to have provided minimal comfort and convenience. Baltimore provided Dickens with

the most comfortable of all the hotels of which I had any experience in the United States, and they were not a few, is Barnum's in that city: where the English traveller will find curtains to his bed, for the first and probably the last time … and where he will be likely to have enough water for washing himself, which is not at all a common case.[1]

Frances Trollope, mother of the novelist Anthony, had also favoured this hotel designed by F. Small and built *c.* 1825, it being referred to as 'a very ornamental building in the heart of business'.

The Tremont House in Boston was a landmark in hotel design by Isaiah Rogers (1827–30), who handled simple classical elements in an effective manner. Four storeyed and with a frontage of eleven bays, it was entered through a Doric portico with a short flight of curved steps up to a rotunda, this relatively modest central space being expressed above roof level as an Ionic pillared cupola. The granite-faced building occupied a peninsular site with three street façades and was among the most imposing of contemporary hotels, characterized by Dickens as having 'more galleries, colonnades, piazzas and passages than I can remember, or the reader would believe'. The Boyden family, when they ran this hotel, broke new ground in training their staff to be guided by respect for the customers, so initiating one of the basic tenets of grand hotel management. One more Dickens quotation merits use as the record of an establishment which he clearly considered exceptional and which was helping to set the pattern for a long succession of ever-larger, ever-grander homes from home:

The [Tremont] House is full of boarders, both married and single, many of whom sleep upon the premises, and contract by the week for their board and lodging: the charge for which diminishes as they go nearer the sky to roost. A public table is laid in a very handsome hall for breakfast, and for dinner, and for supper. The party sitting down together for these meals will vary in number from one to two hundred: sometimes more. The advent of each of these epochs in the day is proclaimed by an awful gong, which shakes the very window-frames as it reverberates through the house, and horribly disturbs nervous foreigners. There is an ordinary for ladies, and an ordinary for gentlemen.

In our private room the cloth could not, for any earthly consideration, have been laid for dinner without a huge glass dish of cranberries in the middle of the table; and breakfast would have been no breakfast unless the principal dish were a deformed beef-steak with a great flat bone in the centre, swimming in hot butter, and sprinkled with the very blackest of all possible pepper. Our bedroom was spacious and airy, but (like every bedroom on this side of the Atlantic) very bare of furniture, having no curtains to the French bedstead or to the window.[2]

The Tremont House with its 170 rooms, 8 bathrooms, 8 water-closets and its pioneering architectural hotel design, was demolished in 1894.

Boston, Tremont House, 1830. This pioneering 170-room hotel attracted presidents and celebrities with its many innovations, including eight bathrooms and lavatories.

Returning to the years 1832–6 in New York, we find John Jacob Astor setting out deliberately to surpass the Tremont House in size and amenities and employing Isaiah Rogers as his architect for this declared purpose. Rogers succeeded in providing in the Astor House 309 rooms, 17 basement bathrooms, privies on upper floors, segregated ladies' and gentlemen's dining-rooms and drawing-rooms as well as many parlours on the ground floor and suites on the floor above. Its appearance was less conventionally classical than the Tremont, though Greek Doric motifs persisted in the pedimented and pilastered main entrance but shops occupied the ground-floor plinth areas at street level, detracting to some

New York, Astor House, built by John Jacob Astor I in 1834 to outshine the Tremont House. Both were designed by Isaiah Rogers, but Astor achieved 309 rooms, seventeen bathrooms in the basements, dining- and drawing-rooms for each sex, twenty parlours, several suites and greater grandeur and monumentality.

extent from the unity of the six-storey façade. The diarist Mayor of New York, Philip Hone, described it as 'the marvel of the age', and the extensive use of black walnut for interior fittings, together with corridors described as being carpeted and decorated on a par with the rooms, indicates that Astor's aims were being realized. It also seems to indicate that the hotel was not built to attract those guests with the tobacco-chewing and spitting habits that so revolted Dickens when on his travels. Attentive lobby staff, a fine cellar, luxurious cuisine and an excessive two dollars a day for the cost of a room all became newsworthy and gave rise to the first reporting, in *The New York Herald*, of social comings, goings and extravagances. The mix of royalty and politics, literary and stage celebrity represented in such early guest lists has remained remarkably consistent in attracting general public interest towards grand hotels.

In the towns and cities of North America during the 1830s more large hotels were built, following the trend for size and amenity, even if they were hardly of Astor standard. In New Orleans the St Charles of 1837 had 600 beds as well as a gilded dome to emulate the Capitol, and the St Louis, built in 1838 and featured in *Uncle Tom's Cabin*, was designed by Jacques Bussière de Pouilly with 'quite spectacular interiors'. Both had burned down by 1850 but their influence had helped to spread new standards well beyond the East Coast and the best early nineteenth-century hotels had taken great steps forward. The four-storey Charleston Hotel in South Carolina, brick-built with stucco rather than granite front facing, had a full-blooded Corinthian colonnade 150-feet long with plinth, entablature and cornice, and must in its prime have added great distinction to the city. It was designed confidently by Charles F. Reichardt, one of the founder-members of the American Institute of Architects. The building contract was let in 1837, and in March of the following year when the hotel was nearing completion (it had much in common with its close contemporary, the Queen's Hotel, Cheltenham), a celebratory dinner was given for investors, shortly after which the hotel was destroyed by fire. It was immediately rebuilt and was ready for use again in 1839, surviving until demolition in 1960, after which came a redesigned successor. One surviving detail is recorded, that the dining-room floor was painted to resemble oak.

Comfort and amenities were gaining ground in the new hotels, and instead of dormitory bedrooms to sleep as many as ten people, and then not necessarily in separate beds, single and double bedrooms had taken over by this time. Individual privacy was considered a necessity and the rooms were lockable, with jug, bowl and soap being supplied – a

Charleston, South Carolina, Charleston Hotel. Begun three years later than the Queen's at Cheltenham, this American hotel by C. F. Reichardt displays a remarkably similar architectural vocabulary.

Chicago, Palmer House, built in 1873 to replace its predecessor, which went up in smoke in the great Chicago fire of 1871. This 'New Palmer House', now superseded, shows the corner turret and dome which became a popular feature for large hotels in the United States and Europe.

notable innovation when this had first occurred at the Tremont. Sprung mattresses resulted from the invention of bed springs in 1831 by J. French of Massachusetts, but were not generally available for another 40 years until mass production had become practicable. The St Nicholas Hotel in New York was furnished with the handmade variety, giving rise to favourable comment by *The Tribune* in 1852. Steel-frame building techniques coupled with the use of hydraulic or electric power to lift, elevate or transport guests vertically in 'rising rooms' resulted in another large technical advance. Hotels could be taller, much taller, and the top floors did not need to be let more cheaply when stair-climbing was no longer such a problem. American enthusiasm for technology and record-breaking statistics led to millions of dollars being spent on building and hundreds and thousands of hotel bedrooms being provided. With great regularity, however, fires continued to destroy these efforts. Chicago suffered a great fire in 1871 and many hotels were destroyed, including Potter Palmer's new Palmer House by J. M. Van Osdel (1811–91), built the previous year and advertised as 'the only fireproof hotel in the world'!

The San Francisco earthquake in 1906 created greater havoc, among its more serious losses being the Palace Hotel, opened in 1875. The building, very carefully designed to withstand movement and well provided with great roof and basement water-tanks plus reserve wells and fire-pumps, survived the quake but succumbed to the creeping fire as these water supplies were commandeered to try and save the nearby municipal offices – which they failed to do. Accommodation lost included 755 rooms for 1,200 people, planned

around a glazed atrium and using solid brick and wrought-iron construction with compartmented iron staircases intended to resist the spread of flame. The hotel had cost the developer, W. C. Ralston, over $4,000,000 and had probably been the largest city hotel in the world, although it was exceeded in size by the summer hotel, the United States in Saratoga, which had almost 1,000 rooms.

Summer hotels sprang up to cater for a seasonal demand away from the heat, infections and congestion of cities. They were sited by the sea, by lakes or near mineral water springs for health treatments, but entrepreneurs usually sought semi-rural or at least non-urban surroundings. Provision of a large number of rooms was an economic necessity if profits were to be made, and expensive building techniques therefore played a smaller part in these than the city hotels required. On the Eastern seaboard, long and relatively low building profiles seemed to answer the fashionable trend and the developers' resources, with maximum advantage being taken of views and fresh air. Pillared loggias that offered shade and private balconies which extended the feeling of space were popular and profitable. Some balconies were of the cast-iron lace pattern but many were, like the main buildings themselves, of timber construction with rough and ready finishes. As early as 1812, the three-storey Congress Hotel on Cape May at the southern tip of New Jersey pioneered this type of hotel. It was built by Thomas Hughes, son of Ellis Hughes, postmaster, who had earlier seen the commercial possibilities of providing increased and improved accommodation on Cape May as the stage-coach and steamship services were accelerating. It was a timber-framed building, timber clad but unpainted, and it only survived for two years before being burnt. A later Cape May hotel, the Mount Vernon, achieved a slightly longer life (1853–6), but had not been fully completed before the fire to its intended capacity of 2,100 guests. Early illustrations show festive elevations with three and four tiers of decorative ironwork balconies. Individual rooms were a standard 9½-feet square in comparison with the 425-feet-long dining-room, and one wonders at the logistics of serving so many meals. It is clear that suites with private dining- and drawing-rooms would be popular with those who preferred a restful holiday and could afford to pay. Charles Dickens had always preferred such privacy, which allowed him to keep away from the intrusive public gaze. Resort hotels of light construction, crammed with temporary visitors needing quantities of cooked food, lighting and heating, all of which must have been under the control of largely untrained seasonal staff, represented an even greater fire hazard than their city counterparts, and few such buildings lived to a ripe old age.

An exception is the Grand Hotel, Mackinac Island, which celebrated its centenary in 1987 and has succeeded in keeping abreast of the changing fashions in leisure and holiday pursuits under the régime of one family for the last 85 years. It is claimed to be the 'World's Largest Summer Hotel' with 317 rooms and was constructed in 1887 for the Mackinac Island Hotel Company, formed by railroad interests and first chaired by Cornelius Vanderbilt. The island, in the straits between Lake Michigan and Lake Huron, was known to

Saratoga Springs, Grand Union Hotel, 1880s. Edith Wharton visualized her fictional Mrs St George and Mrs Elmsworth vying with each other in style and in their attempts to marry off their daughters against the background of this hotel.

have been a tribal meeting-place and Indian graves were found during excavation of the site for the hotel. In the late eighteenth century Fort Mackinac had been occupied as a trading-post, mainly for furs, by the French, British and Americans. The builder of the hotel, Charles Caskey (1851–1933), decided with the aid of his brother-in-law, Alphonse Howe, to become his own architect, and as the hotel book says, 'with some guidance from John O. Plank, the Hotel's first manager' he opted for a semi-classical style loggia design with a central six-bay projecting portico.[3] The roof over this projection is supported on coupled Tuscan-type columns and each side wing has its overhanging verandah roof carried on elongated single columns of matching design. The original right-hand wing ended in normal rectangular manner, but the left-hand end takes a sweep forward and then forms a curved, bastion-shaped corner feature supported on four more plain columns. In subsequent alterations, the right-hand wing was extended by the addition of a similar curved section, increasing the total verandah or front porch length to 700 feet. Other changes have included a complete additional bedroom floor and a neat pedimented roof to the lobby entrance. The central turret now houses a bar but retains its flattened double ogee profile with a gable at lower level on each side. Speed of building was remarkable, the whole being completed in just over three months in spite of an initial confrontation between Caskey and his labour force, which he successfully disarmed.

He was skilled in timber work and used Michigan white pine prepared in his own mill across the strait in St Ignace and hauled in the winter of 1886–7 over the ice to the island. Some subsidence later occurred in the foundations of the building but this is now remedied.

Resort hotels of more substantial design and construction frequently developed in the wake of the railways and, although the holiday resorts were always intended to provide an escape and a freedom from the usual restrictions imposed by daily life, they also needed to offer social activities and diversions. Saratoga, 150 miles or so up-state from New York City, had origins dating back to the discovery of High Rock Spring by Sir William Johnston in 1767, but before then had been long known to the Mohawk Indians for its medicinal waters. Surrounded by mountain scenery and supplied with numerous mineral springs that were progressively discovered to have a great range of therapeutic qualities, it attracted the commercial interest of Gideon Putnam who leased 300 acres in 1789. He built a 'Tavern and Boarding

Mackinac Island, Michigan, the Grand Hotel, 1887. One of the few timber-built 'summer hotels' to escape the risks of fire. The end of the nearer wing and the portico are among later additions.

House' in 1802, followed by the Congress Hall Hotel but unfortunately did not live to see this Federal style building completed, having died after a fall from the scaffolding during construction in 1811.

Steady development progressed, marked by exploitation of Congress Spring with its naturally carbonated water which in 1830 was housed in an attractive small Doric temple building, later superseded by an elaborate neo-Gothic pavilion which in its turn made way for a reconstruction in the original style. Similar changes of architectural fashion appear in the records of hotel rebuildings held by the Historical Society of Saratoga Springs, but the authors of these building designs largely remain anonymous.

First the races in 1863 and then the casino in 1867 set the seal on Saratoga's popularity and drew visitors and money that were unrelated to the respectable spa routines. Those who came for livelier entertainments included Leonard Jerome, subsequently acquiring historic distinction as the grandfather of Winston Churchill, but at that time notable as owner of the first horse to win a Saratoga race. To accommodate this mid-century influx, large establishments were essential, and the United States Hotel, of which a previous 1824 version had been built by Elias Benedict and burnt down

in 1865, arose again in 1875 to claim the title of 'largest hotel in the world' according to Pevsner, who quotes 917 rooms from an 1884 Directory, although exact figures vary according to different sources. Suites and cottages were in demand and families took up residence for a considerable part of the season. Mothers with marriageable daughters made up quite a large segment of this temporary population, ready to seize every social opportunity and appearing to possess many attributes in common with Jane Austen's characters in Bath, two or three generations earlier.

The Grand Union Hotel attributed to John A. Wood in Saratoga Springs was the background to some of these manoeuvrings, as afterwards evoked by Edith Wharton, and was situated in fashionable Broadway near the United States Hotel. After its purchase by A. T. Stewart in 1872 for $532,000 in the bankruptcy sale of the Leland Brothers, the previous

Wentworth by the Sea, New Hampshire, 1879–80. This hotel was built of timber to a relatively sophisticated French-influenced design by C. E. Campbell and C. H. Chase as a summer resort, but has declined in spite of its fine site and awaits possible rescue. In 1905, before the Russo-Japanese War was concluded by the Peace Treaty of Portsmouth, this hotel housed the preliminary discussions and the delegates.

West Virginia, the Greenbrier. This grew from an eighteenth-century spa based on a cluster of mineral springs to be one of the foremost resorts in the United States. The 1913 rebuilding of the main hotel after an earlier fire was in well-proportioned neo-classical style with interiors containing many features in sympathy with late twentieth-century taste.

owners, the Union Hotel became the Grand Union and was extensively enlarged and improved to become another contestant for the 'largest in the world' title. It boasted, with U-shape plan, a Broadway frontage of 450 feet and two wings to complete the U-form, each approaching a quarter of a mile in length and making an open-ended trapezium filled with 'elm-shaded, landscaped gardens'. Among component parts were a 306-feet-long dining-room to serve 1,400 people, 824 guest-rooms, a mile of covered piazzas, two miles of corridors, 12 acres of carpeting and an acre of marble tops and floor tiles. Mention of crystal chandeliers, black walnut staircases and a steam-engine elevator installed by the Otis brothers lends a little more down to earth detail, although one receives the impression of somewhat austere interiors. Henry James's coupling of this with the Congress Hall as 'the two monster hotels' seems perfectly appropriate description.

The 1880s and 1890s saw Saratoga at the height of its fashion, during which period luxurious travel was possible from New York's Grand Central railroad station in less than half a day on the 'Saratoga Limited'. Its widespread attraction and fame as a resort was underlined by the naming of curved-top travelling trunks and boxes ('Saratoga trunks') to contain all the smart and expensive clothes from New York or Paris, the display of which was one of the prime occupations and entertainments of the female guests in *la belle époque*, not forgetting the supporting roles of their spouses and admirers. Life seems to have been conducted mostly out of doors or on the covered colonnades or 'piazzas' by day, followed by dancing in the evening. This, according to Edith Wharton, took place 'for hours every night in the long, bare hotel parlours, so conveniently divided by sliding doors which slipped into the wall and made the two rooms into one' so becoming the hotel ballroom and displaying 'this vista, with its expectant lines of bent-wood chairs against the walls, and its row of windows draped in crimson brocatelle heavily festooned from overhanging gilt cornices'.[4]

Racing and gambling prospered, bands played and flags flew. The spa waters were still popular, still bottled and distributed across the country, but a moral time-bomb was ticking and in 1904 it was decided that the contravention of the gambling laws had been too flagrant and the Casino was closed, taking much of the heart out of the place.

In contrast to the busy picture of New Yorkers seeking racing, gambling and generally animated occupations in Saratoga, the cluster of mineral springs along today's border of Virginia with West Virginia gave rise to early resorts where a southern way of life was lived at quieter pace. Valleys, forests and the Allegheny mountains provided a splendid summer background, and from 1727 onwards small settlements were established variously around the Warm, Hot, Healing, Sulphur and White Sulphur Springs. Tidewater Indians had used the first two of these but it had been left to incomers to develop the wider possibilities of the area. Hot Springs, where there was in 1766 some lodging and a small hotel built by a Thomas Bullitt by 1800 was already by 1838 attracting 6,000 visitors. Its importance had risen through the construction of a timber-framed hotel, the Homestead, in 1832 and by the work of Dr Goode in setting up warm bathing facilities. Competition existed between Hot Springs and Warm Springs and in 1841 'Tanner's United States' described the Warm Springs Hotel as 'a two-storied brick building, about one hundred feet in front, immediately on the road, and having a spacious piazza extending along its whole front'. Mention of a 'large and airy eating room … in which thrice a day is spread a table amply supplied with a variety of good things' follows, with admiring comment on the place-card system whereby new visitors sat at the end of the dining-table and worked their way up to its head according to length of stay, as was the custom in Virginian resorts at the time.

While Warm Springs ceased to hold its own, Hot Springs was aided by Dr Goode's innovative Spout Bath, Pleasure Pool and Plunge, but more crucially by a new branch extension of the Chesapeake & Ohio Railroad from the main line at Covington. The 'old frame hotel' seems to have survived through various alterations and additions until being burnt in 1900. Before this, the Homestead complex of hotel and spa buildings did include a more solidly built bath-house in pleasing neo-classical style dating from *c.* 1890. Rebuilding after the fire was in brick, and by the 1920s the main façade appears with a colonnaded piazza front four to five storeys high, the tiers of bedroom sash windows punctuated by brick pilasters below a white cornice and dentilled eaves detail. The main entrance, with *porte-cochère* and six Ionic columns surmounted by a balustraded roof terrace, emphasize the Southern *ante-bellum* origins of the design. Extensions in all directions ensued in response to continued demand in this exclusive resort where the railroad syndicate had provided imaginative impetus for development in the latter part of the nineteenth century and the regular appearance of Rockefellers, Vanderbilts, Mellons and Fords vindicated their judgement. New York financiers may have come to refresh themselves on holiday, but in the 1920s were nevertheless provided with a broker's office in the Homestead to maintain contact with the markets. Occasionally surrealism erupted to enliven the scene, as it did during a party in 1898 when 'the Chinese Minister in Washington … crowned the evening by rising, in his yellow and gold robes, and declaring

A primitive painting of 1842 shows Virginia Row and Baltimore Row cottages in White Sulphur Springs, now encompassed by the Greenbrier resort. One of the Baltimore cottages on the back row was designed for his own use by J. H. B. Latrobe.

"I must tell you how much I admire your country. Now I will sing your national anthem in Chinese." At which he proceeded to render, rather flat, "There'll be a Hot Time in the Old Town Tonight".[5]

White Sulphur Springs in Greenbrier County also features in the *Geographical, Historical and Statistical View of the Central United States* of 1841 by H. S. Tanner with a good description of the essential service buildings that dominated the groups of accommodation cabins or cottages where visitors to the White Sulphur Spring lived. They consisted of a timber-frame dining-room, which was

about one hundred and twenty feet long, with which is connected a large kitchen and bakery; a frame ball-room, with lodging rooms over it and at each end; two very large frame stables, with eighty stalls each, of which the exterior rows are open to the air; and many rows of cabins tastefully arranged around the larger edifices, and standing on rising ground. The cabins are composed of various materials, brick, frame or logs, and the view of the *tout-ensemble* is very pleasing. Most of the modern cabins are furnished with little piazzas, and shaded with forest trees purposely rescued from the ruthless axe.

A more critical point of view had been expressed a few years earlier by John H. B. Latrobe, the son of Benjamin Latrobe, the English-born immigrant established as the first fully trained architect in the United States and designer of some of its finest buildings, including Baltimore Cathedral and the Capitol in Washington, D.C. John Latrobe is described as a lawyer and an architect who designed a cottage for himself in the resort on Baltimore Row, with altogether more modest neo-classical pretensions in 1834. His strictures about the organization of the resort, the shortage of accommodation and the meal-time rush to the dining-room at the ring of a bell 'like that at the booth at a contested election' may have been attended to in the intervening period. The survival of the White Sulphur Springs resort, where a new hotel, attractively designed in 1913 by Frederick Sterner and now called The Greenbrier, is due to its secluded mountain site and an adaptability to numerous social and historic changes. Far-sighted management and exceptionally skilled interior design in the restoration after the Second World War by Dorothy Draper and Carleton Varney have conjured up the atmosphere of a very well-appointed and comfortable country house.

EUROPE BURGEONING

Industry and Commerce

In Europe during the early years of the nineteenth century the Industrial Revolution was still led by British invention and enterprise. Society in Great Britain had remained intact in spite of the threats of invasion by Napoleon, so after Wellington's victory at Waterloo and the Congress of Vienna in 1815, civil interests replaced military necessity. Concentration on material progress placed the country in the industrial lead, with its natural resource of coal and the refining processes of Henry Bessemer in steel production combining to lay strong foundations for the dominance that was to follow. Travel has always provided a key to power and influence, and the development of railways opened many golden doors. By 1830 England alone possessed railways with steam-powered locomotives – the Stockton & Darlington and the Liverpool & Manchester lines – and stood on the threshold of unimagined transformation. Benefits for commerce, learning, pleasure and the spread of ideas came into view and the construction of private railways went ahead rapidly in a first crescendo of enthusiasm that held its own in the face of local protests and the cumbersome law relating to joint-stock companies that involved a Parliamentary Act and therefore probably a year's delay.

Belgium, France and Germany quickly followed the British process of industrialization, accompanied and assisted by railways.[1] Germany started with a short four-mile length of line in 1835 from Nuremberg in Bavaria, privately financed by the mayor and citizens. British locomotives built by George Stephenson's son, Robert, operated this line with the Adler engine and within four years provided *The Comet* for a Dresden to Leipzig system of 72 miles in length, including a tunnel, in Saxony. In Belgium a line more than twice that length had been started in 1836 to run from Brussels to Antwerp, and this exceeded all other Continental achievements at the time. George Stephenson's experience was widely sought by, among others, Leopold I in 1845 as adviser for the Belgian railways. France had made a start with steam in 1832 between St Etienne and Lyon in the form of 58 kilometres of rail, initially for transport of coal, built by the five brothers Seguin on the basis of a visit to study the Stockton & Darlington system. Paris to St Germain and Paris to Versailles were both built in the 1830s but real advances had to wait for Napoleon III's Second Empire (1852–71) and involvement by the state. Conflict between railways and existing waterways was a factor in France where private companies had been the initiators of early ventures, but occurred less where Government played an increasing part, as it did at later stages in Belgium and Germany, Italy and Russia.

The prospect in the 1830s was of a Continent comprising some large states and many smaller principalities and powers struggling, in the cases of Germany and Italy, towards unification. A new pattern of industry and transport was growing as fast as practical considerations would permit, involving engineering inventiveness, financial restructuring and the acquisition of land. In 1848 railway coverage radiated thinly from Paris and Berlin, giving a west-to-east bias with scattered short lines north of the Alps and in northern Italy. Britain was better served with major lines centred on London but linked to connect east and west, including two sea routes across to Ireland. By 1877 there was a dense railway network in the British Isles and a more open but equally impressive spread in France, Germany and the Low Countries.

Population increases had started in the eighteenth century and continued throughout the nineteenth, creating needs and pressures which mechanization was in part able to answer. Working conditions may have been hard and squalid, but manufactured goods in the form of everyday utensils reached a wider section of the inhabitants and helped to

OPPOSITE The Hypostyle Hall in Atkinson's third Liverpool Adelphi, 1912–14. Its large-scale and lavish neo-baroque style attracted social fashion and created one of the city's favourite meeting places.

improve standards of life. Metal tools, cheap machine-made textiles and pottery all came within reach of the majority. More varied and nourishing food was available, but poverty and hunger did persist in remote and rural areas, most notably in Ireland, Russia, southern Italy and Sicily. Urban conditions offered more possibilities of improvement than did peasant communities as it was in manufacturing industries that money was being made. Against this roughly-sketched background comes the intriguing evolution of new building types to serve changing ways, and one of these, displaying a surprisingly uniform set of standards, was the European grand hotel.

Britain and Early Railway Hotels

Raising capital for large-scale ventures could still be hazardous, as even after the 1837 formation of the Register of Companies, where new enterprises could apply for inclusion from 1844 onwards, the problem of limited liability had not been solved. Investors were deterred by the danger to an individual of total liability if the company should face bankruptcy, and this risk was not satisfactorily eliminated until further Acts in 1855 and 1862 became law. Names of shareholders and directors had to be disclosed, as did audited accounts, but liabilities were limited in relation to investments, encouraging the inflow of investment firstly for the railways themselves and then for the logical step of providing convenient accommodation for rail travellers. Location of this close to the new train systems was much to be desired, provided that endemic noise and dirt could be excluded.

Architecture of distinction had already reached the railway world at the entrance to London's Euston station in the form of Philip Hardwick's Doric Arch or Propylaeum of 1837, an entirely appropriate neo-classical statement expressing the strength and grandeur aptly associated with railway engineering. Soon after the opening of the station, a company prospectus was issued on behalf of the London & Birmingham Hotels & Dormitories, soliciting investment and showing Hardwick's proposed four-storey designs in straightforward late Georgian manner. The scheme went ahead subject to permanent control by the directors of the London and Birmingham Railway and so the Adelaide (later renamed Euston) and the Victoria became in 1839 the first 'railway hotels', although the accommodation at the Victoria

London, Euston Station, 1839. The first railway hotels, the Victoria and the Adelaide (subsequently called Euston), designed by Philip Hardwick the elder to provide basic accommodation for travellers, flanked the famous Doric Arch at the entrance to the station.

was merely designated as 'dormitory'. No visitors were allowed to occupy a room for more than three nights consecutively if railway passengers required accommodating. A near contemporary was the former Royal Western Hotel, Bristol, built in 1837–9 by local architect R. S. Pope (1791–1884) with the collaboration of Brunel and intended for use by Atlantic steamship passengers. Pevsner considered that 'it must at first have been one of the most spectacular hotels in England', and describes its stone façade, thirteen bays wide and four storeys high as bearing comparison with the Queen's Hotel in Cheltenham.[2] Its Ionic colonnade surmounted by pilasters in idiosyncratic Corinthian order form a handsome composition, with dominating end pavilions over semicircular-headed entrances. Although built as a railway hotel, the trade did not develop as expected and from 1855 it was put to other uses. Now, as part of the Council Offices and known as Brunel House, it should not be confused with the later Victorian Royal Hotel on College Green, which recently was restored to full hotel use.

The railway architect Francis Thompson (1808–95), whose elegant station frontage design for the North Midland Railway at Derby had been started in the same year as the Royal Western, was persuaded by the station contractor Thomas Jackson of Pimlico to provide the design for a hotel to complete a spacious neo-classical grouping around the station square. This was approved by the company and opened in 1840 as the Midland Hotel, a substantial asset for travellers, for local citizens and for Queen Victoria on her way to and from Balmoral in Scotland. The hotel still exists and so does the menu for 'Her Majesty's Dinner' on 28 September 1849, being six courses plus 'Roast beef and Roast mutton on the Side Table'.[3]

An advertisement in *The Derby Mercury* for 2 June 1841 states below the North Midland Railway logo and the name 'Midland Hotel and Posting House, Railway Station, Derby' that

J. Hall begs to announce to the Nobility and Gentry that this Hotel under his management is open for their accommodation; and where, he trusts, those who honor him with their patronage, will find the style and comfort of the Establishment equal to that of any in the Country.

Porters are in constant attendance on the arrival of the several Trains at Derby for the removal of Luggage &c., to the Hotel.

This announcement is just one of many that give lively insights into life in the prospering county town, offering variously 'apprenticeships for millinery and dress making' and 'Dr Fox's Patent Coffee Pots and Portable Steam-Baths constantly on hand', a report on 'A VERY MATERIAL REDUCTION having taken place in the PRICE of ... PLATE GLASS FOR WINDOWS', a lecture ('ladies might with propriety attend') on 'SOCIALISM UNMASKED!!! The Town of Derby having been visited during the past week with that worst of moral pestilences misnamed SOCIALISM ...', and finally a leader that presages with considerable accuracy comments recognizable today, remarking that

Her Majesty's Ministers do not sufficiently possess the confidence of the House of Commons to enable them to carry

---

Bristol, Royal Western Hotel, 1837–9, designed by R. S. Pope, a local architect who was associated with I. K. Brunel on this project. Never successful in capturing the railway or steamship trade, it is now in use as Council Offices.

Derby, Midland Hotel, 1840 (*on the right*), formed part of the elegant neo-classical North Midland Railway Station complex (*left*) although it was privately owned until 1862. Its designer was the railway architect Francis Thompson, and it is still in use.

through the house measures which they deem of essential importance to the public welfare; ... *their* doom as a government is sealed ... and, as they have evidently framed their Budget with a series of clap-traps sufficiently hypocritical and daring to catch the applause of the unthinking ... they commit themselves to this nefarious proceeding as a death-struggle for the party ... which yet supports them.

A directory entry for Cuff's Midland Hotel in 1843 gives the following list of charges which included 'attendance of every description':

Bed	4 shillings
Double Bed	1 shilling extra
Servant's Bed	2 shillings
Sitting Room	5 shillings
„ „ fire	2 shillings
„ „ „	Evenings only, 1 shilling
Wax Lights	2 shillings
Bed Room Fire	1 shilling
Breakfast, with cold meat or eggs	2 shillings & 6 pence
„ with chops & eggs	3 shillings
Tea with meat & eggs	3 shillings
Plain Tea	2 shillings

Though John Cuff was running the hotel, Thomas Jackson had retained ownership but went into bankruptcy with enormous debts of £300,000 in 1859 and the hotel was sold. This pattern of enterprise, over-optimistic creation, unmanageable debt and financial failure is so recurrent in entrepreneurial circles of all kinds as to need little reciting. Again according to pattern, a buyer came on the scene ready to take advantage of the previous failure. In this instance the purchaser was the Midland Railway Company, by this time in 1862 seriously engaged in the hotel business which it was to conduct with much success for 85 years.

Another product of the first great railway boom in the decade from 1837 was the Victoria Hotel at Colchester (1843) where Lewis Cubitt, born in 1799 and one of the designers of King's Cross Station, adopted a change of style towards the Italianate villa formula which was becoming fashionable in well-to-do suburbs up and down the country. A lookout tower, Venetian windows and Florentine cornices all owed allegiance to Renaissance features until competition from the Gothic enthusiasts weakened the classical hold in the Battle of the Styles. The Victoria cannot have been a commercial success as it was sold within six years for use as a hospital and has now been demolished. A similar Florentine influence can still be seen in the Royal Station Hotel in Hull (1851) by G. T. Andrews (1805–55), but for the Central Station Hotel,

Newcastle upon Tyne in 1854, John Dobson (1787–1865) moved towards a more sophisticated French Renaissance revival treatment well suited to the character of northern stonework. Some Roman Renaissance details may be recognized in the rustication and the window pediments, but Parisian ideas show in the mansard roof and centre pavilion, speaking more of the Louvre than the Palazzo Farnese.

This small group of pioneering railway hotels shows transition from neo-classical to the beginnings of revivalism in design terms, but a more vital factor affecting railway developments in general had been the railway mania of 1843–7, marked by wild speculations such as those by Thomas Jackson in Derby, followed by widespread collapse not overcome insofar as hotel interests were concerned for the best part of ten years. By the time the market recovered, ideas of size had altered and perceptions of grandeur were being applied to the design of new projects. This change of scale drew much invigorating influence from the Great Exhibition of 1851, which both underlined the need of extensive accommodation for foreign and provincial visitors to such displays and at the same time demonstrated the existence of technical expertise available for ensuring their comfort and well-being.

London Hotels and the Railways

The London railway termini offered hotel locations which were very appropriately placed, within easy reach by cab of clubs, theatres, Parliament and the City, in most cases con-

Newcastle upon Tyne, the Central Station Hotel, 1854, by John Dobson, was inspired by the French Renaissance style and was enlarged from 50 to 133 bedrooms in 1892.

nected directly and under cover with station concourses without need to brave the open air. Such convenience could be offset by the nuisance of noise and dirt from steam trains, depending on ability to isolate bedrooms from the platforms by careful planning and construction. Legislation in the middle of the century was simplifying the financial problems of liability, and many railway companies that had survived the backlash to the overreaching speculation of the 1840s continued to show interest in developing railway hotels. They were prepared to encourage others, or themselves, to build a new breed of hotel which could go well beyond the previous moderately sized descendants of the best coaching inns.

The first London railway terminus to acquire a hotel of grand proportions was Paddington, starting-point of the Great Western Railway, whose engineer, Isambard Kingdom Brunel, lives on in reputation as one of the world's finest. His achievements were in the fields of railway systems, bridges and allied engineering works, steamships and submarine cable laying. As well as having some involvement with the Royal Western Hotel in Bristol, Brunel was interested in the financing of the new Great Western Royal at Paddington in his position as the board's first Managing Director. The design of the hotel was entirely in the hands of Philip Hardwick the younger (1822–92), who incorporated many influences, from the Renaissance classical caryatids, pediment and cornice treatment to the mansard roof from France and the ogival-roofed corner turrets echoing English Jacobean. The figures on the façade by the prolific sculptor John Thomas (1813–62) represented in confident Victorian manner Peace, Plenty, Science and Industry.[4] (Other grand hotels where these or closely related symbolic figures occur include the Windsor in Melbourne and the Metropole in Brussels.) A heavily decorated ironwork *porte-cochère* covered the main entrance but no longer exists, and the lower section of Hardwick's grand front has suffered from unsympathetic alteration. The original exterior, directly in front of the Paddington station train-shed, asserted an impressive presence in the London street scene and was completed in 1854, only five months after the station. The size of the hotel, prompted by the obvious demand by exhibition visitors to the capital in 1851, was large in its day with (sources vary) 103–120 bedrooms and 15–20 sitting-rooms or suites; it was recognized as the finest in the town and cost just under £44,000. Present capacity has been increased to 250 bedrooms.

Lewis Cubitt's railway associations with Colchester and King's Cross were extended in his design of the 69-bedroom Great Northern Hotel (1854) adjoining the latter station, a restrained curved façade and low-pitched hipped roof

London, Paddington, Great Western Royal Hotel, 1854, by Philip Hardwick the younger. This hotel was grand in size and conception from the outset, with 103 bedrooms and features influenced by various sources. It owed its existence to the increase in demand made plain at the time of the Great Exhibition of 1851.

London, Victoria, Grosvenor Hotel, 1861, a further large-scale work this time by J. T. Knowles survives with very little change in external appearance.

with twin ridges, aiming at good proportion without surface decoration but lacking the drama of his King's Cross station building.

At what is now known as Victoria station, the Grosvenor Hotel was built in 1860–61 as a new type of terminus hotel and in fact served two stations, the Brighton line and the adjacent London, Chatham & Dover Railway, colloquially known as the 'London, Smash'em and Turnover', which had been built alongside each other at the northern end of a new rail–river crossing on the site of the old Grosvenor Canal basin.[5] It was designed by James Thomas Knowles (1806–84), whose earlier scheme of 1858 for an 'International Hotel' in the Strand had not proceeded. The main façade fronts Buckingham Palace Road at the west of the station with a 262-feet long symmetrical, semi-classical composition of a slightly recessed fifteen-bay block stopped at each end against a raised two-bay pavilion. These have convex mansard roofs in the French manner, each in its turn being crowned with another smaller pavilion. A wide and heavy Florentine cornice over the fifth floor and repeated horizontal emphases below this all make a solid background to the windows, which vary in shape at each level. Much vigorous stone carving with portrait heads and plant forms is set against the Suffolk white brickwork, and the present appearance of the hotel varies little from its original state. The interior also retains its foyer and grand staircase with stone balustrades of heavily carved leaves. A steam lift had been installed as a novelty but was much needed in view of the eight storeys that dominated that part of the capital for many succeeding decades. Two bathrooms on each bedroom floor seem to have been quite generous for the time.

Charing Cross station brought another new line across the Thames from the south, the South Eastern Railway, which served Channel ports on the Kent coast, benefiting from a shorter sea crossing to the Continent than any of the more westerly harbours. Also, of course, the bulk of passengers were daily commuters from the English towns in the southeast, travelling to work in London. Edward Middleton Barry (1830–80) followed closely in 1863–5 with a very similar design scheme to that of the Grosvenor, making a more compact version of combined hotel and train shed and with capacity of about 250 beds. Owen Jones (1809–74), specialist in interior design, decorated half a dozen excellent first-floor public rooms, from a ladies' coffee-room to a billiard-room, using classical neo-Renaissance French and Italian models with coffered or saucer-domed ceilings, marble columns, scagliola pilasters and vigorous ornamental plasterwork, some of which survive. Externally the horizontal emphasis of the main façade, the corner pavilions, Italianate fenestration and Louvre-inspired roofs with the usual dominating chimneystacks, constituted a more sophisticated but less emphatic architectural statement than the Grosvenor, although at ground level the line of the canopy, terminated at each end with columned entrances, showed an elegance that Knowles's design does not possess. Charing Cross was badly damaged during the Blitz and the hotel was rebuilt in 1941 with the addition of two storeys that, with the further insensitive application of signs and lettering, has destroyed its architectural integrity. Barry's Eleanor Cross replica in the forecourt, carved by T. Earp, acts as a pleasing focus and reminder that the original memorial to Edward I's queen, Eleanor of Castile, whom he 'cherished dearly', stood not

The staircase of the Grosvenor Hotel, planned symmetrically in the central hall area and dividing at right angles to reach the balustraded first-floor corridors. This layout, used a few years earlier in the Station Hotel, Inverness, provides the dramatic architectural setting so favoured in Victorian grand hotels.

The Grosvenor Hotel, Bedroom 232, photographed *c.* 1910.

London, Charing Cross Hotel, 1865. A Staffordshire Pratt-ware pot lid dating from about 1870 shows the hotel and the Eleanor Cross in their original relative positions.

The Charing Cross Hotel, a postcard from early in the twentieth century.

The Charing Cross Hotel, station entrance through a side pavilion in E. M. Barry's vigorous style.

The first-floor Betjeman Restaurant preserves some of the original Owen Jones decoration.

many steps away, where Charles I's statue now is placed in Trafalgar Square. It was the last Cross in a series of thirteen, marking each overnight stop for Eleanor's funeral cortège from Harby near Lincoln, where she died in November 1290, to her burial place at Westminster Abbey.

The apotheosis of railway terminus hotel-building was reached in extravagant terms with Sir George Gilbert Scott's competition-winning adventure into the full-blown Victorian Gothic he had been anxious to use for Government offices in an earlier competition. Scott's drawings exceeded the brief but won the commission, to the chagrin of the second prizewinner. The directors of the Midland Railway Company wished to impress the capital city with the new

hotel and, though engaging in client versus architect arguments along the way, obtained through their general manager, Sir James Allport, the 'grand scale' he had always advocated. Scott (1811–78) may have considered his Midland Grand Hotel design as 'too good for its purpose', and in view of its history of under-use may have been proved at least partially right. As a point of arrival in London from the north, it made for the Midland Railway an unquestionable presence. This was reinforced by the high standards of service that the régime of William Towle and members of his family ensured over several decades in control of Midland Railway Hotels.[6]

The Midland Grand, or more familiarly the St Pancras Hotel, opened in 1873 and became a part of the London scene that has never been ignored, even when standing empty and neglected. Its Gothic profile against the evening sky is memorable and deserves all the preservation it can be given. Full of interest, it departs from the rectilinear formula so characteristic of the general run of grand hotels, leaning towards the more imposing outlines of nineteenth-century town halls in northern Europe. French and Italian elements have diminished in the design, although Ruskinian Venetian Gothic flavours remain. Gothic town halls were fashionable but Gothic hotels were scarce, probably because they were ex-

pensive to build, although a four-storey one of moderate size in Aberystwyth (1864–5, J. P. Seddon), now part of the University, forestalled, as the Castle Hotel, many of Scott's motifs. Scott never fully resolved vertical and horizontal emphases on his main frontage, but detail is excellent and always lively. The exposed interior ironwork is structural and decorative, with strong effective colours and fine handling of spaces in the splendid main staircase. At the time of writing the future of the building is uncertain, but basic conservation works proceed.

London, Midland Grand Hotel, St Pancras, 1873. The architect, Sir George Gilbert Scott (1811–78), was a leading figure in the Gothic Revival movement, and the main body of his work consisted of church architecture, which he considered superior to that of the railway hotel. Ironically, his popular reputation now rests chiefly on the Midland Grand.

The Midland Grand. The main staircase is decorated in High Victorian colour, including the prominent structural steelwork that, under today's legislation, would need protection against fire.

A sitting-room in the Midland Grand provided ample space for the large fireplace, an Erard piano, a table and many chairs. The door was hung with a portière curtain and sheltered by a screen for draught exclusion.

The Randolph Hotel in Oxford, unrelated to the railway network, is another Gothic hotel, dating from 1864 and designed by local architect William Wilkinson (1819–1901) after considerable discussion between Ruskinian partisans and the classicists of the City Council. The resulting compromise was described as 'Scottish Early English' and claimed to provide 'all the comfort and quietude of private dwellings'.[7] The inclination towards heaviness inside the hotel was alleviated in recent decades by the entertaining series of scenes painted by Osbert Lancaster that illustrate the progress of Max Beerbohm's hero, the Duke of Dorset, in his Oxford-based extravaganza, *Zuleika Dobson*.

More serious and suited to City of London ways is the Great Eastern Hotel, adjoining Liverpool Street station, which served the Great Eastern Railway, opened in 1884. It was designed by Charles Barry and Charles Edward Barry, son and grandson of Sir Charles Barry, architect of the Houses of Parliament and the Reform Club in Pall Mall. The Abercorn Rooms were added to the hotel ten years later by Robert William Edis (1839–1927), both parts of the building being in red brick like the Midland Grand, with stucco and stone ground floor and dressings in a mildly classical style. The later part of the hotel turned the corner into Bishopsgate, a setting now made almost unrecognizable by the recent dramatic Broadgate development. This city hotel accommodates two Masonic Temples in addition to the normal varieties of public rooms, unexpected but not unknown as hotel amenities. The Egyptian Temple in the basement, with traditional seating around the rectangular black and white chequered marble floor, contains painted Egyptian lotus bud pilasters, an organ and three freestanding symbolic pedestals in Tuscan, Ionic and Corinthian architectural orders, turned and carved in mahogany. The Grecian Temple on the first floor is in almost daily use and was fitted out to a higher standard in 1912, with organ, complete mahogany panelling and an allegorical pedimented doorway at each end, one in Doric order and the other Ionic, part gilded to match the sunburst ceiling. Bronze Roman candelabra on claw feet are fitted against the panelling supporting torch-style lighting brackets. The same black-and-white sunk marble floor, Masonic insignia and throne-like chairs complete a strongly neo-classical interior with space to seat 108 to 150 members. Elsewhere in the hotel, some original though overpainted decoration remains in the Glass Dome Restaurant and the 600-seat Hamilton Hall banqueting-room. Balls Brothers' Wine Bar and *L'Entrecôte* restaurant, independently run, similarly retain decorative plasterwork. Historical former occupiers of the site included the Bethlehem (Bedlam) Hospital and Hobson's stables of 'Hobson's Choice' fame.[8]

London, Great Eastern Hotel, Liverpool Street, 1884. A combination of stone, brick and stucco by Charles Barry II and his son Charles Edward Barry produced a serviceable City hotel, even if it lacked the glamour present in grand West End hotels. In 1894, banqueting facilities designed by R. W. Edis as the Abercorn Rooms extension became steadily in demand for private and public functions.

Colonel R. W. Edis also designed the Great Central Hotel (1899) to serve Marylebone station, although it was not strictly a railway hotel as the site was developed by Frederick Hotels to be 'A Temple of Luxury' with a tariff 'more moderate than any other Hotel of the same class in London'. Not only was it advertised as being close to Regent's Park, Hyde Park and the West End but also listed as convenient attractions 'Club and Medico Land, the Art World, Lord's Cricket Ground, and Madame Tussaud's'. There was even a cycle track on the roof for exercise addicts, and a dominant central clock tower, possibly used to time the laps. Who could resist all this and more for inclusive terms 'from 15/- per Day [75p] for a stay of not less than One Week'?[9] Edis had considerable experience of hotels for, in addition to the Great Eastern extensions he designed the Chine Hotel,

Two Masonic Lodges were accommodated in the Great Eastern Hotel: the Egyptian Temple in the basement, and the Grecian on the first floor. The latter was lavishly fitted out in 1912 to the designs of architects Brown and Barron. Alexander Burnett Brown, himself a Mason, was in charge of the works, on which no expense was spared. Hand-carved and gilded mahogany chairs were provided for the principal officers, and carved columns represent the three Orders of Architecture. *Skyros Alpha* and *Brèche Violette* marble wall panelling and Roman-style bronze lamps follow the classical effect, with significant black and white chequered marble filling the central rectangular floor space.

The saucer-domed ceiling completes a setting for the ritual with a 'Blazing Star' centrepiece of glass prisms and lights, to which a gilded ladder ascends against a sky-blue background accommodating the zodiacal signs.

Boscombe (1873), the Royal Pavilion at Folkestone (1898) and the Victoria Hotel and Clock Tower in Nottingham (1901), which once formed part of a comprehensive Victoria Station development scheme. London clubs were another of his specialities, and the British Pavilion at the Chicago World's Fair in 1893 was his work.

An exceptional example of a non-railway hotel in Central London, which carried forward the aims and achievements of the grand hotel builders in the mid-nineteenth century, is the Langham Hotel. Because of its consistently well-recorded history and the project's encounter with difficulties that were to repeat themselves in so many other cases, a study of the site, its acquisition and some detail of the building process merits careful attention. The story really starts in the middle of the eighteenth century when, in common with many other cities and towns, London had been developing westwards and then, as the area between the City and West-

London, Great Central Hotel, 1899, now known as the Landmark, was a later work by R. W. Edis, more lively in expression than the Abercorn Rooms at the Great Eastern Hotel. It closed as a hotel in 1939 at the outbreak of World War II, and after Government requisition as housing for troops in transit it became offices for the British Transport Commission, and later British Rail had it until 1986. Purchase and re-purchase by hotel companies ensued, while an imaginative scheme introduced a covered atrium and enlarged the bedrooms while reducing their number from 700 to 305.

By 1993 the Landmark Hotel had combined modern amenities with turn-of-the-century interiors in the public rooms, altering the earlier modestly priced family atmosphere and offering greater luxury.

The Landmark. The early interiors, decorated by Maples, have been
restored to their original state where practicable.

London, Langham Hotel, 1865. Designed by John Giles, this was the largest hotel of its time in London, but was successful only after a false start burdened by debt and inadequate management. Once reorganized it became highly fashionable, particularly in literary and American circles.

minster was built up, towards the north. Established families owned substantial estates of farms, fields and parklands in the area and these, the Portman, Portland, Berners and Bedford estates, were next to be covered by urban development.

The Marylebone estate had been bought in 1708 by John Holles, Duke of Newcastle, whose son-in-law, Edward Harley, Lord Oxford, subsequently launched a comprehensive scheme centred on a new square north of Oxford Street. This was to be Cavendish Square, with chapel and market building respectively sited at west and east ends of the estate. Harley was advised on the general layout by his architect James Gibbs, who later took up several building leases and lived in one of the houses on these plots, at the corner of Wimpole Street and Henrietta Street. Harley's daughter Henrietta became Duchess of Portland, and the Cavendish–Harley estate remained in the Portland family until 1879. Completion of the Cavendish Square developments was slow, but just beyond the northwest corner of the Square, a Harley relative, the third Lord Foley, built in 1758 a pleasing five-bay classical mansion for himself with two octagonal pavilion wings. This house lay across the north–south line of Portland Place which, as a result, became a cul-de-sac or 'close' with access from the new Marylebone Road. Foley House looked north up a gentle slope towards fields and gardens, and the agreement between Foley and the Portlands provided that this view should be preserved in perpetuity. The ground should be left unbuilt upon for ever and a private Act of Parliament legalized the undertaking,

thus retaining the width of Portland Place as the open 125-feet frontage of Foley House.[10]

The Adam brothers had been working on the riverside Adelphi project near Charing Cross from 1768, and in about 1773 they turned their attention to speculative development in Portland Place which, now controlled in an ample width, offered opportunities for grandeur in the form of town palaces or mansions for the aristocracy. In the event this conception, perhaps because of anxiety on account of the War for Independence in America and French intervention in that conflict, did not draw sufficient potential takers. James Adam modified the scale of their enterprise and designed opposing pedimented terraces of houses that were nevertheless of considerable size and great elegance. As long as Foley House sealed off the southern end of Portland Place, the atmosphere wherein residents could parade in evening dress up and down the wide pavements was maintained and the gates at the Marylebone end ensured a degree of privacy and security. John Nash later called this whole architectural composition 'the finest street in London'. Nash himself was involved from 1811 with the planning of Regent's Park as a climax to the triumphal way that had long been an ambition of his royal patron the Prince Regent. Reversion of Crown leases brought its achievement near and Nash's scheme to link Carlton House with the new park by way of Portland Place was approved. This was to be no great swathe cut in monumental manner through the capital but rather a skilled exploitation of the existing ownership boundaries, disguising irregularities by the careful siting of focal points and in using classical architectural vocabulary with slightly unorthodox accents.

Like the Adam brothers before him, Nash had an interest in property speculation and acquired from Lord Foley, for whom he had carried out substantial work in Worcestershire at Witley Court, the small Foley House estate, probably as part of a settlement of outstanding debt. He then sold part to the Crown and part to Sir James Langham, a Northamptonshire baronet, on the understanding that he would also be employed by Sir James as architect for the new town house. Some structural shortcomings – not entirely unknown in some of Nash's work – seem to have occurred during the building process and relations between client and architect broke down, another architect being appointed to complete Langham House. Nash finally forced Sir James to buy at exorbitant cost a further 'ransom strip' of land on which he threatened otherwise to build a terrace of houses, much to his ex-client's detriment. In spite of these dealings, Nash never lost sight of the overall effect that mattered so much to the King, and what might have become an awkward realignment between Upper Regent Street and Portland Place, Foley House having been demolished in 1820, was overcome by the Ionic portico of All Souls Church which he was designing. Circular on plan and surmounted by a fluted sharp-pointed spire, this still remains as the pivotal point of transition between the two streets. Thomas Smith, writing in 1833, describes the road at this point as taking 'a handsome sweep round the elegant mansion and grounds of Sir James Langham … built on part of the site of Foley House'. On this site 30 years later the vast Langham Hotel was under construction, an example of the transformation effected by the Industrial Revolution and the mobility conferred, as we have seen, by steamship and above all by the new railways. This mobility and the rapid increase in population escalated demand for hotel rooms that existing modest-sized Georgian hotels could not supply. The passage through Parliament of the Limited Liability Act in 1862 widened eligibility for those who wished to become shareholders and therefore encouraged initiation of large-scale enterprises. One of these was the Langham Hotel Company, which was formed the same year with a raised capital of £150,000 in £10 shares.[11] The Company immediately proceeded with a limited architectural competition for the new hotel, which had been publicized as a proposed 50 per cent larger than the recently finished Grosvenor Hotel at Victoria Station designed by Knowles. John Giles was the winner, and nine months later, in July 1863, the Earl of Shrewsbury and Talbot, Company chairman, laid the foundation stone. Giles seems to have had James Murray wished upon him as partner or collaborator by the directors, who had presumably seen and liked Murray's previous work in the Westminster Palace Hotel at the eastern end of Victoria Street. His function appears to have been to design the interior, but this association was not a happy one and Murray entered into a lawsuit against Giles in 1867 as to the ownership and rights in the working drawings. Owen Jones, the British architect who was in charge of the decoration for the Crystal Palace at Sydenham and who had published his influential *The Grammar of Ornament* in 1856, was also brought in to contribute to the interiors and furnishing.

Not surprisingly, as work proceeded shareholders were told in 1864 that estimated costs had been exceeded and a further £30,000 must be raised. The contractors, Lucas Brothers, could then continue at full capacity, with brick deliveries of Suffolk whites from Woolpit being resumed. Completion, or near completion, was achieved by the appointed day when the Prince of Wales, later Edward VII, was to open the hotel, the largest in London. The ceremony, followed by a luncheon party and a tour of inspection, was accomplished to general satisfaction and admiration of

the many new amenities. This was on 10 June 1865, but the Langham Hotel Company, not sufficiently experienced in business matters, fighting an economic recession and inadequately supported by the hotel manager, went into liquidation within three years. The first attempt to provide luxury service at moderate prices had failed, and the hotel, which had finally cost £300,000 to build and equip, was sold for £155,715, representing a disastrous loss to the shareholders. Some recouped their loss by investing in the new company that was formed and under which, with a new board and its chairman Henry J. Rouse, cost-cutting and more capable management resulted in profitability. The hotel now succeeded in attracting a fashionable clientèle, and within a few years had improved its services and capacity by adding a new extension to the west in 1871.

Literary figures, politicians, explorers, musicians and royalties patronized this great hotel, which continued to prosper in spite of growing competition. The guest lists included 'Ouida', Harrison Ainsworth, the traveller Richard Burton, artist J. E. Millais, Wilkie Collins, Browning, Longfellow, Gladstone, H. M. Stanley, Bret Harte, Mark Twain, Napoleon III, Prince Hassan of Egypt, Conan Doyle, Dvořák, Oscar Wilde, Alcock and Brown, Elgar and many more whose visits are detailed in Tom Steel's hotel book, which also provides a great deal of background relating to the later use and recent full restoration as a hotel for Hilton International. Visitors from abroad, and in particular from the United States, found the Langham much to their taste. The 1860s building itself must be looked at by the architectural historian in close relation to its nearest predecessor, the Grosvenor, with which in general style it has quite a lot in common. The origins of these two hotels differed, as the Grosvenor was a railway hotel linked, as it still is, directly to the main station concourse and did not have the restraining examples of neighbouring buildings designed by the Adam brothers or John Nash. In comparison, the Langham is a great deal larger, but the handling of component parts shows greater skill and subtlety.

These talents can also be seen in a rather different style and scale of hotel that John Giles built in 1865–6 as the Richmond Hill Hotel in Richmond, Surrey (now the Petersham Hotel, but in the intervening period being called successively the Mansion and then the Star and Garter). From near-contemporary auction sale particulars in 1867 we learn that it was 'designed by an architect eminent in the school of Palatial Buildings, And has been built under the superintendence of another architect as well known for his knowledge of materials and construction'. Its style is idiosyncratic with an elaborate two-storey oriel above the main Romanesque-influenced entrance that leads into the impressive staircase hall. The probable record length of unsupported Portland stone staircase, with pineapple newel for welcome, is crowned with a painted ceiling by Ferdinando Galli, celebrating Annibale Carracci, Michelangelo, Titian and Raphael. This was a relatively small hotel and had originally fewer than 40 bedrooms with 12 private sitting-rooms, but it was unquestionably conceived in the grand manner. The northwest entrance elevation shows a quality that marks John Giles as an architect worth further study.

To return to the Langham design, the site by virtue of its curved frontage opposite All Souls Church, Langham Palace, gave him opportunities for modelling and massing which he used well. The size of this 300-bedroom hotel imposed on the more human dimensions of the surrounding Adam and Nash buildings a sudden, and not very welcome, change of scale, but the Langham itself expresses Victorian aspirations and its developers were proud to describe it as the largest building in London, by whatever method they justified the claim. Not having to incorporate train sheds or cater for the exigencies of noise and pollution inseparable from

railway travel, it escapes the censure of Summerson's comment on the Grosvenor at Victoria, that 'in its deliberate coarseness it speaks for the age of steam'.

The considered balance of the entrance elevation, which looks northwards up Portland Place, is an object lesson in accommodating rows of windows successfully in an eight-storey building without either monotony or self-conscious tricks. Ornament is strictly zoned and subservient to the dominant Florentine cornice and carefully varied or emphasized semicircular headed windows. The entrance, with its carriage porch and, originally, a cast-iron canopy over the pavement, forms the main though understated vertical axis in a seven-bay-wide recess between two pavilions. These are rusticated and stone faced, with projecting window bays to the height of the two main floors. Their parapets are linked by the balcony at third main floor level, forming visually a frame for the main entrance. The façade of the west wing continues in four slightly wider bays of sufficient emphasis to give a suitable stop to the building. On the east side of the entrance a taller corner tower, owing something to P. C. Hardwick's Great Western Hotel with triple windows and

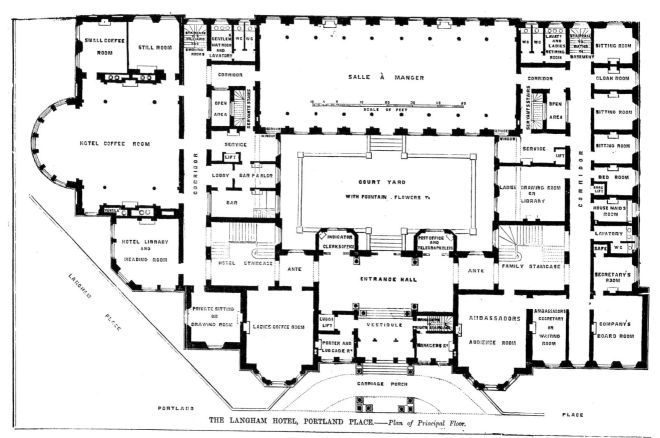

London, Langham Hotel. Comprehensive provision of public rooms for mid-Victorian times; note the Ladies Drawing-room and Library and the adjacent Family Staircase.

heavy upper cornice, has a French-style convex roof, now restored after war damage. This important feature balances the elevation and turns the corner towards Upper Regent Street. Here a further chamfered corner block usefully modulates into the east elevation, where a simple seven-bay grid of windows supports a two-storey many-windowed bow built above the large basement kitchen as the hotel's coffee-room. For all its difference of scale, this elevation appears as a conscious attempt to relate the Langham to the circular porch of All Souls Church yet not to offer unmannerly competition.

Above the stone-faced plinth, tuck-pointed brickwork of Suffolk whites is used, and stonework, except for the important modelled frieze under the main cornice, is generally confined to horizontal band courses, some moulded and some decorated, linking the Florentine and Venetian windows. The main cornice is capped in Portland stone, but the related mouldings and cast decorative panels beneath are in a mix of Portland stone dust, cement and sand. This was discovered during the recent restorations and probably represents an economy measure at a height normally well clear of close inspection. Unidentified portrait heads of similar material fill the roundels of the Venetian windows just below the frieze of the front pavilion projections. The extant principal floor plan from *The Builder* of July 1863 shows clearly the straightforward axial layout through the main entrance and dividing left and right to the two staircases and wings. An open courtyard 'with fountain, flowers &c' separated the entrance hall from the 102 × 40 feet colonnaded *salle à manger* that was serviced at each end from pantries and lifts from below. The right-hand west wing with its 'Family Staircase' and numerous sitting-rooms contained in addition the Ambassador's Audience Room with anteroom for Ambassador's Secretary or Waiting Room, Company's Board Room and Secretary's Room, and a Ladies' Drawing Room or Library. Stairs to the basement led down to the swimming-bath, which was probably under the four western bays of the *salle à manger*. This end of the building would appear to have been the more subdued of the two main wings and 'for persons not of an aspiring character', so no doubt was considered appropriate for the ladies who rarely travelled alone and were normally circumscribed within strict limits of propriety in public places. The east wing was altogether a more public area, with a social club-like atmosphere in the large bow-windowed coffee-room, the library and reading-room, small coffee-room and still room, bar and bar parlour and stairs leading down to the billiard- and smoking-rooms. Finally, and nearer to the entrance hall and the staircase, a large private sitting- or drawing-room and indeed a ladies' coffee-room completed the principal rooms.

PORTLAND PLACE

During World War II the Langham was occupied by the BBC and suffered a direct hit in an air raid. The water storage tanks were ruptured and their contents streamed down through the building. This architects' drawing shows the building in its damaged condition minus much of its corner, which was rebuilt during the Langham's restoration to hotel use in 1991.

Fire precautions had been carefully considered and a patent electric fire alarm was installed at an early stage. All stairs were of York or other hard stone construction with circulation areas being generally supported by shallow jack-arched brickwork vaulting confined between either cast-iron or plated steel girders. A filling of rubble and cement levelled the upper surface, which in some cases was finished with a paving of Portland stone slabs and in others with a thicker layer of concrete. On upper floors the rooms had traditional timber-joisted floor construction and a finish of butt-jointed floorboards. Where unsupported spans exceeded the practical limits of timber, steel or cast-iron members were sub-

The Langham, details of sculpture on the façade.

stituted in a somewhat random manner, as observed by the Halpern Partnership in 1991. Between the joists, sound reduction and a limited degree of fire protection was obtained by filling or 'pugging', and the architects' photographs show an unorthodox use in one area of all sizes of cockleshells packed in for this purpose. Wherever possible the original joists have been retained, but the old dirty pugging material has been removed and soundproofing was obtained instead with alternate layers of mass and air space using modern materials.[12]

Hydraulic lifts were a novelty, the first 'rising rooms' in the world, for guests and also for services, including the vital supply of coal for innumerable open fireplaces throughout the hotel. The kitchen department below the coffee-room was fitted out by Adam & Son, Haymarket, and cooking utensils were supplied by Johnson & Ravey. Coal, gas and steam heated the ovens and other cooking equipment and, from basement kitchen to roof level, two very large chimneystacks are thought to have incorporated ventilation ducts as well as flues and have been adapted for use as part of the 1991 modernization.

In the ceiling of the dining-room (originally *salle à manger*, now known as the ballroom), were three circular ventilation extract grilles two or three feet in diameter. Most details of this or other equipment and services have been destroyed, partly due to war damage to the building and partly at a later date when BBC records (kept by the BBC during their 1941–86 period of occupation) may have suffered fire damage. Water was provided from an artesian well, as became the case for many of the new buildings in London in the mid-nineteenth century, but a mains supply from the West Middlesex Waterworks could be obtained and was used to ensure adequate supply, stored in a very large roof tank until, in the Blitz of 1940–41, the tank succumbed to repeated bomb damage and the water flooded down through the building.

Building alterations had begun in the first few years of the hotel's life, and by 1871 a new western extension had been completed, accommodating extra public and private rooms and a lift. Electric light was used for the entrance and the courtyard, superseding gas, by 1879 but was not extended to the whole hotel until 1888.

The Langham in its heyday was always anxious to keep abreast of the latest ideas in technology and in grand hotel levels of service. Postal and telegraphic offices, telephonic communications, reception, billiard- and smoking-rooms were all advertised to attract custom, as well as the mixed benefits of a steam laundry, telegraphic news service and a select band playing from 6 pm to 8.30 pm every evening

London, Richmond Hill Hotel. This smaller family hotel by John Giles was completed in 1866, was later named the Star and Garter and is now known as the Petersham Hotel. Since its recent renovation and cleaning it indicates Giles's versatility, easily being confused at a glance with late twentieth-century post-modern design.

during the Season. Recent renovation has enabled the Langham to resume its proper role as a grand hotel contributing to the street scene of Langham Place in a state close to the first conception by its architect John Giles.

Scotland and Northern Routes from London

Railways to Scotland and the North usually generated large hotels to cater for commerce in the growing city centres and for recreation where a tourist trade was expanding. Travellers from the Continent and North America belonged to both categories, having interest in industrial progress and being ready to enjoy romantic scenery and seascapes. Karl Friedrich Schinkel, Goethe and Mendelssohn were a few among many who found their way north before the railways, helping to blaze the trail for others. The 1860s was a boom period for travel throughout the industrialized world, served by dozens of new hotels. In the north of Scotland the Station Hotel at Inverness was a forerunner, designed by Jos Mitchell and opened in 1856 under private enterprise; in 1878 it was sold to the Highland Railway. It was built in the mid-Victorian Italianate villa style, a substantial version in stone, with entrance hall and dividing staircase remarkably like that of the Grosvenor at Victoria Station in London, which was four or five years later. Carved pineapple finials on the staircase newels symbolized welcome and may be ascribed to later work by the Aesthetic Movement interior designer

Inverness, Station Hotel, 1856, by Jos Mitchell, was bought by the Highland Railway in 1878.

The grandeur of the Station Hotel staircase in Inverness can be compared with that of the Grosvenor in London, but here the detail of ironwork and woodwork produces a balustrade of greater finesse.

D. Cottier. The Inverness Station Hotel had the distinction of being for many years consistently profitable. Like many hotels of the time, it was absorbed into the LMS Hotel group and benefited from their efficient management.

Cottier was employed on two large houses at Crieff that contain his interior woodwork and stained glass in William Morris style, now used as the Coll-Earn Castle Hotel (1869–70) and the Ruthven Towers Hotel (1882). Both were designed by W. Leiper, and the Coll-Earn has fireplaces by B. Talbert and tiles by William De Morgan and W. B. Simpson. Station hotels at Dunkeld (1856) in Tudor manner and Perth (1888) in Scots Gothic are credited to A. Heiton. Father and son of the same name are likely to have been involved.

The 45-bedroom Station Hotel at Ayr (1886) by A. Galloway offered a package deal in the 1890s of a first-class rail ticket from St Enoch's, Glasgow, plus a full week's board and lodging for £3 10s. Many such bargains were offered under the auspices of Thomas Cook, travel agents, whose scope extended into many parts of Europe and the rest of the world.

Glasgow preceded Edinburgh in railway hotels, St Enoch Station Hotel, now demolished, being the first that, in 1879, was purpose-built by Thomas Wilson, echoing some features from Scott's Midland Grand but handling them with sober restraint. The Caledonian Railway brought forth the Central Station Hotel in 1885 by R. R. Anderson (1834–1921), by which time a mixture of Low Countries Renaissance stepped gables, pedimented dormers and Venetian windows seemed to be getting a little out of hand, although detailing was carefully done.

Edinburgh's dignified answer was the Caledonian Hotel (1899–1903) by Peddie and Browne, in dark red Locharbriggs sandstone, delivered by rail direct from the quarry and worked in neo-Renaissance style. The design was made in about 1867 but long deferred due to lack of funds. It was finally completed to a high standard on a dominant wedge-shape site at the end of Princes Street, and, with its marble, stained glass and Louis XV décor, became one of the favourite LMS hotels. The rival Waverley or North British Hotel (1895–1902) was at the same time being built as stiff competition by the North British Railway at the other end of Princes Street. Rising from the Waverley station platforms in the valley below via four utilitarian levels up to the street entrance, a further five storeys were designed by W. H. Beattie in a blend of Old Scottish with New Town Classical styles, not quite equal to Peddie's elegant luxury at the Caledonian but providing more than 300 bedrooms, 52 bathrooms and 70 lavatories. The plan at street level, almost square, contained all main rooms, entered under a substantial clock tower to entrance halls giving access to the grill room on the left, drawing-room on the right, and the Palm Lounge straight ahead. A spacious coffee- or dining-room further to the right faced a magnificent view towards the west and the National Gallery of Art. The ballroom, 'Mahogany Room' and tea-room completed the hotel's street-floor accommodation, the remainder of the available space within the site being let as shops. Services within the hotel were up-to-date and had double-glazed windows where noise presented a problem. Five thousand electric light fittings, 25 miles of various service pipes for hot and cold water, waste, vent and fire-hydrant purposes and 75,000 gallons of water storage in the entrance tower made quite an impressive list of statistics. Steel and concrete filler joist floors were carried on load-bearing walls and steel stanchions in an exploratory move towards full steel framing. This hotel, now called the Balmoral, initially aroused a certain amount of criticism for its bulky dominance in Princes Street, but by the time it was closed for refurbishment in 1988 the same local society, the Cockburn Association, that objected to it in 1902 acknowledged its acceptability and encouraged historic listing to protect it.

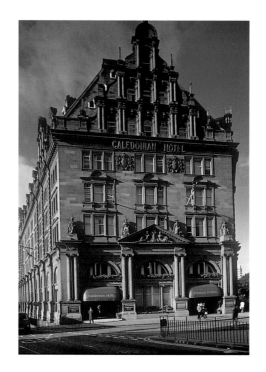

Edinburgh, Caledonian Hotel, 1903, designed by J. M. Dick Peddie, son of the founder of the architectural firm Peddie and Kinnear. The red Permian sandstone lends warmth to the distinguished building on its corner site.

The Caledonian, bedroom corridor, giving an impression of solid quality.

A Scottish railway hotel of entirely different character and cherished by an extensive following of golf enthusiasts was low-built in the domestic vernacular style of the early 1900s. It opened at Turnberry in 1906, served by its own branch line and generously provided with two golf courses, the Ailsa and the Arran. James Miller (1860–1947) was the architect, having been staff architect to the Caledonian Railway Company in 1888 after working in the office of Andrew Heiton (1823–94), Perth, then in various Edinburgh practices. His own practice was started in Glasgow in 1893, and hotel work included Peebles Hydro *c*. 1908 and sketch plans for auxiliary housing at the Gleneagles Hotel, Auchterarder, in 1920 which was then handled by the railway company's architects.

The principal architect for Gleneagles was Matthew Adam, and the hotel was opened in 1924 after a long gestation period of eleven years. Once completed, its golf courses and tennis courts gained worldwide fame, justifying the advertised title of 'Premier Sports Hotel'. The Cruden Bay Hotel near Aberdeen had been first on the golf hotel scene, opening in 1899, designed by the railway company's architect John J. Smith. Although its golf course still exists, the hotel is no more. It was the earliest of a dozen British golf hotels developed by railway companies, who found them to be very popular and good investments.

Moving back a little in time and south to England's industrial heartland, we come to the railway hotels of Bradford and Leeds, Liverpool, Manchester and Birmingham. The dark satanic mills of the Yorkshire woollen towns looked towards Bradford as a manufacturing and trading centre where good rail transport assisted exports and reinforced American and Continental links. Its cultural demands were met by a number of local choirs and good choral societies interspersed with regular visits from the Hallé Orchestra and from touring theatre companies. None of its three hotels, the Victoria (1867) by Lockwood and Mawson, later bought by the Great

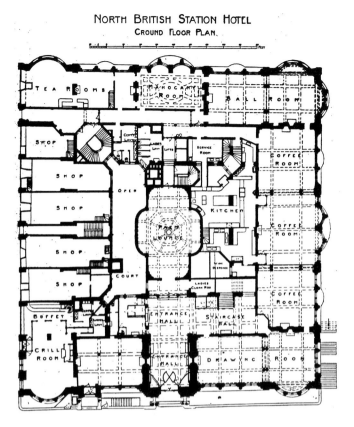

NORTH BRITISH STATION HOTEL
GROUND FLOOR PLAN.

The Balmoral Hotel. An innovative plan combining a series of public rooms with some of the finest views in Edinburgh, and incorporating shops and services at street level.

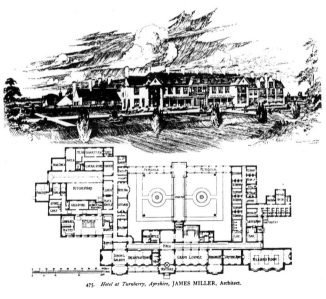

475. *Hotel at Turnberry, Ayrshire*, JAMES MILLER, Architect.

Turnberry, Ayrshire, Turnberry Station Hotel, 1906, was one of several hotels which responded to demand for golfing facilities. Built by the Glasgow & South Western Railway, one of the constituent companies of the London, Midland & Scottish (LMS) Railway, it was designed in a low-built domestic vernacular by James Miller and possessed two golf courses, the Ailsa and the Arran.

Edinburgh, North British Station Hotel, 1902, by W. Hamilton Beattie and A. R. Scott, architects from the Scott and Beattie practice. It is now named the Balmoral Hotel since complete refurbishment, and in the past was sometimes referred to as the Waverley, located as it was above that railway station.

Northern Railway, the privately owned Alexandra (1877) and the Midland (1890), would lay claim to 'grand' status, but the Midland was architecturally important as a precursor of Manchester's Midland, being designed by the same architect, Charles Trubshaw (1841–1917). It is also recorded in theatrical history as the scene of the death of the great actor Sir Henry Irving at the age of 67 during his provincial tour in 1905. The 1850s and 1860s were great decades for Britain's railway systems, and Leeds was a vigorous enough entrepôt to be served by both the Midland Railway and the Great Northern line. Each of these companies built a very substantial hotel of its own, distinguishing Leeds as being the first British town apart from London with two large railway-built and railway-owned hotels. Acts of Parliament were still required to vest appropriate powers in the relevant companies and the Midland acquired these in 1861, enabling the first Queen's Hotel to be opened two years later. Additions were made in 1867 and 1898, but a complete twentieth-century rebuild under W. Curtis Green (1865–1960) and William Hamlyn was made

Leeds, Metropole Hotel, located close to the two railway stations, between the Queen's Hotel and the early Great Northern.

Bradford, Midland Hotel, 1890. Designed by Charles Trubshaw in the best traditions of Midland railway hotels, this lobby, looking out to the horse and carriage park under the station roof, is lavishly tiled with the Burmantofts Company's arabesque designs.

in 1936–7. The other line, the Great Northern, produced a seven-storey square-set Gothic block in 1869, not much further than 100 yards away, large in scale and part Ruskinian Venetian in character, named after the company and designed by M. E. Hadfield (1812–85). It was badly damaged by fire in 1906 but is still in use. The third Leeds hotel, also nearby, was the Metropole (1899) by Chorley and Connon, now looking well in its cleaned terracotta cladding, with very little alteration to its Victorian design. York Royal Station Hotel (1853) by G. T. Andrews (1805–55) was superseded by the Royal York Hotel (1877) by another railway architect, W. Peachey, alongside the well-known curve of the station layout. Its plain buff brick exterior looks out over a sizeable formal garden, and internally the grand staircase with a double well forms an impressive main concourse.

Liverpool flourished as a port orientated towards transatlantic traffic, and the first Adelphi Hotel, built in 1826 and referred to by Charles Dickens as 'undeniably perfect', was superseded by a rebuild in 1876 and then acquired by the Midland Railway in 1892 and again rebuilt in 1912–14 using the new building method of a completely steel-framed structure with stone as non-structural facing. The architect was

The Royal York Hotel, 1877, by W. Peachey, is sited dramatically beside the railway tracks, rendering obsolete the old station hotel within the city walls.

The pleasing formal garden layout of the Royal York Hotel is in scale with the substantial hotel building, but the latter, impressive as it looks in the aerial view, is defaced by a plethora of unconcealed drainpipes.

Robert Frank Atkinson (1871–1923) who had married into the LMS hotel dynasty of the Towles and ran offices in both Liverpool and London. His Adelphi scheme was not fully completed before the Great War and afterwards a modified version was executed by Stanley Hamp of Colcutt and Hamp. The opening, in April 1914, was commented on as

a fitting climax to the career of Mr W. Towle, who … has retired after fifty years' active association with the Midland Railway hotels. … The hotel is of six storeys, and has a massive and imposing exterior, the architecture being in a chaste Neo-Grecian style. The stately entrance-hall gives access to the central hall which is of considerable size, and forms a very luxurious lounge.

The *Caterer and Hotelkeepers' Gazette* goes on to mention the French restaurant and drawing-room as inspired by Fontainebleau, a ballroom, smoke-room and a quiet and shady garden with fountain court. A 'Masonic Room' and 'Gentlemen's Sitting Room' were provided and two other sitting-rooms were furnished and decorated by well-known firms, one by Waring & Gillow and one by Maples. Technical facilities included room telephones for service and 'to all parts of Great Britain and the Continent'. Steam heating, well distributed through concealed vents, supplemented by coal fires for bedrooms, all warmed the building very satisfactorily and the old kitchen areas had all the necessary food and fuel stores, with further available space to allow for butchering and baking under the same roof. One of the first hotel swimming pools in addition to Turkish and other baths were installed as were Otis Elevators' lifts and, more surprisingly, squash- and lawn tennis-courts and a miniature rifle-range.

Not far away from the Adelphi, the North Western Hotel, which fronted Lime Street Station, has a majestic turreted Victorian presence, designed in 1871 by Alfred Waterhouse (1830–1905). It was closed as a hotel in 1933 but now is achieving a second lease of life. Its fine profile, still intact, deserves better treatment than Waterhouse's later hotel design for the Metropole at Brighton (1888), where the addition of extra storeys mutilated its sea-front façade. In Liverpool the North Western and the Exchange Station Hotels both suffered upstaging by the wide range of amenities and comfort the more modern Adelphi was able to offer.

The outstanding railway hotel in Manchester, the Midland, attracted virtually unanimous approval when it opened in 1903. Four years of intensive preparation and building had taken place under the direction of the Midland Railway Company's manager and genius, William Towle, and their distinguished architect Charles Trubshaw. Towle's dedication, mentioned above in connection with the Adelphi opening, subsequently won him a knighthood. The Manchester site between the Town Hall on one side and the old Central Station (now G-Mex) on the other had been occupied by warehouses, a music hall called the Casino – or colloquially 'Old Cass' – and the Gentlemen's Concert Hall. It was at subscription concerts in this hall that Charles Hallé first appeared in Manchester and there, in 1857, formed his own Hallé Orchestra. After difficult negotiations the Concert Hall part of the two-acre site was sold to the railway company on condition that a theatre or hall 'which should be as commodious as the old one' must be incorporated in the new hotel. The *Guardian* took the opportunity to remark that the 'latest enterprise should have some effect upon the social life of the city' and made the point that the planned hotel had residential suites of rooms which were understood to be in 'widespread demand'.

Now that Manchester was obtaining its first grand hotel after Towle and Trubshaw had studied the latest ideas and

Liverpool, the Adelphi. The vigorous rebuild in 1876 failed to keep abreast of rail and steamship traffic and was demolished, to be superseded by a third, still larger hotel by R. Frank Atkinson, 1912–14, completed after the end of World War I by Collcutt and Hamp.

The Adelphi. A private dining-room in a more restrained manner, furnished by Waring's.

innovations in Europe and America, little expense was to be spared in supplying all the best amenities and schemes of decoration for exterior and interior. The building was designed to express the superb confidence of the Edwardian age in the city of cotton, culture and cricket on the basis that, if you are spending a lot of money you should be able to see the results. One of the most striking interiors in the new building was the theatre required in the purchase agreement. With its own separate entrance the auditorium was rectangular in plan with columns of two-storey height along each side to support the shallow barrel-vaulted ceiling and first floor balconies, all finished with the ornamental plasterwork of the *belle époque*. When filled to its capacity of 800, the

An Adelphi bedroom with advanced layout
and fittings, built-in wardrobes, cupboards,
dressing-table and washbasin, all supplied
with fixed mirrors.

Liverpool, North Western Hotel, 1871.
A railway hotel by Alfred Waterhouse that
stood empty for many years until recently
redesigned for student accommodation.
Its roof contributes an impressive profile
to the city skyline.

theatre and its patterned marble staircase must have swelled Mancunian civic pride. In the period before the Great War, theatregoers could watch the Pelissier Follies, Edward Terry and Mrs Patrick Campbell, the French Comedy Theatre and Miss Horniman's troupe – the first repertory company in England. The theatre closed in 1922 and was divided horizontally to add in its place three bedroom floors, leaving as a reminder of more glamorous days only the occasional forgotten scrap of decorative plasterwork.

The original hotel was six storeys high with many public rooms on the ground floor and 300 bedrooms. A choice of four or five restaurants was available and a tea-room with access to a roof terrace among the chimney pots; the trellised Winter Garden at ground level and the two-storey Octagon Court were popular meeting places with cane furniture, palms, hanging baskets and wrought ironwork introducing an occasional touch of Art Nouveau. The French restaurant retains its Louis Seize décor and the present Stanley suite, formerly the Gentlemen's Library, keeps the original mahogany panelling. This type of interior finish also survives unchanged in one or two bedrooms, deliberately preserved with their original fittings also. The Octagon has lost its dome, but the stairs from Mount Street down to the German Restaurant, now the Goblet Wine Bar, still display the authentic decorative wall tiles. The glazed covered way which linked the hotel to the Central Station was a casualty, along with the Winter Garden, of alterations in 1936.

For the structure, a full steel-framed construction was decided on by Trubshaw, a method that was still regarded as innovative and a step forward from his Midland Hotel at Forster Square Station, Bradford, which had been completed in 1890. The general ground plan was of irregular wedge-shape built on the upper floors around two light wells, bedrooms being planned on both sides of the corridors, many with private bathrooms. A red Aberdeen granite plinth, red brick walls and teapot brown Burmantofts faience form the exterior facings, but comparison with the much smaller and more classically orientated Bradford Midland ceases with the faience and with the use of octagonal domed corner turrets. Both composition and style in the Manchester Midland remained unresolved, but the complexities of planning for multiple uses and the careful attention to practical and aesthetic detail helped to conceal these shortcomings. Fireproofing measures were embodied in the building, and the great water tanks common to all grand hotels were supported at roof level in the centre of the building. A form of air conditioning included careful filtering of the city pollution and double glazing reduced street noise. Every bedroom was fitted not only with a bedside telephone but also with an elec-

Manchester, the Midland, 1903. Built by Charles Trubshaw as a proud statement of the city, and containing a theatre (as it originally did), this robust hotel became both a cultural and a social centre. Rolls met Royce here, setting a stamp of quality.

The brass bedsteads and free-standing washstand in the Midland were up-to-date, but comparison with Atkinson's later Adelphi (*illustrated on pages 68–9*) shows the amount of change that occurred in the intervening decade.

tric clock dial over the door which could be illuminated by a switch near the bed at any time. 'It seems to have been the particular study of the management to relieve the visitor of the smallest care', recorded *The Manchester Evening News*: 'a world of kitchens below ground level and three huge boilers, besides immense stores and wine cellars. Twenty-three hydraulic lifts are in the building.' Private dining-rooms, rooms for smoking and billiards, reading and writing, Turkish baths, a post office – the only one in a British hotel – and a business bureau extend the list. Ladies had their own tea-room, foyer and whole block of rooms where dressmakers, milliners, hairdressers and domestic servants functioned. The only dissatisfied Mancunians seem to have been competing hoteliers, who soon lost trade to the glorious Midland.

Birmingham was becoming an important rail junction in the 1830s and existing accommodation was soon insufficient. Various short-term expedients took place to house travellers at Curzon Street station, with Philip Hardwick's design for conversion of the railway company's ballroom in 1839 being

one. The Ionic columned station building was extremely handsome, but the standard of accommodation was inadequate, and even with a further hotel wing in 1840–41 by R. B. Dockray (1811–71) and a new name as the Queen's Hotel, the problem was not solved. A new hotel with the same name took its place in 1853 (William Livock), and with extensions in 1911, 1917 and 1925 the satisfying classical building failed to meet twentieth-century standards and was closed prior to demolition in 1965.

From among the remainder of mid-century hotels, two in the Northeast of England stand out as being of exceptional interest. Henry Pease, member of the well-known Darlington Quaker family which had been to the fore in early promotion of railways was a director of the Stockton & Darlington Railway and saw possibilities in the development

Saltburn-by-the-Sea, Zetland Hotel, 1863. William Peachey, an architect with railway associations, produced a Victorian essay to dominate the coastline, with a central viewing tower as its distinctive feature.

of Saltburn-by-the-Sea as a seaside resort with sandy beach and a mineral water spring. The necessary Parliamentary bill was enacted by 1861 allowing a branch line and hotel to be constructed. No time was wasted, and William Peachey, architect to the railway company, advertised for building tenderers in May 1861 and achieved completion ready for the opening ceremony for the 50-bedroom Zetland Hotel to be carried out by the original landowner, the Earl of Zetland, on 27 July 1863. Although divided into separate flats since 1988, the building retains its character as an excellent example of mid-nineteenth-century hotel architecture. It has considerable presence, with a cylindrical viewing tower looking out to sea, imposing Renaissance-style entrance steps and terracing and the special amenity of a domestic-sized train shed and platform literally on the back doorstep. The station track has gone, but in those days a station-master in frock coat and silk hat officiated. Cream-coloured brick with worked stone dressings and a continuous balcony at first-floor level add vigour to the Italianate style. The envisaged development of Saltburn as a resort was never completed, although pleasure gardens were laid out, descending into a sheltered ravine and including a folly in temple form made out of the Corinthian portico moved from Barnard Castle station in 1867. For a guidebook of 1876 it was noted that

the Pleasure Grounds are open to visitors to this hotel *free*, a concession not granted to any other establishment … At the upper end of the gardens, close to the wood, ground is laid out and used as a croquet lawn, and for the new and fashionable game of lawn tennis. A handsome structure, called the Albert Temple, affords from its summit a splendid view of the whole of the grounds.

The popularity of this part of the coast persisted for some time in a modest degree as the building of the Coatham Victoria Hotel (*c.* 1871, C. J. Adams) demonstrates. It 'abuts upon the magnificent Promenade recently constructed by Arthur Turner Newcomen Esquire', but the Promenade Pier did not succeed owing to both competition from Redcar Pier and depression in the ironworking trades, and further ideas for development were shelved.

The second historic hotel on the Northeast coast, which announced in no uncertain terms that the day of the grand hotel had arrived, was the Grand at Scarborough, not this time a railway hotel although owing its viability to the rail connection that had reached Scarborough in 1845. For the size of building which the hotel syndicate had in mind, efficient transport had to be available, although the first train from York on the day the line was opened took 3¼ hours, allowing for extra time needed to acknowledge acclamations

en route. A site for the hotel on St Nicholas Cliff was obtained, close to the new bridge that linked south with north Scarborough across a 70-feet-deep cleft, and an architect was then appointed. This was Cuthbert Brodrick (1822–1905), whose masterpiece, Leeds Town Hall, had been finished in 1858, a few years before this new commission. Local myth had it that components of the design he now produced symbolized the seasons, months, weeks and days of the year, with four towers, twelve floors, 52 chimneys and 365 bedrooms, but the real figures were not so exact and 300 was nearer to the true number of bedrooms. The conception was magnificent and vast in scale, achieving ten storeys from beach level to the roof. The three lower floors were on the sea frontage only, being built into the cliffside up to the general ground level where the third-floor roof formed a terrace accessible from some of the main public rooms. Above this the bedroom floors came together in a truncated v-shape, finished along its southern end with a large curved bay. The four corner towers that mark out the trapezoidal site are surmounted by domes and supporting decoration now assimilated into the vocabulary of hotel design on the French Côte d'Azur and elsewhere. They were discovered as a design device particularly appropriate to the awkwardly shaped sites and the multi-storeyed, multi-windowed façades of so many grand hotels, where repetition only too easily turned into dullness and where pivotal corner features could disguise asymmetry. Brodrick was well-travelled and obviously found inspiration in Parisian Second Empire style. *The Builder* magazine described the materials he was using as 'exterior surfaces … of white brick, with ornamental moulded red brick jambs, and enrichments of terra-cotta and some of the jambs and cornices … of tooled Yorkshire stone', while the size of 'the main block of the building is about 220 feet long, 174 feet wide at the northern end, and 70 feet at the south end, and may, speaking generally, be called ten stories in height'.

After two years of building, the hotel works in 1865 ran out of money and progress had to be stopped. The story of unsuccessful attempts to raise further financing followed by sale to a new company willing and able to complete the project then unrolled, with a Dr John Deakin Heaton of Leeds taking a very active part in the rescue. Eventually the hotel was finished in 1867 and a great opening dinner took place on 23 July. A ball was given the next evening and guests, including Dr Heaton, were for the first time 'lodged and boarded' in the hotel. The interior could be inspected and its merits assessed as a summer resort hotel planned partly on the lines of many new American models in the matter of management. The main street-level floor contained a central hall and magnificent staircase, one of the most widely known in hotel history. This rose to the upper floors in a rich mixture of bronzed baroque metalwork balustrades, giant arcading and robust plasterwork with marine motifs. Much of the decoration has now been covered up for, one hopes, future restoration. The large bay-windowed Coffee Room facing south commanded a sweeping view of the bay and cliffs, while at the north end an even larger dining-room could take 300 people at a sitting. The main drawing-room, as at the Queen's in Cheltenham, was above the Coffee Room, and many other sitting-rooms catered for the leisure activities of visitors.

In the notorious scarcity of conventional hotel archives, special episodes have embedded themselves in the lore of well-known hotels and reached by press or word of mouth into the wider world. The Scarborough bombardment by the German navy that struck the Grand Hotel on 16 December 1914 was a case in point, not forgotten to several generations. Three German battleships in a naval squadron which appeared off the coast fired about 500 shells into the town as a salutary warning that their navy was an active one. Seventeen people were killed, scores were injured and damage in the town was extensive. From the restaurant at the foot of the cliff to a bedroom on the third floor, the Grand Hotel sustained some injury to property but not to people and so, fortunately, was able to show its war wounds without undue distress except for the £10,000 repair costs.

So far we have concentrated chiefly on the development of large hotels in Britain as they related to the railway networks, spreading from 1830 onwards. Once the novel idea of steam traction had really arrived, few hotels of any importance were built in complete disregard of accessibility by rail. Railway hotels were primarily linked with business and industry, but a minority of seaside towns, smaller spas and even some hotels in London continued to rely on the old horse-drawn carriages to deliver their visitors, at least for the last stage of their journeys.

Hydros, Spas and the Seaside

The vogue for hydropathic establishments is part of grand hotel history and 'Hydros' arose in substantial bulk to cater for the ailments of those magnates and their families from industrial centres who might have been inclined, among other things, to overwork, overeat and possibly drink too much. Whatever the cause, this particular form of 'taking the cure' seemed to justify provision of numerous rooms on at least four floors, facilities for immersion and consumption of locally recommended waters and sparse diet. To balance the

Scarborough, Grand Hotel, 1867, by Cuthbert Brodrick. This extensive edifice is one of Brodrick's few surviving major works and served well the demands of fashionable Scarborough. Music, dancing and the Cricket Festival all presented attractions in the town.

The fine staircase balustrade of the Grand was encased in damaging concrete during military occupation in World War II and the hotel has never been restored to its earlier glory, being now in use as a Butlin's family hotel.

austerity, fresh air and panoramic views were offered. In Wharfedale the earliest baths were built by the Romans but a Hydro at Ben Rhydding, the eastern end of Ilkley, was one of the earliest of its type on the edge of the moors and built in Scottish Baronial style in 1843–4. It owed its existence to Hamer Stansfield, Mayor of Leeds, and at a cost of £30,000 for the building, was advertising its treatments for asthma, rheumatism and skin infections. Used as the Wool Control Secretariat in the Second World War, it never resumed business as a Hydro and was demolished in 1955. Another local Ilkley development of higher architectural quality was Cuthbert Brodrick's Wells House (1858), which became a hydro hotel and still survives although the grounds, pleasingly laid out with small stream and waterfall by Joshua Major after correspondence with J. C. Loudon, have been curtailed by additional building for a College of Education. Both these establishments preceded construction of the railway but were within carriage-driving distance of Leeds and Bradford. Harrogate, as a spa and in the nineteenth century a dormitory town for Leeds, has three existing pre-grand hotels, the Crown (1806) where Byron stayed, the Granby (c. 1820) and the County (1830). The White Hart Hotel, now a hospital (1846), the Prospect, now Imperial (1859), and the Prince of Wales (1860–61) approached the change of rank in a well-mannered way, but a final leap into the grand category came with the Majestic (1900) by G. D. Martin, a large brick and stone building five to six storeys high with central cupola above an uncomfortable pair of Dutch-gabled bays but overlooking well landscaped sweeps of lawn and shrubs on an attractive site.

The Duke of Devonshire's interest in the town of Buxton had given it a good start as a remote and remarkably sophisticated spa in the eighteenth century. It has the benefit of some of the best urban architecture of the period in the form of the stone-built crescent near St Ann's Well dating from 1780. This was the result of the Duke, vying with the splendours of Bath, choosing as his architect one of the best of his time, John Carr of York (1723–1807), and spending £120,000 on the whole enterprise. In quality of design this crescent needs to make no obeisance to Bath's Royal Crescent although it is considerably smaller. Hotel accommodation always occupied large sections of Carr's building, there being first of all the Grand, the Centre and St Ann's Hotels as well as shops and the Assembly Room. Attention to the serious damage caused to the main hotel, the Crescent, by subsidence may ultimately enable it to be restored to full use. Elsewhere in the town, contributions by Wyatville, Joseph Paxton and Frank Matcham have all helped to maintain high standards of design. Returning to the 1860s, we find the seventh Duke

Harrogate, Majestic Hotel, 1900, by G. D. Martin. Well-sited in large grounds convenient for the spa, it is now a centre for conferences.

Buxton. St Ann's and the Crescent Hotel occupy a Georgian crescent to rival Bath, designed by John Carr of York on the Devonshire estate at the end of the eighteenth century.

The Palace Hotel. Staircase detail with quatrefoil-pierced supporting beams and the same motif on a small scale in the decorative iron balustrade.

supporting the Buxton Palace Hotel Company, substantially enlarging his shareholding when, almost inevitably, the Company ran into financial difficulties. The Palace Hotel 'elevated most salubriously' was opened on 6 June 1868, and in speaking of the Duke's generosity, the Chairman, Mr R. Broome, noted that 'it should not be overlooked that His Grace was previously the owner of seven hotels in Buxton, and the fact that he took shares in the eighth could only be accounted for by his well-known liberality.' The London architect Henry Currey had been introduced by the previous Duke, and was also lauded by the company chairman for his skills and for the fact that he had taken no payment for his work but would accept in due course any benefit due to him in the form of shares in the enterprise. The appropriately named Palace Hotel stands on a dominant site conveniently near the station that had been completed the previous year by the London & North Western Railway. This company also took up shares in the hotel and received appreciation at the opening dinner. The lengthy account of this occasion in *The Supplement of the Buxton Advertiser*, for Saturday, 6 June 1868 mentions that the dinner-table was laid *à la Russe*, for serving the meal as successive courses rather than using previous methods of displaying everything, hot or cold, at the same time. The opening menu for the Palace Hotel (reproduced overleaf) was certainly an impressive one.

Buxton, Palace Hotel, 1868. Henry Currey, a London architect known to the sixth Duke of Devonshire, used a five-part scheme for his design which incorporates French-influenced pavilions and a central tower linked by mansard roofs. The seventh Duke opened the hotel, to which he had contributed substantially.

SOUPS
Turtle. Printanier.

FISH
Salmon. Fillets of Sole à la Normande.
Eels à la Génoise. Turbot and Lobster Sauce.
WHITEBAIT.

ENTREES
Fillets of Beef, with Mushrooms.
Mutton Cutlets, Soubise Sauce. Lobster Cutlets.
Braised Sweetbreads and Green Peas. Compote of Pigeons.
Curry of Chicken.

RELEVES
Roast Lamb. Capons à la Béchamel. Ham.
Spring Chicken au Cresson. Langue de Bœuf au Macédoine
de Légumes.
Roast Ducklings.
Sirloin of Beef. Quails and Lobster Salad. Leverets.

SWEETS
Sir Watkin Pudding. Cabinet Pudding à la Windsor.
Gelèe en Macédoine de Fruits.
Crème à l'Italienne. Charlotte Prusienne. Gelèe de Dantzic.
Lemon Cheese Cakes. Pàtisserie Francaise.
Génois aux Pistaches. Méringues à la Romaine.
Ice Pudding à la Palace.
DESSERT.

The French-influenced symmetrical exterior of the building, with central and end pavilions, was an exceptionally well-balanced composition, an interesting version of the formula that was everywhere emerging as the accepted grand hotel hallmark. The gardens were and are expansive, terraced at the upper levels near the entrance; croquet and archery grounds were promised for outdoor entertainment as a future attraction. The public rooms for dining, coffee, withdrawing, reading, smoking and billiards were all of generous size and height. Stone corridors and stairs were 'substantial and fire-proof'. Thorough ventilation and 'modern appliances for lighting, warming etc., etc.' were recommended, as were suites on each floor for families, with separate entrances. These seem to have been much in demand in the new hotels as offering the welcome package of freedom and luxury without sacrificing comfort or privacy.

In the same district, Matlock played a crucial part in the hydropathic movement under the driving enthusiasm of John Smedley. Once again ambitious plans were assisted by the building of the railway – the Midland – up the valley from Derby in 1849. Smedley was a rich man with boundless energy, many talents and the ability to fire others with confidence and devotion so that his aims could be achieved. Reviving a Matlock family business at Lea Mills was his early enterprise but he progressed in other directions, first as a churchman then at chapel to become a nonconformist preacher with a temperance message. The fact that he caught typhoid fever was not entirely a disaster, for he was sent to Ben Rhydding Hydro for the hydropathic water cure. Not only was it an apparent success but he was converted into an ardent supporter of the method, and, with a few successful trials on his own millworkers, set up in the hydro business himself, buying a small going concern in 1853. Business grew and a new building on its present site with two subsequent additions made it the leading establishment of its kind in the country, without a single qualified doctor in sight for nearly two decades. Having the confidence to act as his own untrained doctor, Smedley also took on board the responsibilities of being his own architect and his hydro, now used as offices by Derbyshire County Council, initially consisted of the 1867 crenellated four- and five-storey block of eleven bays, straightforward and with little ornament. From the garden side a would-be classical wing to the right (1885) was linked to the older building by an unrelated pavilion feature. A third section made yet another change, but as this is a glazed winter garden the discrepancy is more acceptable. Smedley appeared unworried by this jumble of styles, and in the interior it is hard to put a name to that of the main entrance hall and stairs, but probably 'eclectic' is the best adjective. Carved Corinthian fluted columns appear in the old sitting-room, now members' room. The billiard-room retains all its Siena marble columns, fretted woodwork and alcoves lined with banquettes. Above these a series of painted and stained-glass panels depicts sports being decorously practised by the ladies – golf, croquet, hockey, cricket, tennis, archery and billiards, with what moral conclusion is not exactly obvious.

A sensible, if severe, régime was instigated with fresh air, exercise and rest; no smoking or drinking of alcohol. It worked, gained great popularity and revived Matlock as a spa, helped no doubt by at least fourteen editions of John Smedley's own handbook on *Practical Hydropathy*, 'including plans of baths and remarks on diet, clothing and habits of life'. Smedley seems to have been one of the few entrepreneurs in the business to finance and run such a pro-

Brighton, Grand Hotel, 1864, by John Whichcord. This presents
a light 'seaside' effect, with its new western wing extension (*on the left*)
carefully blended with the original building.

ject at a substantial profit, even at a fee of two guineas a week.
He died in 1874 and a hydro company was formed within
a few months, paying out very gratifying dividends for a
number of years. Others followed him, and this particular
branch of the hotel industry appealed to a large middle-class
clientèle, preponderantly in Scotland and the north of
England.

The Scottish Hydro boom centred on the 1870s was not
long-lived, although efforts were made to attract holidaymakers rather than confining the market exclusively to
patients. The hotel elements were therefore emphasized,
but this was not successful for long and expensively-built
assets were sold off by receivers at give-away prices. The
most dramatic single loss was Callander Hydro, which cost
£54,000 and was finally sold for £12,000. As buildings the
most notable were Crieff (1867) by R. Ewan, neo-Jacobean
in style, Dunblane (1875) by Peddie and Kinnear, soon closed,

and the Atholl Palace Hydro at Pitlochry (1875) by A. Heiton,
which cost £93,000 to build and raised only £25,000 when
sold to a Mr MacDonald who was already a hotelier.

Sporadic building continued to provide health-orientated
establishments in Harrogate, Malvern, Tunbridge Wells,
Torquay and other minor spas, offering rather more socially
respectable backgrounds for wives and children than some
fashionable resorts. Bournemouth was approved and grew
quickly after the railway arrived in 1870, with the Royal Bath
Hotel being extended in 1878 by C. C. Creeke, harking back
to the classical core of 1837–8 by the prolific church architect
Benjamin Ferrey. The Chine Hotel (1873) by R. W. Edis was
built as the Boscombe Spa Hotel for Sir Henry Drummond
Wolff, but the later Burlington Hotel (1893) by T. E. Collcut,
a large brick composition with corner turrets, is more
distinguished. Bournemouth received royal visits from the
Prince of Wales, the Empress Eugénie and the King of

Sweden, the King laying the Mont Doré Hydro foundation stone, but even this did not fend off early failure. In Blackpool the Imperial Hydropathic Establishment (1867) by Clegg and Jones, followed Mr Smedley's precepts and spread into a new wing (1875) by Mangnall and Littlewood. Perhaps the ten different kinds of baths available, from Turkish to warm, cold and sea water helped to engender interest and confidence to overcome the depressed economy of the 1870s. The Imperial reorganized itself as a hotel and a 'wildly Edwardian part' (1904) was added to J. B. Broadbent's design, still being used by seemingly endless conferences of all political shades. The Metropole, on an excellent island site near the north pier reached its optimum size in 1896, complete with pepper pot turrets and sea view. Ballroom dancing developed into a favourite Blackpool pastime, and hotels including the Metropole engaged professional dancers to raise the standards by example and tuition. Derequisitioning after the Second World War left this hotel at a low ebb until rescued by the popular approach of robust entertainment and value for money offered by Butlin's Holiday Hotels in 1955.

Brighton maintained its attractions although respectability was not its most important preoccupation. Railway service had existed since 1841, but fresh ground in hotel design was broken only in 1864 with the construction of the Grand – the first to bear that name in England and just ahead of the one in Scarborough. Originally it had 260 rooms, designed by the architect John Whichcord junior (1823–85) to vary in size, allowing versatility in allocating different rooms for differently sized functions. Private suites were included as usual and great attention was paid in contemporary reports to the hydraulic lifts, a total of five for service and passengers, operating to serve seven of the nine storeys. An

From the age of fifteen, William Towle (1849–1929) had worked for the Midland Railway Hotels company, becoming a legendary figure at the head of this profitable enterprise and receiving a knighthood for his work in 1920. This photo, at the Adelphi Hotel, in 1912, was taken one year after his elder son Francis had been the first in the Towle hotelier family to be similarly honoured.

Brighton, Metropole, 1890, designed by Alfred Waterhouse for Gordon Hotels. Many features including the arched window heads are in common with the Liverpool North Western Hotel, also by Waterhouse, built in 1871. To the right is the Grand.

impressive well-type staircase behind the restricted foyer space is lit from mezzanine windows and crowned with a glazed dome. Separate coffee- or dining-rooms for gentlemen and ladies were each accompanied by a conservatory 'lined with some of the most exquisite specimens of Minton's decorated tiles and they remind one strongly of the Courts of the Alhambra in the Crystal Palace'. Externally the location was ideal, facing the sea and close to the centre of the town. Whichcord's stucco façade, while overweighted by two Italianate pavilions at roof level, has a certain attraction in the contrasting lightness of wrought-iron balcony balustrading and five-storey bays which recall Brighton's Regency pedigree. A letter to the Manager in 1883 paints a realistic picture of the protocol that obviously formed part of the manners of the day. The aide-de-camp of H.S.H. Prince Edward of Saxe-Weimar wrote that the Prince would be commanding the Easter Monday Volunteer Review and would require the same rooms as in the year '81 viz: 1 dining room, 1 drawing room, 1 double bedded room with dressing room

Bathroom at the Metropole Hotel, Brighton.

attached, 1 room for maid near this room and another single bedded room on the first floor. H.S.H. will also require stabling for 3 horses and rooms for 4 men servants ... I shall let you know further particulars later on.

In the first years the management did not seem to have made an impressive start, as the appointment of George Quiddington as manager after four years had elapsed was exceptionally warmly received. When he came to retire on health grounds nine years on, his supporters who produced 'The Quiddington Testimonial' were referring to his initial need 'to clean out the Augean stable', after which 'from that day the vessel began to right itself'. He was presented with a volume of tributes, including one from E. M. Barry Esq., RA, who was a director of the Grand Hotel Company, and also a candelabrum, 300 guineas and the offer of a seat on the board. Of this proposition *The Sussex Daily Post* remarked 'When a manager

is fagged, when ill health compels him to give over the command, and he needs rest and repose it certainly seems inconsistent to offer him almost equal responsibility' as managing director 'with but a tithe of the renumeration'. From apprenticeship at the Old London Tavern, Bishopsgate Street, he had been a hotelkeeper for 38 years, and his retirement was much regretted.

The incident most likely to gain the Brighton Grand Hotel a place in history was the explosion of a delayed fuse terrorist bomb in the hotel during the Conservative Party Conference in October 1984. This was aimed specifically at the then Prime Minister, Margaret Thatcher, and her Cabinet, of whose members and wives as well as hotel staff, five were killed and several more badly injured. Mr and Mrs Thatcher and others escaped injury through sheer good fortune. The owners, De Vere Hotels, rebuilt the swathe of damage which almost cut the hotel in half and took the opportunity to insert a second file of well-appointed rooms on all the upper floors and to provide more staff accommodation in the turrets, all without destroying the main roofline. At the same time the west wing was extended by three extra floors, and thanks to the construction team under the direction of architect Igal Yawetz, virtually all trace of the damage has been removed. Decorative brackets under balconies and a chimneystack which collapsed have been replaced by glass-fibre reinforced plastic substitutes to reduce weight and fire risk. The fact that no fire had followed the bomb explosion must have saved many lives.

If we look back to the first decades of the Grand, a different hazard was threatening. In the 1880s an even larger hotel by Alfred Waterhouse, then President of the Royal Institute of British Architects, was under construction for Frederick Gordon almost next door, in brick and terracotta, a Gothic central spire and French pavilioned roof giving it a presence that has vanished with the twentieth-century alterations. This was the Metropole (1890), and with its 700 rooms it far exceeded the size of the Grand, which suffered badly from its competition. The whole of the interior decoration and furnishing was handed over to Maples, with whom there was a close business connection. The usual public rooms were large and lavish, three dining-rooms when opened into a single space being able to seat 500. Baths offered a choice and a Moorish tinge and were prefaced by an Apodyterium or dressing-room; duty-paid stock of 185,000 bottles filled the wine cellars. The fine marble staircase and a carved chimneypiece by Prince Victor of Hohenlohe were offset by decorations in golden brown graduating to ivory white. At the back, away from the sea view, there was a terraced Italian garden but this – and the royal chimneypiece –

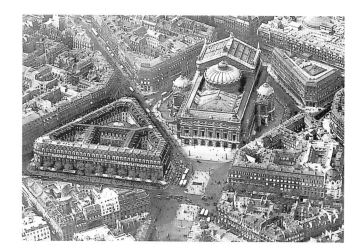

France, Monaco, Holland and Germany

Continental Europe was subject to a great deal more political and dynastic ferment than Great Britain in the years following Napoleon's defeat at Waterloo, and this instability inevitably tended to delay new building schemes. We have looked briefly at the speed of change to industrialized manufacture and trading as soon as the quantum leap from muscle to machine power had been made. The propagation and culture of hotels in the Alps can be left aside for the moment as it deserves special study, but France with Monaco and Belgium, followed by the constituent parts of Germany, became aware as the nineteenth century progressed of the pressure building up on an international scale for high-class accommodation. A background was being set that brought into use such technical advances as extensive coalmining for industry and the development of steel as a structural material. More noticeable introductions in society were telegraphic

ABOVE, BELOW & OPPOSITE Paris, Grand Hôtel, 1862, by A. Armand and others. The convergence of Haussmann's boulevards formed a seemingly vast open space which was to become the Place de l'Opéra. The main façade of the Grand Hôtel occupied the whole extent of the site on the Boulevard des Capucines, containing the main entrance as axial to the plan.

have long since disappeared, although there is still a sense of style and space in the remaining public rooms.

Eastbourne, some twenty miles to the east, still has a Grand Hotel dating from 1877, designed by Robert Knott Blessley in a succession of four-storey bays directly facing the sea with pedimented central entrance and end pavilions all in stucco, manifesting Victorian classical treatment of considerable character before the symmetry was upset by additional building. The earlier Cavendish, dating from 1872, was more Frenchified, but no concessions to the nineteenth century were made in the fiercely uncompromising modernity of the mid-twentieth-century east wing. Many more British spa or seaside grand hotels could be listed but the pattern becomes repetitive, and before studying further Anglo-Saxon steps forward we need to look across the Channel to see how hotels were developing there.

communications, which only usurped the carrier pigeon in the 1850s, and the improvement of M. Louis-Jacques Daguerre's 1829 discoveries that, by the 1840s, resulted in photographs of good-enough quality to provide a realistic record never before achieved.

Napoleon III had consolidated his position as Emperor and was pursuing a policy of encouragement towards the enhancement of Paris, based on an overall plan prepared by Baron Georges Eugène Haussmann (1809–91) under his close practical interest. Many fields lay open to imaginative enterprise, and the Péreire brothers, Portuguese in origin but settled in Bordeaux, had been cooperating on the financing of railway building with the Rothschild family before aligning themselves with Napoleon in his grandiose rebuilding schemes. Paris, not unnaturally, was striving to lead the field with a vast project that materialized as the Grand Hôtel du Louvre in 1855. This was a hotel for the capital city, not directly associated with railway systems but aimed at accommodating visitors to the International Exhibition of that year.

The Grand Hôtel by night, with Garnier's Opéra to the right.

OVERLEAF The Grand Hôtel's *Salle des Fêtes* could have been described on completion as the grandest such room in existence and was without rival in the remaining years of the Second Empire.

Paris, after the Revolution, had instigated as a statement of the new régime a national exhibition in the Fourth Year of the new calendar (1798), making further similar displays in 1806, 1834 and 1844. Across the Channel the idea expanded to form the Great Exhibition of 1851 in London, bringing in an international dimension of world trade, industry and art. Paris replied with the above-mentioned Exposition Universelle and its attendant Palais de l'Industrie, in 1855, and an irregular series was established. Wherever such exhibitions were being planned, there became obvious needs for greatly increased lodging space, and all levels of hotel building benefited. Coverage stretched from Vienna in the east (1873) to Philadelphia (1876) in the west, and by the 1880s Australia was showing its wares in company with the commercial centres of Europe. Chicago in 1893 and Hanoi in 1903 were relative outposts in a trading world in which the industrial European cities still dominated. There occurs an obvious symbiosis between exhibitions and urban hotels, both being interdependent products of the rising volume of industry and trade. London, Paris, Vienna, New York and

Melbourne come immediately to mind, their resulting off-spring being, respectively, the Great Western at Paddington; the Grand Hôtel du Louvre, the Continental and the d'Orsay; the Imperial, Britannia and Donau; the La Farge House; and the Grand (now Windsor).

The Grand Hôtel du Louvre came into existence in the Rue de Rivoli and far exceeded the favoured English size of 200–300 bedrooms by providing at least 700 behind a 500-feet frontage. Part of the city centre rebuilding was financed through purchases of bonds by enthusiastic small investors, but this new hotel was in the hands of Emile and Isaac Péreire and however magnificent the public rooms might be, business and pleasure and 'toutes les classes de voyageurs' were to be sought after. The largest in Europe, it was to be the general rendezvous for all tourists. A glass-roofed courtyard with monumental staircase and galleries formed an excellent background for this purpose and gave access on the first floor to a *table d'hôte* dining-room beyond which was another high-class restaurant. Other public rooms were on this level, the salon being 133 feet long, and billiard-rooms were equally of ample size. Also to be appreciated in the hotel as innovative were the numerous bathrooms on all floors and twenty lavatories. At ground-floor level, shops occupied the street frontages in this fashionable quarter. The life of the building as a hotel, designed by a team of architects – Alfred Armand (1805–88), Jacob Ignaz Hittorf (1793–1867), Charles Rohalt de Fleury (1801–75) and Auguste Pellechet (1829–1903) – did not last for very long as it was gradually taken over for retail trade until the whole became a department store in the 1870s and 1880s.

On a prime triangular site in the same quarter, flanking the large square plot designated by Haussmann for the future Opéra, another similar enterprise was emulating the Louvre, this time to be christened simply Grand Hôtel. Alfred Armand was again the architect and the Péreire brothers, having formed La Compagnie Immobilière, were the developers. A professed aim was to demonstrate to the world the achievements in science, art and industry under the Second Empire. The adjoining Place de l'Opéra acts as a hub for the converging boulevards created by Haussmann but at the time was considered immense, empty and useless. It is now crowned by Garnier's Opéra House, opened in 1874 after delays occasioned by the war with Prussia and the defeat of Napoleon III, and its conception as the nineteenth-century focus of 'Nouveau Paris' has been fully justified.

The Grand Hôtel itself was built in fifteen months (5 April 1861 – 30 June 1862) by working day and night under arc lamps. The architect Rohault de Fleury assisted Armand especially in the neo-Renaissance Louis Quatorze style of the

elevations, which were intended to follow a pattern set for the entire district.[13] De Fleury had prepared a matching scheme for the Opéra House but this was never used. In size this Grand Hôtel exceeded the Louvre Grand with 800 rooms and 65 salons (1,000 rooms had been mooted) and the city's first hydraulic lift. Building stone came from St Maximin 60 kilometres away, ready cut to size and numbered, on horsedrawn carts. Marshy ground caused foundation problems but steady progress continued uninterrupted. Interior decoration, sculpture and painting were carried out by well-known artists, and much of the busy hotel activity could be watched taking place in an internal glass-roofed courtyard. In greater privacy, the ladies could see all without being seen themselves from an adjacent *Salon des Dames*. The concierge, the letter-box, the telegraph desk, reception, carriage service, couriers and interpreters, cash desk and foreign exchange, theatre-ticket desk and a *café-divan* with excellent billiard tables; all these were available to the visitor and, in addition, a laundry, a wine cellar holding a million bottles of wine, a model dairy near Paris and a further wine reserve in Bordeaux were on hand for supplying the endless needs of hundreds of guests. The management of such a vast establishment must have been organized on highly disciplined lines.

No other Parisian public building expressed the spirit of the age more faithfully than the Grand Hôtel, and no other salon exceeded the great D-shape *Salle des Fêtes* or *Salon Opéra* on its ground floor in creating a dramatic backdrop for the banquets, balls, dinners and receptions of the Second Empire. On the joint occasion of the Grand's inauguration and the foundation-stone laying for the new Opéra on 5 May 1862, the Empress Eugénie, having made a detailed tour of the hotel on the arm of Emile Péreire, told him that it was 'absolutely like home; I feel that I am at Compiègne or Fontainebleau'. Nevertheless, it must be admitted that the brilliance of the gas lighting and the *élan* of M. Jacques Offenbach's conducting with Madame Patti's singing would have dazzled super-critical eyes from distinguishing plaster-work figures and decoration from solid sculpture and carving. Today the *salle* looks startlingly magnificent; in its 1862 freshness it must have astonished even the most sophisticated Parisians.

For the rest of the century royalty, statesmen, artists, writers and explorers constituted elements in a clientèle very similar to the corresponding visitors to the Langham and other London hotels. From the Grand in 1869, J. G. Bennett, founder of *The New York Herald Tribune*, sent H. W. Stanley off to search for Doctor Livingstone at the head of the Nile. In 1884 Count Ferdinand de Lesseps presided over a gala

Paris, Hôtel Inter-Continental in the Rue de Castiglione was formed behind the uniform arcading so characteristic of Haussmann's Paris. Ex-Empress Eugénie made it her favourite Parisian home in her later years, when it was called the Continental.

dinner given by the Geographic Society to representatives from the Transvaal, and 1896 saw Sarah Bernhardt receiving acclamation from the Paris press in the *Salle des Fêtes*. George Augustus Sala, writer and traveller, was a regular visitor, and on one occasion after a violent brush with the Prefecture in the uncertain year of 1870 he watched from his bedroom a small piece of history in the making. On the façade of the Opéra opposite his room the inscription 'Académie Impériale de Musique' was visible, but the reign of the Emperor had ceased only three days previously on his defeat and capture by the Prussians at Sedan. Sala was able to see the name 'Impériale' cut out and 'Nationale' being substituted.[14]

In 1878 a faulty casting in the lift structure resulted in an accident: the lift-cage fell, killing three passengers. Hotel equipment had obviously begun to age, and new inventions replaced old. Four thousand gas jets were replaced by electricity throughout the Grand Hôtel in 1890 and faster lifts were fitted eight years later. Steam heating was installed in 1901, making the sale of baskets of firewood on the various floors unnecessary. More alterations took place in the twentieth century when in 1905–7 Paul Henri Nénot (1853–1934), architect for the new Sorbonne, changed the main entrance from Boulevard des Capucines to Rue Scribe, making the courtyard into a splendid Winter Garden and Tearoom, covered by a glazed dome. The hotel, surviving its 133 years remarkably well, continues in full use as the Grand Hôtel Inter-Continental Paris.

Let us return for a moment to observe the expectations of those in charge of architectural education in the 1860s. The École des Beaux-Arts in setting a design programme in 1865 for the Grand Prix chose 'une vaste hôtellerie pour les voyageurs' as its subject. The site had to be on a Swiss lake and to contain the following accommodation:

Ground floor: Reception etc., Vestibule, Waiting Room for arriving guests, Ladies' Room, Telegraphic office, Central hall rising to the top of the building, one Grand Staircase or more, Dining room for 150, rooms for private dinners, Breakfast Room, Reading Room, Billiard Room, Smoking Room, Ladies' Salon, Washrooms (well ventilated).
Basement: Kitchens.
First floor: The lake side to have suites, the other sides small rooms and lavatories.
Second and third floors: Rooms with fireplaces, which can be made to communicate.
Stables, Coach Houses etc. to be in subsidiary buildings.

When the design entries were received, criticism cited forced symmetry and a lack of practical sense – defects which are still sometimes repeated in architectural design.

The Beaux-Arts description had already been overtaken in the two hotels mentioned above, the Louvre and the Grand, and these were added to in 1878 by a third, the Continental, designed by Henri Blondel (1832–97), son-in-law of Charles Garnier, whose new Opéra had been completed three years before and which must have inspired some of the Baroque element in Blondel's eclectic *belle époque* interiors found behind the regular colonnaded Rue de Rivoli and Rue de Castiglione façades. The magnificence of the hotel is announced by a splendid pair of gilt-bronze candelabra in the outside arcade, ten to twelve feet high and rich with sphinx supporters, scrolls and elegantly perched half-nude female figures, originating from a palace in St Petersburg.

The attachment felt by the ex-Empress Eugénie for this hotel is commemorated on a plaque by the entrance. For more than twenty years she made it her home for regular extended summer visits, having a second-floor apartment with bedroom and two salons commanding a view across to the Tuileries gardens. Her last visit was made in 1919.

The overall plan of the hotel was in the form of a large quadrangle enclosed by four wings. The three principal salons, all listed in the *Inventaire des Monuments Historiques*, show French interior design at its best, of top quality and ornamented with the work of some of the best artists and craftsmen available. The Salon Impérial (29 × 13 metres) has a fine Corinthian order as its basis with an entablature and coved and panelled ceiling above. The columns are fluted and gilded with deep cream and light-brown colouring. Works by Laugée, Faustin-Besson, Mazerolles and Delaplanche are shared between this room, the Salon Napoleon and Salon de l'Aiglon. Bronze chandeliers and chimneypieces are finely

ABOVE & BELOW Paris, Hôtel (Concorde) Saint-Lazare, 1889.
Designed by Juste Lisch, it was built on a palatial scale and opened
within a few days of the Eiffel Tower and the Exposition Universelle.
Solid pink granite columns support exposed steel beams and a
coffered and decorated ceiling in the entrance lobby.

OPPOSITE Candelabra in the arcade flank the entrance to the
erstwhile Continental Hôtel, a foretaste of its lavish historic interiors.

The Hôtel Saint-Lazare's grand hall is one of the most
spectacular in Paris.

executed, a Delaplanche astronomical clock being particularly outstanding for the sculptured figures. Ceiling panels painted by P. F. Laugée took the theme of the Four Seasons, adding Love and Night in the most important spaces. Mazerolles painted the Napoleon ceiling on a Jupiter and Mercury theme and Faustin-Besson took marriage as his subject in the Aiglon salon. A winter garden and adjoining Moorish salon reported in the press of the day as 'a part of the Alhambra brought to Paris by a fairy's wand' and regarded as 'one of the most wonderful oriental [interiors] in Paris' by virtue of some careful authentic detailing, both disappeared under one of the modernization schemes to which hotel interiors regularly fall victim in the need to keep abreast of fashion.

Whereas in London, railway terminus hotels tended to precede the fashionable haunts of society, in Paris the reverse applied. Multiplication of railway companies in Britain introduced a strong degree of competition and sense of pride. Catering for passengers and providing them with accommodation was a part of the railway line's identity, in a manner largely absent in the centralized and state-aided French systems, although international or *universelle* exhibitions in France did stimulate accommodation near to the railheads from Channel and transatlantic ports. Le Grand Hôtel Terminus-Saint Lazare (1889) in Paris thus germinated in time for the Exposition Universelle, which was to celebrate the centenary of the French Revolution. This happened also to be the first year of the Orient Express service through to Constantinople, probably accounting for design influence from the Terminus spreading to the Pera Palace Hotel. Juste Lisch, the architect for the Saint Lazare enterprise, was to design both railway station and a grand hotel with about 500 rooms. The idea of integrating both elements had been current in London since the Great Western Royal at Paddington station in 1854, where access on foot directly from the hotel foyer to station platform was even more convenient than that devised by Lisch in the form of a covered footbridge. From outside, the Terminus displays no great distinction, its plain rectangular form and six storeys being dominated more by the heavy chimney stacks and pedimented former windows than by any points of architectural importance. The outer and inner halls provide much more interest and, like the exterior, have suffered little alteration during the hotel's life. A combination of exposed structural steel with traditional classical columns of pink granite in the entrance hall gives way to the less conventional three-storey central hall, where coupled iron stanchions support an arched gallery reached by the double staircase. A second gallery surmounts the first, and all was finished in Pompeian

wall decoration. The eccentric mixture of styles proves very unexpected within such non-committal street fronts. Technology obviously attracted the enthusiasm of the management, whose handbills waxed lyrical on the various subjects of saving time, money, trouble and fatigue because of the easy access from the station, of the rapidity of the telephone room service, and the magic of two-way switching from bedside and main room lights. 'One would believe oneself in Houdini's company.'[15] Alterations in the 1930s by Henry Pacon added a French-style billiard-room with eight competition standard tables, the last such to be retained in any Paris hotel. After the Second World War it was for a short time an American Services Club, and in the early 1990s modern standards have been met by reducing the number of rooms from 500 to about 300, to increase individual space and improve amenities.

At the turn of the century a second railway station and hotel complex included the Hôtel du Palais d'Orsay (1900) by Victor Laloux (1850–1937), of which there remains some lavish baroque decoration in first-floor rooms now forming part of the museum.

Away from the metropolitan influence of Paris, recreational interests and activities generated hotel-building centred to a great extent on the seaside and split between, in the north the Channel and North Sea with, in the south, the Mediterranean. The impetus for development given by Napoleon III did not spread widely beyond Paris, although he built a summer palace at Biarritz in 1854 for Eugénie de Monteijo, his Spanish Empress who had kept a fondness for the place since her childhood. This royal Villa Eugénie ripened into a stylish court which attracted many other European royalties each summer and established a focus of high fashion outliving the demise of the Second Empire in 1871. The villa was then sold to the Banque Parisienne and was used for a time as the Casino (1880) and then as the Hôtel du Palais. In the days of the Empire the social pattern had been well established, and transformation into a hotel did not destroy the magnetism it held for the *beau-monde*.

Sea coasts everywhere were changing from fishing villages into alternative places of residence, and the Riviera was among the foremost to respond to this demand. The Mediterranean climate with its mild winters and exotic vegetation had been discovered by the English nobility as an ideal refuge from cold northern temperatures and many others followed. In Cannes and Nice hotels began to change the scale of building to match the new sophistication that was reaching the Côte d'Azur. The Beausite in Cannes was built in 1842, and the advent of the railway in 1864 coincided with the opening there of the Grand Hôtel by Vianay, who later added to the

Menton, Riviera Palace, 1883. Abel Glena and Alfred Marsang as architects incorporated classical and Renaissance motifs into the design. A popular social focus when Menton was fashionable, particularly with the English, the hotel is now converted into private apartments.

Menton, Winter Palace, 1880–90. Its architect, Ceruti, created a twin to the Riviera Palace; this has also been converted into apartments.

Beausite in 1880. At a later date the reputation of the Beausite was enhanced by the Renshaw brothers' construction of seven hard tennis courts, an innovation in France, which attracted such glamorous doubles as Suzanne Lenglen and Mrs A. E. Beamish (Geraldine Ramsey) making a four with the King of Sweden and the ex-King of Portugal.

At Antibes, the Grand Hôtel du Cap was transformed from convalescent home to hotel in 1863, but its real fame came later when the Eden Roc extension (1914) housed the rich and fashionable and found a role in Scott Fitzgerald's *Tender is the Night* as the Hôtel des Étrangers. Nice had the Hôtel des Anglais and developed extensively along the water-front, which was called the Promenade des Anglais. Menton was very much approved by the English as a winter resort, with the Riviera Palace (1883) by Abel Glena and Alfred Marsang having an impressive entrance foyer leading to a little theatre with sliding roof, popular, no doubt, for enter-tainments. The Winter Palace Hotel (1880–90) by Ceruti is of similar style, perched high above the old town, and the Oriental Palace nearer to the station displays Moorish motifs. This is now used as offices, while the two other palaces are divided into apartments.

The history of the Principality of Monaco and the Casino in Monte Carlo which created for it so much wealth under the rule of the Grimaldi family entered the grand hotel scene with an aura of luxury and excitement. Casino and theatre, largely the work of Charles Garnier, epitomized the idea of lavish indulgence, but below the surface, in contrast, a hard-headed administration was formed. The original Sea-Bathing Company was formed by Monégasque Prince Charles III as a front for the development of Monte Carlo in 1863 and established itself as the Société des Bains de Mer. Sea-bathing was altogether a more proper occupation than the projected casino would offer and may originally have disarmed puritanical objections from nearby France, where gambling was forbidden. Prince Charles's secretary, Eynaud, had visited Bad Homburg in Bavaria, where a comparable development had attracted 'two million wealthy visitors'. Attempts made in the 1850s to emulate this in Monte Carlo had not been a success and it was only when Eynaud per-suaded the French casino manager from Bad Homburg to take on Monte Carlo instead that fortunes changed. When François Blanc agreed and acquired a 50-year franchise, a new history commenced. He was to operate the SBM, which controlled gambling, public services, entertainments and developments, including hotels. No local citizens other than employees were to be allowed in the Casino.

From trailing behind Nice and Cannes in terms of fashion and development, Monte Carlo was rapidly transformed by

Monte Carlo, Hôtel de Paris. The building underwent many changes, from the first Gobineau de la Brétonnerie designs in 1862 through those of Jean-Baptiste Dutrou, 1865, and reached what may prove its definitive size and character under Edouard Niermans in 1908.

The glazed dome over the inner hall lights up the opulence of the hotel's interiors and sets an Edwardian baroque style.

As restaurant cum ballroom, the Salle Empire follows a white and gold Second Empire decorative scheme with sculptured plasterwork and the mural of the Three Graces typifying Monégasque *joie de vivre*.

BELOW Lighter in effect is the Louis XV room, equally sophisticated and well-executed.

outstanding success. Blanc instigated the building of nineteen establishments of various types. One of the immediate projects was the completion of the Hôtel de Paris originally designed by Gobineau de la Brétonnerie in 1862 and destined for at least seven alterations to date. Jean-Baptiste Dutrou (b. 1814) extended the building well beyond the two-storey original size in 1865, and when further changes were made in the hotel, the Grand Hôtel near the Opéra in Paris could have been a model. A reconstruction of the public rooms was carried out by Edouard Niermans (1859–1928) in his usual lavish style in 1908, and the glazed dome over the inner hall was almost certainly his inspiration. Throughout the period interiors in Monte Carlo there is a *leitmotif* of idealized female nudity; the large 1909 Paul Gervais fresco of the Three Graces in the Empire Room is a prime contributor to the sumptuous white, gold and marble setting. A much-reproduced bronze bust, 'La Bacchante aux Roses', repeats the general theme, which has survived many variations though the overall interior style seems to have been consistent.

It was during the years of startling development in the 1860s that the Nice–Menton railway line was built through Monte Carlo in 1868 and increased its influx of visitors, according to an article in *Le Figaro*, to 'a veritable Californian Gold Rush'. Nice, along the coast, was getting jealous and campaigning for closure of the Casino, but the Prince resisted pressure, although after the French defeat at Sedan François Blanc did close it for a few months. When he opened it again, comments came from the hotels in Nice that without Monaco's gambling, their trade fell severely as well. Blanc made a generous gesture of 120,000 francs to support French national defence, largesse which seemed to heal the rift. After all, he only took 5,000,000 gold francs in the Casino that year. By the time Blanc, who was 57 when he came to Monte Carlo, died in 1877 he had seen 35 hotels built. Competition arose between the Hôtel de Paris and the Grand Hotel, although the latter could not be a competitor in style or decoration. It could, however, boast César Ritz as manager for the next few seasons and, with a brilliant young chef, was making money at the expense of the Paris. Before long his star was lost to direct poaching by his rival but Ritz,

Monte Carlo, Grand Hotel. The hotel opened in 1882, when a Moorish style became fashionable in the wake of the French expedition to Tunis the previous year.

Amsterdam, Amstel Hotel, 1867. Cornelius Outshoorn designed a palace hotel for the owner, Dr Sarphati, and this indeed became something of an annexe for the royal family, a number of whose important celebrations have taken place there.

always resourceful, had discovered the name of the man who had taught his prodigy and offered him the job. The resulting appointment led to an association that would bring fame for both of them and last for the rest of Ritz's working life. The chef's name was, of course, Auguste Escoffier (1846–1935). In 1881, the reputation of the cuisine at the Grand Hôtel drew Edward, Prince of Wales, who unexpectedly left Cannes to 'follow Ritz'. Superhuman efforts were made to create a royal suite for him in next to no time and, as so often in Ritz's life, he achieved the scarcely possible.

On the Channel coast the Grand Hôtel, Cabourg, was built in 1862, in modest château style, then in 1881 rebuilt with five storeys of columned, arcaded and decorated stucco suitably ornamented with shell motifs. There were further additions in 1907–8 (discussed in chapter Seven). Houlgate squeezed into the Second Empire time span with its Grand Hôtel in 1870, designed by Baumier, with mansard roofs, pavilioned ends and one corner dome upsetting the symmetry. Vittel in the Vosges mountains had a Grand Hôtel de l'Etablissement as early as 1862, decorated by Charles Garnier in 1884 but demolished in 1911, giving way to a new hotel by G. Walwein (1912) on the same site.

France in the 1870s saw the foundation of the Third Republic and the rise in Paris of the republican Commune in the aftermath of the war with Germany. The indulgences of the Second Empire were past and repression took their place in the severe presidencies of Adolphe Thiers and Marshal MacMahon. Uncertainty discouraged investment in luxury trades and hotel building was cut back until greater political stability could be observed. Industry proved resilient, and the sense of progress that pervaded much of the nineteenth century returned as a constituent of the *belle époque* society which played out a long last act before the tragedy of the Great War began in 1914.

Holland in mid-century was represented by the Amstel Hotel in Amsterdam, this being the first Dutch venture into grand hotels, inspired by the Beaux-Arts school in Paris. It was designed by Cornelius Outshoorn (1810–75) in 1867 and was intended from the beginning as a palace by its owner Dr Sarphati, fulfilling these expectations in being consistently a favourite of Dutch royalty. Amsterdamers followed its construction closely and watched it grow from the foundation stage upwards. A waterlogged site necessitated unexpectedly deep foundations and cost estimates were exceeded, thus work was slowed down as additional capital had to be raised. Not only was this done by a new share issue but spectators were charged for admission to the building site that had aroused so much interest in the city. More financial problems intervened before the hotel was opened – pleasing outside

and luxurious within – but then success rewarded persistence and good management.

The exterior is brick-faced with stone and stucco dressings, and the additional floor, added in 1899, has not destroyed the visual effect of a riverside palace conforming to the symmetrical five-part Beaux-Arts formula of central emphasis, mansard roof and pavilioned wings. Second Empire interiors by Ivan Gosschalk commence in a fine galleried and stuccoed staircase hall with lion masks all in white with gilding limited to garlanded 'A' monograms. Elegance and satisfying proportioning are present through a range of banqueting and smaller rooms, from the Stadthouderszaal and Sarphatizaal to the Spiegelzaal, while terraces and a glazed dining area overlook the river and the Sarphati bridge. Bedrooms have in recent comprehensive renovations been reduced from the original 111 to 79 so that more space could be allotted, according to present demand, to amenities and modern communications equipment. Designers and craftsmen whose work enhanced the original decoration included Nina Klaassen (painter), Frederick Zaalberg (carpenter) and Gawein Groeneveld, who executed sculptures and ornamentation. A Royal Suite in one corner of the building amounts to a full two-bedroom apartment with living-room, dining-room, butler's pantry and guest powder-room. The suite claims a long and distinguished list of occupants, from the Tsar and Tsarina of Russia to Elizabeth II and most of her contemporary crowned heads in Europe. It has been the particular prerogative of the Amstel to house the celebrations given by the Dutch royal family. In modern times the most outstanding occasion has been the silver wedding party of Queen Juliana and Prince Bernhard in 1962 while their own Soestdijk Palace was being restored.[16] Eminent visitors in earlier years were Empress Eugénie of France, a connoisseur of hotels, also Ferdinand de Lesseps and Gustave Eiffel, having achieved fame respectively as chief authors of the Suez Canal and the Eiffel Tower. Until he moved to Wiesbaden, the services of Dr John Mezger as house physician and osteopath appealed to many who sought relief from aches and pains. Advertising aimed at potential guests was, in 1892, offering complete electric lighting and elevators to all rooms. In the winter months rooms would benefit from a special tariff.

Subsequent history in the Second World War meant that the German occupation hit hard and the hotel lost its general manager Rolf Belinfonte to anti-semitic Nazi persecution. A successor in the post, Dick de Bes, had joined the hotel as assistant to Belinfonte in 1932 after experience on the French Riviera, in Paris, Barcelona, Saragossa and Majorca. He came to be, after the war, one of the great hoteliers, with unequalled tact, skill and organizing abilities, which were all applied in good measure to the 'special event' of the royal silver wedding.

Business, banking and shipping interests patronized the Amstel, many with American and East Indian links both before and after independence of the colonial Dutch East Indies was declared in 1948. Internationalism was fertilized by ease of travel and in the new world of instant communication. These sprang up at the same time as the political face of Europe was searching for a suitable degree of union. All these factors affected the future plans for the Amstel and other important hotels that were looking towards re-equipping in the new technical age. Affiliation with the Inter-Continental hotels organization in 1981 helped the Amstel to manage the necessary transformation and to make the difficult decision to close for a period of two years to enable the necessary work to be carried out. This was done in 1990–92, and the hotel re-opened with full confidence for a successful future, abreast of any near competition. These references to the Amstel's life in the twentieth century digress from a proper time scale but still leave us with a largely unaltered exterior, blending with older buildings and doing credit to its designers.

In Germany the grand hotels came of age as enlarged versions of the older spa hotels, and their nineteenth-century history forms a continuation of the earlier story. Geography and politics proved the main influential ingredients as there was no seductive Mediterranean coast beckoning and the unification of Germany became a preoccupation with confederation and nationalism at issue. Prussia was at the forefront, anxious to keep up with western neighbours in industrialization. Friedrich Wilhelm III had sent his Privy Councillor for Public Works, Karl Friedrich Schinkel, with Peter Beuth, head of the Trade and Industry department, to France and Britain in 1826 on a tour to collect ideas and information relating to advancing technology not then available from Prussian sources. Through all the various phases of unification, finally arrived at in 1871 with the proclamation of Wilhelm I as German Emperor, railways and industry had gradually spread to include Austria and the majority of the spas established previously in the German states.

The further history of the Nassauer Hof in Wiesbaden can be pursued here from its earlier stage in establishing itself as a well-known spa hotel during the first half of the nineteenth century as described in chapter One. The plain and severe building was constantly being improved and extended from 1864 onwards, when Philipp Hoffmann built the Marble Hall in a much more elaborate style. In 1872 the Casino was closed under the stricter laws that followed the advent of

Prussian rule which had occurred six years before, but Kaiser Wilhelm II patronized the spa, though not the Nassauer Hof, regularly bringing trade and prestige to Wiesbaden. Complete rebuilding of the hotel took place after long negotiations with bureaucracy, drawings by the local architect Alfred Schellenberg receiving approval in 1897. A Wilhelminian neo-baroque style had been adopted for the exterior and, from 1900 until 1945, when gutted by fire from incendiary bombs, the Nassauer Hof filled an important role in the town.

The Goetz dynasty, whose interest in the hotel had started in about 1819, had lasted almost a century until the death of Frederick Goetz during the Great War when trade dwindled and heavy losses were sustained. Even after the war, subsequent years remained uncertain until a wealthy industrialist, Hugo Stinnes, perhaps the richest man in Europe according to report, planned to indulge his personal ambitions to own luxury hotels which could be used as impressive settings for his business meetings. This was surely a grand precursor of the conference trade which has swept through the whole hotel world. He already owned the Atlantic Hotel in Hamburg and the Esplanade in Berlin but died in 1924 before the Nassauer Hof work was completed to his satisfaction. His company pursued modernization and extension plans in a somewhat different direction, taking the needs of the automobile into serious consideration. After the bombing in 1945 only a shell of the hotel remained, but this has been preserved and repaired in the form of the old façades, with a new interior replacing the original.

A very long history attaches to the top-ranking German spa of Baden-Baden on the fringes of the Rhine valley, a good 100 miles south of Frankfurt. The evolution of the Badischer

Baden-Baden. The Badischer Hof was converted from monastery to hotel by Friedrich Weinbrenner, neo-classical architect of distinction, in 1809.

Hof from Capucin monastery to nineteenth-century grand hotel may be seen as the essence of the story of the spa.[17] After the closing down of the monastery the government of Baden acquired the land and buildings, giving much consideration to their future use, including the suggestion that a china factory might prove feasible. Further deliberation favoured Grand-Duke Carl Friedrich's desire to attract tourism by providing a new hotel, and this won the day, leaving the question of finding a suitable buyer to be solved. The price being asked by the official state buildings director Weinbrenner was 25–30,000 guilders, but finally, after a low offer of 10,000 guilders, a publisher from Tübingen, Johann Friedrich Cotta, completed the purchase for 13,000, on behalf jointly of himself and writer–publisher Johann Ludwig Klüber. The latter was well informed as to the extent of their purchase, having studied in detail the secularization of the monastery and its dependencies, publishing as a result *Baden at Rastatt* at the instigation of the Grand-Duke. Two benefits came with the property, one in consideration of its use being restricted to that of a spa hotel and permitting permanent rights to a supply of thermal spring water and the other, never fully exploited, which allowed gambling in the hotel. Friedrich Weinbrenner (1766–1826), distinguished in his capacity as architect, made the best of the existing buildings on a limited budget. Neo-classicism was flourishing at the time (1807–9), and the three-storey dining-hall created in place of the old courtyard was columned and galleried to give access to bedrooms on all floors, lit from above by a domed glass roof. The church was converted into a 'ball, music, gambling and conversation room'. A new bath-house accommodated 26 single and two communal baths and 33 horseboxes with hayloft were built as a separate stable block. Toilet accommodation in the Badischer Hof was specified in detail by Klüber to have a self-closing door which always shut and 'a little shelf on the wall for the light to be put on. The seat-board should be tilted so that any water immediately runs off it, should it be wet ...'. Great care was taken in the garden planting, completed in 1810, and included, according to extant delivery notes, silver maples, dwarf birches, olive trees, black American walnut, Persian wine-trees, red-flowering acacias, American arborvitae and many others. The hotel received favourable comment from treasury president von Vinke, and the composer Carl Maria von Weber thought 'the beautiful lofty dining room ... the tasteful casino room and the beautiful stone baths' were far superior to 'other establishments'. Success enabled profitable buying and selling to take place and it was bought in 1830 by Joseph Schmidt, for once in *hôtellerie* making money at the handsome price of 65,000 guilders. Schmidt died five years later and his widow remarried a

Martin Hotz. Their daughter Marie grew up to be heiress to the Badischer Hof hotel and in due course married another hotelier in 1858. Her husband Emile Dupressoir extended family business prospects by being heir to the lessee of the casino, Edouard Benazet. In this favourable position they rebuilt the hotel, retaining its general characteristics and appointing as director Franz Ziegler to run it in great style. Their adequate resources maintained standards and kept everything up-to-date for the next 30 years. The first railway in Baden had been laid in 1843, but more vital was the Black Forest Railway, completed in 1873. Closure of the casino by order of Bismarck the previous year signalled a disappointing change of circumstances, although Ziegler continued in management for another seventeen years. The Dupressoirs' son-in-law Baron von Diesburg ran the hotel for a short time, selling it in 1900. The Great War and severe competition depressed business until the casino opened again in 1933, but the Second World War extinguished the short revival. Wartime turned it into a military hospital and occupying forces then made it into an administrative centre. By 1949 the Steigenberger régime had taken over and renovation was in progress as part of a continuing policy for reviving Germany's war-torn building inheritance. Unfortunately, the nightmare of hotelkeepers lay in wait and a serious fire swept through the domed atrium damaging staircase and rooms again before the reopening. Restoration work recommenced, incorporating additional improvements, and the delayed resurrection took place in 1950.

The Europäischer-Hof or Hôtel de l'Europe was built in 1838–40 on land inherited by Franz Xavier Meier on which a tannery and the municipal wash-house both stood. The site, close to the Baden spa and the casino, was ideal and Meier's hotel of neo-classical design not only opened with guests from Hamburg, Frankfurt, Cologne, Paris, Metz, London and Ireland but later welcomed celebrities including Prince William of Prussia, Russian Chancellor Gortschakov, Giacomo Rossini and Franz Liszt. Baden was certainly a cosmopolitan spa, more for its delights of society than the merits of its cure, and it became the 'European mecca of all who enjoy a spa, who need spa bathing and indeed of all tourists'.

One of the most highly-rated hotels in Germany today is the Brenner's Park Hotel in Baden-Baden. Like all notable hotels in the town, it continues in the spa tradition dating from Roman times, offering a variety of health-giving springs and waters, one of which claims to be the hottest spring in Europe, at a temperature of 154°F (67.8°C). In 1860 the resort was already becoming a fashionable place for the courts of Europe to frequent, and a new palatial hotel building

Baden-Baden, Brenner's Park Hotel, started in 1872 with this Hôtel Minerva, which established standards of quality and service that have since become traditional.

erected by Alexandre and Joseph Beaussier from France welcomed Napoleon III as its first guest. After Bismarck's victory and the fall of Napoleon, German interests came to the fore and the first member of the Brenner family, Anton Alois, who was a master-tailor to the Prussian court, bought the building which was known as the Hôtel Stephanie-les-Bains in 1872, starting a long history of successful hotel-keeping. His son Camille at this time was gaining all-round experience and knowledge as a cloth merchant in London before returning to take charge of the hotel in 1882 and in the following year to buy it from his father. Soon the Villa Stephanie and the Villa Impériale were built as annexes for use by royalty and other distinguished visitors, being linked by bridges to the main Hôtel Stephanie. This extension provided about 100 rooms, regarded as a desirable size for maintaining the individual service they wished to give. César Ritz at this stage appears once again, he having had a lease on the neighbouring Hôtel Minerva and where, therefore, a prestigious clientèle might be within reach. Camille Brenner took over this lease from Ritz to extend his hotel complex further by building in its place the Sanatorium Stephanie in 1912.

Brenner guest-lists were able to record Dom Pedro of Brazil, Grand-Duchess Olga of Russia, the Sultan of Johore and King Chulalongkorn of Siam, familiar travellers all. Kurt and Alfred Brenner, grandsons of the founder, inherited responsibility for the hotel on their father's death at the beginning of the Great War and in 1919 named it Brenner's Park Hotel. Kurt had been to the Waldorf-Astoria in New York and the Ritz hotels in Paris and London for his training and, with Alfred, successfully overcame the problems of the Great

Depression, only to succumb financially in 1941 during the Second World War, when the majority of shares were sold to the Oetkers of Bielefeld. Revival and modernization returned after the 1950s, and the excellence of service and comfort that Brenner's has always sought has been maintained under the direction of Richard Schmitz, who has declared as his guiding principle 'Who stops improving has stopped being good'.

Moving from spa to capital city, the Kaiserhof in Berlin, built in 1875 by Hennicke and Hermann von der Hude was a hotel of moderate size with 232 rooms and straightforward classical style, while the slightly later Grand Hotel Alexanderplatz of 1883 introduced gabled northern Renaissance features. In Frankfurt, the Frankfurterhof was given a more interesting configuration by local architects Carl Jonas Mylius and Friedrich Alfred Bluntschli, planned around three sides of a square with an arcaded screen on the fourth side.[18] The design embodied neo-Renaissance elements deriving from the Louvre in Paris and was approved by the city planning council in 1873. The enterprise took the usual course for raising capital of forming a stock company, and the building construction occupied a period of two years. For the interior design an architect from Interlaken, Edouard Davinet (1839–1922), was employed. Davinet made a speciality of hotel work and attained a capacity of 250 rooms with 350 beds, 20 salons, a dining-room to seat 800, lifts, steam heating and a kitchen 21 feet (6.5 metres) high. Concurrently he was working in Switzerland on the second Rigi-Kulm Hotel and the Grand Hotel Schreiber, being recognized as among the most eminent Swiss hotel architects. The initial building

Frankfurt, Hotel Frankfurterhof, 1876. Carl Jonas Mylius and Friedrich Alfred Bluntschli were the architects, Edouard Davinet the interior designer. In World War II it was reduced to little more than a shell, but has been painstakingly rebuilt within the old structure by Albert Steigenberger.

cost of the Frankfurterhof was 4.75 million marks. From its opening in 1876, new technology when obtainable was readily adopted and a hotel telegraph office soon developed into a post office which, in 1891, provided the first public telephone in Frankfurt. Soon after this, electric lighting was installed.

Economic difficulties in the 1890s resulted in the leasing by the hotel company for five years to a management consortium under César Ritz, which bought out the original Aktien-Gesellschaft in 1899 shortly before the lease expired. The new régime carried on with Ritz on the board for ten years, then under one of the original board, Georges Gottlob, and Ferdinand Hillengass, a pupil of Ritz's, entered a long period of stable and effective management. This international element and the success that for a time it brought, emphasizes the extent to which in the late nineteenth century, the clientèle for grand hotels had become mobile. Recommendations circulated among relatively small groups of affluent people, exerting competitive pressures, so that rivalry between hotels was keen.

Bomb damage sustained during the Second World War left barely a shell of the Frankfurterhof standing, but a devotee, Albert Steigenberger, bought it in 1940 and rebuilt it in modern terms behind the façade. Gradual progress over a decade made possible the opening of a substantial part of the hotel in 1951.

Italy, Austria, Sweden and Greece

Italy did not invent travel, but has the distinction of having been in Europe the oldest and greatest magnet to draw those interested in art and architecture, classical study or simple enjoyments of the Italian scene. Italy's culture has no equal and yet its existence as a unified nation was not finally accomplished until about 1870. Travellers of increasingly broad social levels pursued the itineraries of the Grand Tour long beyond the eighteenth century, the dominance of the English still being evident. Unsettled politically and with hazards of revolution and war in 1831, 1848, 1859 and 1866, Italy's material development was restricted and mechanized industry and transport were slow to spread. The disparate regions, as always, existed in differing time scales, and facilities for travellers followed suit. Prior to the end of the nineteenth century a main method of developing hotels took the form of extending and converting existing buildings, which often happened to be villas or palaces on historic sites.

The Grand Hotel Villa Serbelloni at Bellagio, as its name indicates, is one such hotel, perfectly sited at the point which

Bellagio, Grand Hotel Villa Serbelloni, 1850 and 1872. Rodolfo Vantini and Giuseppe Pestagalli respectively designed the villa and the additional two wings to form a hotel. The symmetrical nineteenth-century garden layout has been curtailed since a new swimming pool was built.

ABOVE & OPPOSITE Cernobbio, the Grand Hotel Villa d'Este, adapted to hotel use in 1873. It was originally a palace designed by Pellegrino Pellegrini and built in 1568, and is included as an exceptional example of palatial grandeur, contributing its style to the demands of the nineteenth-century hotel.

divides Lake Como into two arms.[19] Romans and Gauls successively found it to be a strategic site, but Pliny the Younger, a native of Como, built himself two villas on the lake – named Comoedia and Tragoedia – the second of these occupying a dominant position on the promontory. Goths and Vandals may have fought each other here and fortifications are said to have been the work of Theodoric. At a much later date Galeazzo Visconti, Duke of Milan in 1375, had the castle demolished to eliminate unwelcome use by outlaws and the cycles of rebuilding and destruction continued until the

Renaissance, when the Sfondrati family gained ascendancy over the rival Medici and retained the property until 1788. From them it was acquired or inherited by Count Serbelloni, of a rich and powerful family whose unexpected claim to fame arose by way of their son's tutor, Giuseppe Parini, who championed a girl the Duchess Maria Vittoria had vigorously slapped. His dismissal was instant, but ridicule rebounded on the family after Parini's satire *Il Giorno* made them 'the laughing stock of Milan when the alleged impotence of the husband and the loose morals and infidelities of the wife were suddenly brought out into the open'. The hillside villa that had been built in 1539 was neglected during the difficult years of the *Risorgimento*, but it was in use as a hotel at the end of the nineteenth century and then had a succession of owners until 1959 when the Rockefeller Foundation took over. The Grand Hotel is on a site closer to the lake shore and the town, where the Villa Frizzoni was built for a patrician family in

Sanremo, Hotel Royal, 1871. The architect was Alessandro Cantù; an extension was built in 1874 by Pio Soli and an outdoor heated swimming pool by Gio Ponti was completed in 1948. Additional accommodation at roof level was achieved in 1989 by Luigi Vietti with little detriment to external appearance.

A cascade fills the basin of the Villa d'Este's nymphaeum, which overlooks formal gardens to Lake Como.

Unobtrusive but design-conscious public spaces in the Royal at Sanremo contain family portraits and a limited amount of decorative plasterwork, enabling views of sea and garden to prevail.

1850 to the design of Rodolfo Vantini (1791–1856). Much of the Pompeian and Roman Renaissance revival interior design remains intact. Vantini, who qualified as 'Ingegnere-architetto' in 1810, became professor at the Liceo di Brescia in 1819, and his other works include the Porta Orientale and Barriera di Porta Venezia in Milan. In 1865 Milanese merchants and bankers purchased the lake shore villa with a hotel enterprise in mind and symmetrical wings were added in very compatible style by Giuseppe Pestagalli (*fl.* 1840–72), another Milan architect and professor who adhered to the current trend for neo-Renaissance decoration. In 1872 it was opened as the Grand Hotel Bellagio in very much the same form it retains today, modest in size with less than 100 bedrooms but undoubtedly, through its unequalled location and unobtrusive high standards of service, among the most enjoyable of grand hotels. The Bucher family have owned it since 1918 and in 1930 altered the name to Grand Hotel Villa Serbelloni, emphasizing both domestic and patrician aspects of its history and underlining these with antique furniture and works of art. Gilded candelabra and Turkey carpets evoke the nineteenth-century atmosphere. A fine mid-century garden, although it does contain a modern swimming-pool, has not lost the neo-Renaissance formality of terrace, arbour and double balustraded staircase down to the private jetty.

It is tempting to stop at the Villa d'Este, also on Lake Como and converted to hotel use in 1873 after centuries of private occupation and a distinguished architectural heritage. Citing it as a prototype of building suited to such transformation is an excuse for mentioning the original palace design by Pellegrino Pellegrini for Cardinal Gallio in 1568 and the extensive neo-classical alterations for Caroline of Brunswick, Princess of Wales, in the early nineteenth century.

Contemporary with these two hotels was one on the Italian Riviera built at Sanremo near the French frontier immediately after the advent of the railway. Menton, Nice and Cannes were then popular on a modest scale but did not represent competition in the grand hotel world for at least another ten years. The Hotel Royal, built by and still under the ownership of the Bertolini family, was the offspring of an enterprise created by Lorenzo Bertolini in the mountaineering centre of Courmayeur and also called the Hotel Royal.[20] There he ran a hotel to serve climbers and more fashionable visitors to the resort, among them the Queen of Italy, Margharita of Savoy, whose achievement was to cause the first bathroom in Courmayeur to be constructed for her use. Seeing possibilities latent in the pleasant climate of the Ligurian coast, Bertolini, a knowledgeable engineer, com-

missioned Alessandro Cantù to design a luxury hotel suitable for the discriminating clientèle he had been building up in Courmayeur. A five-storey rectangular building with about 150 bedrooms offers no surprises but, with plain ironwork balconies, green Ligurian window shutters and elegant stucco-work on the classical façades, expresses quality and restraint. Marble columns with bronze capitals complement the interior stuccoes; paintings and busts from different periods complete the decoration but attention tends always to be wandering through the palm trees towards views of the Mediterranean. The site is terraced down in the direction of the sea with a large private garden space, an important asset which has been treated with care in its planting and in the insertion of a sea-water swimming pool designed by Gio Ponti (1891–1979) in 1948. The palm trees along the promenade adjoining the garden were a novelty when given to the developing town by the Russian Grand-Duchess Maria Alexandrovna. The climate and the owners' interest, perhaps also encouraged by the proximity of the Hanbury garden near Ventimiglia, have resulted in the formation of a fine subtropical plant collection, of which the hotel is proud, having issued a list of its botanical garden plants. Success with this hotel stimulated further investment and development, helped by the presence of European royalties, scientists, writers, performing artistes, diplomats and tycoons of the business world who widened its fame and added to its reputation in America as well as Europe.

The history of the Grand Hotel des Iles Borromées at Stresa on Lake Maggiore was somewhat similar, although built earlier for the Omarini brothers and dependent originally on lake steamers rather than railways for transport. A new wing was added in 1868 to the flourishing hotel, just five years after its opening, and its domed and stuccoed presence dominates the lakeside, looking towards the Borromean Islands.

Austria in the middle of the nineteenth century was losing not only the dominance she had held in Germany after 1815 but also territories in northern Italy – Lombardy and Venetia – where nationalistic movements were active. As a counterbalance she acquired Turkish Bosnia-Herzegovina but the static politics of the Habsburg Monarchy had been, in the posthumous instructions of the Emperor Franz to his successor Ferdinand in 1835, 'Govern and change nothing'. By mid-century Franz Joseph ruled, and in 1867 was crowned King of Hungary also, thus establishing the Dual Monarchy but failing to solve the political turmoil in a central Europe urgently in need of reform.

Meanwhile, on the domestic scene, where such distractions were no doubt welcome to many, Austria, or more specifically Vienna, had entered the world of exhibitions and was engaged in an ambitious Parisian-style replanning of the city based on the new Ringstrasse as the key to its grandiose design. A number of hotels contributed to the desired amenities, and most of these were built on the ring boulevard which had been started in 1858. Two were designed by Heinrich Claus (b.1835) and Josef Grosz (b.1828), named the Britannia, finished in 1870 and the Donau, 1870–80. A third was the Metropole, with about 300 rooms, by K. Schumann and L. Tischler, which like the others was made ready for the 1873 International Exhibition. Most attractive of all was the sumptuous – but never used – palace of Duke Philippe of Württemberg, built for him in 1867 by Arnold Zenetti and Heinrich Adam but converted by Wilhelm Fraenkel into a hotel six years later. From then onwards, christened Imperial by the Emperor himself, it was the height of fashion, in constant favour with the great and the glorious until the Second World War. Taken over by the Third German Reich, it several times accommodated Adolf Hitler as well as suffering serious war damage and then was in Russian use until 1965. It has been completely restored to previous internal and external appearance of nineteenth-century glory and maintains its leading place in the city centre.

But there is still one further world-famous hotel to investigate in Vienna, the Sacher, directly across the road from the Opera House.[21] Eduard Sacher, a butcher in the city, extended his business with a delicatessen and a restaurant, both of which soon became profitable and exclusive. In 1880 he took the next step of buying the site where the old Kärntnertor Theatre had been replaced by a new building and which he proposed to transform into a hotel to fulfil the growing fashion and demand for well-appointed accommodation. Here too, the idea of living in palatial rooms at will and without responsibilities had caught the imagination of the well-to-do. In the closely-knit establishment of Imperial Vienna, where intrigue and gossip were indigenous, he foresaw that private dining-rooms would be extremely useful as adjuncts to the public restaurant, and so it proved. The exterior of the building by Fraenkel was in the heavy neo-Renaissance manner used extensively in Vienna in the 1870s with only slight relief by way of balustrading, rustication and ornament. This proved no obstacle to the international status soon acquired after Sacher's innovative arrangements were presented to the clientèle. Another valuable asset came his way in the person of one of his trainee staff, Anna Fuchs, a pretty and capable young woman whom he promptly married and who then matured into a powerful personality. Her unwritten but well-understood rules of complete discretion made possible the maintenance of privacy in circles

Vienna, Imperial Hotel, 1872. This was transformed from its original unused purpose as the Duke of Württemberg's palace by Wilhelm Fraenkel in time for the International Exhibition of 1873. Zenetti and Adam's palace design lent itself to grand hotel use, and its fashionable status lent it immediate success.

The carved wooden bedroom furniture of the Imperial proclaims the Viennese style.

of power and influence without conceding any tarnishing of the hotel's reputation. Her husband, though technically in charge, faded into the background and led a peaceful life in 'his' hotel for twelve years until his death. The rule of Anna proceeded with quite a lot of Viennese frivolity, and the 90 rooms available to the selected circle brought in a most satisfactory income. Serious affairs of state often had the Sacher Hotel's private dining-rooms as their background, with the picturesque Austro-Hungarian army looking anxiously at Serbia and talking of military theory and Balkan problems. The Emperor Franz Joseph, who reigned for 68 years, never visited the hotel, but his extended family exceeded 60 members and many of them were regular visitors. Austrian Arch-Dukes, Russian Grand-Dukes, Serbs, Czechs and Hungarians all passed through and enjoyed the luxury. Operettas and more serious music were delighted in, but the Habsburg Empire was living out its last decades, to end in effect with the assassination of Arch-Duke Franz Ferdinand at Sarajevo in 1914.

The picture in Sweden was very different in the 1860s and Stockholm was undergoing changes at its own pace, transforming itself into an industrial and administrative centre with rail communications and an active port developing as a result of steam power. Hotels had existed before the first railway station in 1860 but most were still of the inn type, although the Hotel Garni, in Drottningatan 3, was opened in 1832 with a reputation for luxury and a clientèle from amongst diplomats and aristocrats. The story of a much-needed new hotel for Stockholm, a city of 200,000 people, includes some very familiar elements.[22] The first such hotel was the Rydberg, named after a merchant and shipowner Abraham Rydberg, whose philanthropic aim was to use its profits to maintain a boys' training ship. The site was in Gustav Adolfs Torg and the hotel designed by A. Tornquist, was completed in 1857. An interest in *haute cuisine* was increasing and, by way of Paris and St Petersburg, a young Frenchman from the Hautes Alpes, son of innkeepers there, found himself as chef in the household of Count Jacob Dashkoff when the Count was appointed Russian Minister to Stockholm. Jean Francis Régis Cadier (1829–90) was this chef, destined to achieve his ambition to be an hotelier. The Dashkoff family lived on Blasieholmen for twenty years, and during this period Régis Cadier married the Countess's lady's maid, Caroline (Lilly) Roberg. Cadier, like most ambitious would-be hoteliers, tried always to benefit from opportunities and had made contact with Swedish royalty by way of an incident at the Military Club where Dashkoff and Prince Oscar were in fierce dispute at the luncheon table. Cadier was said to be in the Club kitchen at the time and rushed out

Stockholm, The Grand Hotel, 1874, by Axel Fritjof Kumlien. The Grand was described in Murray and Stanford's *Cook's Tourist Handbook* for the succeeding three years.

An altered façade simplified the front view of the Grand in the 1920s, as seen from the quayside.

to separate the two, earning the Prince's gratitude and a future appointment as royal chef. The next step in Cadier's career was to open a French restaurant with his brothers in Gustav Adolfs Torg under the title 'Les Trois Frères Provençaux'. The lighter food and attentive service were novelties and the restaurant proved very successful. Another innovation was the provision of a clean table napkin for each person, replacing the established practices of either using a communal one hung up on the wall or one left on the table by previous users but folded to present the cleanest surface to the next customer, food hygiene being then obviously unknown.

Careful saving put Cadier in a position during the booming 1860s to buy the Hotel Rydberg when its original management failed and, in addition, he was able to buy the Alhambra on Djurgården. The first-floor restaurant at the Rydberg boosted his catering success and established a reputation for quality and fashion that brought in money and stimulated further ambition as, even with an extra rented annexe, the available space was too small. His aim was to create from scratch the best hotel in Stockholm, large enough to satisfy public demands and fully up-to-date in both design and equipment. His own lively taste and temperament had to be gratified and it is to be expected that his years of training in Paris and subsequent experience of the diplomatic world with Count Dashkoff exerted their influence. He formed a syndicate to raise the necessary capital but seems at all times to have maintained the lead and direction of the whole enterprise. The site chosen on Blasieholmen – originally an island but now a peninsula – faces the Royal Palace across the water and is close to the site of the old Fersen mansion where Cadier had spent his first years in Stockholm. Little time was wasted in commissioning and briefing the architect, Axel Fritjof Kumlien (1833–1913), or in accepting the builder's tender and giving him instructions to start. Kumlien's five-storey rectangular design was neo-Renaissance in a northern manner, in 25 bays along the front elevation to the quayside with a central pilastered feature over the main entrance. Other decorative detail consisted of crested ironwork to the roof, œil-de-bœuf windows to the attics and pierced stonework balustrades to a number of the balconies.

The opening of the Grand Hotel on 14 June 1874 was an important occasion, with King Oscar II participating together with the Crown Prince and Dukes of Gotland and Västerbotton. Cadier and the city of Stockholm were understandably proud of the 400-bedroom hotel, built of Swedish materials and incorporating electric light, steam-powered lifts, telephone, piped gas and water. The public water supply was expensive and use was made of water pumped directly from the Stockholm Stream for general utilitarian purposes, those arrangements remaining in force until 1905 when large institutions were allowed a rebate on the public supply charges. Baths were scarce – just two being provided in the basement – and toilet facilities appear to have been similarly primitive. Public rooms in contrast were well provided for dining, sitting, coffee, reading and billiards – in fact the standard selection. The Banqueting Hall designed by Kumlien was inspired by Brunelleschi's church of S Lorenzo, Florence, but was superseded in the reconstruction of 1898. The Porcelain Café with wall and ceiling tiles in lime green was a popular rendezvous with access directly from the street, as was its counterpart 'The Pit', which discharged the role of a men's club for notabilities of the day.

Régis Cadier must have been one of the few hoteliers to make an immediate financial success of such a large enterprise. The building cost 1,800,000 thalers (now kronor), and the first room rates were 1.50 kronor a night. At the same time, Cadier was still running the Hotel Rydberg with its flourishing restaurant and 150 bedrooms. Unusually for someone in the hotel trade his services were recognized by the honour of appointment as Knight of the Order of Vasa. Many further developments continued to uphold the standards and reputation of the Grand Hotel, summarized in several steps. The purchase of the Bolinder Mansion adjoining the hotel (1889) was followed by extensive reconstruction after sale to AB Nya Grand Hotel (1898). New interiors were designed in 1902 and another purchase, that of the Grand Hotel Royal at the rear of the site, increased the size very substantially. Another major reconstruction changed the face of the building in 1925–8. Further alterations to enlarge and improve single rooms are planned.

The Bolinder Mansion or Palace was built as a private house for the founder of the Bolinder Engineering Works in 1877, next to the southeast end of the Grand. Jean Bolinder commissioned Helgo Zetterwall to design a grand house in sympathy with his artistic tastes and incorporating by way of structural or decorative features any items that could be made in cast iron by his firm. Apart from the use of semi-circular headed windows, roundels and pilasters there is little direct borrowing from the Venetian style and a hangover from the German *Rundbogenstil* of the 1830s and 1840s might have left its mark. The interesting oriel turrets on the corners could only belong to the end of the nineteenth century. The interiors, under advice from Academy of Art Principal George von Rosen, are more definitely neo-Renaissance, with much Pompeian decoration backed up by dark colours and gilding, all in a good state of preservation. When Cadier bought this

The Bolinder Mansion in Stockholm was added to the Grand's property in 1889. Its staircase represents neo-classical elegance among a variety of ornamental styles.

property it was constructed as three residential flats and he made the first floor unit his home. One of the most striking rooms, Mårten Winge's Room, can now be seen and hired for private functions, although its original wealthy occupier, before Cadier's purchase, was L. O. Smith, the Schnapps King. Well-known Swedish names in addition to Mårten and Hanna Winge included Fredrik Wilhelm Scholander (1816–81), Carl Larsson and Gothard Werner as painters and Ansgar Almquist as sculptor, employed by Bolinder to execute the decoration. Mouldings and plasterwork and high-quality inlaid timber floors all play a part in the rich nineteenth-century effect, although the character of the staircase in the Bolinder mansion is unreservedly neo-classical. Ownership of the mansion passed out of the hotel company's hands in 1928 only to return again in 1970 after transactions too numerous to list.

Régis Cadier had died in 1890 aged 61 and his widow Lilly carried on for a year with both hotels, selling the Rydberg in 1891 but remaining in charge of the Grand until 1897 when she sold it to Axel Burman who formed AB Nya Grand Hotel (the New Grand Hotel Company Limited). An extensive modernization scheme was put in hand, an extra storey was built, wrought iron took the place of stone for balconies, and steep decorative gables, small corner cupolas and a central tower were added by the architects. Ludvig Pettersson and Thure Sternberg were aiming to achieve 'the bright, new, lighthearted façade of the Grand Hotel, which contrasts with

OPPOSITE The Hall of Mirrors in the Grand drew inspiration from Versailles. It became the prime site for Stockholm's most prestigious functions until the new City Hall was built in 1929.

the heavy, clumsy appearance of the old version'. A new French restaurant, an Indian café (in the Bolinder building, demolished 1929) and an extension of Cadier's wine cellar to hold 120,000 bottles were accompanied by a newly fitted kitchen in the souterrain floor where the centrepiece was 'two huge Bolinder's hotel stoves, equipped with every modern convenience for hot water etc. unsurpassed of their kind in Europe and America. Such a stove is no mere toy. They can produce a meal for 1000 persons.' An automatic spit from A. Senking of Hildesheim is mentioned, long enough to take fifteen chickens, and the duties of the 170-strong kitchen staff are described. Ice carving and sugar sculpture are wondered at; so is the laundry. Best of all in this 1898 reconstruction is the Mirror Room in place of the old banqueting hall which, inspired by the seventeenth-century Galérie des Glaces at Versailles, Thure Sternberg created as a highly decorative white and gold neo-baroque interior. It is carefully scaled, with lightly painted compartmented ceiling and a deep cove pierced with blind œils-de-bœuf, all ornamented with gilded urns and cornucopias, garlands and ribbons. Below the cornice, semi-circular headed bays of mirror, doors and niches alternate with composite pilasters, and at each end two pairs of fully gilded Corinthian columns frame respectively a small stage and access to the quayside salon with its dramatic view of harbour and Royal Palace at the opposite end. From 1901 until 1929, when the new City Hall was built, the Nobel Prize banquets were held in this room. Jugendstil found its way into the Grand in 1902 chiefly in ground-floor alterations by Lars Israel Wahlman to form a café in place of the billiard-room.

The acquisition of the Grand Hotel Royal made a more significant change in the hotel accommodation, just as the advent of Wilhelmina Skogh as general manager that same year was the signal for a more positive direction. As Wilhelmina Wahlgren she had made her remarkable way in a man's world, being a manageress in Gävle at the age of nineteen and a licensee of a railway station restaurant five years later. At 29 she was a hotel owner, full of novel ideas, such as farming her own vegetables and animals or raising a boiler flue by two metres to improve the draught when the engineer had failed to get adequate performance out of the generator. She married a wine merchant, obtained the most important hotel job in Stockholm and started to create a legend. It fell to her to negotiate with the Marshal of the Court in relation to acquiring the site at the back of the Grand, royal property previously used as a mews in Sophia Albertina's time, and which was ripe for redevelopment for the Duke of Skåne. Agreement was reached with the Sophia Albertina Foundation in 1906 for a form of building lease, and the Grand

Hotel Royal went ahead with Ernst Stenhammer as architect and Carlsson and Löfrgren as contractors for the sum of 780,000 kronor. Building works involving interiors and the necessary linking with the Grand were carried out under the architect Edward Berhard. The consideration paid by AB Nya Grand Hotel to the Princess Sophia Albertina Foundation in 1910 was 2,600,000 kronor. The design, on a corner site approximately 60 metres square, was inventive and extended the scope of the Grand Hotel substantially with four- and five-storey accommodation enclosing a large Winter Garden. This is capable of serving 1,000 people at a cocktail party or 700 for dinner, and a curved corner proscenium provides for entertainment or ceremony. In this attractive and versatile space Venetian Gothic influence is strong, with terracotta coloured rendered walls, arched and pointed windows and well-placed balconies, from one of which Manageress Skogh was able to keep an eye discreetly on the happenings below. Paintings by Lotten Rönnquist of Drottningholm (1906–8) and a series of frescoes by Elis Aslund (1926) are among the decorative pieces in the Winter Garden, which is roofed with shallow glazed geometric domes that look deceptively modern.

Another reconstruction of the main building changed the scene yet again in 1925, to the designs of Ivar Tengbom during which the façade to the quayside was simplified and much-needed replacements or improvements were executed for the new owners, the liquor monopoly AB Vin & Spritcentralen. Services and equipment were updated and the foyer was re-designed in a twentieth-century version of neo-classicism with bas-reliefs by Nils and Robert Olsson and Axel Wallenberg, Nils Olsson also carrying out pictorial decoration.

The Stockholm Exhibition of 1930 brought visitors and trade from abroad, and before long air travel became practicable. Financial difficulties and the Second World War led to more transfers of ownership, but since 1967 the hotel company has been owned by the Wallenberg family and a steady programme of renovation has been pursued in this unique group of buildings, the Bolinder mansion, the Grand Hotel Royal and the original Grand Hotel, under whose distinguished name all three operate as one. For the whole of the Grand's history a remarkably intimate connection has existed between city and hotel to the extent that it would be difficult to envisage one without the other.

A comparable hotel in respect of its importance in the social structure of a capital city can be seen at the far end of Europe, in Greece. There, in Athens, the Hôtel Grand Bretagne developed in a similar way over an extended period and owing its reputation and existence, as did the Grand in Stockholm, to the vision and ambition of a single young man setting out from obscurity to make his mark among the small kingdoms of the grand hotel world.

Athens in the mid-nineteenth century witnessed the downfall of King Otto after 30 years on the throne, partially under his uncle as regent, partially in his own right. In 1863 a new dynasty began, with a Danish prince as George I, King of the Hellenes. Social life had hitherto managed to survive as a recognized focus that supported theatre, opera, receptions and balls, although 21 changes of government within eleven years proved there was little political stability. It was during this uncertain period that Stathis Lampsas was growing up, nurturing an ambition to start a hotel in Athens equal to the best in Europe. His father, a Greek peasant, had moved to Russia, where Stathis was born, then returned to Athens, where the boy found work in the Royal Kitchens.

Stathis's dedication and hard work won him the opportunity to learn cookery at the Maison Dorée restaurant in Paris with the aim of his return to take charge of the royal *cuisine*. Instead of this he remained in Paris where his skill and imagination as a chef enabled him to repay the loans that King George had sponsored. Later, having married a French woman and also acquired considerable savings, he returned to Athens, went into partnership with Savvas Kendros, then owner of the down-at-heel Hotel Megali Bretannia, and set about realizing his dream. The basis for the hotel was the Dimitriou mansion, a building well-sited near to the Royal Palace and designed on an ample scale by Theophil Hansen (1813–91), a Danish architect, in elegant neo-classical style. It was three storeys high, arcaded at ground-floor level and set apart from much so-called classical building of its time by its direct Greek pedigree and absence of western European mannerisms.

Extensions which have been added to the original building follow its early inspiration, but inevitably the increase to eight storeys in height and a façade of eighteen bays along Panepistimiou have changed its character, although without damaging its power to draw visitors. On the death of his partner Kendros in 1888, Stathis Lampsas took up his interest in the hotel and pursued, as sole proprietor, modern trends, such as electricity, with the first power generator in Greece and, in following winter seasons from 1894, a series of highly popular dinner dances.

The Hôtel Grande Bretagne consistently made and maintained its status as the prime hotel in Athens, a magnet for all prestigious guests, while the Greek capital, so designated only as late as 1834, grew slowly and sometimes not very steadily in consolidating its supremacy. The revival of the Olympic Games and the founding of the International Olympic Committee in 1894 to set up and manage the

An austere elegance pervades the public rooms of the Grande
Bretagne, Athens, maintaining the relatively unchanged style
of the turn of the century.

occasion benefited both Athens and the Grande Bretagne in
presenting many opportunities for the accommodation and
entertainment of organizers, participants and spectators in
the first modern Olympiad, which took place in 1896. The
reputation of the Grande Bretagne had been enhanced by
the Games, and its management was dynastic by the time the
torch passed on from Lampsas to his son-in-law Theodore
Petracopoulos in 1918. Two wars interrupted his long régime
in charge of the life of the hotel, but innovation and extension took place when practicable, and as a meeting place for
the eminent and powerful, as well as for more questionable
intriguers, it continued to represent the heart of Athens.
Petracopoulos died in 1963, ending the personal intimacy
between his hotel and the political scene, but the tradition of
quality and hospitality remained.

These attributes are touchstones in judging a hotel's success and this was realized fully by the Swiss, whose mastery
and perfecting of the hotel trade in all its aspects is the subject of the following chapter.

Opened in 1874, part new and part incorporating the Dimitriou
mansion, the Grande Bretagne is a fine neo-classical building
designed on palatial lines by the Danish architect Theophil Hansen.

THE SWISS GENIUS

Swiss expertise has occupied consistently a unique place in all aspects of hotel development and hotelkeeping since the genre came into being. Switzerland would not have seemed the most likely breeding ground for such a culture; a small land-bound territory where industrialization arrived late and political federation suggested the likelihood of disintegration rather than unity. The first railway as an aid to communication was not built until 1847, but in the preceding twenty years there had been reform among the 22 cantons with the aim of introducing more democracy and solidarity. This was contested by the Catholic cantons in a shortlived civil war during the same year, and although they lost the fight a conciliatory peace agreement gave birth to a new and successful constitution under stronger federal government and universal male suffrage. In 1848, therefore, when France and Italy were being upset by revolutions, Switzerland was able to enjoy tranquillity in which to guide its economy into a more up-to-date world. Transport did not develop quickly, hampered by the difficult terrain and the lack of engineering skills in craft-centred communities. Tourism was nevertheless persistent, following the footsteps of Goethe and Byron and fostering a hotel environment to supply the wants of the eminent and wealthy from all Europe and beyond. Swiss hotels were not developed on a grand scale for the Swiss themselves, but as a service industry for the foreign visitors whose predecessors had shown their attachment to travel and exploration by crossing the Alps in conditions of extreme discomfort for the benefit of the pot of gold at the end of the rainbow. By the early nineteenth century the pot of gold was less a discovery of unknown wonders and was sought more in terms of ease and comfort to be appreciated in fresh surroundings away from the cares of everyday life.

OPPOSITE St Moritz, Suvretta House, designed by Karl Koller and built in only eight months, it opened in 1913.

Travel in the Mountains

Switzerland had its background of lakes and mountains, and society's upper ranks were looking for indulgence in romantic scenery and good living. The spark between them was waiting to be lighted and when this happened a new age began. Austria, in fact, had been first in the field of mountain railways with the Semmering Line in 1854, when the Emperor Franz Joseph was conducted over its spectacular course in the first passenger train to run on this important artery. Switzerland's rail network advanced spasmodically, influenced by pressure from the surrounding states of France, Italy and Germany, whose need for good transalpine links steadily increased. The line from Germany to Switzerland was completed in 1857 and main lines of access constructed after this connection involved tunnelling, these being the Mont Cenis (1871) followed by the Gotthard (1882) and the Arlberg (1884). Branch lines scaled many of the steep approaches when new mountain localities attracted fashionable travellers, but horse-drawn transport was still relied on for the final stage of virtually all journeys until ousted by the internal combustion engine in the twentieth century.

Luxury hotels did not necessarily wait for easy travelling and, from a start in the older towns, waves of development ran along lake shores and up into the Alps during a half-century which reflected social aspirations and demonstrated the ways in which they could be satisfied. In the words of the actress Fanny Kemble, writing letters in the 1870s:

The railroad now runs all the way from Geneva to the foot of the Simplon, an easy journey of less than 8 hours, and nobody wants to stop halfway at Villeneuve. Then, too, there is really almost a continuous terrace all along the lake from Lausanne to Villeneuve of hotels like palaces, one more magnificent than another, with terraces and gardens, and fountains and bands of music, and such luxurious public apartments, and *table d'hôte*.

And she continues:

Fashion directs the movements of the great majority of the people and for the last few years there has been a perfect insane rush of the whole tourist world to the valley of the Upper Engadine, to the almost utter forsaking of the formerly popular parts of Switzerland.

The claim for first position as a de-luxe hotel, opened in 1834, is made by the Hôtel des Bergues in Geneva, on a prime site next to the river Rhône and advertised as the only hotel from where one could see Mont Blanc. Its name is derived from the seventeenth-century philanthropist Jean Kleberger, who had owned the land. During the intervening century a wallpaper factory existed there but, after this had declined, improvement and development, in particular on the 'right bank' of the Rhône, was being considered under the initiative of Colonel Guillaume-Henri Dufour, the city engineer. His ideas were rapidly approved and the Société des Bergues was formed to carry out a comprehensive programme of public works. Roads, bridges and a new quay were to be augmented by the building of housing and other accommodation and the Société acquired the wallpaper factory site for the construction of a grand hotel, to be 'le fleuron du nouveau quai'.[1] An architectural competition took place in 1829, won by a young Lyonnais architect, A. Miciol (1804–76), but the actual building of the hotel was put in the hands of a local architect, François-Ulrich Vaucher, whose sober neo-classical design still overlooks Geneva's waterfront. Superfluous ornament had been excluded, and even the pilasters above the central front entrance did not appear on the original drawings. At a cost of 500,000 francs the new five-storey hotel, opened in 1834, was then the largest hotel in Switzerland.

Other hotels quickly followed – at this pre-railway period for reasons of access they tended to be well-placed town hotels – in Zürich the Baur-en-Ville (1836) and then the Baur au Lac (1844); in Vevey, the Trois Couronnes (1842); in Basle, the Trois Rois, a very early foundation in 1026 but updated into the mid-nineteenth century; the Schweizerhof, Lucerne (1845), and another Schweizerhof in Bern (1857). Less risk was incurred by building in centres where a tradition of inn-keeping was there to support new and larger-scale ventures. Confidence increased as the above few luxury hotels achieved recognition and it became clear that there was a wider potential market for top levels of service at top levels of pricing.

The Hotel Dynasty Beginnings

The career of the hotelier was taking shape somewhat surprisingly among villagers from the mountains, who in the first generation had learnt down-to-earth trades varying from *paysans de montagne* through coopering, shoemaking, baking, soapmaking and ironmongering to customs officer

Geneva, Hôtel des Bergues, 1834. The architect François-Ulrich Vaucher was responsible for the building, basing his design on ideas from the French architectural competition winner, A. Miciol.

An elegant staircase embodies the neo-classical style of the entire hotel.

Zürich, Baur-en-Ville, 1838. Architect Daniel Pfister and his friend and hotel enthusiast Johannes Baur were able to launch this enterprising neo-classical design as part of the city centre redevelopment. Its 140 bedrooms were considered excessive in number and size, but demand proved Baur's foresight correct. Much alteration to the original building has taken place.

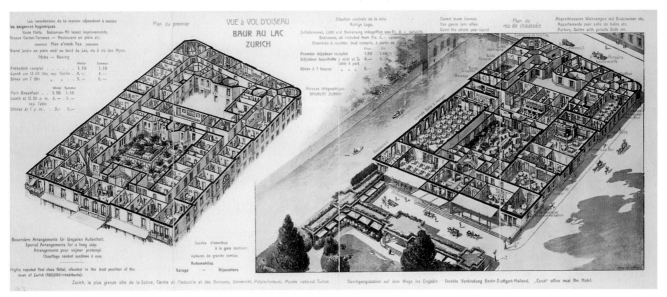

'Bird's eye view'of the Baur au Lac in Zürich around the turn of the century. Automobiles were beginning to replace horse-drawn carriages and a garage is advertised.

Royalty and other eminent guests soon found the Baur au Lac to their taste and its reputation has lasted for more than 150 years. The arrival of Kaiser Wilhelm II of Germany is here expected by a crowd of sightseers in September 1912.

and, occasionally, to building or architecture.[2] Mutual regard often arose between mountaineers and their Swiss guides, who in their turn had been nominated by local innkeepers, opening useful channels of communication. Unsuccessful aspiring hoteliers went largely unrecorded, but those who carved out their own profession as hotel developers shared visions of remarkable sophistication coupled with practical talents. What has come to be regarded as a typically Swiss ability in financial affairs was spiced with a gambling element and the recipe was complete.

Johannes Baur (1795–1865) could be regarded as the founder of *hôtellerie*. He was the son of a customs officer who also seems to have been innkeeping at the Lion Inn at Götzis in Austria, in addition to his responsibilities as mayor of that town. His son Johannes began to learn the bakery trade but was more interested in designing buildings, particularly large hotels. He became friendly with a talented young architect, Daniel Pfister, who had similar interests and, at a time when the centre of Zürich was being replanned, was closely involved with the project for a great hotel opposite the post office and overlooking the new market-place. Local financial backing was obtained, and by 1836 the neo-classical Zürich Hotel, well-designed by Pfister with a giant Ionic order on the main façade, was scandalizing the citizens with its enormous size and capacity (140 beds). Experience vindicated Baur's judgement to the extent that a second hotel was built by him in 1844 by the lakeside. This was designed by Johannes Jakob Keller and also was derided because the main façade with its six balconies actually faced the lake instead of looking inwards to the centre of the town. The two hotels, both resulting from Johannes Baur's enterprise, became known later as the Baur-en-Ville and the Baur au Lac. In 1862 Johannes relinquished the business to his son Theodor, who joined with Jacques Tschumi, hotelier at the Beau Rivage, Ouchy, and founded the first Swiss hotel school at Lausanne, selling the Baur-en-Ville.

Johannes Baur in Zürich and Alexandre Seiler in Zermatt made exceptions to the usual financial practices, providing their own capital on a personal and not a company basis. Baur's son-in-law Karl Kracht took over in 1890 when the second wing of the Baur au Lac was complete, and ownership still remains in the Kracht family.

Alexandre Seiler (1819–91) represented an alternative approach through the business of innkeeping, from a start as candlemaker to fulfilment as an entrepreneur on a larger scale. He was an incomer from Blitzingen in the Conche valley who succumbed to the spell of Zermatt from his first sight of it in 1851. He was encouraged by his brother Joseph, who had previously moved there, and found in it and the surrounding mountains his life's work. The mountaineer Edward Whymper, writing in his *Scrambles Amongst the Alps* (1871) of his visit in 1863, describes the circumstances:

Zermatt itself is only a village with 500 inhabitants (about thirty of whom are guides), with picturesque châlet dwellings, black with age. The hotels, including the inn on the Riffelberg, all belong to one proprietor (M. Alexandre Seiler), to whom the village and valley are very much indebted for their prosperity, and who is the best person to consult for information, or in cases of difficulty.[3]

Seiler had achieved this position having first leased and then purchased and extended the Mont-Cervin (Matterhorn) Hotel in 1852 and the Mont-Rose in 1855. He was therefore well-established enough to serve all the unsuccessful mountaineers attempting the Matterhorn as well as the successful, though tragic, effort of the Whymper party in 1865, during which four lives were lost. Whymper knew Seiler well from many expeditions and commended his 'friendly and disinterested acts' by which 'Monsieur Seiler has acquired his enviable reputation'. Nevertheless, Seiler had to wait for a long time before achieving citizen status, and even then the *farouches Zermattois* had to be pressed into accepting him among themselves by the cantonal authorities.[4]

An exact contemporary of Seiler was Johannes Caspar Badrutt (1819–89), second son of a stonemason who had moved from near Arosa to Samedan in the Engadine, where Johannes was born. At secondary school in Chiavenna his taste for Italian art was formed, but innkeeping seemed to be his goal, and after his marriage to Maria Berry from a good family in Chur, they jointly leased the Berninahof in Samedan as a first venture. St Moritz was slightly higher up the valley, with an ancient pre-Roman mineral spring and a small spa for which an Engadiner consortium of Fluegi, von Planta and Dr Bruegger had renegotiated a further 50-year licence. Johannes and his wife saw future possibilities in the place and, when the old Pension Faller came on the market in 1856, they interpreted two omens in favour of their high-flying ambitions. The first was when an alternative prospective purchaser of the pension nearly cracked his skull on the door lintel, when both parties were inspecting the property, and then withdrew; the second came when Maria slipped and sat down on the ground – obviously meaning that she was destined to settle there. For whatever superstitious and other reasons, they leased the property immediately and eighteen months later were able to buy it outright for 48,500 Swiss francs, backed by Rudolf von Planta and Toendury, a banker from Samedan.[5] From the basic twelve-bedroom pension a grand hotel of 130 bedrooms, large public rooms, bakery, laundry, flushing lavatories, maintenance workshops and farm buildings metamorphosed as the Grand Hotel Engadiner Kulm, close to the old church of St Moritz, of which only the leaning tower remains. Badrutt's invention – or at least the development – of the winter sports season is widely known. At the end of the 1864 summer season, four Englishmen were commiserating on its end when Johannes offered them a bet in support of his claim that winter in St Moritz provided sunshine so warm that shirtsleeves could comfortably be worn. They took up his challenge and agreed to come as his personal guests at the Kulm just before Christmas. If his claim was false, he would pay all their travelling expenses to and fro. If not, they could still stay until the end of the winter at his expense. When they in due course arrived, all of them thickly wrapped up for arctic conditions and sweating as a result, Badrutt greeted them with only shirtsleeves, as wagered. Their appreciative but losing entry in the visitors book on departure, after acknowledging the warmth and brilliance of the weather, ended with handsome value for the future of St Moritz:

The lake affords the opportunity to those who love the art of skating to do so without interruption for five months.[6]

So began the skating, skiing and tobogganing which gave such international renown to St Moritz.

The Badrutt family continued to extend their Grand Hotel ambitions, and the construction by another generation of the Badrutt or Palace Hotel was to widen their achievement.

The background of Bernhard Simon (1816–1900) was altogether different, for he started with architectural abilities that he exercised as a young man in the Russian court at St Petersburg, building grand houses and palaces. Returning to his native Glarus in 1855 he became involved as inspector of railways for St Gall, then went on to serve as director of reconstruction works in the town, which had just suffered devastation by fire. Spas were less common in Switzerland than in nearby Germany but one had existed at Ragaz under the auspices of the Pfäffers monastery with its Prince Abbot's Palace, centred on a thermal spring at the bottom of the Tamina Gorge which had been accurately analysed by Paracelsus in the early sixteenth century. The cantonal government of St Gall had acquired the whole site in 1838 when the monastery was dissolved and developed it as a spa. It was greatly improved two years later when engineer Adolf Neff piped the spring water into the town, thus avoiding the need to negotiate the alarming gorge. Simon was becoming interested both in the overall spa layout and the old monastery which functioned as the Grand Hotel Hof Ragaz, see-

ing possibilities of comprehensive development. He bought the whole domain and a licence to use the thermal spring for 100 years, subject to building a casino, baths with pump room and an additional new hotel 'to European standards'. The resulting Hotel Quellenhof, in straightforward villa style with wrought-iron balconies, was opened in 1869 with the innovation of an indoor thermal swimming pool being completed in 1872, the first in Europe. Although credited with the design of two churches in Bad Ragaz, Simon was now primarily a hotelier and, with useful Russian connections and the practical ability to supply the service guests required, he ran the establishment for twenty more successful years. In 1892 he handed over to his sons and Simon family ownership was maintained until 1943. Then, after more than a decade of inaction due to the Second World War and the resulting economic problems, a revival was achieved by Hans Albrecht, Swiss Member of Parliament, whose energies began to reinvigorate many of Simon's original ideas.

Another success story originated with Franz Joseph Bucher, native of Sarnen, trained for no trade and said to speak only his local patois. In 1863 at the age of 29 he met Joseph Durrer, who was already an entrepreneur, and they set up a furniture and flooring workshop before launching themselves on the hotel world. Among all kinds of enterprise they built three hotels in Bürgenstock, converted the monastery at Lugano into the Grand and Palace Hotel with 200 rooms, and bought the Euler at Basle. Their dealings spread to Genoa, Milan and Rome and even reached Cairo, where they built the now-vanished Semiramis in 1906, and did not stop at hotels. Tunnels, lifts and cable cars were all on their agenda, which included regular buying and selling, and set them up as pioneering creators of an international hotel chain.

Sons of poor families were spurred on because they had little to lose and sought entry into worlds which had been far from their birthright. Others started from greater advantages, with the same dreams of grandeur but able to raise capital without the years of hard labour which their less fortunate colleagues in *hôtellerie* had to undergo. Maximilian Alphons Pfyffer von Altishofen, a colonel from a distinguished Lucerne family, had fought in a Swiss regiment for Francis II of Naples in 1861, but after completion of his army service he revived the early studies of architecture and engineering which he had pursued in Munich and channelled them towards the creation of a luxury hotel in Lucerne. In association with the brothers Segesser de Brunegg, who were also involved in the building and design of hotels in Lucerne, he built the Grand Hotel National there on a lakeside site not far from the Schweizerhof. Acting as their own hotel managers this small consortium failed to make it a profitable enterprise, but Pfyffer was sure of success and personally bought shares heavily when a limited liability company was formed. Losses dimmed but did not extinguish his expectations for the luxurious baroque-influenced hotel, which had deteriorated through the intervening neglect and inefficiency. It was not until he asked his protégé, César Ritz, to take over the management that the hotel was rescued and a close relationship between Pfyffer and Ritz developed, later to be carried on by Pfyffer's two sons.

Thoroughness of preparation was a ruling characteristic of another Swiss devotee in the hotel business, Anton Sebastian Bon (1845–1915), son of the owner of the local sawmill and Mayor of Ragaz. Before embarking on the construction of his hotel empire Bon had worked in England, Marseilles and Rome for experience, had married in 1879, and then rented the Hotel Bodenhaus und Post in Splügen before buying the Rigi First in 1885, a summer hotel he kept until 1929. The Park Hotel, Vitznau, was his next purchase, and after a few years he built (1902) a new hotel on the site, relegating the old one to annexe status. In preparation for this he had taken his architect, Karl Koller, on a study tour of 'les habitations des lords anglais et des princes allemands'.[7] Two more building projects, the Waldhaus, Sils Maria (1908), and the Suvretta House, St Moritz (1912), were both designed by Koller, who appeared to have greater affinity with the taste of German princes than with that of the English lords whose country houses he and Bon had inspected. Of Bon's five sons, two became colonels, one a major and one a captain during their Swiss army service, and all except the youngest took to the hotel trade. Anton, the eldest, learnt English in England, worked with his father at the Vitznau Park Hotel and had a distinguished career at the Dorchester and Brown's in London, in addition to directorships of the Esplanade, Berlin, and the Gordon Hotels. He became chairman of the Swiss Hotel Keepers' Association, but in the 1930s took up residence in England. His brother Hans listed experience at the Quirinal in Rome, Naples, the Rigi and Vitznau Park, and Primus went to Vitznau and then ran the best-known Station Restaurant of all at Zürich.

The ancient name of the Armleder family is said to have originated with marauding bands in areas of southern Germany who wore leather armbands as means of recognition. First records of it as a surname date from 1583 at Altstadt-Rottweil in Württemberg. Adolphe-Rodolphe Armleder (1847–1930) was a descendant whose father worked as a cooper in very limited circumstances, but the son pursued the idea of working in the hotel trade from his early years and left their village, Rottweil-am-Neckar, at the age

of fifteen, no doubt with this ambition in view. Little is known of the following years except that in working up the ladder he had experience in England, Ireland and then Italy. Geneva in 1875 pinpoints his first modest success, when he rented the Riche-Mont Pension. This was already a small going concern with accommodation for 25 guests and its bias was towards good food. Marriage to Victorine Francoz from nearby Annemasse produced a son and daughter, Victor and Valentine, but it was only a short time before Armleder was left a widower and asked his sister Marie for help with the enterprise. Rooms at the time were equipped with marble-topped washstands for jugs and basins, candles or spirit lamps and open fireplaces for lighting and heating. The table staff had to subsist on gratuities alone and the house staff received about 25 Swiss francs per month for 15- to 18-hour days. No holidays were given, but even with this strict régime a good level of service was provided. A general economic crisis in 1880 slowed down the pension's prospects and it was not until an exhibition in 1896, when he leased accommodation for the extra influx of visitors, that expansion took place, adding 25 more beds. The name had been changed to the Richemond Family Hotel when Anglo-Saxon travellers augmented previous German and Russian nationalities. Absence of adequate capital meant grindingly hard work, but appearances were maintained and the reception of guests met by carriage at either of the two railway stations was impressive. Irrespective of whether he had been on his knees sewing carpet repairs or carrying out a variety of other necessary tasks, Adolphe-Rodolphe would make a dignified entrance in frock coat, with stiff white collar and cuffs, to welcome them and offer refreshments in the salon. When presiding over the *table d'hôte* meals, for which a gong sounded at 1 pm and 8 pm, his presence was equally imposing.[8]

In the following generation Victor (1883–1927), to whom his father passed control in 1906, died at the early age of 44. He left a widow, born Emilie Spreter from a restaurant family in Rottweil, and three daughters and one son, Jean, then eleven years old. Meanwhile, another Rottweil family was entering the Richemond scene, destined to play an important part in its history with their devotion and expertise. The father of the family, Gottfried Lang, had risen in the recognized manner from waiter to manager, holding secretarial and chief receptionist jobs en route, contributing his skills in the service of the hotel for more than 50 years, including the vital period after Victor's death. His wife, Thérèse, was all her life the Richemond's dedicated housekeeper. The sons of the two families, André Lang and Jean Armleder, grew up together as good friends, the former to become manager in due course and the latter to widen his experience by travelling until the advent of the Second World War brought him back to take charge. In the difficult wartime period, trade dwindled and Jean acted as general factotum, just succeeding in keeping the business afloat. His good fortune was that he married Ivane Kuhn, the daughter of an American family resident in the hotel, and secured the succession in the arrival of Victor II and John Armleder.

Architectural history of the Richemond is sparse, with an absence of grandeur which indicates steady building up from the original pension in harmony with Adolphe-Rodolphe's temperament. No grand rebuilding schemes changed the quiet style of urban Geneva in the last half of the nineteenth century, and the increase in accommodation which was completed in 1950, adding major public rooms and 54 guest rooms, continued in the same tradition in the hands of the architect, Charles Liechti. Most notable in the impression given by the hotel is the interior furnishing, including a fine collection of antiques, many acquired by the enthusiasm of Ivane Armleder.

An acquisition from the hotel's early years, accepted reluctantly by Adolphe-Rodolphe in payment of a bill, lay unrecognized in the attics until rediscovered by his grandson Jean and revealed as a substantial work, a *Paysage Bernois* by the penniless customer who became the well-known painter Ferdinand Hodler (1853–1918).

The Armleder family has generally preferred to concentrate on this one hotel with only a few outside ventures,

Geneva, Richemond Hotel. Founded in 1875 and remaining in the Armleder family for about 120 years, the building grew with purchases of adjacent property, becoming renowned as one of Geneva's best hotels.

such as the National Hotel bought by the founder, Adolphe-Rodolphe, at the turn of the century, and an interest in the Beau-Séjour at Sempel, of which he was a director. Like many of his hotelier colleagues he had a strong interest in the future of hotelkeeping in Switzerland, which he and his contemporaries had created. There is still no easy route to excellence in the profession to which they had all contributed, but formal training as started by Baur and Tschumi at the Hotel school in Lausanne and supported by Armleder made a most valuable foundation.

César Ritz, King of Hoteliers

Few people have occupied such a dominant position in their chosen field or have contributed so much to the creation of their chosen profession as César Ritz (1850–1918).[9] He was born in the village of Niederwald in the Valais, the thirteenth child of the Mayor, Anton Ritz, whose family had lived in the small Swiss community for generations. He went to school in Sion, and his father arranged an apprenticeship as wine waiter for him in the Hôtel des Trois Couronnes et Poste at Brig, but this lasted no more than one year. His employer then terminated the arrangement with the seventeen-year-old, whom he considered to have no aptitude for the hotel business. César tried again, at the local Jesuit seminary, but was dismissed from that post for neglect of religious observances, although he managed to secure a brief appointment as sacristan there for a few months, until news of the 1867 Exposition Universelle drew him to Paris. There he pursued the well-known process of gaining experience from the lowest levels upwards, by this time having decided after much vacillation that he wanted to be known in the outside world, and restaurant or hotelkeeping was probably the best path to take. From boot-boy to washer-up to assistant waiter he was in and out of work, but for the moment the Restaurant Voisin in the Faubourg Saint-Honoré was his target, being fashionable with artists and statesmen in the last years of the Second Empire. Having risen already to the level of manager in one Paris restaurant, he abandoned status to learn the style that Voisin's could offer and accepted the rank of assistant waiter there.[10] Bellenger, the owner, was an ideal master, teaching his staff all aspects of the business with strict attention to detail and with the ability to attract leaders of fashion and society. Edward, Prince of Wales, was a frequent visitor when attending officially the Exposition Universelle, and an illustrious list of names included Boulanger, Blondeau, Thiers, MacMahon, Grévy, Gambetta and Clemenceau from the establishment, Gautier, the Goncourts and Dumas *fils* from the literary world, and George Sand, Sarah Bernhardt, La Païva and Cora Pearl, a group representing eminent women able to disregard the convention that excluded ladies of social standing from public restaurants.

The surrender of Napoleon III to Bismarck at Sedan in 1870 ended the Second Empire in France. The Emperor was a prisoner of war, his Empress Eugénie fled to England, and the Prussians laid siege to Paris, where social life largely disappeared and many retired to the South. Voisin's restaurant continued to serve members of the new republican government, Bellenger's forethought enabling him to stretch out recognizable foods for two or three months, during which cats, dogs, rats and zoo animals were being eaten by the populace, rats being offered at one franc to one and a half francs each. Eventually Voisin's had to resort to the following and many similar menus:

Purée de Lentilles

Sardines à l'Huile

Vol-au-Vent

Selle d'Épagneul (spaniel)
Haricots blancs et rouges

Oranges[11]

A young French chef patronized by Marshal MacMahon had been making his name in Paris at the same time that Ritz was learning his trade. This was Auguste Escoffier (1846–1935), who found himself in the war situation working as *chef de cuisine* in the army's General Headquarters at Metz, where he became aware of the great need for better food preservation methods. His later close connection with Ritz has been mentioned already, but his war experience led him to prove that tinning and bottling food which could be cooked in large quantities was practicable and he continued to improve the processes, reaching also a luxury market with his scarcer products.

Ritz had managed to leave Paris in the spring of 1871 but returned in the following year, finding work at the Hôtel Splendide and gaining fast promotion to *maître d'hôtel*, using his persuasive skill to good effect on the influx of Americans who had made fortunes and were willing to spend lavishly while discovering Europe. Wanamaker, Gould, Vanderbilt and Morgan – Ritz served them all and picked up advice and friendships by his attention and tact. For a young man who was forming very definite ideas about standards of service, these opportunities were beyond value and more than replaced the deficiencies in Ritz's formal education. Part of his success resulted from knowing individual quirks and

preferences of such possible future customers and, years afterwards, being able to put the knowledge to apparently miraculous use. An insatiable appetite for hard work year after year without relief may ultimately have played a part in curtailing his career, but not until his reign as 'King of Hoteliers' had gained worldwide recognition. In 1873 he was still looking for the best possible chances of training himself further and he turned to Vienna for the International Exhibition there. A waiter's job at the Restaurant les Trois Frères Provençaux placed him near the Imperial Pavilion where some of the restaurant's best staff were loaned and where, as always, Ritz took every advantage to observe and remember European royalty, their entourages and their foibles. Wilhelm I, German Emperor, with Crown Prince Frederick, Bismarck and Moltke were there in strength, receiving due deference from Franz Joseph of Austria. The Prince of Wales, friendly with the ill-fated Prince Rudolf, Vittorio Emmanuele, King of Italy, Leopold of the Belgians and Tsar Alexander II with the Tsarina constituted a glittering assembly with equally glittering hotel backgrounds available as already mentioned, but here under close inspection by a 23-year-old waiter whose own future fame was to shine at least as durably as theirs.

The opinion among fellow hotel and catering staff was against good prospects in Paris where turbulence might again erupt and in favour of the Mediterranean coast for seeking a winter job. A good hotel in Nice offered Ritz the restaurant managership for the season – the Grand Hotel, large and well-known if not well-run. During his time there Ritz met Herr Weber, director at the Rigi-Kulm, who appointed him as restaurant manager for the following summer season. As the name suggests, the site was a dramatic one near the top of the mountain between Lake Zug and Lake Lucerne and highly popular in a romantic age for the purpose of watching the sun rise in a magnificent theatre of lakes and snow-covered mountains. Access was not easy, although the Vitznau-Rigi-Staffelhöhe rack and pinion railway was built in 1871 and ran a twice-daily service under steam, the first of its type in Europe. A branch line extension to Rigi-Kulm in 1873 and a new Arth-Goldau line approaching from the north in 1875 were soon electrified, halving the journey time. The same year saw also the opening of the third Rigi mountain hotel, designed by Edouard Davinet (1839–1922) and known as the Grand Hotel Schreiber. Davinet, interior designer and experienced hotel architect, had made a previous report embodying important considerations on the design and ideal siting of grand hotels, but referring especially to the Victoria-Jungfrau, Interlaken (1866):

The affluence of the tourists who come to taste the great beauties of our lakes and glaciers increases unceasingly year by year. Encouraged by the example of our neighbours on Lakes Geneva and Lucerne, we have found an exceptional location for building an entirely first-class establishment … The property which we look forward to purchasing is known for its magnificent view, it dominates Interlaken from the approach through Unterseen and certainly enjoys the best position in the area … The main building is intended to be between the two roads bordering the site on the north and south. In that way it will be easy to lay out the rest of the plot as parkland with paths and secluded garden areas planted with large trees. Knowing well that the success of such an enterprise rests primarily on the good organization of the establishment, we shall not draw out the present proposals without first incorporating lessons learnt in the comparable Swiss hotels from Geneva to Ragaz.[12]

The end of season at Rigi-Kulm provided a good Ritz anecdote when the central heating broke down on a particularly cold autumn day and which coincided with a last-minute booking by Thomas Cook's in Lucerne wanting luncheon for a party of 40 Americans who were coming up for the wonderful view. All attempts at repairing the system failed; Ritz had 40 bricks well warmed-up in the ovens and the table laid in the red drawing-room for a modified menu designed to raise the temperature – from *consommé* to *crêpes flambées*. Four large copper *jardinières* taken from under the potted palms contained methylated spirit and acted as welcoming flambeaux for the visitors. Heated flannel-wrapped bricks as footstools completed the conjuring trick, and not one cold or miserable murmur came from the satisfied guests.[13] This episode gave rise to a visit by Colonel Pfyffer to the Rigi-Kulm Hotel, as Ritz had become acquainted with his sons who spent school holidays among the mountains and frequently used the hotel bar. Pfyffer had Ritz in his sights, but it was 1878 before he decided to offer him the job of manager to set to rights the Grand Hotel National in Lucerne which he owned. Immediate improvement occurred as soon as Ritz took up the task, and many of his established customers from other locations gave him support. The cuisine remained below standard and some tactful manoeuvring elicited a suitable comment from the gourmet Duc de Maillé to Pfyffer, who immediately pounced on his slack and lazy but not unskilled *chef de cuisine* with the desired result. The hotel regained its proper standards within a very short time and continued to build up a European reputation for elegance and luxury that was held for a decade. Royalty and the fashionable worlds of Paris, London, Rome and New York became its clientèle.

Ritz's peripatetic lifestyle had before this taken him to several different hotels in the winter seasons and in 1876 he was at the Hôtel des Îles Britanniques in Menton, the year when Queen Victoria, accompanied by John Brown, had taken a villa there, making a busy period for the town. The next year he was at the Hôtel Bellevue, Enghien-les-Bains near Paris, and in 1878 his first independent enterprise was to rent the buffet of the Jardin d'Acclimatation for winter months when the Exposition was open, making a satisfactory profit. An unexpected and ill-judged summer switch from the National at Lucerne to Les Roches Noires at Trouville in partnership with Ehrensberger, his old employer at the Splendide in Paris, showed a sizeable loss although Ritz absorbed valuable experience in the responsibilities and risks of investing in catering at gourmet level. Colonel Pfyffer behaved magnanimously and reinstated him for the next summer season in Lucerne. Winter came to mean the Grand Hotel in Monte Carlo, owned by the Yungbluths, relatives of his wife-to-be. Mention has been made of the poaching of chefs between the Grand and the Hôtel de Paris in Monte Carlo, resulting in the long and fruitful association between Escoffier and Ritz.

The two perfectionists became a team that wrote much of late nineteenth-century catering history, completely transforming earlier conceptions of vast meals centred on meat, fish, poultry and game mainly boiled, baked or roasted. In the early part of the century, Marie-Antoine Carême (1784–1833) had made a place for himself in the culinary world, reaching eminence by way of ornament and alimentary architecture just as much as by his skill in cooking. He began as a *pâtissier* in Paris, sculpting confections with great skill. This obtained him a post as gourmet chef to Talleyrand, where his 'arts of the table' inspired by the architecture-based designs of the goldsmith Odiot created a fashion. Small-scale temples, columns, garlands, archways and other architectural fantasies, sometimes edible, sometimes *garniture*, were displayed on the buffets of the great and gluttonous, but this style did not continue to be acceptable in the new world of luxury hotels and sophistication. To Escoffier and Ritz these ponderous table settings were out of date and should have no place in their world of *haute cuisine* and sensitive management. Their views frequently coincided and they constantly discussed practical and theoretical aspects of hotel management and the cuisine that formed such a vital element in its success. Ritz rebelled against the heavy ornament and furnishings of Empire decoration, the plush, the velvet and the fringes, just as Escoffier turned towards simplified though elegant presentation of food.

Lister's first use of antiseptics in 1865 and Robert Koch's discovery of the tuberculosis bacillus in 1882 give a reminder

Lucerne, Grand Hotel National, 1871. Maximilian Alphons Pfyffer von Altishofen in association with the Segesser de Brunegg brothers operated on a design-and-build basis. The western (left-hand) end of the hotel as seen from the lake employed the accepted five-part form with pavilioned ends and neo-classical treatment. For many years it was a favourite of international society.

This dramatic mountain view was the backdrop for the historic Trapani betrothal party in 1885, organized by César Ritz and reaching its climax with fiery beacons lit on the summit of Pilatus – centre right – followed in sequence on the Rigi, the Urirotstock and the Stansterhorn.

Lucerne, Hotel Schweizerhof, 1845, by Melchior Berri. The wings
were added in 1854–5 and a fine *Grosse Saal* by Leonard Zeugheer
in 1865.

Geneva, the Metropole, 1854, built by
Joseph Collart, has much in common with
the classicism of the Hôtel des Bergues and
was refitted in 1982 for a return to luxury
hotel use after a chequered career, including
occupation by the International Red Cross.
It was saved from destruction by a popular
referendum in 1976.

of the elementary state of pathology at mid-century. New discoveries in medical science and the importance of hygiene had received little or no attention in application to everyday life outside the medical profession, but both Ritz and Escoffier gave serious consideration to questions of infection and disease based on the limited knowledge available. Ritz hotels were the first in Europe to provide private bathrooms for each room or suite, and even these were not installed until the 1890s – the Grand in Rome (1893), the Ritz in Paris (1898), the Carlton (1899) and the Grand Hotel National, Lucerne, in the remodelling which took place in 1900. By contrast, the new Palace Hotel at St Moritz in 1896 was only providing one bathroom per floor on the grounds that visitors would not wish to pay the necessary price and they had another eight years to wait for this amenity. The Hôtel Bristol in Paris also had only one bathroom on each floor until 1898, and the Prince of Wales, a regular visitor, had, according to Madame Ritz, to have a portable bath with tanks of hot water delivered to his bedroom. There was much interest in the fresh ideas embodied in the Hôtel Ritz, Paris (1898), and a magazine report soon after the opening of Ritz's favourite hotel, in which he tried to incorporate all his mature experience, indicated growing public awareness of health and cleanliness:

Were I afraid of catching tuberculosis – the most contagious of diseases – I should go to the Hôtel Ritz. Every bedroom faces south, and has wide, high windows that solicit light. There are no bed curtains. The window-curtains are of white muslin, so as to be often washed. The white walls would show the least speck of dust; so would the highly polished furniture. I cannot think where a microbe could take refuge, unless in the carpets; and even there the oxygen from the great continuity of gardens and the southern sunlight must soon make short work of them … The bathrooms are roomy. One can walk about in them to bring on a reaction after a cold douche. The douche may be warm if one chooses. The bath is marble, and the walls are faced with Dutch tiles. The whole room might be 'scalded' with steam.[14]

Palatial Decades

Returning from the international stage that Ritz increasingly dominated to the state of Switzerland's *grande hôtellerie*, the most prolific building decades were the 1860s and 1870s, with growth maintained when in other parts of Europe and in the United States various political instabilities led to recessions in trade and development. With the probable exception of the French Riviera, the Swiss lakes and mountains produced

César and Marie-Louise Ritz in 1888.

the highest concentration of nineteenth-century grand hotels. The terrain was simultaneously providing a magnet for tourism and, on mountain sites, creating severe difficulties in the construction of the desired accommodation. Industrial and technical advances were being applied to overcome the practical problems, and Swiss neutrality in otherwise changing Europe was attractive to wealth and royalty. Proximity of good transport in towns and country still influenced location of the new building ventures, while the wonder generated by pioneering grand luxury hotels had matured into easy acceptance of their improved standards.

In Europe it was never the aim to accommodate such vast numbers as American hotels were able to house, and a size range between 100 and 300 bedrooms was usual. English predominance among eminent guests could still be expected, and the enthusiasm for hotel life on the part of the Prince of Wales, assisted as it was by the exceptional service offered to him by César Ritz, stimulated a fashionable clientèle wherever he led.

The building of grand hotels always presented an aesthetic problem in placing hundreds of windows to create interesting and well-proportioned exteriors, and function too often dominated over elegance of form. Occasionally semicircular-headed windows of Renaissance derivation were introduced, as in both Baur hotels in Zürich, where, though different architects were involved, each displayed a crowning feature of such windows on the main front. Aimed at some escape from the very formal Swiss neo-classical style, these departures formed one strand of design until baroque and romantic tendencies found freer expression towards the end of the century. An example of the traditional face for such public buildings, imposing in its symmetry, is the newly renovated Metropole in Geneva (1855). A neat horizontally emphasized seventeen-bay frontage facing the lake has two main bedroom floors and a well-defined cornice forming the next stage with an attic storey above. The three-bay central entrance is the only feature, with pilasters and Ionic engaged columns, to project slightly, relieving the rectangular façade. The remodelling of the roof with a plain mansard treatment did not greatly disturb the overall proportions.

The Schweizerhof on the lakeside in Lucerne was established as a luxury hotel as early as 1845, designed in formal neo-classical manner by Melchior Berri with two wings added in 1854–5. In 1861 the three brothers Gottfried, Albert and Adolf Hauser purchased it, the first of five generations of the Hauser family up to the present time, running it as a hotel of distinction and nineteenth-century character. The west wing or annexe was linked to the central building across a roadway in 1863, and two years later a fine columned and gilded *Grosse Saal* or ballroom of considerable architectural quality was completed. Its designer was Leonhard Zeugheer, expert in the proper use of the Corinthian order and able to present it in full glory just before the visit of Napoleon III and Empress Eugénie. Previous historic occasions in the hotel had been the visits of General Dufour when accepting the capitulation and dissolution of the Sonderbunds cantonal alliance in 1847 and by William III's widow Queen Sofie of The Netherlands in 1853. Also in the 1850s Leo Tolstoy and Richard Wagner paid visits, the latter before he came to live in his house 'Tribschen' on the other side of the lake, completing *Tristan and Isolde* in his room overlooking the water. The German Kaiser Wilhelm II and his wife were received at the private jetty, stone obelisks with bronze lamps being erected in their honour.

The hotel interiors remain in an excellent state of preservation, the foyer with marble columns, tessellated mosaic floors, oriental rugs and comfortable late nineteenth-century furniture, all of which could have remained unchanged for more than a century and will, hopefully, survive for many more years. On the bedroom floors, matt white paintwork, historic bathroom fittings and heavy iron heating pipes all form essential components in preserving the authentic atmosphere.

In Lausanne-Ouchy the Hotel Beau-Rivage (1857–61), like the Schweizerhof, maintained the tradition of symmetrical classicism inherited from the eighteenth century. In a competition organized by the Société Immobilière d'Ouchy for the development of the fishing village which was becoming fashionable, François Gindroz submitted the winning hotel design, although the two second prizewinners, Achille de la Harpe and Jean-Baptiste Bertholini, were entrusted with the execution of the scheme in a modified form. A glance at the original plans conjures up a monumental town hall rather than the setting for relaxation and enjoyment, and the modifications were likely to have been made to alleviate such severity. An annexe, 'Le Châlet', was added in 1864 to increase the number of rooms, but the ambitious plan to build a 'Palace' block and link it to the original building by way of a neo-baroque rotunda had to wait until 1908 for its realization. For this future stage, Eugène Jost was to be employed, an architect who would ultimately have the Grand Hotel de Territet (1888) and the Palace Hotels at Caux (1893), Montreux (1906), Villars (1914) and Lausanne (1915) to his name along with Lausanne public works in the St Francis Square post office and, in Montreux, the railway station and civic hall. His commission for the major extension of the Beau-Rivage, to be carried out with help from the architects Louis Bezencenet and Maurice Schnell, was for a transformation into the Beau-Rivage Palace. The core of rooms in the link between the old and the new comprises the restaurant and adjoining salon, both confusingly named Rotonde, with a further Grand Salon or ballroom able to seat 500. Rich decoration was contributed by E. Diekmann in the main cupola, the neo-rococo painter Otto Haberer undertook frescoes in the rotunda, and Thiebaud of Paris made bronze chandeliers and wall brackets. Stained glass in the stairwell, similar to that in the Hôtel Ritz, Paris, was executed by Chiara.

As one of the most fashionable Swiss hotels of the 1870s and 1880s, the Grand Hotel National, Lucerne, mentioned previously for the position it held in the hotel management and social scene, bears further comment on the building itself. A shrinking tourist interest was aggravated in the hotel's first years by the results of the Franco–Prussian War, but during this period the city of Lucerne was proceeding with the building of the new National quay, extending from the Schweizerhof to the Casino beyond the hotel. This was

Lausanne-Ouchy, the renamed Beau-Rivage Palace Hotel, 1908, saw the integration of the earlier work by Gindroz, de la Harpe and Bertholini with a rotunda and new wing by Eugène Jost.

The reception and sitting-room areas have acquired a more self-conscious 'period' atmosphere.

Its neo-baroque exuberance still retained elegance, assisted by some of the best artists and craftsmen of the time.

Montreux, Le Montreux Palace, 1906; another of the baroque-influenced hotels by Eugène Jost.

Art Nouveau characteristics also appeared in some areas, though these may not have been part of the original décor.

A more familiar style is seen in the grand salon with its stage and perspective-painted backdrop.

a most useful asset, forming a pleasant promenade and increasing the width of ground between the Haldenstrasse and the lake, allowing space for garden planting and outdoor tables. With Colonel Pfyffer as the instigator and the brothers Xaver (1814–74) and Joseph Plazidus Segesser (1803–78) completing the joint design and building team, the application for approval of the project had been signed by Xaver as 'Hotel Manager' and, being known as architect and art master, Joseph Plazidus was credited with much of the design in association with Pfyffer. The first section of the building was conceived in orthodox terms, strongly influenced by French Renaissance precedents in the form of a symmetrical five-part classical façade. A two-story rusticated plinth, three floors of bedrooms and a mansard roof were kept well within a very conventional architectural style. The son of Joseph Plazidus, Heinrich Victor (1843–1900), formed an architectural practice and is thought to have contributed to the design, although another Segesser, Paul, is recorded as the designer of a new dining-room to the east of the original block, where an extension was built in 1897. The Lucerne architect Emil Vogt (1863–1936), who was a specialist in hotel design and later became architect of the King David Hotel in Jerusalem, had responsibility for a much larger addition to the eastern end of the National in 1899–1900, almost doubling its original size. He changed the main entrance from south to north, added public rooms and a new eastern entrance and provided more rooms and suites or apartments on upper floors. In this part of the building an indoor swimming pool has since been constructed. All additions and alterations were carried out in harmony with the style and detail initially used, but the formation of a corridor in the east wing to improve access to some of the salons, carried out by Vogt in 1910–11, had the effect of emphasizing the narrowness of the site.

A tradition under the present owner, Umberto Erculiani, maintains uniform interior furnishings of Biedermeier style throughout the bedroom floors, in support of the classification of the house itself as a historic monument, listed in 1984. The 40 residential suites and 80 bedrooms of today are spacious and well-equipped but no subsequent period could equal the great days of Pfyffer, Ritz and Escoffier as they devised new comforts, entertainment and cuisine for the delectation of their royal and eminent patrons of the *belle époque*.

A slightly later hotel with similarly high ambitions was the Maloja Palace (1882–4) at the head of the Upper Engadine valley near the Maloja Pass. The accepted symmetrical formula remained in use for this, designed in so-called neo-Renaissance style by a Belgian architect, Jules Rau, for a Belgian client, Camille, Comte de Renesse. This E-shape

plan for a 300-room hotel contained two enormous dining-rooms and an equally large ballroom possessing a small stage where, as part of the luxurious lifestyle intended to be on display, two concerts a day were given in the summer months, often performed by musicians from the orchestra of La Scala, Milan. Externally, curved window heads for ground and top floors relieve an overall barrack-like appearance, as do the coloured frieze and horizontal string-course. In common with many more palace hotels at the outbreak of the Great War, it closed down. No longer a hotel and having had a spell of use as a barracks for the Swiss army it suffered removal of a central cushion-domed roof and lost its attractive tiered balconies. At the edge of the Sils lake where a formal garden has been laid out and where swimming was a regular pastime, the flat-topped mutilated building still manages to provide a useful home for Belgian schoolchildren on holiday.

Attempts made to break away from the rectangular plans and elevations on which so many grand hotels were based and experiments with a trefoil layout resulted in the Hotel Bernina, Samedan (1864–6), designed by Johann Jacob Breitinger of Zürich with a minimum of classical ornament and the Hotel Roseg, Pontresina (1870), by Jacob Ragaz (1846–1922), more fully neo-classical in treatment. At Rigi-Kulm the Grand Hotel Schreiber (1874–5) by Edouard Davinet combined a similar plan with added neo-baroque embellishment. This, though popular with the tourists who came to watch the dawn, ultimately attracted strong disapproval from the landscape preservationists, who considered it to be out of place among the mountains, resulting in its demolition.[15]

Pontresina in the Upper Engadine abounds with large hotels dating from the turn of the century. The Grand Hotel Kronenhof, although flourishing in the *belle époque* had a much earlier beginning in 1850 as a guesthouse, but with many alterations and additions by Nicolaus Hartmann the elder (1838–1903) it had by 1877 become the Hotel Kronenhof and Bellavista and the doyen of Pontresina. The brothers Ragaz, Jacob (1846–1922) and Georg (b. 1847), were practising architecture in the late 1890s and extended one of the wings with a tavern restaurant and various offices added asymmetrically to a ground-floor plan that started life as an open rectangle. These extra spaces illustrate the escalation in the number of public rooms, which were in demand to deal with a variety of indoor leisure and entertainment activities. A tally of a few of the top hotels shows that there were 30 salons at both the Victoria-Jungfrau, Interlaken, and the Grand Hôtel de Territet, five dining-rooms at the Baur-en-Ville, Zürich, in 1838 and, when Johannes Badrutt had the Engadiner-Kulm in St Moritz, he provided not only a library

Vitznau, Park Hotel, Vierwaldstättersee, 1902, built by Karl Koller for hotelier Anton Sebastian Bon. The lakeside site attracted summer visitors and the semi-château style hotel had many additions, carefully respecting the design of Koller's original conception.

and many old paintings but 'En cas de mauvais temps, de vastes salles, des vestibules avec des terrasses et des galeries permettent aux étrangers d'avoir leurs recreations presque comme en plein air.'[16]

The standard entrance hall or foyer and a large dining-room which might have to double as a ballroom were augmented in the Grand Hotel Kronenhof by the end of the nineteenth century to include the second restaurant with verandah, a café with attached French billiard-room, a bar adjoining the English billiard-room, the bridge-room, a small *restaurant à la carte*, two salons and an extension to the foyer. Two or three more private rooms, a ski room and space for toboggans were all to be found on the ground floor. In style the interior has been well done with neo-baroque entrance hall or foyer and an inventive but unclassifiable mix

of decoration in the dining-room, which incorporates Pompeian, Empire, Louis Seize and precursors of Art Nouveau motifs, to which Queen Anne dining chairs are added incongruously but without destroying, in spite of all the above, a certain pleasing atmosphere. A frescoed ceiling and frieze by Otto Haberer (1866–1941) depicts the Four Seasons represented entirely by female figures. This decorative painter from Bern between 1895 and 1914 executed ceiling paintings in many other hotels, including the Victoria-Jungfrau, Interlaken, the Schweizerhof, Bern, the Palace Hotel, Caux, and the Montreux Palace. The lightness of touch in these and other late interiors is in contrast with earlier use of marble columns with gilded or bronze capitals and bases, marble or wrought-iron staircase balustrades and moulded or coffered ceilings. Surviving examples of the heavier 1860s style are the Euler and the Schweizerhof from Basle; the Grand Hotel, Neuchatel; the Grand Hotel de la Paix and Beau-Rivage, Geneva; Park Hotel Kurhaus, St Moritz; and Hotel Quellenhof, Bad Ragaz. The last two are no longer called 'Grand' but have at least avoided demolition.

After Classicism – Attempts at Change

By the 1850s the building boom in Switzerland was beginning to lose its impetus and the mid-century enthusiasm gradually changed in character. In the 1880s there was a searching after new distractions and entertainments – famous parties and some new venture like the Maloja Palace Hotel which should, according to its developer, have formed the nucleus of an unequalled new mountain and lake resort 'das Monte Carlo der Alpen'.[17] Politically, countries bordering Switzerland had outlived their worst difficulties, and, in a quest for fresh fields, taste moved to Baden-Baden and Monte Carlo, where the Prince of Wales had pursued César Ritz to the Grand Hotel and society had followed. The Mediterranean coast did not escape further problems, however, with the 1883–4 cholera epidemic and the 1887 earthquakes.

No clear direction marked progress in Swiss *hôtellerie*, and in the face of strong competition consolidation was more vital than new building. City hotels may have housed prospering businessmen, but the fashionable world moved about freely and new whims could have disastrous effect in the hotel trades. Manners still remained formal but grew more international as the élite of different nations mixed. Long lists of royalty and other celebrities continued to be entered in Golden Books, exotic rulers attracting attention often by the size and composition of their retinues.

After initiation by Caspar Badrutt (1848–1904) at the Kulm in St Moritz some twenty years previously into the delights of winter sunshine and skating on the lake, the English had taken seriously to the enjoyment of such sport and the Swiss had seized the opportunity to indulge the new taste. St Moritz and Davos generated skating clubs and tobogganing which changed dramatically from their utilitarian origins to highly competitive and skilful sports. In Davos the English author John Addington Symonds set up a short toboggan race, and by 1883 a Davos Tobogganing Club held an international event over two miles. The local post conductor from Klosters, Peter Minsch, and an Australian visitor from St Moritz, George Robertson, ran it to a dead heat in a five-nation field of 21 competitors. At St Moritz they were already well aware of the benefits of attracting winter holidaymakers. Initiative was centred on the Kulm Hotel with Peter Badrutt, son of Johann, being involved and a fast run between St Moritz and the village of Cresta was carefully planned away from the existing road and banked up in snow. The decisive touch was to ice the surface to give it durability and much more speed. The Cresta Run then took an immediate place in the history of sport. Skiing, an even wider subject, cannot be dealt with here in detail, but it must not be isolated from the study of hotels among the Swiss Alps. Its growth from being a pastime for the few moved in the direction of the many during the twentieth century until, after the Second World War, it lost entirely its exclusive aura and came within reach of a great number of independent young people who discovered the pleasures of an energetic winter break in the mountain resorts. But all that lay far ahead: many years of the *belle époque* were still to run, finding a place for the greater freedom of outdoor occupations without for some time abandoning long-established and strictly regulated behaviour. Women were engaging in, even pioneering, skating, tobogganing and primitive forms of skiing. The English still held pride of place among visitors, and St Moritz was a focal point for these emergent winter sports which would transform the tourist trade in our own century.

The Badrutt family in its second generation of hotel-keeping spread from the Engadiner Kulm, which had become a company, to Austria, where Peter Robert Badrutt bought the Bellevue at Voslau near Vienna. His two sisters ran the Privat Hotel in St Moritz, a nephew bought La Margna at Sils Maria, and Rosina Rocco, another sister, would with her husband build the Waldhaus (1906–8) by architect Karl Koller, on a site above the village and the end of the lake, the Silsersee. Caspar had greater ambitions, although in 1866 he had bought in a casual way the Beau-Rivage in St Moritz Dorf, supposedly for a friend who was

Davos, the Belvedere, 1875, built by a German developer J. C. Coester; it was several times extended, becoming a favourite hotel for English tourists.

Visitors no doubt used this terrace as a suitable place to read the newspapers and magazines that were made available for them.

Long stays were the norm when Davos blossomed into a resort, and impressive spaces for entertainments, like this *Grosse Festsaal*, were obligatory.

absent at the crucial time. On returning, the friend decided that he did not wish to buy and Caspar was left with the property. This was to become the nucleus for a grand hotel full of new ideas for the dawning century and was to depart entirely from the accepted regular plan. Designed by the Zürich architects Alfred Chiodera (1850–1916) and Theophil Tschudy (1847–1911), it was at Badrutt's request to be in Baronial style, expressed in the rough granite and timber that dominates in the forecourt where the old hotel has been skilfully absorbed into the new design. The interior takes on a Gothic character from the pointed arches and pine panelling ornamented by carving in the large lounge hall, offset by oriental rugs on the wood floors.

The ground-floor plan also accommodated a verandah with extensive views over the lake and mountains, a large restaurant and ballroom with stage. A grill-room, two bars, reception area, library, bridge-room, staff offices, cloakrooms and several staircases extended the accommodation list that was completed by a hairdressing salon, a bowling alley, skiroom and covered tennis court, all integrated under the same roof.

St Moritz, Badrutt's Palace Hotel, 1896, by architects Alfred Chiodera and Theophil Tschudy. An unusual plan and style, instigated by Caspar Badrutt. A new dining-room or restaurant extension was opened in 1913, designed by Nicolaus Hartmann the younger.

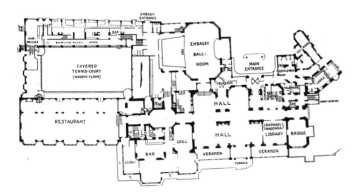

Badrutt's Palace, St Moritz, plan of the ground floor.

The baronial style with accompanying antique furniture shows at its best in the spacious halls.

The genesis of the new hotel derived from the background of the Engadiner Kulm Hotel in which Caspar's father Johannes had been inspired by a visit to the 1878 Paris exposition to install electric lighting, water-powered from a generating plant situated in a gorge on the river Inn where it flowed out of the lake below St Moritz. This had been a pioneering departure, the first of its kind in Switzerland, and was followed by a further novelty when Johannes installed a telephone line down to the valley at Chur. Caspar Badrutt therefore was well prepared to accept fresh ideas in spite of his reluctance, earlier mentioned, to provide private bathrooms. The Palace certainly had electricity, Otis lifts and English plumbing. Open fireplaces were also in the English style and, with hot-water radiators, combined to heat the building in the best available manner while German, French and Italian craftsmen and manufacturers contributed to the fitting-out of an extravagant setting. It was given the name 'Palace' in place of 'Badrutt's', and was recognized as a symbol of the thriving community of St Moritz, which it still dominates. Alterations and extensions in 1907 were in the hands of Chiodera and Tschudy, and a new wing and dining-room were designed by Nicolaus Hartmann the younger (1880–1956) in 1912–13. Much later, in 1983–4, Josef Troxler designed additional apartments spreading down the slope of the site. The complex of buildings is in a mixture of styles, more like a small village than a hotel, but it makes a very positive contribution to the town with its distinctive silhouetted roof line. The dominating tower was badly damaged by fire in 1967 but was soon rebuilt to restore its proper character to St Moritz.

Princess May of Teck, partnered by Caspar Badrutt, had opened the inaugural ball on 29 July 1896, and as she subsequently married the heir to the British throne and then became Queen Mary, the British connection and its royal pedigree were kept alive. Status as a fashionable and exclusive hotel was quickly achieved and the *Almanach de Gotha* was well represented in the guest lists of the first decade. Wealthy Americans had no difficulty in spending money on high living there, and John Jacob Astor and his wife gave a dinner for fourteen to the Prince of Liechtenstein on New Year's Day 1899, a daunting twelve courses being served. Since various social revolutions were to transform life in the twentieth century, the strong devotion to winter sports that existed proved to be crucial for the survival of the Palace and the Badrutt dynasty through two major wars and many changes of economic fortune.

Several other grand St Moritz hotels came into existence as the town developed. The Schweizerhof (1898) was designed by Chiodera and Tschudy in an Art Nouveau style quite at variance with that of the Palace. In 1909 Karl Koller, well-known in the area, designed the vast and heavy Grand Hotel not far from the Palace, one of the largest buildings in Switzerland at the time, which burned down in 1944. Koller also added to the Schweizerhof in 1909 and built the Suvretta House, completed with great rapidity for the owner, Anton Bon, in 1912, using a free adaptation of the non-classical 'Swiss style'. Emil Vogt, the Lucerne architect, designed the Carlton, which was opened in 1913 but subsequently altered.

For more than half a century the architectural language used in the design of grand hotels had been based on some form of classicism, but movements – and not only in Switzerland – were gaining ground that rejected this approach as outworn. Both the jumble of styles in the Grand Hotel

Maloja, Upper Engadine, the Maloja Palace Hotel was opened in 1884, the Belgian architect was Jules Rau and the style termed neo-Renaissance. Later removal of the central domed roof and reductions of balconies and projecting bays changed its appearance.

Kronenhof, Pontresina, and the semi-historicism of the Palace, St Moritz, show symptoms of a desire for change. Domestic architecture in Switzerland acquired a romantic nostalgia for the traditional timber buildings that might loosely be described as 'Swiss chalets' and which were the focus of a revival of historic timber building styles or the *Schweizer Holzbaustil*.[18] When the Palace Hotel was celebrating its opening in St Moritz in 1896, a forerunner of the movement, the architect Jacques Gros (1858–1922), was seeing the first trenches dug for a new hotel at the edge of forest land above Zürich that was to prove his masterpiece in this style, the Dolder Grand. Gros played an important part in this slighter parallel to the Arts & Crafts Movement in Britain, which sought to recover the practical skills on which earlier craftsmen had relied. Gros had worked for a time in the woodworking business of Bucher and Durrer in canton Obwalden as 'Spezialist für Holzarchitektur'. Bucher and Durrer were to become hotel entrepreneurs on a large scale while Gros, in 1890, set up an architectural practice in Zürich and continued to study timber design and construction, repeatedly exhibiting and publishing excellent architectural drawings and watercolours. The vogue for country backgrounds led to development at the head of a short and steep railway from Zürich, the Dolderbahn. The scheme was to provide a station building, restaurant and the hotel or pension Waldhaus, built among the trees and offering a quiet retreat from the city below. Gros was the architect, and after his success with this complex he was offered the commission to design the Grand Hotel Dolder to be built higher up the hillside, taking advantage of the sweeping views of lake and mountains. As befitted the son of a landscape gardener he sited it well in forest and parkland which adjoined the Waldhaus land, leaving enough space to plan a nine-hole golf course. The hotel opened in 1899, the golf course in 1907 as a special attraction and innovation for Zürich. A central tower with needle spire and two large splayed wings formed the essence of the hotel plan, and the whole building had abandoned all suggestions of classical derivation except for the pink granite columns in the main foyer. Eclecticism in details, square corner towers with smaller spires, balconies and oriel windows together with the asymmetry of the wings announced firmly that this was the *Holzbaustil*, but the scale of the structure seems to deny the nature of its material. It is, however, a timber-framed building – with the exception of modern additions – constructed on stone foundations in oak and pine. Fire-resistant coatings have later been applied to the timber work, including very large load-bearing members.

Built originally as a seasonal hotel, open only from April to October and serving many local residents and families, the pattern changed to all-year-round use with a reputation for fine cuisine, seeking to serve a discriminating business clientèle among those who preferred the peaceful semi-rural situation. Ownership has remained largely consistent between the Hürlmann and Wehrli families – the Schweizer, Wehrli management company being currently represented in house by Andreas Wehrli.

The Palace Hotels in Caux (1902) and Montreux (1906) were both designed by Eugène Jost using differing means to pursue lines of extravagance more suited to the *belle époque*. At Caux the long splayed south façade and spired turrets bear a resemblance to the Dolder Grand, although the style is of the fantasy château and not *Holzbaustil*. Classical motifs are present here and at the Montreux Palace, used for exterior and interior ornament. Both the hotels contain theatres, that in the Montreux being the grander and larger of the two and, with its painted glass dome, making a dramatic demonstration of Jost's 'audacity and imagination'.[19]

In Lucerne, the Palace (1906) by Heinrich Meili was a Bucher-Durrer enterprise of less magnificence on the lakeside near the Casino and designed with British visitors particularly in mind. It was stone built, conforming to the accepted semi-classical pattern. Externally it bears a limited amount of Art Nouveau decoration, and internally more lavish neo-rococo decoration remains in a number of the rooms. Some of the large blocks of limestone used for the building were from material excavated during tunnelling for the railway in the previous century.

Other major hotels in the years that we now see as sliding towards the Great War but which then had no such disastrous perspective, were the Waldhaus, Sils-Maria (1908), a Badrutt family investment in romantic castle form by Karl Koller containing some Jugendstil interiors; the Hotel and Pension Eden au Lac, Zürich (1909), by Scheel, and a final group of Palace Hotels at Gstaad (1913), Villars (1914) and Lausanne (1915), the latter again by Jorst, and built as an answer to the Beau-Rivage Palace at nearby Ouchy. From this time onwards, Swiss *hôtellerie* suffered badly. The large numbers of tourists who had created such a boom in preceding years dwindled sharply, and uncertainty about the future reduced investment. In any event, the supply of hotels exceeded the demand and managements only survived by efficiency and skill. Political neutrality was useful in various ways but these scarcely compensated for the absence of so many visitors. There were just too few people to fill the 100 or so top-class hotels that had been built. Figures for registered arrivals in Lucerne fell from a level of 200,000 in the years 1910–13 to 104,000 in 1914 and a mere 30,000 in 1915. A scheme was

ABOVE, BELOW & OPPOSITE Pontresina, Grand Hotel Kronenhof, by master-builder and architect Nikolaus Hartmann the elder, 1870–82; rebuilt by the Ragaz brothers, Jacob and Georg, 1896–8.

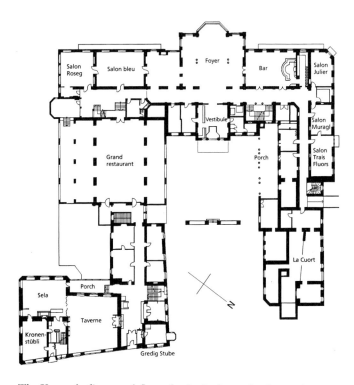

The Kronenhof's ground-floor plan in the form of an inverted U was the work of the Ragaz brothers and gave the hotel much of its present form, incorporating the previous Hartmann building.

ABOVE St Moritz, Suvretta House, bold use of carved natural wood characterizes this dining-room.

RIGHT Interlaken Hotel, Victoria-Jungfrau. Horace Edouard Davinet's central tower dominates the long neo-classical frontage, for much of which design he had been responsible.

The Kronenhof's Grand Restaurant is a fine example of the many Engadine hotels which competed in luxury for the growing spa, sport and tourist trade in the area at the end of the nineteenth century.

Zürich, Dolder Grand Hotel, 1899. Jacques Gros pioneered the new timber-built architecture which began the rejection of accepted classical design.

Gstaad, Palace Hotel, 1913. Dutch architect Adrien van Dorsser and Italian master builder Mainardi were involved in the design and construction respectively of the fairy-tale château-style hotel.

entered into by many hotels for the treating and housing of wounded soldiers from the belligerent countries at the low rate of 4 Swiss francs per person per day, and even at this level it saved their continuity. The Palace in Lucerne was one of the first to be turned into a hospital on this temporary basis and was occupied by British and French troops, as was the Montreux Palace. The Swiss army also mobilized to defend its frontiers and the existence of many more hotels was secured by the income derived from requisitioning. The Bellevue Palace in Bern had the quaint experience of maintaining its civilian role while in partial use under military orders.

Unfortunate owners found themselves surrendering their hotels into the hands of the banks, and this financial distress extended well beyond the war. Among the best-known were the Engadiner Kulm, St Moritz; the Grand Hotel Beau-Rivage, Interlaken; Hôtel des Bergues in Geneva; and the Baur-en-Ville and Eden au Lac, Zürich. Post-war conferences and diplomacy brought in cosmopolitan names once more and the benefit was felt particularly in Bern at the Bellevue Palace, the Bernerhof and the Schweizerhof. The Lausanne Palace and the Beau-Rivage Palace, Lausanne-Ouchy, received many old habitués, although the former staged the first auction of jewels sold to pay overdue hotel bills.

Schemes of improvement helped to encourage the recovery in the 1920s, and many other changes followed in the wake of the motor car. The biggest loss of grand hotel buildings did not occur finally until after the Second World War, and by 1990 the 91 that were categorized by Thierry Ott as true grand or palace hotels had diminished to only 56. There was no longer the need in Switzerland to build new luxury hotels on a large scale. Most of the society that had generated such intense desire for the lifestyle they offered had vanished or moved elsewhere.

Vernacular timber-work did not invade the interior of the Dolder Grand Hotel in Zürich (*see illustration on previous page*), and two handsome pink granite columns in the *Steinhalle* set the tone for simpler and less innovative decoration.

Interlaken, the Hotel Victoria-Jungfrau, based on two large hotels of the 1880s and '90s, linked at the end of the century by Davinet to form a single composite unit. The photograph dates from 1900.

A 'modern look' respects the massing of the Victoria-Jungfrau, but has eliminated much of the ornament, changing the visual emphasis from vertical to horizontal.

5.

FIN DE SIÈCLE

The Swiss contribution to recognition of a grand hotel style did not take place in isolation from other European countries although it was, by virtue of relative stability at the right time, able to take a lead in perfecting the type. Fostering and satisfying the demands for luxury and convenience lay in the hands of a few far-sighted pioneers whose influence reached international standards. A clearly defined way of life had been created and crystallized over quite a short period and could not have existed independently of the buildings in which it functioned. There is no way of improvising a grand hotel. The multiplicity of big hotels with lavish interiors and dressed externally in variants of late nineteenth-century classicism can be seen as centred on Switzerland but had earlier roots in French precedents. By the 1880s, examples of the style were being reproduced on many sea coasts from the North Sea and English Channel to old and new Mediterranean resorts, but awareness was creeping in that some new ideas would be welcome. Few areas were so intensively developed as the French and Italian rivieras between Hyères and La Spezia, where the provinces of Savoy and Nice had been ceded by Piedmont to France in 1860 as part of the Italian unification negotiations.

In France and Monaco, The Netherlands and Belgium, individual ventures spread the grand hotel culture, reacting to local circumstances in the absence of overall trends. London and Switzerland were alike in finding the 1890s to be active years, and on the other side of the Atlantic the development of the Canadian Pacific Railways and their attendant hotel chain outstripped achievements in the United States. As seen in chapter Five, restlessness was occurring in the world of design, although its products of Art Nouveau, Jugendstil, Liberty and *floreale* styles were scattered thinly in comparison with the expressions of grandeur that seemed to speak more appropriately in a classical language.

OPPOSITE A scene in one of the French-decorated salons in London's Hyde Park Hotel.

Holland and Belgium

The Kurhaus at Scheveningen had, as its name suggests, origins connected with a small 'cure' establishment that was almost on the sea shore and also within convenient distance of The Hague. It was in the form of a wooden bathing-house built in 1818 by one Jacob Pronk, who used two bathing-carriages to convey users directly into the sea for their treatment, which seems to have consisted chiefly of sea air and salt water. A Grand Municipal Bath House superseded this in 1826, possessing hotel rooms, a library, billiard- and dining-rooms as well as bathing facilities. Having made a considerable success of the business, Pronk sold out his interest to the city council, which was considering a competitive scheme of development for Scheveningen to counteract the popularity of the Belgian spas down the coast. Under the proposals four Dutch businessmen obtained sole rights from the council as developers until 1958 at a yearly rent of 25,000 Dutch florins. The old bath-house was demolished and replaced by the first Kurhaus Hotel, opened by the Mayor of The Hague, J. C. Patijn, in 1885. The German architects Johann Friedrich Henkenhaf (1848–1908) and Friedrich Ebert (b. 1852) with experience of building the Krasnapolsky Hotel in Amsterdam were appointed and provided the great hall or Kurzaal, two restaurants and 120 to 150 bedrooms. Hot and cold running water and a lift were among the amenities and a private gaming club was housed in the building, which had cost 600,000 florins to complete. Fire, the old enemy, burnt it down the following year but rebuilding was carried out rapidly, though subsequently it was discovered to have been to a poor structural standard. Additions were made to create a self-contained summer resort, offering a respiration centre with inhalatorium, sea air and sea water as basis for many treatments. A pier, a shopping gallery, two more hotels, the Kurhaus bar and the Circustheatre augmented the attractions, and interest on the part of the Dutch royal family was started by the 13-year-old Princess, later Queen Wilhelmina,

Scheveningen, Holland, The Kurhaus Hotel, 1885 (rebuilt 1886)
by architects Johann Friedrich Henkenhaf and Friedrich Ebert.
This photograph dates from the 1920s and recent renovation has
followed as far as possible the original design and materials.

A view of the Kurzaal, *c.* 1890, the home of many music festivals.

being the first to sign the visitors' book. The page on which
she wrote was charged with insignia and elegantly framed in
a design of ribbon and *rocaille* with a putto bearing the crown
above her careful inscription.

Architecturally the heavy baroque neo-classicism of the
last decades of the century dominated the design, and an axial
composition was centred on the large octagonal-domed
Kurzaal supported by four corner turrets. Two L-shape wings
formed an open court facing towards the sea, more impressive in general appearance than in detail. Internally the
Kurzaal was the main attraction, invaluable as the scene of
almost daily concerts during the season, which built up a high
reputation in the musical world. A special feature was its ceiling, executed in 1904 by a team of 30 artists under the leader-

Young Princess Wilhelmina's signature inaugurating the Kurhaus's much-valued Golden Book.

ship of N. Van Hoeck from Belgium, who accomplished the upper tier of panels and the lower pendentives of the vaulted frieze in the course of one month. The appropriate subjects were hunting, fishing and musical scenes, the signs of the zodiac and the essential presence of Neptune.

The hotel won approval at many different social levels and continued as a favoured summer home of royalties and other heads of state whose preference for sleeping accommodation tended to be the adjacent Palace Hotel because of its quieter position. International conferees from The Hague often found their way out to the Kurhaus and many ceremonial dinners and celebrations took place there. The first inter-parliamentary peace conference was housed there in 1894 and the Imperial Chinese Foreign Minister Li Hung Chang was given a Government reception in 1896, some three weeks after a Persian delegation had enjoyed its hospitality. Crown Prince Wilhelm of Prussia was an incognito visitor in 1901 and the Grand-Duke of Saxony-Weimar took a suite with a sea view each summer. Fashionable life went on until the Great War, but then the structure of society was dissolving and could no longer sustain the old patronage. Congress delegates began to supplant nobility and ideas about health and exercise made fresh air and sea bathing into a pleasant recreation, no more a medicinal régime – a tendency gaining ground in spas generally.

Many hotels kept 'Golden Books' for their important guests to sign as a valuable record, but at the Kurhaus this acquired special interest when Goldbeck, the director, invited a number of well-known artists to provide paintings or drawings for it.[1] H. W. Mesdag, Josef Israëls, C. Bisschop, B. J. Blommers, P. C. Gabriël and Jacob Maris all contributed, representing the Hague School with their quick but atmospheric sketches of the 1890s. Art found its way also on to the dining-table, this time as a menu-card design for a journalists' banquet celebrating Queen Wilhelmina's coming of age investiture in 1898. The artist J. W. Toorop was pioneering Dutch Jugendstil and drew three suave female figures with swooping hair and draped garments offset by a severe head-and-shoulders male in the foreground who presents the menu itself. Toorop's work is occasionally known as 'salad oil style' on account of his famous poster for the Delft Salad-Oil factory that gained him notoriety.

Music was an integral part of the Kurhaus attractions from its inception, under the hotel's first director M. A. Reiss, who brought a German fondness for the Viennese classics to present in 1895 the Berlin Philharmonic Orchestra. The programmes featured Beethoven, Brahms and Schubert with ever-popular Strauss waltzes in the role of lollipops. These concerts, having discovered a public appetite for good music, indirectly gave rise to the formation of the Amsterdam Concertgebouw Orchestra as a native Dutch counterpart. Busoni (1899), Nikisch (1911), the eccentric Schneevoigt (1919–28), Stravinsky (1928) and Mengelberg (1938), created a fine tradition. (More recently, Marlene Dietrich and Herbert von Karajan performed there in the 1960s and Yehudi Menuhin, after many earlier visits, played Mozart in 1983. This was at a fund-raising dinner for his Live Music Now Foundation, and the pastrycooks under chef Hekkelman had prepared 40 life-size confectionery violins which were auctioned, realizing 10,000 florins to add to the 40,000 proceeds from the dinner.)

The inter-war years saw no major changes in the hotel, which had remained a high-class summer hotel until 1952 when installation of central heating extended practical use of the building. Music in the Kurzaal was still a magnet, and official gala celebrations remained in the social calendar. The secretary of the Scheveningen Development Corporation

(EMS) from 1927–62, A. Adam Zijlstra, kept musical events in the public eye at the Kurzaal and he was also a co-organizer of the very successful Holland Festival in 1947.

It was not until the 1970s when public and private money combined in a redevelopment project that new forward-looking building activity materialized. Demolition of the run-down hotel had been proposed, but public opinion against it was very strong and a consortium for renovation or reconstruction was put together. The Hague city council secured participation from contractors Bredero and some finance from Nationale-Nederlanden insurance to rejuvenate the hotel, which by then had become listed as a national monument. Investigation started and much inferior structural work dating from the 1887 rebuild was uncovered. Far more drastic treatment than had been visualized was unavoidable, including demolition and complete rebuilding of the two wings. Some economies were made, decorative stonework being replaced by cast concrete, but materials were matched as nearly as practicable to the originals in consultation with the National Monuments department. In the Kurzaal the 1887 timber dome and N. Van Hoeck's ceiling paintings on canvas of 1904 were saved and reinstated but those relaxing in the space beneath no longer hear orchestral music, this part having been converted into the Grand Café and Bar. Total costs mounted to 110 million guilders, of which 50 million was a Government subsidy. The architect Bart van Kasteel was in charge of the restoration, which took five years, and the interior designer was Bernd Schmigalla. Princess Beatrix reopened the hotel in 1979 and it now operates as the Steigenberger Kurhaus Hotel.

Brussels in the 1890s was a polyglot city of 400,000 people, the centre of an industrially developed country with a sophisticated artistic culture which was taking a lead in Art Nouveau or Jugendstil design. Politically, Leopold II had long been a stabilizing influence, although Socialist ideas were being expressed in the Parliament which had acted as a model for new constitutional monarchies since 1831. Some of this unrest was finding expression on the streets in more aggressive form.

The owners of the Café Metropole on the Place de Brouckère, Prosper and Edouard Wielemans, were looking optimistically to the future and, after opening the Café in 1892, proceeded to convert the remainder of the Savings Bank premises they had purchased into a grand hotel with a magnificent interior and 100 bedrooms. The bank had been designed by Gédéon Bordiau but the interior redesign was in the hands of Alban Chambon, born in Varzy, France, in 1847 and settled in Brussels at the age of 21, where he was much in demand and executed numerous contracts at the

ABOVE & OPPOSITE Brussels, Hotel Metropole, 1894. Alban Chambon created a series of high-quality interiors inspired by neo-Renaissance influence from Italy and France. Art Nouveau design, much favoured in Belgium at the time, contributes to plain and coloured glazing panels and more assertively to the original electric chandeliers.

Law Courts, the Stock Exchange, theatres and palatial private houses. His reputation spread abroad and work included the Krasnopolsky Restaurant in London in 1891. Chambon secured the Metropole commission and produced a fine, largely neo-Renaissance essay in marble and gilt, wrought iron, carved wood and bronze. Teak from Asia with Numidian breccia and Tunisian marbles set the scene for a rich parade of public rooms. Distinctive electric chandeliers of elaborate design, stained glass by Brigode, furniture by Thonet and sculpture by Julien Dillens contributed to the display of talents. Technical equipment was not neglected and the lift was built by the French firm Edoux who had supplied the lifts for the Eiffel Tower in Paris.[2]

The property was augmented by purchases of adjoining buildings as they became available, until 420 rooms could be provided. In this, 'the only nineteenth-century hotel in Brussels', as the Metropole describes itself, Chambon managed to integrate diverse influences with his own originality.

Brussels, Palace Hotel, 1905–10, the Art Nouveau façade by architects De Leener and Antoine Pompe.

Coffered ceilings of the François I period combine with marble walls and pilasters, Indian and Byzantine motifs inspire the reception area and dining-room respectively, the climax being reached with the Italian Renaissance banqueting-room. Ornament on the exterior is limited to a single sculptural group above a podium at mansard-roof level, representing Abundance and Peace, two seated figures supporting a central and triumphant Progress. Sculptor Jacques de Haen symbolized electricity and steam power by placing a thunderbolt and propeller in the left hand of Progress and a traditional torch in her right.

Quality and a degree of restraint among the richness of ideas and materials have fortunately been preserved, as have the grand hotel traditions through two world wars, enabling the Metropole, with considerable panache, to retain a dominant position in a Brussels at the heart of the new Europe. It accommodated the unsuccessful British delegation led by Edward Heath in 1961–2 and has seen the subsequent evolution towards European union that could never have been envisaged by the founders of the Café Metropole in the last years of the nineteenth century.

The Wielemans family occupied a central place in the Belgian beer industry and bred at least four generations of hotel dynasty in, first, Prosper and Edouard then their respective sons Leon and Paul followed by Claude and Eric, sons of Leon, with Patrick, son of Eric, and Jean-Pierre Bervoets, great-grandson of Edouard, representing the youngest generation. Always interested in the visual arts, the family built a large cinema in 1924 at the back of the Metropole with seating for 2,900, and had it decorated by the sculptor Ossip Zadkine with interior frescoes measuring five by fourteen metres. A panel containing three Muses was interpreted by the then eight-year-old Eric Wielemans as representing his aunts. The architects for the cinema were Blomme and Richard, the latter from France, and although the new building contained 50 new rooms for the hotel connected by a covered walkway, the style looked forward to the 1930s, not backward. Leon Wielemans, in charge of the hotel at the time, resisted similar modernization in the hotel proper and, with valuable foresight and against the only too common practice of replacing work of a previous generation by fashionable modernity, preserved Alban Chambon's 1893 décor. A 1920s Egyptian banqueting-hall interior at lower-ground-floor level was dismantled and preserved for reinstatement in 1955 by the designer Brunard. Existence of the cinema attracted as guests many film stars, Pagnol and Raimu reminding us that not all stars grew up in Hollywood. In the hotel itself, a prestigious scientific International Conference in 1911, organized by the Belgian scientist Ernest Solvay, gathered a triumvirate whose distinction would be difficult to equal: Marie Curie, Albert Einstein and William Rutherford.

The Metropole's staff became known over the years for their expertise and abilities. Immediately after the Great War had ended, Monsieur Deliens arrived as general manager from the Adlon in Berlin and was succeeded by a widely-experienced Ernest Strainchamps, who almost reached the age of 80 while still in harness. Marcel Goffin, his deputy, had a long career at the Metropole and after him, François Bursa came from Reid's Hotel in Madeira and remained until 1976. The present manager from Luxembourg, Serge Schultz, in a late twentieth-century world of high-velocity travel and hi-tech infrastructure should have the last word. When asked what was the most difficult aspect of running a hotel he replied:

Succeeding in giving a proper welcome to a foreign head of state and then two minutes later advising on the washing-up, having in the meantime popped along to check the workings of the boiler room.[3]

London Fashion

London in the 1880s saw the beginning of a surge of hotel building that lasted for the rest of the century and beyond. After leading the way in railway terminus hotels and their fitting culmination in Sir George Gilbert Scott's great Gothic exercise, the Midland St Pancras Hotel, there was no development in the 1870s to match the proliferation in Switzerland. Three Frederick Gordon Hotels were built in central London during the decade – the Grand, Trafalgar Square (1881), the First Avenue, Holborn (1883), and the Metropole, Northumberland Avenue (1885) – but the most important of the new generation of hotels for the Nineties was undoubtedly the Savoy (1889).

The site on which the Savoy was built had a long history dating back to a grant of land by Henry III to the uncle of Queen Eleanor, Peter II, Count of Savoy, in 1246. It was situated on the north bank of the Thames between Westminster and the City of London in an area favoured by noble families down the centuries as convenient for their grand houses with gardens and direct access to the river thoroughfare. Peter built himself a palace there but this French connection never blossomed in England and he left 'the fayrest mannor in Europe', later to be occupied instead by the Duke of Lancaster, John of Gaunt. Gaunt held it for twenty years, during which a stipend was paid out to Geoffrey Chaucer through

the Manor of Savoy for his good services. John of Gaunt's son ascended the throne as Henry IV, merging the dukedom with the Crown and perpetuating the precincts of the Savoy palace as a 'Liberty of the Duchy of Lancaster', still extant. During Richard II's reign, Wat Tyler's rebellious mob attacked the palace in 1381, threw most of its valuable contents into the river and contrived to ignite barrels of gunpowder, destroying most of the buildings. Rebuilding as a hospital for the poor, use by the royal court as a rural retreat in plague times and formation of schools for Catholic and Protestant alike, all contributed to its history, but in the eighteenth century the properties were allowed to decay. Remnants of the palace were removed for the Waterloo Bridge construction in the nineteenth century and only the Savoy Chapel, with its royal prerogative restored as recently as 1939, retains a physical link with the medieval palace.[4]

Richard D'Oyly Carte, impresario and chief patron of the Gilbert & Sullivan operas, after establishing the most successful light opera team ever to take the London stage, bought the freehold of land in the Manor of Savoy and built a new theatre, the Savoy Theatre, to house his company. Designed by C. J. Phipps, it opened in 1881, and was the first theatre in the world to be electrically lighted. D'Oyly Carte then attempted a larger house for more serious opera but was less fortunate with his presentation of Sullivan's *Ivanhoe* and sold his opera house, the Palace Theatre, to Augustus Harris. During this period D'Oyly Carte had taken advice on planning the theatre from T. E. Collcutt (1840–1924), who became involved as architect with his next speculation for the construction of a luxury hotel next to the Savoy Theatre.[5] The impresario's travels in the United States to deal with Gilbert & Sullivan copyright problems had made him aware of the advanced aspects of their best hotels, where capacity and size were linked with use of all available new equipment and services. The Palace Hotel, San Francisco (1874–6), with its covered atrium enclosing six storeys, 850 bedrooms and 437 bathrooms, may have inspired his celebrated demand for similar ratios, which elicited from the contractor (George H. Holloway) when the Savoy Hotel was being built the response that D'Oyly Carte must be expecting his guests to be amphibious.

D'Oyly Carte knew that he had an ideal site, on the river yet close to theatreland, if the right atmosphere could be created. With the cooperation of his wife he proceeded to incorporate all those facilities that might attract a new wealthy American trade. Helen, born Couper-Black and of Scottish background, had a good degree and, as Helen Lenoir, took to the stage and then worked for D'Oyly Carte first as secretary and later as business manager before they married in

1888. Her influence towards all modern comforts and innovations in the hotel was of considerable value. T. E. Collcutt was assisted by Arts & Crafts architect A. H. Mackmurdo (1851–1942) as consultant for interior furnishing and decoration. For the structure, fire-resistant steel joists were cased in concrete and faced with terracotta, a material popular with Collcutt. He used it in the near-white matt glazed Carrara Ware version from Doulton to give modern-looking festive finish to a hotel that was well ahead of most of its competitors in appearance and amenities. There were 400 rooms, six lifts and electric lighting throughout, but only 70 bathrooms despite the contractor's earlier exclamation. The Savoy was opened in 1889 but its development continued in a series of extensions and improvements by Collcutt in 1905 and 1910 when, with a large west block for offices, the in-fill between the Strand and the 'River Block' and the addition to this Block itself, it reached its final size. A pictorial section in *The Illustrated London News* in 1911 represents the whole establishment from Strand to Thames Embankment. Its detailed treatment recreates the architectural and social setting that Arnold Bennett was to draw on so comprehensively in his novel *Imperial Palace* (1930). We see the 500-feet-deep artesian wells each yielding 240,000 gallons of water per day, a brine cooler behind the ice lift, engine rooms and boiler house, enormous wine vaults, stairs leading to the Vienna bakery, pastry kitchen, storage and lifts. In the drawing the kitchen is cut away so that foyer, restaurant and ballroom can be seen and, as part of the background, St Paul's Cathedral in the distance.[6]

Creation of the hotel in its physical form did not automatically ensure the sort of establishment or attract the clientèle D'Oyly Carte had in mind. Financial backing had been obtained through city, court and social circles, the hotel company board listing such names as R. B. Fenwick and A. H. Weguelin, financiers, the Lord Chamberlain, Earl Lathom, Arthur Sullivan, Michael Gunn from Dublin's Gaiety Theatre and Hwfa Williams from the Prince of Wales's circle. This alone was no guarantee of success and no instant technique was in place to launch the Savoy with the necessary crew of imaginative and devoted staff. In this situation it joined one or two other slow starters with deficiencies in their personnel teams. The Grand Hotel National, Lucerne, and the Frankfurterhof, Frankfurt, come to mind as examples of badly run hotels where over-optimism was not backed by either the knowledge or the devotion needed on the part of key members of the staff. In both cases a poor situation was turned into a success by the gifted hotelier César Ritz, who was able to see weak links in the organization and to substitute imagination and skill for the laxity that had

meant operating at a loss. In Lucerne it was he who answered the call of his early patron Colonel Pfyffer and turned the National into a hotel for fashionable Europe. In Frankfurt Ritz was again involved, holding a one-third interest with two Hillengass brothers as partners whom he bought out, replacing them by Georges Gottlob, formerly reception clerk at the Hôtel Ritz in Paris and who as manager under Ritz's direction rescued the Frankfurterhof.

D'Oyly Carte had decided that Ritz was the man he wanted to run the Savoy, having been impressed by his management of the Grand Hotel at Monte Carlo, which had received the cachet of a visit by the Prince of Wales in 1881. But Ritz was not anxious to work in England on account of impressions given by his English clientèle relating to restricted licensing and other laws, together with a culture that had not accepted dining in public. D'Oyly Carte persisted in his vision of a luxury hotel in London to the standards Ritz was creating in Lucerne and Monte Carlo but received no positive response. Seasons went by and the Savoy building was going ahead but Ritz was busy with additional commitments in Baden-Baden, Nice and Cannes. Even so, he could not refuse an invitation to the opening on 6 August 1889, when he was asked if he would stay for a few days in the hotel to make any suggestions he thought fit and lend his reputation to D'Oyly Carte's achievement, all for a substantial fee. The patrons who tended to follow the Ritz trail would indeed be worth acquiring. Marie-Louise Ritz, his wife, lists those whom Carte sought to attract as

the Marlborough House set – Lord Rosebery, Lord and Lady Elcho, Lord and Lady Gosford, Lord and Lady de Grey, and the Sassoons, the Roman princes, Rudini, the Crispis, the Rospigliosis, the Radziwills, and so forth; the best of the theatre and opera crowd – Patti, the de Reszkes, Coquelin, Bernhardt; the Grand Dukes, and the smart Parisian crowd – the Castellanes, the Breteuils, the Sagans; he wants the Vanderbilts and Morgans, he wants the Rothschilds. He wants to make his hotel the hotel de luxe of London and of the world.[7]

There it was all set out, the material for the 1890s assembled in London, hub of the Empire and rich with the fruits of Victorian achievement. Nevertheless, six months into its life as a new wonder, the Savoy was showing the lack of management inspiration that Ritz had foretold and finally, after much further persuasion and an offer to name his own price, he succumbed to the brilliance and potential of *belle époque* London and agreed to collect his own staff and take over the management, reserving six months in the year for his own interests in Cannes and Baden-Baden. His chief deputy was Louis Echenard, who had long hotel experience and thorough knowledge of wine and had been tried and trusted since their first meeting in Menton. He would be backed up by William Autour from Ritz's own hotels. The restaurant manager Henry Elles was half French, half English and the *maître d'hôtel* François Rainjoux came from Monte Carlo. Devoted Agostini the cashier was another trustworthy pillar of the organization of which August Escoffier provided the keystone as *chef de cuisine*. Dismissal of the previous manager caused some difficulties but the new carefully chosen personnel served D'Oyly Carte well. One of his particular wishes was to encourage and make socially respectable the habit of eating in public restaurants. The promotion of after-theatre suppers was a milestone in this direction and, as stiff Victorian attitudes began to ease, society came to absorb them as an acceptable facet of London life and manners.

Since his American travels D'Oyly Carte had successfully sought for the hotel a transatlantic reputation and this was followed by wealth from South African sources. The Savoy has consistently maintained strong Anglo-American links in the fields of business and politics in addition to the previous clientèle from stage and artistic circles. The old European contacts did not cease but a younger generation was growing up and D'Oyly Carte's death in 1901 underlined the change. The gap left by the departure of Ritz in 1897 had been dealt with by the appointment of George Reeves-Smith of the Berkeley Hotel to the board of the Savoy Company. In order to overcome the breaking of his contract with the Berkeley, the hotel was bought into the Savoy Group. Shortly before D'Oyly Carte died at the relatively early age of 56, Reeves-Smith took on the Managing Directorship of the Savoy while still living at the Berkeley, an arrangement which must have been very satisfactory. His long and distinguished tenure took London's favourite hotel through good and bad years until the Second World War, being acknowledged in 1938 by the bestowal of a knighthood.

The D'Oyly Carte connection was maintained through Carte's son Rupert, who became chairman of the board and who took responsibility for all necessary interior decoration. His daughter Bridget sustained the tradition after his death in 1948. Self-sufficiency in matters of interior design, furnishing and upholstery persisted in Savoy workshops as long as D'Oyly Cartes were in charge, but outside designers were brought in for the larger projects when later alterations were made. Repairs and maintenance could usually be dealt with rapidly by the hotel's own staff, and the occasional regular guests who kept in store their own furniture could rely on a complete transformation of a room or suite to a familiar background of their own choice.

In many respects the Savoy would be a front runner in any

Count Peter of Savoy presides over the Strand entrance to the Savoy Hotel.

worldwide hotel championship but there would be many near-rivals to contest the crown. In comfort, cuisine and service the Savoy in London has been a leader, but as in other great capitals, a number of the best hotels uphold similar standards of excellence for their fortunate clientèle for whom, in the end, individual taste will be the deciding factor.

Another large end-of-century London hotel to acknowledge the benefit of César Ritz's advice was the Carlton, designed by C. J. Phipps (1835–97) in 1891 in the Beaux-Arts tradition on a fine site at the corner of the Haymarket and Pall Mall. With Her Majesty's Theatre it covered a substantial area and the building operations took until 1899. Within the perimeter of the block there were also shops and arcades with heavily-corniced classical detailing rising to a mêlée of chimneys, mansard roofs and baroque pediments between domed cupolas. Half of this block was demolished in the 1950s to be replaced by New Zealand House, but the theatre still gives an indication of the original style of the hotel.

London, Savoy Hotel, 1893. Thomas Edward Collcutt was employed
by Richard D'Oyly Carte, who had already started to build the first
block of the Savoy, to make improvements and to take over as
architect for the remainder of its development, which continued until
1910. Collcutt carried out much work for the interior design of P & O
liners and for the Galle Face Hotel, Colombo, and the Reina Cristina
Hotel, Algeciras. Nearer home he added London's Wigmore Hall to
his achievements.

The Savoy river frontage, which was
superimposed as an extension to the first
building, giving a few feet of extra floor
space throughout.

London, Carlton Hotel, 1899, by architect C. J. Phipps with H. L. Florence. Now half-
demolished, but Her Majesty's Theatre remains.

1. View from the Victoria Embankment.
2. Restaurant Balcony, South View, Overlooking Gardens and River.
3. Angle of Courtyard.
4. General Reception-Room.
5. A Flemish Corner.
6. Entrance to Courtyard.
7. Restaurant.

THE SAVOY HOTEL.

An artist's cross-section in 1911 indicating all the functions of the Savoy. At the same time as the new river front was built, a ballroom and banqueting hall for 2,000 were added in celebration of its twenty-first anniversary.

For design of the Carlton interiors, Mewès and Davis were commissioned as César Ritz had a close interest in the hotel and they were familiar with his carefully considered requirements. His was the expensive demand to lower the level of the Palm Court and introduce a flight of stairs for the effective entrances and exits of London's best-dressed ladies.

London, Hyde Park Hotel, 1890. The front lobby in marble and bronze with a staircase rising from entrance door to hall is uncompromisingly impressive. Its marble wall panels were at one time panelled with wood and papered until rediscovered by John Mulhall in the 1970s, then in charge of maintenance, and revealed in a painstaking restoration process.

One of the French-decorated salons in the Hyde Park Hotel is occupied by a chefs' meeting.

Henry Louis Florence (1841–1916) worked with Phipps on the development and Mewès and Davis were employed for the interior planning and design of the hotel. Ritz contributed his usual careful attention and skill to the creation of ease and comfort for guests of both sexes. One of his strengths, shared also by Escoffier, was consideration for female taste and preferences. This had never been taken seriously before the Ritz era, but the latent power of femininity soon became a factor in successful hotelkeeping. In the Carlton, double windows reduced noise, each room had its own large bathroom, wardrobes and cupboards were carefully planned and, for reasons of hygiene, walls were painted not papered. Indirect lighting was another Ritz hallmark, allied to shaded lamps to give pinkish tinges to feminine complexions. A further innovation was the sinking of the Palm Court entrance hall below the dining-room level to create an element of theatre, enabling splendidly dressed ladies to sweep up or down the steps in dramatic display. A small balcony at the upper level gave a degree of privacy behind a screen of palms where the Prince of Wales could enjoy on his regular visits a vantage-point over the Palm Court.

The Hyde Park Hotel, 1890, was designed by Archer and Green as gentlemen's chambers, presenting an interesting roofline on the edge of Hyde Park.

Georges Auguste Escoffier – as a key member of César Ritz's team he contributed new and valuable ideas on *cuisine*.

Furnishing of the Carlton was chiefly in English eighteenth-century styles, executed by Waring's under Mewès's eye and all of high quality. Floral decorations reinforced the impression of luxury and welcome in the charac-

teristic Ritz manner. Extravagance reigned and Lady de Grey, a leader of London society, took the entire cast of the play *Véronique* to late supper there on one occasion. The Carlton was large but its size did not deter the Maharajah of Bikaner from taking a whole floor for his retinue. Not all happy occasions were lavish, and at one staff party the men were dressed in bath-towel togas to salute the master of all hoteliers with 'Hail César', responded to by Ritz in flippant pseudo-Roman manner.

The Hyde Park Hotel had been designed by Archer and Green and built in 1890 as gentlemen's residential chambers. It gained such notoriety by its great height of 10 to 11 storeys that legislation was passed to limit future height of buildings to '90 feet and two storeys'. In its brief life as Hyde Park Court it had 200 private rooms and for 'club' use was well-equipped with drawing-, dining-, smoking- and billiard-rooms together with its own theatre club. As private

When, after various financial difficulties and a fire at the turn of the century, changes of taste had called for more public grandeur than the resident club use required, Mewès and Davis were again brought in to create a luxurious atmosphere, French neo-Renaissance with baroque leanings. The smoking room seems to have had an intermediate style, some panelling, some garlanded classical pilasters. After the re-opening in 1908 the hotel became well established in the London scene.

chambers the enterprise was involved in the collapse of Jabez Balfour's fraudulently based property empire in 1892 that terminated for him in a fourteen-year prison sentence. Conversion to hotel use did not require much alteration and took place under the Hyde Park Hotel Company Limited, which belonged to the Bennett family of hoteliers. The building style was French château in origin, executed in brick with stone dressings, but a fire took place at the turn of the century and new interior work was carried out by Mewès and Davis while advice on detail and management was once again obtained from Ritz.

After the official opening in 1908 its clientèle developed with a strong bias towards the peerage, gentry and army, and their close courtly connections. Politicians also found it a pleasant and convenient meeting place. Towards the end of the Great War it was used in part as a military hospital, and Queen Mary participated in various charitable activities there. Its proper hotel establishment comprised 28 valets, 42 chefs, 69 waiters, 30 launderers, 6 doormen, 12 hall porters, 112 domestics, 12 French polishers, 14 seamstresses, 12 cellarmen and 18 barmen, but this complement was obviously not sustainable in wartime.[8] Problems in obtaining food were eased by contributions of produce from the country estates of regular patrons, and after 1918 the hotel was ready for the wild social life of the Roaring Twenties. Formal balls and coming-out parties were still very much in the social calendar and the royal family, especially the Prince of Wales, later Edward VIII, came frequently. There was a sad decline during the Second World War but social revival came in the 1950s with the royal patronage still in evidence. In 1968 it was bought by Trust Houses Ltd and a careful renovation progressed over many years during their ownership.

Other contemporary large and grand hotels beside the Carlton that have disappeared include the Grand in Trafalgar

London, Claridge's Hotel. Starting life as a lodging-house known as Mivart's, Mr and Mrs Claridge took it over fully in 1854 and raised it to hotel status. Forty years later, under the auspices of Richard D'Oyly Carte, a new hotel was built on the site to designs by C. W. Stephens with interiors by Ernest George and Yeates, completed in 1898.

Most of Claridge's early decoration was replaced in subsequent schemes, leaving only the staircase and what is now the First Ballroom as reminders. Art Deco designs by Basil Ionides dating from the 1920s have been preserved in the Front Hall (*opposite*) and Restaurant (*left*), and in one of the suites (*above*).

Square (1881) with 500 rooms, long defunct as a hotel although the building remains and has recently been restored, the Northumberland Avenue (1887) with 500 rooms, and the Cecil (1896) with 800 rooms. Claridge's, the Connaught and St Ermin's (1887) still exist and flourish.

Claridge's dates back to the early nineteenth century when, on behalf of James Edward Mivart, Lord William Beauclerk applied to the Grosvenor Estate for permission to use the house in Brook Street (later no. 51) as a hotel. Use as a private lodging house was tacitly permitted and Mivart proceeded to extend his business to other adjacent houses with little regard for restrictions. Some rumour of the Prince Regent's use of it as a bolt-hole was current, though Mivart's was plainly known in the 1820s as a fashionable discreet address for senior *corps diplomatique* personnel.[9] When Mivart retired, William and Marianne Claridge who had been running Coulson's next door, took over in 1854 and made a single business of 'Claridge's'. Empress Eugénie of France during a stay at the hotel received the distinction of a visit from Queen Victoria, who was said to be 'very impressed', to the undoubted delight and benefit of Mr and Mrs Claridge. From such an auspicious recommendation it has received consistent patronage from royal visitors from all parts of the world throughout succeeding years.

In 1894 it was bought by Richard D'Oyly Carte as principal in the New Claridge's Hotel Company and rebuilt to the unremarkable designs in red brick of C. W. Stephens. Interiors by Ernest George and Yeates derived from the English eighteenth century. The building, for which Lady de Grey had laid the foundation stone, was seven storeys high with 260 rooms and took four years to build by contractors George Trollope and Sons. The outside appearance with façades to Brook Street, Davies Street and Brook's Mews has not been greatly changed by additional storeys or a new main entrance. Public rooms on the ground floor accommodated the usual activities, with those required specifically by one or other sex being divided according to the manners of the time. The central winter garden and the restaurant served both sexes as dining and socializing in such public places was becoming more commonplace. With the exception of the Drawing Room, now in use as first Ballroom, and the sweeping main staircase, none of the Ernest George and Yeates interiors have survived. Some conflict persisted between the hotel and the ground landlord, the Grosvenor Estate, when any extension was envisaged, but in 1909–10 a ballroom overlooking Brook's Mews was approved and executed in French manner, with René Sergent as architect, reliefs by Marcel Boulanger, lighting by Baguès and paintings of Watteauesque character. Basil Ionides introduced pioneering Art

Deco interiors in 1925–6 in place of the earlier decoration, but most of his own work in turn fell victim to the next modernization in 1929–30 and then, in 1930–31 when the freehold was acquired, to major eastward additions. Both these changes were dealt with by Oswald Milne, and the new reception hall with carpet by Marion Dorn and skylight by the Birmingham Guild showed Art Deco at its best. Architects Stanley Hall, Easton and Robertson coupled with Betty Joel furnishings carried out other Modern interior schemes. Rapid change of design and decoration is a particular characteristic of urban grand hotels where interiors receive more attention and pressure to become fashionable than those with rural settings or spectacular views to attract the eye and relax tension.

Preparing precise chronicles of their history has therefore been made difficult as hotel managements have seldom kept adequate archive material, being more absorbed by their day-to-day problems. The author was told that, when rebuilding of the Grand Hotel, Brighton was taking place after the terrorist bombing in 1984, in the interests of rapid return to normal service, roomfuls of old hotel records in the basement were thrown away. With interest in older hotels increasing, more historical studies of individual ones are being commissioned, indicating that more attention may be paid to preservation in the future.

Also on the Grosvenor Estate in Mayfair, a hotel similarly emphasizing quality above quantity is the Connaught, built as the Coburg after road alterations on the Estate by the Duke of Westminster had created Carlos Place and a new layout. The previous leaseholder, August Scorrier, wished to rebuild his earlier hotel premises and received permission in 1892 subject to a restriction preventing him from including a bar. This was apparently invoked to protect other clients of his solicitors who happened to be brewers. From a short list of three architectural firms supplied by the solicitors, Scorrier selected Isaacs and Florence, who had designed the Holborn Viaduct Hotel, the Northumberland Avenue Hotel and the basic structure of the Carlton. Scorrier then nominated Langdale, Hallett & Co. of Brompton Road as contractors and the work of demolition and rebuilding was probably complete in December 1896 although unfortunately he did not live to see it finished.[10] A new Coburg Hotel Company had been formed to deal with the final works and to manage the hotel. Sir Blundell Maple was a director, and probably chairman, of the Company, and Maple's records indicate that they were responsible for supplying all furniture and furnishings. Externally the Coburg, on a curving corner site, is a well-mannered building in red brick and stone with no indications of grandiosity. Named originally

London, Holborn Viaduct Hotel, 1874, designed by Isaacs and Florence for Spiers and Pond. The French Renaissance-influenced dining-room, now demolished, was photographed in 1901.

BELOW Menton, Hôtel Impérial, 1913, the last hotel among the works of Hans-Georg Tersling, maintaining his consistent neo-classicism.

Aix-les-Bains, a spa town from Roman times, was developed further after the opening of the casino in 1949. Of the hotels built in the second half of the century the Splendide, 1883, by Antoine Guy (1842–92) later became the Beaux-Arts, core of a group of hotels with the Excelsior, 1906, and the Royal, 1914, both by Alfred Olivet, being built on either side. This complex is now converted into apartments, the photograph showing the Splendide section in the centre and the Excelsior to the left. Both Antoine Guy and Alfred Olivet were Genevois architects.

Monte Carlo, Hotel Hermitage, 1890,
created by Jean Marquet as an opportunity
for festive architecture which expressed the
raison d'être of the principality.

The Restaurant Belle-Époque is aptly
named and decorated accordingly, repeating
the colonnade motif of the hotel façade.

after Prince Albert's family, the hotel altered its title to become the Connaught during the Great War, a time when German names were unwelcome. It had made a propitious start with a first-rate manager, Kossuth Hudson, who had been well-trained under one of the Gordon group managers on the Riviera and so could set standards for this custodian of excellence in hotelkeeping.

France, Monaco and Italy

Development of seaside Mediterranean towns, given impetus as we have seen, some 25 years earlier with the advent of the railway, continued in the 1890s and spilled over into the twentieth century.

Prominent on the architectural scene was Danish-born Hans Georg Tersling (1857–1920), who spent most of his life in France, living and working chiefly on the Riviera coast from Monaco to the Italian frontier. Hotels and villas constituted the main part of his output, but the Casino at Menton might be considered his most important work. His style was unreservedly neo-classical, developing within the practical disciplines of woodworking and technical school training through the Royal Academy of Architecture in Copenhagen, which he left, showing artistic promise, in 1879. Architecture had become his only aim and, with contacts in Menton and some practical experience in Paris, he was able to build up a successful practice. Menton in the 1890s was a busy scene of development and Tersling gained entry into the social world, quickly winning recognition, and throughout his career commissions to design grand hotels came his way. These were the Metropole, Monaco (1888), the Grand-Hôtel du Cap-Martin (1891), the Hôtel Bristol, Beaulieu-sur-Mer (1898), Hôtel du Golf, Sospel (1900), and Hôtel Imperial, Menton (1913). Cap-Martin was a particularly fashionable area, and the Villa Cyrnos (1892) which he designed for ex-Empress Eugénie, then living as the Comtesse de Pierrefonds, helped to develop his style in the form of neo-classicism as used in the Second Empire and which she so admired. The Metropole is still in use within close range of Garnier's Casino at Monte Carlo from which Tersling's design with *œil-de-bœuf*, cupola and split pediment features may have gained inspiration. At Cap-Martin, a headland on the edge of Menton, the scale of the Grand-Hôtel du Cap-Martin was larger and the design less ornamented, harking back to the 1880s and the less baroque style of G. Rives, which was again present as an influence in the later Imperial. Demolition of the mansard roofs has blemished the appearance at Cap-Martin and at the Bristol at Beaulieu where fire

damage was the cause. In the design of the latter, which was also curved on plan, Garnier's influence dominated again, producing monumental treatment of the plinth area, which was deeply rusticated, and a more elaborate scheme of decorative stucco-work. All the furnishing of the Bristol was carried out by Maples under the supervision of Sir Blundell. The Golf Hotel, Sospel, visited on several occasions by Emperor Franz Joseph, was more modest in size and simpler in design with a rectangular thirteen-bay front and some Art Nouveau embellishment of the classical pilasters.

The Hermitage in Monte Carlo was designed by Monegasque architect Jean Marquet with considerable panache in 1890. With a main block five storeys high and sixteen bays wide he manipulated an assortment of motifs into one of the most festive façades that even Monte Carlo could deliver. Above a *sous-sol* built on the natural rock, a neo-Florentine arcaded loggia rises to vaulted, decorated ceilings emulating the Prince's Palace. Projecting balustraded balconies surmount all the columns of the arcade, making a counterpoint with the two tiers of windows above. At frieze level are five central bays of sculptured stucco-work between the tapestry-like pictorial panels in coloured mosaic. The top floor below the main cornice is punctuated by two curved and domed oriel windows flanking the central 'Hermitage' sign. Shadow effects by day and imaginative lighting by night emphasize the rococo quality of a delightful design. Behind this bedroom wing is a large quadrangle and the floor plan was extended in 1906 in a modified w-form to link up with the rooms which had first been part of a private villa before becoming the nucleus of the hotel. Two very notable public rooms formed part of the previous separate and inconvenient arrangement. The domed winter garden is the more unusual, with Art Nouveau ironwork structure, painted glazing and a great parasol-shaped central chandelier. It makes a spectacular effect and has in recent years been carefully restored by the management of the Société des Bains de Mer, which purchased the property in 1928 when a first renovation programme had been put into operation throughout the 200-room hotel. The grand dining-room, rectangular in shape with an apsidal end and a 'side aisle', has rose marble columns and lavish gilded ornamentation. The ceiling, painted by Gabriel Ferrier, holder of the Prix de Rome and gold medallist at the Paris International Exhibition of 1889, has as its theme the amorous graces of Boucher and Fragonard, which were favourite subjects of the period.

Italy at the time could offer no similar concentration of *belle-époque* settings but a grand hotel project involving the ubiquitous Ritz materialized in Rome. The Eternal City was long accustomed to visiting travellers, pilgrims and Grand

Tourists, so numerous inns and hotels were already available to supply straightforward board and lodging. Unification of Italy, with Rome once again as its capital, inevitably increased the needs inseparable from a central administration. Unlike France, Italy was hindered by its geography, but although history and temperament delayed complete integration of the provinces, the governmental, judiciary and military systems all drew attention and traffic within and from beyond its borders. Technology was advancing in the later nineteenth century, and provision of sufficiently well-equipped and sophisticated standards of hospitality pointed naturally towards the need for the prestige of suitable grand hotels. One of the most notable, though not built until 1894, 24 years after political unification, is the Grand in the Via Vittorio Emanuele Orlando near the Piazza delle Terme. The sponsors brought in César Ritz and Auguste Escoffier for advice and organization of the management and catering. Cavaliere Giulio Podesti (1857–1909) was appointed architect and produced a building in the traditional mould to suit the wishes of Ritz and therefore almost automatically the approval of the leaders of society whose wants he could divine so sensitively. The Grand is larger in scale than other Ritz hotels, but with fewer than 200 rooms keeps within limits that allow for personal service. Even in Rome there is evidence of French influence in the classical orders with pendant garlands in their decoration, and Mme Ritz's taste may be evident in this. Flattened arches and moulded panelling also are reminiscent of Louis Seize style but painted or coffered ceilings, marble and rusticated stucco speak the local language, and all the materials used were said to be from Italy. This included fine bronzes and paintings. The *piano nobile* with foyer at the top of the double staircase provided a fitting background for the rich and distinguished who attended the inaugural banquet. The Mayor of Rome, Emanuele Ruspoli, and Ritz were among the speakers.

At ground-floor level an imposing lobby gave access to a winter garden, salon, private rooms, smoking-room, American bar and billiard-room 'with separate table for Italian, English and French players'. Two conservatories led from the restaurant and dining-room into the garden. Advance publicity mentioned that the restaurant was accessible 'even without residing in the hotel', and the cooking was to be 'the finest imaginable and entrusted to the supervision of two famous chefs, Mr Escoffier from the Savoy Hotel, London and Louis from the Grand Hotel National, Lucerne'. This indicates the extent to which *hôtellerie* had become international, and its leaders in all departments were being sought after to please the clientèle.

Bohemia

In Bohemia, now in the Czech Republic, the Central European spa town of Carlsbad, now Karlovy Vary, provides us with a useful focus on many of the circumstances common to the gestation of grand hotels. Mineral springs, ordeal by fire, the favours of royalty and a high degree of cultural sophistication were all present, as we shall see, in the historic background of the establishment that became the Grandhotel Pupp. The spa itself had developed by the end of the fifteenth century, but the hotel traces its genealogy from the eighteenth. The enterprise started when a large assembly room later known as the Saxon Hall was built by Andreas Becher, mayor and pharmacist, in 1701 at a sharp bend in the river Teplá. This attracted visitors that included the Margrave of Saxony and later Augustus II the Strong, King of Poland, and initiated 30 years of spa development in a period of blossoming Baroque architecture. At a great banquet in 1682 the Margrave had appeared dressed as an innkeeper, so presumably had the interests of hospitality at heart. Peter the Great of Russia, the philosopher G. W. Leibniz and J. S. Bach stayed in the town, which was fast becoming a focus of culture and fashion for much of Europe. Here it was that Bach's Brandenburg concertos were commissioned.

In 1757 fire swept through Carlsbad, starting at the Three Moors Inn and destroying 224 houses. Rebuilding took place to an improved standard to reflect the town's status and in the same year Count Rudolf Chotek came as a visitor to take the cure, bringing in his retinue the pastrycook Jan Jiří Popp of Veltrusy.[11] Popp was attracted to the place and the opportunities it offered him so he returned the next year to work in Mitternach's *pâtisserie*. He settled in the town and married Mitternach's daughter Frances in 1775, who was in a position to buy one-third of the Bohemian Hall which Becher had built next to the Saxon Hall, from his widow. This cost her 300 gulden and was the first of three instalments, the second being 732 in 1776 while the third and last payment of 1,000 gulden was paid in 1786 by her husband, now beginning to be known as 'Pupp'. After the fire new planning and building regulations came into force. Streets were more spacious and stone or stuccoed brick replaced timber as a building material. In 1802 the town council granted a two-year tax relief to owners of timber houses who had them rebuilt in stone. A new spa régime was also introduced by physician David Becher, with the consumption of mineral water and walks taking the place of long baths and large but unspecific imbibing of spring water. Combination of these two aspects of development resulted in the building of the delightful

Rome, the Grand, 1894, designed by
Cavaliere Giulio Podesti in the manner of
a Renaissance *palazzo* for the Savoy Hotel
Company. Ritz and Escoffier prepared
the brief and saw it launched, adding
distinctively to the relatively few luxury
hotels of Rome. Ritzian hallmarks are
evident in the hall and staircase.

A furniture arrangement that could well
have been inspired by the interior furniture
and furnishing schemes in which Marie-
Louise Ritz had been deeply involved.

The smaller hall, photographed in 1901, has been restored with remarkably little alteration to its ebullient sculpture and plasterwork.

Karlovy Vary (Carlsbad), Czech Republic, Grandhotel Pupp, 1896–1913, by Ferdinand Fellner and Herman Helmer shows a complete departure from the standard rectangular treatment, with a set-back forecourt, elaborated balconies and window surrounds.

The Grandhotel Pupp's larger ceremonial hall with stage and arcaded upper storey continues similar themes of decoration and metalwork, with an organ providing facilities for concert performances.

colonnades that form such a feature of the town centre.

As owners of the main assembly hall and its park-like approach through lime tree avenues, the Pupp family were at the centre of social life and amusements. The founder, Jan Jiří, lived on into the next century until 1810 to see the spa receive as visitors Frederick the Great, Catherine the Great, Prince Clement von Metternich, Marshals Landon and Schwarzenberg, Goethe and Schiller and to continue drawing west Europeans away from resorts that were less pleasingly appointed or situated. Architecturally a latter-day comparison with Bath comes to mind in the distinguished neo-classical colonnade of the 1870s. It was called Mlýnská and designed by Josef Zitek, a worthy addition to the public face of Carlsbad. The Viennese architects Ferdinand Fellner and Hermann Helmer followed with another colonnade, the Vřídlo (1879), now demolished. These two architects had de-

signed about 50 theatres from Hamburg to Odessa, and in Carlsbad their theatre interior was decorated by Gustav and Ernest Klimt and Franz Matsch. Their major work at the Grandhotel Pupp was made possible as a result of more than a century of tenacious planning and expansion by the Pupp family, who already in 1810 had become wealthy. Josef, son of Jan Jiří, died after a relatively short period managing the Bohemian Hall and his cousin Jindřich eventually bought out his widow. He rented part of the site in the avenue to the town council, on which in 1862 they had built 'in Swiss style' a hall for an international congress of natural scientists. This he bought back at bargain price after the congress was over, named it 'Café salon' and instituted series of concerts. One of the literary evenings held there included Turgenev and Tolstoy reading from their own works.

Jindřich Pupp's three sons, Anton, Julius and Jindřich, inherited in 1864 and steadily added to the family holdings until in 1890 they were able at last to buy the Saxon Hall and complete the long-cherished aim of creating a cultural centre and grand hotel for the spa. A joint-stock company was formed and Fellner and Helmer were instructed to plan a new complex with Festival Hall, restaurant and two hotel wings. This they did in neo-baroque style which must be rated among the finest of hotel architecture, retaining a firmness of line combined with a lightness of touch reminiscent of the true spirit of the eighteenth century. The building period of 'L'Établissement Pupp' seems to have covered the years 1896–1913 and displayed exceptionally well-modelled exterior features, decorative Corinthian pilastered recesses and balconies effectively avoiding monotony. The large Festsaal and its smaller companion were beautifully done, the former with a double storey colonnade and delightful corner staircase, the hall lit from above through Art Nouveau patterned glazed ceiling, a fine plaster and metalwork completing the scene. The smaller hall leaned more towards rococo style with shells and c-scrolls in plaster, draped putti and lively semi-caryatid figures all well executed and uncoloured in good Austro-Hungarian tradition. The Parkhotel and the Grandhotel flanked opposite ends of the Festsaal and supplied luxurious living under the successive management of the three brothers, each of whom served his turn as president of the hotel company. When Karel Pupp took over in 1903, the accommodation was modernized with private bathrooms and central heating. Music remained a part of the hotel life with the spa orchestra and various chamber groups taking part and with a grand concert organ from Otto Rieger of Krnov in the Festsaal, costing 260,000 crowns. The same organ builders reconstructed the organ in 1989 for 1,500,000 crowns.

In the years following the Second World War, the Habsburg monarchy was barely a memory and the 'Établissements Pupp' as such were no more. In the 1940s and 1950s, state control and occupation by army officers for holiday purposes took their toll of wear, tear and fire damage in the hotel, then known as the Grandhotel Moskva. The fire in 1951 destroyed the top floor and roof with its corner towers, including some valuable contents. Rebuilding in the 1960s was to a poor standard and very little effort was made to restore any of the original design. A more thorough and sympathetic restoration had to wait until after 1980. The democratic revolution nine years later has brought a new spirit into a reviving Grandhotel and Parkhotel Pupp, enabling it to come full circle with proper conservation, as advised by Karel Nejdl, giving it renewed life more worthy of the Pupp name.

While in Karlovy Vary we should see the Hotel Imperial which looks down on the town from above, on a steep wooded hill and served by two cable cars. It has no long pedigree like the Pupp but was designed in 1912 by Ernest Hébrard, a château-style building with two conical-roofed towers and containing enough accommodation to back its claim as the largest new hotel of its time, surrounded by its own park and gardens. In Carlsbad during the Communist era visitors were directed to hotels of official not personal choice, and those being sent to the Imperial for 'the cure' or merely for a holiday tended to be Russian guests of the Czechoslovak government. Neglect just stopped short of complete decay, awaiting rescue in better times. Hébrard had made contributions to other spas in 1909 with the designs for the Mirabeau at Aix-les-Bains and the Royal at Evian-les-Bains. All three of these were alike in being planned on raised sites, large in bulk and symmetrical in conformation. The Royal – in France but with an Alpine look contributed by the spiky *flèches* of the roof – survives to give visitors fine views of Lake Geneva and the surrounding mountains. Hébrard's style reacted against French *belle époque* revivalism and the new Viennese Secession movement but was not a convincing alternative to the stacked-sandwich effect prevailing in many large hotels.

FOUNDED IN EMPIRES

Canada

Moving from the European complexities of the preceding chapter to a steady westward expansion in Canada, we can see the orderly pattern of hotel growth depending almost exclusively on the rail travel system. It was nearly two generations after the first railway hotels were built in England to serve a well-established network system that construction of the transcontinental Canadian Pacific Railway was, in 1885, completed. It had been built within fifteen years of the Canadian Government's promise to do so as a political step to secure British Columbia's entry into their federation. Great cost had been incurred and much ancillary work remained to be done to protect the track from snowfall and avalanche and strengthening the roadbeds. Precautions against extremes of weather had to be taken by providing heating fuel dumps and carrying survival rations for staff and passengers. The railway syndicate had the good fortune to employ as general manager William Cornelius Van Horne, a man of exceptional talents working as general superintendent for the Chicago, Milwaukee & St Paul Railroad and who came to the CPR in 1881 at the age of 38. In spite of practical problems, the opening deadline for the new Canadian railway was met and services started.

The usual over-spending difficulties had arisen and the need for encouragement of profit-making tourism pointed in the direction of hotel building. 'Restaurant stops' were the first attempts, being initiated in 1886 to designs by Thomas

Sorby, an English architect living in Victoria. The Mount Stephen House in Kicking Horse Valley, the Glacier House below the Illecillewaet Glacier and the Fraser Canyon House at North Bend were all built to a type plan – the Mount Stephen being a reversed version – with six or seven bedrooms in addition to the restaurant that supplemented cars too heavy for mobile use on the steep mountain sections of line. They were pleasant buildings in a neat symmetrical châlet style that would not have looked out of place in prosperous suburbs 25 or even 50 years later. Management problems arose, possibly owing to the smallness of size, making profitability and quality of service difficult to reconcile.

Van Horne looked to larger projects for the next stage of development and to the CPR Pacific terminus at Vancouver, a town in its infancy but growing fast until checked by a fire which destroyed most of it just before construction of the Hotel Vancouver began in July 1886. Sorby was again asked to prepare the designs, this time for a luxury hotel to cost half a million dollars. In 1888 when it was opened, the four-storey brick and tile building suffered unfavourable criticism, being

Between the Rocky Mountains and the Bow and Spray rivers, the Banff Springs Hotel grew over several decades to a size that gives it a presence even among such scenery.

OPPOSITE Canada, Banff Springs Hotel, 1888. Bruce Price took the châteaux of the Loire for some of his inspiration in designing the original CPR Banff hotel and this, combined with the picturesque needs of the rural site, gave rise to the Canadian 'château style'. Price died in 1903 and the south wing shown in the photograph was not built until the late 1920s when J. W. Orrock, succeeding Walter S. Painter as architect, designed it along with a new north wing to replace the last remaining timber-built section, which had been consumed in a fire in 1926.

The pool area helped to provide some of the leisure activity in a community which needed to be largely self-contained in order to succeed.

CPR hotel composite advertisements at the turn of the century.

An early interior designed by Kate Reed, whose interest in the fitting out of Banff Springs Hotel started in 1905.

Quebec, Château Frontenac Hotel, 1893. A letter from the architect, Bruce Price, to Thomas G. Shaughnessy in January 1894 with practical suggestions for improving service in the dining-room.

likened to an asylum, a workhouse or a 'sort of glorified farm-house', none of which seems justified if the CPR advertising literature was accurate. In following up Sorby's reported remark that it had been 'built without the architecture', it does, however, seem possible that features were omitted from his own conception, resulting in a much plainer appearance.[1]

The next hotel project was the Banff Springs Hotel, envisaged by Van Horne as a tourist centre that would satisfy all possible needs for comfort and service and would make accessible full enjoyment of the mountain scenery. Scottish influence, always to the fore in Canada, was responsible for the Banff naming after the native county of Lord Mount Stephen, president of the CPR from 1881 to 1888 and whose name had also been used for the first of the restaurant stops. The site chosen was forested land among the Rocky Mountains at the meeting of the Bow and Spray Rivers, with the added benefit of hot sulphur springs in the immediate neighbourhood. For Van Horne's ambitious vision, care in the selection of a suitable architect was taken. The New York architect Bruce Price (1845–1903) had been employed by the CPR to design Montreal's Windsor Station in 1886 and in the same year he began to receive Van Horne's scribbled ideas on the backs of envelopes from which he proceeded to design his own interpretation of the General Manager's challenging commission. With his training under Henry Hobson Richardson he inherited a view of nineteenth-century architecture which, in the United States, reduced historical references to a minimum and paid attention to the massing of the building and the relationships of solids to voids. Though Price was to develop the 'Château Style' and in so doing to derive inspiration from some of the Loire châteaux, at Banff Springs his design for a five-storey two-winged building largely in timber-frame construction confined the French influence to steep roofs and small corner turrets.

Finance for this flagship hotel was not begrudged and Horne sanctioned the cost of 250,000 dollars as a good investment. Extensive advertising, consistently a strong point of the CPR in Van Horne's time, preceded the opening in spring 1888 of the Banff Springs Hotel, offering beds for 250 guests at the high price then of $3.50 a night.[2] Tourists were attracted by the comfortable hotel and magnificent mountain scenery, and after fifteen years extensions built in more durable masonry increased its capacity. The building programme was more or less continuous for a period of ten years on a piecemeal basis until a real transformation took place with the commissioning of Walter S. Painter (1877–1957), whose 'Painter Tower' became a grand focal point linking the two wings with its considerable plan size of 70 by 200 feet. The facing stone from Mount Rundle quarried nearby was

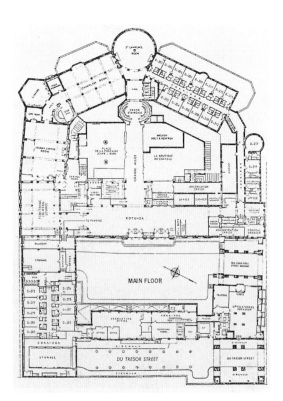

Like the Banff Springs Hotel, the Château Frontenac was subject to many major extensions to keep pace with demand. The Château Frontenac too suffered a fire in 1926 in the Riverview wing and the main floor plan shows proposals for rebuilding and enlarging that Edward and William S. Maxwell were to carry out.

Another CPR advertisement showing the dominance of the Château Frontenac.

laid by Italian and Scottish labour, giving a sense of massive stability with its brown and grey tints and thickening of lower sections of wall battered inwards to give added strength. This was completed in 1912 and introduced the extra amenities of Turkish baths and hot and cold bathing pools. Demand for rooms outran the space available, and from 3,890 guests in 1902, had exploded to 9,684 in 1904, with similar growth in following years. Even the expedient of extending the summer season by an extra month did not eliminate the problem, as the volume of travellers on the CPR seemed to remain ahead of the bed spaces at all their hotels in the Rockies however fast expansion schemes progressed. Mountaineering with the full attendance of Swiss guides was extremely popular, helped by local transport and supply concessions granted to William and James Brewster by the CPR. This was done by their hotels manager, Hayter Reed, who was aware of the additional opportunities for sports and indoor entertainments it could encourage. Photographers too found excitement in the grandeur of the Rockies. Byron Harmon led those who produced picture portfolios, demonstrating the accessibility in conditions of comfort to glaciers and rivers at least equal to those in the Swiss Alps.

Developing in the 1890s alongside the Banff Springs success was another brain-child of Van Horne. He and others formed the Château Frontenac Company to take advantage of a ten-year tax exemption offer by Quebec City Council to any developer realizing the long-talked-of project for a large hotel. This was in 1892 and by the end of the following year a good site had been leased, Bruce Price had been commissioned as architect and the Château Frontenac Hotel had been built – though a trifle late for its advertised convenience for travellers en route to the 1893 Chicago World's Fair.[3] Five of the nine company members had CPR connections and the enterprise was aimed at capturing new traffic to the Orient from among East Coast or around-the-world travellers. Standing dramatically above the St Lawrence river on the site of the old Saint-Louis Governor's fortress it expresses the Château style in emphatic terms. With light-red brick from Scotland and steep French Renaissance roofs and turrets it at once became an attraction for its own sake in addition to its strategic position as an internationally convenient staging-post. Named after Count Frontenac, the seventeenth-century Governor of Quebec who supported the search by La Salle for an overland route to Cathay, the spectacular property became railway property through purchase of the company's shares in 1894 and 1898. Major extensions of the original 170-room horseshoe-shape plan were soon added to meet the rising demand. The first of these was the Citadel wing and pavilion by Bruce Price in 1897–9, the second by Walter Painter, the Mount Carmel wing, in 1908–9.

Price had acknowledged a debt to earlier abortive schemes prepared by the Irish architect W. H. Lynn in 1875–8 and by Roth and Tilden and also Eugène-Etienne Taché in 1890, all of which incorporated borrowings from the châteaux of the Loire. His own particular inspiration, in addition to his Richardson background, seems to have been the Château de Jaligny, to the relative simplicity of which he applied an increase of scale and change of proportion in accommodating 170 rooms, 93 with bathrooms, together with all public rooms and ancillary services. The location of the site provided a theatrical element, and no other hotel has exceeded the Château Frontenac in status as a prized national possession. Major extensions have increased its capacity to a total, after the 1993 completion of the Claude-Pratte centenary wing, of 610 rooms. The first additions resulting from the profitable American and Canadian trade closed off the open end of the horseshoe plan. The style remained basically unaltered although Price increased the vertical emphasis with the steeply pitched dormers and added turrets, giving a lighter effect than the vigorous horizontal banding of the original. He did not limit his attention to the architecture alone and his handwritten letters in scrupulous detail to Van Horne and his successor, J. G. Shaughnessy, indicate close identification with all aspects of his clients' needs. In 1894, fine points of management relating to service of meals are noted after a discussion with Van Horne and then passed on to Shaughnessy, relating to 'how the subject works out in my mind in re Frontenac … No menu cards except for dinner':

To effect this properly bring the service up to the mark of the service in the St James club and conduct it on the same principle. Therefore have the men in livery, no vests, green cutaways and metal buttons and pumps; and train them and drill them like club servants.

Get the table in the Dining Room arranged differently. i.e. take the service trays away from the windows and put guests' tables in their place. This space is too valuable and attractive for dirty dishes. Have serving tables like those in St James club Dining Room in four places (say) in the body of the room.

Does not this seem to be the spirit of the Frontenac?[4]

As an undercurrent to this advice, we can distinguish an authentic cry from the heart of an architect who fears for the misuse of his cherished creation.

When further expansion was planned to cater for the growth of ten more years, a new architect to succeed Price had to be found for the work. A million and a half dollars was estimated as the cost of the proposed new Mount-Carmel wing and the Detroit architect responsible for the Quebec

Auditorium (now the Capitol) and who had been chief architect to the CPR since 1905 received the commission. He, Walter Painter, was similarly to be appointed for the Banff Springs Hotel extension during the next year or so. At the Frontenac his new design pursued the lighter style of Price's Citadel wing, and Painter's Mount-Carmel wing, of reinforced concrete structure, was faced in matching materials. The work was executed by the Provincial Construction Company of Toronto, and when completed in 1910 the building, with its dominating northern tower, over-topped all other buildings in Old Quebec and won the distinction of being Canada's largest hotel. The view of the hotel towards this new wing, from the Dufferin Terrace, became a familiar one, widely used in contemporary advertising material. Painter's scheme for a formal garden to the west was never carried out, but in 1915 his rebuilding of the bridging link between the Mount-Carmel wing and the Price building as a five-storey turreted in-fill gave additional rooms and integrated the two façades.

Next in the continuing line of distinguished architects who added to the hotel were the Maxwell brothers Edward (1867–1923) and William (1874–1952), known to Van Horne from work on his own houses, and commissioned in 1919 by the CPR to double the accommodation. Their solution to this difficult brief in the absence of really adequate space was to demolish the service wing of Price's building and in the resulting available area to build both there and in the *cour d'honneur* another accommodation wing on the Saint-Louis frontage and a seventeen-storey central tower containing two floors of public rooms and dominating not only the hotel but the city itself. Repeated visual references to the Loire châteaux helped to maintain overall unity of design and another suggested back reference was to Richardson's Trinity Church in Boston, Massachusetts. England and France were scoured by Edward Maxwell for period antiques and models from which reproductions could be made for furnishing the sixteen tower suites, but he died before the project was completed. William then amalgamated with Gordon McLeod Pitts (1886–1954) and concentrated on completing the interior design. Many Canadian craftsmen were employed, including Paul Beau on fine metalwork and George Hill on carving and sculpture. Furniture and decorative features in several mediums were made in the early 1920s by the Bromsgrove Guild of Applied Arts.

Two grand staircases, spacious halls, the Ballroom, the Jacques Cartier and Palm Rooms formed part of the Maxwell additions in this period, with interiors in a semi-classical manner augmented by both heraldic ornament and the application of freer plant form designs originating in Art

Nouveau. In January 1926 a serious fire caused damage in the Riverview wing. Rapid reconstruction took place, being completed in six months to the exact Bruce Price exterior design but introducing a reading room and the Champlain Room as Maxwell and Pitts's improvements. Kate Reed, whose interior design abilities will be further mentioned below, exercised her talents and influence towards elegance and lightness of colouring, always avoiding oppressiveness that could have threatened such a large and complicated building. Renovations and replanning in 1973 with a 'French-Canadian village' and various down-market novelties destroyed some of the Frontenac's traditional style and various artefacts were lost. Design policy was redeemed for the occasion of the centenary and the historic approach reappeared, coupled with improvements to the older service installations. The necessary modernization of equipment with the new Claude-Pratte wing adjoining that of Mount-Carmel resulted in a very acceptable design blending with existing work, by ARCOP Associates. After long consultations with the management and at a cost of 65 million dollars, the needs of the next decade and the conservation of a unique building complex were projected and fulfilled to the furthest possible extent.

Before the Maxwells were fully engaged on the Frontenac they had completed another CPR hotel, the Palliser in Calgary (1916) to serve the tourist trade under the title 'The Gateway to the Rockies'. Designed on an E-shape plan, it was built with a basement and eight storeys, with 315 bedrooms and private sitting-rooms plus 249 private bathrooms. Public rooms included the usual large dining-room, an oval drawing-room, palm room, and the general lounge or reception area that in Canadian hotels at the time was invariably called a rotunda regardless of shape, which was more often rectangular than circular. The Palliser design was a straightforward one, decoration being reserved for some Edwardian elaboration of plasterwork in the dining-room and good neo-classical detailing of chimneypieces.

Two other widely-separate CPR hotels carried on the successful château idea, the Place Viger in Montreal (1898) and the Empress in Vancouver (1908). Bruce Price had again found an individual solution for the Place Viger in combining an inventive tower and turret composition with the arcaded ground floor which was occupied by a new Montreal station and, as an experienced designer of New York skyscrapers, planned skilfully for first-floor dining- and ballrooms with a further four floors providing 88 bedrooms. His death in 1903 ended a very fruitful collaboration with the CPR. The Place Viger was closed as a hotel in 1933 but the building remains.

Extension of Canadian Pacific enterprises had in the

meantime spread into shipping and its tourist business increased both east and west. On the Pacific coast, Victoria on Vancouver Island saw itself as a western gateway, meriting a counter-balance in the form of a luxury hotel to the Château Frontenac's position across the continent. Influential citizens persuaded the city council and the CPR to support the project and the new hotel site on the Inner Harbour was secured. The architect of Victoria's parliament building, Francis Mawson Rattenbury (1867–1935), was commissioned and produced a new château hotel, the Empress, opened in 1908. It was named after the CPR's steamships, the 'White Empresses of the Pacific', which served luxuriously on the rail and sea tours around the world that had proved so popular and profitable in the 1890s. In a fresh, simpler treatment of the characteristic style with its roofs and dormers it was subsequently enlarged in 1911 and 1928.

A non-château CPR hotel, the Royal Alexandra, Winnipeg (1904–6), designed by William and Edward Maxwell, was more modest as befitted its location and sported no exciting rooflines, although it appears to have been comfortable for visitors. It was reported in a Winnipeg newspaper that

The work of decorating the new hotel in Winnipeg will be along simple but most artistic lines, and could be in no better hands

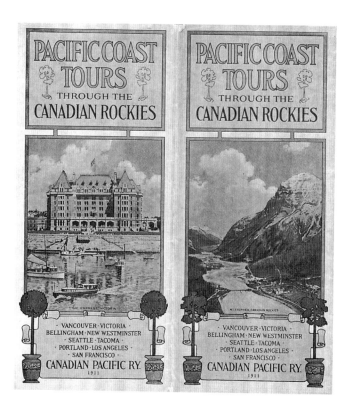

Victoria, Vancouver Island, the Empress Hotel, 1908. Francis Mawson Rattenbury designed this CPR château-styled link in their round-the-world touring itinerary.

than those of Mrs Reed, whose eye for color and effect is unerring and whose taste is always of the best.[5]

This accurate comment referred to Kate Armour Reed (1856–1928), wife of Hayter Reed the manager-in-chief, CPR Hotels Department, who made a considerable contribution to the interiors of all the railway hotels and indeed to the standards and manners of Canadian hotel culture generally. Her background as daughter of Ontario's Chief Justice led to a first marriage into the legal scene and a life in New York's upper social levels of the 1880s. She acquired a detailed knowledge of art and antiques that was put to good use in advising serious art collectors on her return to Canada after the death of her husband. One of her clients was Van Horne, so after she had married Reed in 1894 her interests expanded as a full-fledged professional career at the service of CPR hotels. From a start in decorating the Château Frontenac she travelled to Britain and the Continent in search of suitable items that would create the qualities of atmosphere and comfort that she had in mind. English models seem to have predominated, with Jacobean walnut and Chippendale mahogany visible in surviving illustrations, but more contemporary touches of Mackintosh and Art Nouveau were not excluded. All-embracing attention to detail was applied to household linen as well as soft furnishings, with fresh, light colour schemes replacing the earlier fashions for dark finishes. Interiors of the Place Viger were under her direction and for the Empress she also designed the gardens. When the older hotels began to need attention, her flair and sureness of taste continued to be employed.

Competing with the Canadian Pacific Railway Hotels, the Château Laurier, Ottawa (1912), developed vigorously all the characteristics of the château style. The site was ideal, along the Rideau canal leading to Lake Ontario, which had been cut on instructions from the Duke of Wellington when he was Britain's Prime Minister, and in view of the Parliament Buildings. The hotel was connected to the Grand Central Station by a tunnel from the reception area and made good use of a terrace the length of the 285-foot length of canal frontage. The Montreal architects Ross and MacFarlane were inspired by early French châteaux and created a romantic pinnacled skyline for the building. External walls were finished in Indiana limestone with corbels and brackets emphasizing the historical background of the style and its descent from such examples as Chantilly or Carcassonne. No chimneys were constructed, reliance being placed on electric extract fans to remove smoke and fumes.

Although outside the advertising network which gained so much for the CPR, the Château Laurier under the auspices of the Grand Trunk Railroad quickly made its mark, named after Wilfred Laurier, the first French-Canadian Prime Minister. Public rooms were very grand in scale, with an entrance portico leading into the rotunda measuring 50 feet by 45 feet by 24 feet high (15.2 × 13.7 × 7.3 metres). The floor was in marble – Napoleon grey inlaid with Belgian black – and the walls imitated Caen stone. Ceilings generally were coffered and beams or brackets were moulded or carved. Decorative friezes and wood panelling included heraldic shields, masks and cornucopias. Leaded Tiffany glass in the rotunda and cast bronze for light fittings, balustrades and grilles added to the impression of quality. A marble stair led up to the first floor ballroom 70 feet by 40 feet by 20 feet high (21.3 × 12.1 × 6 metres) decorated in Louis Seize style with gilded and painted plasterwork. No fewer than 22,000 electric lamps of 25 candle-power were used for lighting the building, and an ice-making tank provided five tons of ice per day. Of the 305 bedrooms, about three-quarters had private bathrooms; for public use there were eleven lavatories for women and twelve for men. The building contractor organizing and executing the whole complicated process was George A. Fuller, with many specialist firms under his control. There was an interesting comparison in the contemporary *Construction* magazine relating to daily water usage for domestic purposes in Canadian cities, averaging 143 gallons per head as against 25–27 gallons in Great Britain, with no known explanation of the discrepancy.

Fort Garry Hotel, Winnipeg (1914), was another Grand Trunk Pacific Railway hotel, and the architects, now practising under the name Ross and Macdonald produced a 14-storey E-shape plan with many decorative design ideas showing affinity with the Château Laurier. In this hotel the ballroom was on the seventh floor and each bedroom floor was provided with a service kitchen and a clerk's desk. The majority of the 222 rooms had their own bathrooms but 68 of the rooms shared a bathroom with one another. Double rooms predominantly had twin beds. In the Macdonald Hotel, Edmonton, designed by the same architects for the same railway in 1916, the plan was a modified L-shape with a corner entrance. It was praised for its 'refined taste' and the absence of gorgeous display and extravagance. In the same year, Thomas Sorby's Vancouver Hotel of 1888 was replaced by one designed by Francis S. Swales (1878–1962) for the CPR and in association with Walter Painter. This was of palatial size with neo-Renaissance plasterwork and panelling but it closed in 1939, being superseded by the present Hotel Vancouver, and was subsequently demolished.

After the Great War, Canadian Pacific concentrated on its steamships and sea travel, popularized by efficient advertis-ing, and marketing the cruise idea at the expense of the big mountain hotels. The motor car also competed with the status of the transcontinental railway and independent travellers looked for quieter places and less expense. Special festivals and organized holidays helped to fill the existing hotels but rival railway lines, merged into Canadian National Railways by 1922, increased the competition. The heyday of new hotel building was over but outside the CPR empire a few independent commercial ventures entered the market.

In Montreal the old Windsor Hotel had been designed by W. J. Bounton of Chicago and opened in 1878 offering all up-to-date amenities and elaborate interior decorations. It became a favourite among British royalty, for whom Canada always held a special attraction, and housed all visiting celebrities before the Place Viger was built. The Ritz-Carlton followed in 1913, agreeing certain standards as a condition of permission to use the name. Ritz himself was no longer active in the Ritz Hotel Development Company at the time, but amongst the Ritzian requirements were a bathroom to every bedroom, a service kitchen to every floor and a cuisine in which dishes were not to be 'spoiled by strong sauces'.

The prolific firm of Ross and Macdonald designed Montreal's Mount Royal Hotel in 1923 on an elaborate plan of two E's back-to-back in order to achieve the necessary daylighting for the 1,046 bedrooms. Technical equipment there was well advanced and banqueting facilities on the top floor could accommodate up to 2,500 people. Claiming the title of 'largest hotel in the British Empire' it was an exuberant addition to the city.

Toronto provides the last Canadian examples and could offer to its important visitors adequate hospitality as early as 1856 in a hotel which from 1862 was called the Queen's Hotel. It, too, drew in the royalty and Governors-General, the Red Parlor as reception room for the royal suite providing a setting for ceremonial occasions and political events. By the 1920s its charm had been overtaken in the rapid development of the city and demolition was inevitable. The Prince of Wales inaugurated the new and vast Union Station in 1927 and two years later, on the very brink of the great depression, the CPR's Royal York Hotel took its place on an adjacent central site. Ross and Macdonald were again the architects, making use of their experience of high-rise city centre buildings. The sixteen storeys were designed on a simpler plan than the Montreal Mount Royal, and historical influences were subordinated to the massive modernity of the hotel that won for itself the name of 'largest in the Commonwealth'.

Toronto, Royal York Hotel, 1929.
The architects Ross and Macdonald used
their experience in high-rise building to
provide 'the largest hotel in the British
Empire', which title had previously been
claimed by the Mount Royal Hotel in
Montreal. Massive in bulk, the exterior
design of the Royal York gained balance and
scale through application of semi-classical
motifs and groups of tall arcaded windows.

Australia

In contrast with Canada, a single representative only from
Australia has survived through many crises that could have
brought its long history to an end. Fortunately the Windsor,
formerly called the Grand, in Melbourne escaped some
serious threats to its existence and has lived long enough to
benefit from the worldwide resurgence of appreciation for
nineteenth-century hotel grandeur and ideals of service.

During the 1880s Melbourne was a growing town – or
city – and was the seventh largest metropolis in the British
Empire. Its vitality had won support for the International Exhibition of 1880 which had been held in a splendid new building with a gilded dome, designed by Joseph Reed and built
by David Mitchell. Such an impressive example fired the
imagination of George Nipper, whose ambition to build his
own new grand hotel became fixed despite the 250 Melbourne hotels already in existence. The New Treasury, the
Old White Hart, Imperial, Excelsior, Star and Melbourne
were just a few of those in the area of Little Collins and
Spring Streets near to the town centre on which he had set
his sights. Theatres and the Opera House, the Exhibition
Building and the Eastern Market were all within easy reach,
and the Parliament Building for the State of Victoria was
under construction in Spring Street. Nipper, born in 1838,

Melbourne, the Grand Hotel, now the Windsor, 1883. The entrance carries bold reclining figures of Peace and Plenty by James Simpson Mackennal.

RIGHT Bold design in the form of sturdy granite columns carries through into the entrance hall in character consistent with the exterior.

BELOW The British-born architect Charles Webb expressed in its façade Victorian design at its best.

had emigrated from England and, with John See, built up businesses in grain and produce with interests also in shipping. Three separate plots of land comprised the site he required and he managed to acquire these between April 1882 and January 1883, creating a prime site of 120 × 122 feet for the realization of his dream. Successful in trade but not excessively rich, he had employed Charles Webb (1821–98) to design his own house and commissioned him, as a well-established and distinguished architect who had come from England in 1849, for the new venture that was to be Webb's only large hotel project.[6] He contributed greatly to the public face of Melbourne, building at least four churches and a synagogue, Wesley College and Grammar School in St Kilda's Road, the Royal Arcade, Alfred Hospital and South Melbourne Town Hall – all between 1850 and 1880. After this, as a founder-member of The Victorian Institute of Architects, he became their President in 1882–3.

The new hotel as built in 1883 by contractors Thomas Cockram and William Comely represented less than half the present nineteenth-century façades, six storeys high, brick built and cement rendered, with solid bluestone foundations and 100-feet-high square corner towers, making it a landmark even before the completion of Webb's overall design some five years later. All window openings were semicircular-headed with three tiers of arcading for the lower floors being surmounted by two more bedroom floors below the main cornice and pediment. Accommodation included 94 bedrooms, 16 parlours and 47 servants' bedrooms. Each wing had one bathroom per floor and lavatories were similarly scarce, those for men at one end of the corridor and for women at the other. Gas was installed for cooking, for steam heating and to run an engine for the goods lift. Hydraulic lifts came a few years later. Completion of this first stage of the hotel coincided with the dissolution of Nipper's business partnership and he put his cherished hotel up for sale in 1886.

A strong Temperance movement was sweeping through the country at the time and hotels that abandoned the serving of liquor often adopted the name 'Coffee Palace'. The Grand was caught up in this turn of fate, which changed for a time its whole identity when it was sold by Nipper to the Grand Coffee Palace Company Limited, whose managing director James Munro had been able to raise the requisite capital. Two Scottish directors, James Balfour and David Beath, were named with Munro in the title deeds and with company members George Walker and William Baillieu were fully committed to alcohol-free hotel management. Finding their new régime for the hotel successful enough to support expansion they employed the original architect, now practising as Charles Webb & Sons, to double its capacity, taking in additional land that Munro had been able to purchase. The completed Spring Street front was based on the well-tried five-part formula of a central entrance feature between two symmetrical wings, each terminating in an end pavilion. The design of the first part of the building was accurately imitated and Webb may well have contemplated this sort of addition at an earlier stage as a unified composition resulted, the only weakness being the smallness of the central pediment, hinting at cramped space along the road frontage. This did not inhibit the scale of the central main entrance, where large figures of Peace and Plenty, owing incongruous deference to

Michelangelo, support Australian and British coats of arms. These figures were modelled by James Simpson Mackennal (1832–1901), a plasterworker responsible for much work in the Parliament House and whose son Edgar Bertram Mackennal made his reputation as a sculptor.

Whereas the first stage had cost £50,000, the second building contract, with C. Butler & Son, is given surprisingly at a final account figure of only £38,000 and even this was some £6,000 above the tender sum. This included a grand main corridor about 20 feet wide, a dining-hall 103 feet by 33 feet, new kitchens and 275 bedrooms. Oregon pine, kauri, cedar, jarrah and red gum were among the timbers used and decorative Minton tiles were imported from England. Electricity and gas were installed throughout and new hydraulic Waygood Balanced Lifts provided. Fire precautions received much attention, with two cantilevered stone staircases, three fire hoses on each floor and 32 roof water-tanks of 600 gallons each with a standby pumping engine. Work was virtually complete in 1888 and the Grand Coffee Palace accommodated visitors to the Centennial Exhibition of that year. The Exhibition succeeded in most things with the exception of profit, leaving behind a £250,000 bill for the State of Victoria. This in no way helped a declining economic situation in the 1890s and Melbourne lost interest in staging exhibitions. Hotels in the city had mostly become 'coffee palaces', but few rivalled the Grand in size or quality. The Grand was to have troubles again when the slackness of Munro's management contributed to a decline in trade and his financial manoeuvring in land speculation led to liquidation of his and his family's companies. This uncovered very doubtful dealings in large sums and the Real Estate Bank lost over £1,000,000. Munro had entered politics in the 1880s and been State Premier and Treasurer in 1890. His convenient appointment as Agent-General to London for the State ensured his absence from Melbourne when enquiries were instigated. At the same time the hotel's accounts were under inspection by shareholders, revealing a net loss where profits had been shown in the manager's accounting. This smaller scandal was dealt with by his resignation and that of the previous chairman of the board, R. G. Wilson. The manager, J. H. Durant, repaid £300 cash and forfeited his farm to the company, but no further proceedings were taken in the drastic financial situation of Melbourne generally, when insolvency and unemployment were commonplace.

The hotel board with the investigators Thomas Smith and William Bates together with F. T. Warren appointed a new manager, August Frederick Beker, and attempted to straighten out the finances, but one difficulty persisted. Secret – or semi-secret – drinking of alcohol brought in from outside had been rife and yet the hotel received no benefit from this profitable commodity. Shareholders discussed the possibility of abandoning temperance and at the 1897 annual general meeting agreed on making a re-licensing application for the hotel, which in due course was granted, to the Grand's immediate gain. Beker left the following year, becoming proprietor of the next-door hotel, the Old White Hart, and W. H. Burgess, the head steward at the Melbourne Club, took up managership for the next seven years. Modernization and redecoration, so often connected in the hotel world to the appointment of a new manager, was embarked on around the turn of the century to make use of new public utilities that were improving life in Melbourne. A mains sewerage system had been the first, under construction in 1897 to obviate the bad conditions which gave rise to the town's epithet 'Smellbourne'. The Grand was connected to the drainage in 1898. Next came the improvement of the telephones into a proper network with nationalized exchanges throughout the state, installed from 1887 onwards and superseding a private enterprise called Henry Bryan Moore's Telephone Exchange Company, which had opened in 1880, earlier than London's first service. Refrigeration and ice-making were other facilities for which appropriate equipment was available.

Fashion in the form of bright colours for decoration had reached the Grand with the new century. Oriental influence brought into the sophisticated world of luxury furnishings in peacock blues and greens mixed with bronze, copper and terracotta. A new Moorish lounge in the Grand (1904) contained Indian and Persian motifs, hanging lamps and fretwork accompanied by armchairs, divans and an array of potted plants. Music from a string orchestra accompanied meals in the main dining-room and a separate dining-room for nursemaids with children kept the generations apart. Public rooms were still segregated by sex to a considerable extent, with both a smoking-room and a writing-room for the men and corresponding ladies' drawing-room and writing-room on the first floor near the main staircase. Private bathrooms were still confined to the few suites, and those for public use remained, together with lavatories, segregated on each floor as before. Shops offering services were at ground level within the building near the Spring Street entrance and a pharmacy, tobacconist, hairdresser and dentist were all conveniently placed.

On 9 May 1901 the first parliament of the Commonwealth of Australia was inaugurated by the Duke of York, and the Parliament House in Bourke Street close to the hotel became the seat of government until it transferred to Canberra in 1927. As a result the hotel's profit rose from about £3,000 in 1901 to £5,468 the following year only to fall back to less than £1,000, where it remained for several years. Drought was a prime cause, regional arable and sheep farmers whose custom was valuable being badly hit and therefore absent from their normal social haunts. Food prices and wages rose and the hotel's battle for survival continued. The Great War, a smallpox epidemic in Sydney and further wage increases called for radical remedies and in 1916 the conversion of suites into six private apartments created a vital regular income. Post-war influenza, which killed 3,530 in the city, delivered another hard blow and the hotel company again looked for a buyer. Melbourne Hotels Ltd under the leadership of Sir Arthur Rickard, property developer, acquired it in 1920 and promised complete renovation and refurnishing of the Grand with a scheme to redevelop the adjacent Old White Hart site in the future. The two hotels were merged into one management with T. Hardman in charge and the renovation works began early in 1921. Robinson and Marks from Sydney were the architects in charge, closing the hotel half at a time so that business could have continuity. A local architect, Henry Hardy Kemp, had served on a previous board of the hotel and was very familiar with the building and usefully involved with the work. Structural deterioration was repaired, hot and cold water services and a telephone in each bedroom were installed. Suites and double rooms ranked their own private bathrooms but single rooms fared less well.

Interior design schemes reacted against the late nineteenth-century heaviness and was simplified accordingly, having more in common with the first decorations of 1888. Furniture was reduced in size and quantity and most

The Grand's Moorish lounge of 1904 followed the trend of fashion at the time, as did another Melbourne hotel lounge at the Menzies.

noticeable was the removal of accumulated pictures and bric-à-brac. On completion of the £90,000 renovation by 1923, there was accommodation for 200 in bedrooms, 300 in suites, with 75 more available beds in the Old White Hart annexe. At this point the hotel name was changed to Windsor, commemorating royal visits, as the royal family had taken the name in 1917.

A few years of stability ensued with an adequate stream of visitors, long-term residents and faithful staff to create the right atmosphere. Eating and drinking habits did undergo changes, some of them mourned by the clientèle. One was the disappearance of the free counter lunches, which had been available as bait for further expenditure since the 1870s. This perquisite finally resulted in substantial losses as the free food consumed cost more than the profit on the extra drinks and was discontinued. The 'six o'clock swill' caused by licensing laws after the Great War, which only allowed half an hour between the end of the average working day and closing time for drinking alcohol, made it quite unnecessary for any bars to have chairs and tables as the crush was so intense. Evening drinking in Melbourne was not allowed until 1966, so it was only then that comfortably furnished bars came back into use.

Recent history benefited from the presence of Richard S. Nesbitt as general manager, managing director of the hotel company and lastly chairman over a total period of 40 years, 1928–68. The Windsor was fortunate that all changes were carried out with respect for the original design, leaving the appearance of the main block much as it was in 1889. In the 1970s it was nearly lost to developers in company with the Ress-Oriental, the Occidental, Scott's, the Federal and the Menzies, all of which fell to the rocketing site values. Listing gave some protection in 1972 and, to summarize recent history, a conditional new lease was granted in 1980 at a greatly increased rate for two years with a 20-year option to Oberoi International Hotels. The founder of this group, Rai Bahadur Mohan Singh Oberoi, had built it up after starting as hotel clerk at the Hotel Cecil in Simla. In this Indian hill station under the British Raj, an association and partnership with Ernest Clarke left Oberoi as owner of two hotels run by himself and his wife in Simla and Delhi when Clarke returned to England in 1934. By way of the Grand Hotel, Calcutta and the Mena House, Cairo (both described below), his taste for restoration of historic hotels led to the Windsor while at the same time modern luxury Oberoi hotels were being built in the Middle East and India.

At the Windsor, Oberoi's willingness to take on restrictions and onerous conditions of operation had probably won him the lease. A joint expenditure of approximately $2,500,000 (Australian) split between Oberoi International and the Government of Victoria Public Works Department was projected for reinstatement of structure and decoration. It became obvious that, as no local fund of experience existed, specialist consultants were needed to create the necessary historic authenticity. With Graeme Holdsworth as project co-ordinator, Suzanne Forge and Peter Lovell patiently evolved restoration of a chosen period scheme from among the varying alternatives uncovered during their research. Oberoi and his son Biki had previously acquired experience of likely difficulties through their interests in a consortium which renovated and restored the Australia Hotel, Adelaide. The Windsor project, at treble the estimated cost, at least rewarded them by receiving two architectural awards.

South Africa

'Quiet dignity and gracious living' were the qualities attributed to the Mount Nelson Hotel in Cape Town by the *Union Castle Chronicle* in 1953 when it was already more than 50 years old. Cape Colony was served by fast steamships that by 1890 had reduced sailing time from England to fifteen days. The ships were well appointed but no hotels at the end of the journey could offer any similar standard. The Colonial Governor and the British press took the matter up and canvassed the acute need if the colony was to survive and develop. In this context, when a family estate with interesting historical background came on the market in 1890, a new-formed hotel company bought it as well-suited to their aims.[7]

There had been some settlement by the Dutch in the eighteenth century during the active years of the Dutch East India Company, and a young adventurer from Amsterdam, Baron Pieter van Rheede van Oudtshoorn, who was on his way to seek a fortune in the Far East, stopped off and decided to remain instead in the Cape Colony. This was in 1743, and he received the encouragement of a generous grant of land, to which he later added by purchase, thus forming a farm estate. For 22 years he remained there, whereupon he inherited an uncle's property in Holland and returned home to take possession of his new domain. His 'Garden of Oudtshoorn' estate on the lower slopes of Table Mountain was sold in 1771 to Adrian van Schoor. Scarcity of water affected farming, and after twenty years van Schoor divided the land, selling the western half back to the Baron's son in 1791 and then the remainder to the Revd Christiaan Fleck. On each half a new homestead was built, the latter being where the Mount Nelson Hotel now stands. Resale, subdivision and development followed each other in the early

Cape Town's Mount Nelson Hotel, 1899, was designed by a London practice of two young Scottish architects – William Dunn and Robert Watson – known to the Castle shipping line chairman.

A domestic atmosphere rather than any monumentality suited the Mount Nelson. Art Nouveau ceiling decoration and reproduction chairs of freely interpreted Chippendale style achieved the right combination in the original dining-room.

Garden history is visible in this original fountain dating from the second half of the nineteenth century, when the estate, before the hotel was built, was owned by the Hamilton Ross family.

1800s when Britain, in the cause of checking Napoleon's ambitions, reinstated control of the Cape. In the northern hemisphere four months before the Fleck homestead was resold to a William Maude, a crucial battle had been fought at sea off the southern coast of Spain near Cape Trafalgar. The British fleet destroyed superior French and Spanish forces but their hero, Admiral Lord Nelson, died in the action. His legacy was British supremacy at sea and immortality among his countrymen, hence the renaming of Maude's estate as 'Mount Nelson'. This title was first used in the *Cape Town Gazette and African Advertiser* for 30 August 1806, and the property changed hands in 1812, 1820 and in 1843 when purchased by a Briton with 50 years of residence in the colony, Captain the Hon. Hamilton Ross. It remained in the family for three generations, but the perpetual hazard of financial insecurity led Ross's great granddaughter Maud Maria to make an immediate sale of her inheritance.

The Cape Land Company bought this estate and extra adjoining land to build a high-quality hotel that would fulfil the obvious demand, but it was not until 1897 that transfer to the subsidiary company African Lands and Hotels Ltd was accomplished under the shipping magnate and Castle Line chairman Sir Donald Currie. Just as the Canadian Pacific Railway enterprise was material in the development of Canada, so the Union and Castle Lines – to be merged as Union Castle – played a large part in the opening up and popularizing of South Africa at the end of the nineteenth century. Trade, sport and tourism were at the head of Currie's interests, and his influence, in spite of all intervening happenings, can still be traced, not least in the Currie Cups for rugby football, cricket and swimming.

While the Mount Nelson site lay undeveloped, other entrepreneurs were attempting to fill the accommodation gap in Cape Town. In 1894 the Union shipping line built a Grand Hotel in Strand Street on the site of the previous Parkes Family Hotel, with electric light, a lift, carpeting throughout, and a dining-room to seat 250 and French cuisine available. Before this the Parkes Hotel had been at the top of the list, succeeding in 1848 Mrs van Schoor's boarding house, where Clive of India and Prince Frederik Hendrik of Holland had lodged. Other hotel names listed are the White House, the Hercules' Pillars, Army & Navy, Queen's Arms, Hotel Hamburg, St George's, Royal, Poole's and British Queen. None of these offered competition with the standard the Grand presented to possible customers.

Sir Donald Currie had employed two young Scottish architects with a practice in London on his own property in Perthshire, Glenlyon House, and then commissioned them in 1897 to design Castle Line offices in Adderley Street, Cape Town, and the luxury hotel that had been so long in materializing. To William Dunn (*c.* 1867–1934) and Robert Watson (1866–1916) with their burgeoning practice in London, this was a wonderful opportunity. A fine site and clients whose aim was to build a hotel equal in standard to the best in Europe would be any architect's dream. By 1 March 1899 the 150-bedroom Mount Nelson Hotel was opened and acknowledged as well fulfilling its owners' ambitions. The exterior showed Queen Anne Revival characteristics in a Norman Shaw manner suited to the domestic scale of the building. A modest English country house approach combined with Dutch gables, ogee window heads and a strong cornice produced the atmosphere that has always made the Mount Nelson a favourite hotel.

The British architect Herbert Baker lived in Cape Town from 1892 to 1912, and during this period acted as local agent for Dunn and Watson for the building of the Mount Nelson. His only hand in the design seems to have been for a laundry, boiler room, drainage works and alterations to the pantry – humble work for the man who later in London changed the face of Soane's handsome Bank of England in Threadneedle Street by the addition of its upper storeys, but a preserved link between the Mount Nelson Hotel and the London architect who was to become distinguished and receive a knighthood later in his career.

The hotel's scale may have been far from monumental but, from the 30 × 40 feet reception hall 'used as a common room and as a lounge by ladies and gentlemen' to the drawing-room, writing-room, restaurant and main extendable dining-room (80 × 40 and 14 feet high), space was clearly adequate. A musician's gallery and conservatory augmented this ample dining area decorated with classical oak-panelled walls surmounted by Art Nouveau reliefs and painted decoration. Amenities were up to date in the large kitchen and a sophisticated Pasteur filtration system for drinking water was in use. The wine cellar could hold 20,000 bottles. Superb ventilation, electric lighting, hot and cold running water for baths were all described as 'amazing technical innovations', and at last steamship passengers who were very well looked after on the Castle and Union Lines could look forward to the same living standards when they disembarked at Cape Town. But in a matter of months republicanism and violent conflict intervened, crowding the Mount Nelson with a different clientèle from the European tourists who had enjoyed its first weeks. The South African War (1899–1902) between Boers and Britons was bitterly fought in the twilight of Queen Victoria's reign, and administrative needs in the prosecution of it had the effect of building up rather than destroying the importance of Cape Town's newest hotel (nicknamed 'the

Nellie'), which British forces regarded as a welcome base and where their relatives, journalists and a variety of opportunists enjoyed themselves during their brief or extended visits. An 'officers only' rule was introduced, not without some bad feeling, by the experienced Swiss manager Emile Cathrain. Wild incidents inevitably occurred, and on one occasion a British journalist, H. F. Stanford, was tarred, feathered and thrown into a fountain for gatecrashing an officers' private party. Reverberations reached London as his adjudged claim of £1,500 damages awarded in Cape Town remained unpaid until years later when Lord Kitchener ordered a court martial, which the defaulters were recalled from India to face.

Winston Churchill was one young war correspondent who rubbed shoulders with Kitchener and others at the Mount Nelson, Churchill's mother staying there with him after his escape from a Boer prison camp. Churchill thought the hotel a 'most excellent and well appointed establishment which may be thoroughly appreciated after a sea voyage'. Cecil Rhodes, Joseph Chamberlain, H. G. Wells, Arthur Conan Doyle and Rudyard Kipling are all recorded in its early guest lists.

The deep wounds of the South African War healed only slowly, but material development in the four self-governing colonies was more active and these – the Cape of Good Hope, Natal, the Transvaal and the Orange River Colony – united in 1910 as provinces of the Union of South Africa. Cape Town remained the chief port and commercial centre, and life at the Mount Nelson proceeded with little alteration through the years of the Great War until its second manager, Aldo Renato, instigated improvements and redecoration. Thirty additional bedrooms and many new bathrooms were accompanied by space for 100 more dining places and a ground-floor kitchen to replace the old basement one. A total of £53,000 was spent over three years, ending on 31 December 1921 after a disputatious contract in which client, architect and hotel manager seemed each to have had different opinions. In the name of modernization much good reproduction furniture was jettisoned and the grand piano for gentle entertainment vanished. Uniformed and turbaned staff upheld the hotel's style and tradition of service and the comfort of guests remained paramount. Restoration of the efficient steamship services after the Great War kept up the supply of visitors who were travelling for work and pleasure. Cape Town, like Melbourne, was struck by the virulent influenza which spread from Europe, and in February 1919 the *Kenilworth Castle* arrived to the news that 'flu was already rampant in the town so crew and passengers would be kept aboard in quarantine for their own welfare'. The Mount Nelson had been acknowledged by the local health department to be a 'plague-free zone', so after some delay passengers were at least allowed there.

Other developments were put in hand in the 1920s with a handsome neo-classical gateway leading up a new palm-planted drive to the hotel. This was constructed to the designs of Kendall and Morris to celebrate the enthusiastically welcomed visit of the Prince of Wales in 1925. The alterations made necessary the demolition of the badly deteriorated old Ross house, Oak Lodge, but good workmanship on the gateway by the contractors A. B. Reid helped to make an improved first impression.

The gardens from the time of John Ross onwards had always been well-planted and looked after and were described in a Cape Land Company brochure of 1890 as

well wooded or in a high state of cultivation. The gardens are laid out in sixteenth century style with formal hedges, fountains, tub plants etc. … The turf is of that velvety softness which only age can give; there is an old deer park and there are vineyards and gardens yielding forth the fruits of the earth in abundance, while along the west gable of the old Mansion House of Mount Nelson, and covering a long trellis-walk, climbs the famous vine, patriarch of its race.

As well as the *phoenix canariensis* palms planted 70 years ago for the then new driveway (these are now well-grown), there are tall statuesque Norfolk Island pines and at least one century-old oak, and interesting planting still carries on the tradition. Very few relics from the old estate still exist, two modest-sized globe-topped columns mark the footpath by the 1925 gateway approach road and a seated heraldic lion holding a shield is placed near the northeast façade of the hotel. Most interesting is the one surviving fountain from among John Ross's 26 – a globe carved with lion masks and acanthus leaves discharging spouts of water from its position at the top of a chevron-carved supporting column, all these motifs being credited with family associations. The garden and plant collection give much pleasure and add important visual support to the 'Pink Lady', as the hotel is also affectionately called by its many admirers because of the colour of its walls.

Durban in the early days of its settlement went under the name of Port Natal and made one of its first priorities the founding of the Natal Agricultural and Horticultural Society in 1848. Presumably to explore the fertility of farming conditions the society energetically extended its activities into acquiring and planting land to form the Durban Botanical Gardens within the subsequent two years. The base for these ventures was a very modest Commercial Hotel in the ownership of Hugh McDonald, which had been extended from a thatched wattle-and-daub trading post to fulfil requirements for bed and board and to act as a centre for the community. Law courts were held on the verandah and occasional public dinners in the hotel. From McDonald's Commercial it became Winder's Masonic Hotel in 1857, leased by Hugh McDonald's widow and altered to accommodate family needs and a Masonic Lodge, no. 1040, approved after a visit to England by Farquand Salmon to gain authorization from the hierarchy. Freemasonry flourished, multiplying into nine lodges in 26 years.

A British infantry regiment, the 45th, spent several weeks in Durban in 1858 and enlivened social and sporting occasions, reinforced by their regimental band. An exotically turbaned entertainer called Ali-Ben-Sou-Alle performed very capably on the piano, clarinet and 'turkophone' in the Masonic Hall, though the spice of oriental mystery was dissipated with the discovery of the musician's real identity as Patrick Sullivan from Ireland. George Winder sold the hotel to William Wood, who had the honour of a brief visit from Prince Alfred, Queen Victoria's second son, in the eventful year of 1860, when the 'First Railway in South Africa' was opened by the Acting Lieutenant-Governor, Major Williamson. Cricket made its debut and the hotel's cuisine came up to scratch with the employment of a fulltime professional chef. The Royal Visit encompassed a strenuous programme for the nineteen-year-old prince, whose deportment and civility met with all-round approval. After a very strenuous day, coming to its climax when he opened the celebratory ball with the Mayoress, he was allowed his one night's rest in the hotel. His departure the next day started with a journey on the new railway, timed at 2 minutes and 40 seconds, to take him to the Point from where he was rowed out to *HMS Euryalus*. Thenceforward the Masonic Hotel rose to the rank of 'Wood's Royal Hotel (by Special Appointment)'. With status assured, sale and resale occurred, with Farquand Salmon becoming the owner of the hotel and adjoining property in 1861, then selling it to George Jessup and buying it back three years later after a long stay in England. The colony was suffering from the revival of the American cotton market at the end of the Civil War and Salmon paid only £1,400 for his Royal Hotel. Fortunes rose and fell but development of diamond diggings at Kimberley introduced capital into the area. Immigrant staff from India were also available to supply a more polished standard of hotel service. Cecil Rhodes was a visitor in 1870 on the way to join his brother on his cotton estate, and reported to his mother that he had

Stayed at the Royal Hotel in Durban and was as comfortable as if I had been at one of the best hotels in England, everything being done in fine style.[8]

Charles Smythe, who later became Natal's Prime Minister, stayed there in 1872 at the age of nineteen and reinforced Rhodes' comments. H. Rider Haggard also came as a young man in 1875, in the train of the new Lieutenant-Governor, Sir Henry Bulwer, and gathered experience for many of his novels. Anthony Trollope was the next writer to receive impressions of the place (in 1877), although he stayed at the Durban Club.

The next owner, Thomas Crane, commissioned the well-known local architect Philip Dudgeon to prepare a design for an entirely new building, but this came to nothing and in the depressed years after the Zulu War of 1879 the Royal was on the market once again. One of the casualties of the war had been Prince Louis Napoleon, only son of Napoleon III and Empress Eugénie of France, who as a volunteer had joined Lord Chelmsford's army and had visited the hotel shortly before being killed in an ambush while on a reconnaissance mission.

Frederick Leonard Jonsson then acquired the Royal from Crane for £6,600 in 1881 and entered into a long spell of undisturbed ownership. He was Swedish, with ten years of life in London behind him and already at the age of 24 a string of shops of all kinds in Durban was under his control. His English fiancée Anne Jacob had come out in 1862 to join him, and their long reign as hoteliers brought stability and better days to the hotel. Architecturally the Royal had grown by degrees and remained a conglomeration of unrelated buildings without unified character. Although socially it was regarded as the obvious stopping-place for important people, there were few ideas of grandeur except for the impeccable white uniforms of the Indian staff. Building alterations created the 'Ulundi Square' in the 1880s as a covered lounge with winter garden atmosphere, using a courtyard space between the various detached sections of the hotel. Philip Dudgeon's Natal Club building was incorporated into the hotel as the Grill Room but bore little relationship to the older core structure. Dudgeon was an accomplished designer with important buildings to his credit, including the Town Hall, a neo-classical competition winner not far from the Royal. Jonsson's next programme in 1894 consisted of a new stable yard, extra bedroom wings to increase the capacity well beyond that of the previous 50 rooms and a tall dining-room with kitchen below and gallery above. It appears that Dudgeon's practice had been taken over by William Street-Wilson, who was in charge of these works and whose drawings for them have been preserved.

Durban's Royal Hotel developed spasmodically from recognition as Winder's Masonic Hotel in 1857 to its title as Royal Hotel in the 1860s when, as indicated in the Natal Almanac, 1868, it could offer a good range of amenities at competitive prices.

By 1894 more ambitious building work was completed under the direction of William Street-Wilson, who appears to have taken over the leading architectural practice in Durban of Philip Dudgeon. The dining-room formed a part of the new accommodation and established a tradition of smart presentation and service.

The distinctive loggia, which survived until a substantial rebuilding in 1958, dated from 1908 and was designed by J. Wallace Paton.

A railway connection with Johannesburg stimulated travel to Durban and Mark Twain, who was on a lecture tour in 1896, wrote of the Royal in *More Tramps Abroad* as a

curious jumble of modern and ancient, city and village, primitiveness and the other thing. Electric bells, but they don't ring. If asked why they didn't the watchman in the office said he thought they must be out of order – he thought so because some of them rang, but some of them didn't.[9]

A mains power plant made the electrical supply more reliable in the following year. Jonsson died in 1899, five years after his wife, and after interim management by Horace Twine during the period of the Boer War, it was sold in 1902 to the Royal Hotel and Estate Company for £70,000. A royal visit by the Duke of York, later George V, had recently taken place and was good for the prestige and confidence of the new company. There was competition from the good-looking Marine Hotel designed by Ing and Jackson, but that was to be totally demolished in 1972.

The Royal was again extended in 1908 by a new Grill Room with bar, kitchens and the distinctive Loggia building on the Smith Street frontage, designed by J. Wallace Paton who had become Street-Wilson's partner. Paton was London-trained and it is not difficult to link the Loggia's semicircular entrance arch and side piers with the similar motif used on a much larger scale by Lewis Cubitt at King's Cross Station in London in the 1850s. This Loggia was to be a casualty of later redevelopment, but Wallace Paton's dining-room of 1917 managed to survive in recognizable form, maintaining a thread of architectural tradition between modest nineteenth-century origins and late twentieth-century high-rise.

Madeira

The island of Madeira in the Atlantic Ocean off Morocco was colonized by the Portuguese in the fifteenth century and is well positioned on the sea routes to Cape Town and South America. A Scottish cabin boy, William Reid, went ashore there in 1836 in search of better health than Scotland had provided for him and which he hoped to find in a warmer climate. At the age of fourteen, with £5 in his pocket and plentiful ambitious ideas, he started to make a new life. He did not live to see the full fruits of his years of work when his two sons styled themselves 'Hotel Keepers and Wine Merchants by Appointment to the Duke of Saxe-Coburg and Gotha (HRH Duke of Edinburgh)' in a local guide of about 1891 just after their new hotel was opened, but his far-

sightedness had made it possible.[10] Reid, like Johannes Baur in Zürich, had worked first as a baker's boy for a firm in Funchal, moving on into the Madeira wine trade. In just over ten years from his arrival he was the owner of a wine-exporting business and looking about for further opportunities. British medical wisdom in *The Lancet* and elsewhere was recommending Madeira's temperature range as ideal for sufferers from lung and other diseases, particularly consumption, as a relief from cold foggy winters. Reid saw the possibilities in the letting and management of *quintas* or small estates to such visitors and made it his next field of action. Through this activity he met and married in 1847 Margaret Dewey, the travelling companion of one of his first customers, Marchioness Camden, who had taken a two-year lease on one of the properties. He and his wife then embarked on hotelkeeping, buying the Quinta das Fontes for the purpose. The second son of Queen Victoria, Prince Alfred, whose visit to the Royal Hotel at Durban has already been described, also held the title of Duke of Edinburgh and, through his naval career which took him often to Madeira, he was acquainted with Reid and permitted use of his name. The property therefore became the Royal Edinburgh Hotel. Two other hotels, the Carmo and the Santa Clara, were added to his estates and he cast his eyes on the ideal promontory site high above the Atlantic belonging to an English physician, Michael Comport Grabham. An offer too good to be refused made Reid the owner of this *quinta* and he embarked on the realization of every hotelier's wish, to build his own ideal hotel. Architects were appointed, George Somers Clarke junior (1841–1926) and his partner John Thomas Micklethwaite (1843–1906), both of whom had been pupils of Sir George Gilbert Scott. Clarke was resident in Cairo, an antiquarian and ecclesiologist in addition to his architectural profession, which had won him a good reputation. The planning of Reid's Hotel was dated as 1887, a year before Reid died, and Clarke was also commended for the design of Shepheard's Hotel in Cairo, which was rebuilt in 1891.

The guiding grand hotel principles of comfort, cuisine and service were understood by both Reid and Clarke. Special aspects of Reid's vision related to his available site and to the climate, his determination being to form a pleasure garden exploiting to the full all sub-tropical fruit, flowers and vegetables and to form protected swimming pools in the volcanic rock of which the site consisted. Cultivation had to depend on a good soil, and this had to be brought in and spread by hand to achieve the required lushness and variety of planting. The mature garden covering ten acres contains an extensive plant collection, with specimens from Brazil, China, North and South America, Australia, Africa, Korea,

Funchal, Madeira, Reid's Hotel, 1891–2, designed by George Somers Clarke junior and John Thomas Micklethwaite on a dominant clifftop site above the Atlantic Ocean.

Reid's New Hotel as advertised in *A Guide to the Canary Islands and Madeira* by Ellebeck (1892).

Japan and Mexico as well as the more familiar but still spectacular Mediterranean flora. Bougainvillaea in numerous graduations of colour, bignonia, wistaria, solandra, strelitzia and passiflora mix with jacaranda protea and an unusual schottia, to give potential hours of pleasure to the occasional visitor or dedicated gardener.

The character of the Clarke and Micklethwaite building with gabled dormers and tiers of small balconies has an informality and domestic scale which may have influenced the Mount Nelson Hotel in Cape Town a few years later. Green painted window shutters against the background of cream walls, and the terracotta tiled roofs, gables and dormer windows were varied at the Mount Nelson as pink walls and buff-coloured roof, but each colour scheme expresses the greater freedom of taste and ease which accompanied much of colonial life. Before the Great War, Habsburgs found their way to Reid's, with Empress Elizabeth I of Austria recovering there from the loss of her son, Crown Prince Rudolf, in the shooting episode at Mayerling. In an apparent suicide pact he had, at the royal hunting lodge, shot his mistress Marie Vetsera and then himself. British celebrities relaxed at Reid's: Field-Marshal Earl Roberts in 1900, Sir Austen

Chamberlain, later Chancellor of the Exchequer, in 1903, the royal Duke of Connaught in 1905; the explorer Captain Robert Falcon Scott visited it from his ship *Discovery* on his way to the Antarctic. Shut for the duration of the Great War, Reid's reopened to a different world, and had to deal with royal exiles and refugees from the Austro-Hungarian melting pot. A lighter and improbable occurrence was during a long holiday and working visit spent at Reid's in 1924–5 by George Bernard Shaw, when he was photographed while learning to dance the tango under the eye of the hotel's dancing-master, Max Rinder. Shaw arrayed in swimming attire is scarcely less hilarious.[11]

The Reid brothers had made the mistake of venturing into the unknown scene of banking and commerce and by 1925 were in such difficulties financially that they had to sell the hotel to an English company, Reid's Palace Hotel (Madeira) Ltd. This proved no permanent solution and the company went into voluntary liquidation, the hotel continuing in business as the Island Hotel (Madeira) Ltd. This introduced the hotel to the Blandy family who, as wine, coal and shipping merchants, produced a further £35,000 to rescue it. Under new management major alterations were started, the east wing being completed just before the Second World War. Once again the hotel went into mothballs, opening appropriately for the next chapter of history in time to welcome Winston Churchill and his wife at the beginning of 1950 to a standing ovation. At a dinner in his honour, Churchill, having heard the history of a particular bottle of Madeira wine to be served, insisted on doing the honours, which he did with a napkin over his arm. Dating from 1792, it had been part of a pipe (105 gallons) taken to St Helena in 1815 with Napoleon into his exile. Because of the gastric trouble from which Napoleon suffered, the wine – never paid for – was returned unconsumed in 1820 after his death to the Madeira merchant who had supplied it. Charles Blandy had bought it in 1922, and Churchill poured it with the exclamation 'Ladies and gentlemen, here is a famous wine indeed, vintaged when Marie Antoinette was still alive'.[12]

Egypt and Israel

When thinking of hotels in the Middle East, Shepheard's, to the westerner, was for long synonymous with Cairo. It found a place in the itinerary of every traveller or journalist who could find even a remote reason to stop there. Soldiers frequented it too, mostly from the British Army, although there was a strong French interest during the construction of the Suez Canal by Ferdinand de Lesseps in the 1860s. From a

George Bernard Shaw practising the tango under the watchful eye of the dancing instructor, Max Rinder, 1924–5.

Breakfast overlooking the pool and ocean.

Cairo, Shepheard's Hotel, rebuilt in 1891 when George Somers
Clarke junior appears to have been responsible for some of this work.
Until Shepheard's was destroyed in 1952 it had a reputation second
to none among travellers to the Middle and Far East. This famous
Terrace was a central magnet for social life.

Cairo, Gezira Palace, 1865, by Alfred Chapon for the Khedive Ismail
(now the Cairo Marriott Hotel).

ABOVE & OPPOSITE Cairo, Heliopolis Palace, 1909, by E. Jaspar.
Visitors in the garden (*above*), and the main lounge (*right*).

start as Napoleon's headquarters in his Egyptian campaign
and existence as a harem under Turkish rule in 1841, buildings on Shepheard's site were converted for use as the Hôtel
des Anglais, well-run and with delightful gardens. French
and British were not the only visitors to take advantage of
its unusually agreeable standards and in 1860, already in the
hands of Samuel Shepheard, it became Shepheard's Hotel
and achieved legendary prestige. When officers of the British
10th Hussars were moved suddenly from Cairo to the war in
the Crimea, leaving many unpaid bills, Shepheard personally
pursued the debtors as far as Sebastopol, where he claimed
to have 'settled all within fifteen shillings'. He was soon to
retire but his name was perpetuated and the hotel's reputation was maintained under the Swiss management of
Charles Baehler, who had risen from errand boy to hotelier,

an ambitious achievement that is now familiar to readers
of this book. The first rebuilding had taken place in 1891,
attributed to Charles Somers Clarke junior, but a mid-
century stucco façade garnished with Italianate details had
been applied before then. The 1891 cast-iron verandah gave
excellent views from its terrace over the passing scene of
Cairo's street life, and rooms, even in the extended building,
were hard to come by in the winter season. Further trans-
formations took place in 1899, 1904, 1909 and 1927, giving
an indication of its ever-growing popularity. Travel to and
from the East meant that Cairo – and Shepheard's – served
as an ideal staging-post.

The hotel provided the welcome luxuries of electric lighting from its own generator, steam laundry facilities and
access to French cuisine, all no doubt appreciated most by
expatriots returning from India and beyond in the 1890s.
Local colour was literally on the doorstep, from where
donkeys could be hired for exploration of the sights, bazaars

Cairo's Gezira Palace started life as royal guest house for the Empress Eugénie among others, before conversion in 1894 into a luxury hotel. Embedded now between two modern tower blocks, the whole (now the Cairo Marriott Hotel) encloses a swimming pool with formal terraces and looks outwards towards the Nile.

ABOVE Cairo, Heliopolis Palace, 1909, by E. Jaspar, built for the Belgian Baron Empain's garden city development.

Modern versions of the traditional style have been maintained.

and teeming street life. Shops and a post office were housed within the hotel and a cool refuge might be found under the trees and palms of the large garden. The explorer H. M. Stanley, Lord Kitchener and T. E. Lawrence in their turn frequented Shepheard's, Lawrence during the Great War when it was used as British headquarters in the Near East. Shepheard's then had 550 rooms and 270 bathrooms, and the tale was that after the evacuation of the Dardanelles by the British forces, each of 200 generals who descended on the hotel claimed a private bathroom to himself. Mark Twain, C. G. Leland and Ralph Waldo Emerson all stayed there while exploring the antiquities. Next door to Shepheard's was the Hotel Continental, founded in 1860, rebuilt in 1880 as the Grand Continental and favoured by French visitors. Under the ownership of George Nungovich it was again rebuilt and became the Continental Savoy, opening with great celebrations with Auguste Wild as manager in 1898. At an earlier date the Semiramis (1886) had come nearer to competing with Shepheard's but never achieved the same *cachet*, although it acquired a reputation for style, with a European-style night club on the roof, good cuisine and a location near the British Embassy.

Before looking further into the development of Cairo's hotels we should consider the historically important inauguration of the Suez Canal, which revolutionized contacts between East and West by shortening dramatically the major line of communication. Such a ceremony was planned to gain maximum attention for the sponsors of the Canal and for the prestige of Egypt. Accordingly the Khedive Ismail established Mena House as a rest house within sight of the Great Pyramid of Cheops for his important guests. All visitors considered an inspection of the pyramids obligatory, and on this occasion no expense was spared to smooth their path. Empress Eugénie was his guest of honour, and for her overnight stop and entertainment at the pyramids a new road was built to cover the eight miles from the centre of Cairo and her own chalet was specially constructed. For the main part of her stay in Cairo itself, the Khedive had built another more grand royal guest house, the Gezira Palace of 1865 (now the Cairo Marriott Hotel) attributed to the French architect Alfred Chapon, who worked for the Compagnie de Suez. In 1869 Eugénie, an inveterate traveller, performed the opening ceremony for the magnificent work of engineering that Ferdinand de Lesseps had achieved. As an appropriate compliment the Khedive had provided apartments emulating those of her own in the Tuileries in Paris. The remainder of the Gezira Palace building owed more to the Alhambra in Granada, especially after its final transformation in 1894 from use for official hospitality to the demands of hotel

Luxor, Winter Palace Hotel, *c.* 1910, which after a period of decline has recently been revived successfully without drastic alterations.

Aswan, Old Cataract Hotel, 1899. Its design is credited to 'an English architect long resident in Egypt', and stylistic clues perhaps point to Somers Clarke.

guests. As a matter of record, a performance of Verdi's *Aïda* was not given when the Suez Canal was opened, as commonly stated, its first performance not being until 24 December 1871 in the Cairo Opera House.

The Gezira Palace was acquired as a hotel by the new 'Grands-Hotels' offshoot of the Compagnie International des Wagons-Lits in an attempt to integrate luxurious travel in their trains with hotel accommodation of equivalent comfort at strategic points on their routes. Winter in Cairo presented an exotic alternative to winter on the Côte d'Azur, and from 1894 to 1914 tourist trade in Egypt expanded and supported competing hotels of international standard. The

Gezira Palace vied with Shepheard's, poaching their manager Luigi Steinscheider in doing so. Georges Nagelmackers, the Belgian director of the Wagons-Lits and pioneer of European sleeping cars in the wake of George Pullman's American innovations of 1859, donated several thousand pounds from his company towards the staging of a grand gala at the Gezira Palace in 1896. Egyptian pageantry was again on display, centred on Rameses the First making a ceremonial entry into Thebes surrounded by his pharaonic soldiers, musicians and camels. The Comité des Fêtes organized it for the benefit of Cairo but the Wagons-Lits and the Gezira Palace gained much of the publicity. At different times the hotel acquired the names Ismail Palace and Omar Khayyám and its latest title is the Cairo Marriott Hotel. Nagelmackers bought out Shepheard's but the Wagons-Lits excursion into the hotel business was not pursued and came to an end in 1914. Shepheard's had suffered some fire damage just before the Suez Canal opening and had been immediately rebuilt in time for that great occasion, acquiring a new courtyard and two small but authentic antique sphinxes to guard the entrance. Shepheard's in its historic and much-loved incarnation ceased to exist when destroyed by fire in 1952, victim of an anti-British riot and flimsy building construction. The modern replacement in no way evokes the old extraterritorial Britishness, which had come to the end of its days.

A later entrant among Cairo hotels was the Heliopolis Palace (1909) designed by E. Jaspar for the northeast outskirts as an important feature in a garden city development by the Belgian Baron Empain in a style that adapted traditional *mauresque* vocabulary within a European symmetrical framework. Pierre Loti reacted harshly when writing in 1908 before it opened:

What is all this? What have we come to? You would think you were in Nice or on the Riviera, or Interlaken, or any one of those exuberant cities where bad taste comes from the whole world to frolic during what are supposed to be the elegant months … Everywhere blinding electricity; monstrous hotels showing off the false luxury of their would-be alluring façades; along the streets everything is fake, coats of whitewash over clay walls; a jumble of styles, the rococo, the romanesque, the gothic, *art nouveau*, the pharaonic and, above all, the pretentious and ludicrous.[13]

Martin Meade, writing in the 1980s, refers to the Heliopolis Palace interiors, viewed over the mellowing of three-quarters of a century, as 'a most effective and well adapted revival of the late Mamelouk and Ottoman styles of architecture in Cairo'.[14]

The history of the Mena House at Giza, after its spell as a royal guesthouse, began with its purchase by a well-to-do English couple, Hugh and Ethel Locke-King, in the late 1880s. It had passed through the hands of other English admirers of Egypt, Frederick Head and his wife, who had called it Mena after the first of the pharaohs of Upper and Lower Egypt as listed on the tablet of Abydos. Under their ownership as a private house it had been extended, and the Locke-Kings could visualize it as a luxurious hotel. They made further additions and began to collect excellent antique furniture and fittings, obtaining fine examples of *mashrabia* carved lattice work which were quite easily obtained, only being appreciated then by discriminating collectors. They bought furniture inlaid with ivory and mother-of-pearl, medieval metalwork, carved doors and old floor tiles in blues and greens to provide an ambience of high artistic quality. Relying mainly on their own taste, the Locke-Kings created a dining-room in the form of a mosque, domed and arched and decorated with many of their acquisitions. Comfort was well-considered and large fireplaces, very unusual in Egypt, gave warmth against night-time desert cold. The sun terraces they arranged outside most of the bedrooms were another innovation. With this combination of an English country house and an oriental atmosphere they made a name for their 'First Class Family Hotel at the foot of the Pyramids'.

Their ideas of hospitality did not always satisfy adequate business practice, although their Polish friend, Baron de Rodakowsky, improved matters when engaged as manager. He initiated the building, with the Swiss architect Brugger, of the 'Villa', the stables and a swimming pool, which became well-known as one of the earliest at a hotel. As the Locke-Kings withdrew to pursue their interests in England – Shire horsebreeding and building the Brooklands race track in Surrey for motor-racing – the Mena House was left under the direction of the Baron until he too left for England. Hugh Locke-King died in 1900 and Ethel granted a lease to Emil Wickel and his colleague Schick. A subsequent sale to George Nungovich of the Egyptian Hotels Company grouped most of the important Cairo hotels under the same management. The appointment of Auguste Wild, previously manager for the Krachts at the Baur au Lac in Zürich, to the group's Savoy Hotel maintained a Swiss connection and high standards of *hôtellerie*. Wild's organizing ability and imaginative skill in presenting great occasions followed the pattern of César Ritz's example.

During the Great War Auguste Wild Bey, unusually honoured as 'Bey' by the Khedive and thenceforward known as Wild Bey, was placed in charge of turning several Cairo hotels into hospitals, many of whose first patients were sick and wounded soldiers from Gallipoli. Mena House operated

Giza's Mena House (Oberoi) Hotel near Cairo was developed as a hotel in the 1880s by Hugh and Ethel Locke-King, who incorporated antique furniture and *mashrabia* lattice work in the interiors. The exterior balconies followed similar Arabic patterns on the old bedroom wing.

as one of these. The inter-war years were a period of fame and fulfilment, with great and royal names constantly in the visitors' book. Further expansion took place, a golf course appeared and the manager, Oscar Geyer, when he took charge revolutionized the garden to include a small poultry flock for supplying fresh eggs. A later manager, Fred Herrling, re-designed the golf course in 1932 and planted 5,000 eucalyptus saplings, which grew into a shade-giving minor forest. Numerous anecdotes originated in the hotel where every visitor seemed to have a good time until the Second World War began. Egypt was strategically critical, and even after the hard-fought Desert War was over it remained at the centre of affairs. The Mena House was chosen as the venue for a 'Big Three' conference of Churchill, Roosevelt and Chiang Kai-Shek in 1943. Herrling and his staff, augmented by a company of Scottish soldiers, had only three days to clear the hotel and set up a fully equipped and protected centre for the crucial talks. Political uncertainties followed in the decades after the War without great changes taking place in the Mena House. The tendency for international groupings to acquire or build chains of hotels situated in all areas of tourist interest did increase greatly as a result of air travel,

and new money for the Mena House came from one such chain, the Oberoi Group. In the later 1970s the Group became its owners with the fortunate result that their policy of conservation in historic hotels has preserved much of the spirit and many of the unique interiors put together by the Locke-Kings.

Experiencing many of Egypt's antiquities involved long journeys up the Nile, and in the nineteenth century a few stopping places were desirable in addition to the steamboats that were the main form of travel for tourists. Thomas Cook & Son were granted a monopoly of passenger steamers on the Nile by the Egyptian government in 1880 and proceeded to offer an attractive selection of itineraries. Egyptology was an increasingly popular subject in the last decades of the century, and the climate that took Locke-King to Giza primarily for health reasons drew many more invalids and travellers to Upper Egypt and its monuments. The Thomas Cook vessels which plied up the river as far as Aswan were effectively self-contained mobile hotels equipped to a good standard of comfort and satisfying the expectations of the majority of tourists. A need still existed for more permanent provision of accommodation for the longer-stay winter

Effective Moorish décor of the 1920s houses
the restaurant at Aswan's Cataract Hotel in a
spacious pavilion. At the same period the Art
Deco style was used elsewhere in the hotel.

RIGHT & OPPOSITE Jerusalem, the King
David Hotel, 1931 was the work of Emile
Vogt of Lucerne, built as a result of widespread, chiefly Jewish, sponsorship from
Egypt, Britain and America. Rectangular
with plain projecting pavilions at each end,
the design relies much on the warm quality
of local stone for effect.

ABOVE & OVERLEAF Marrakesh, Morocco, Hotel La Mamounia, 1925, by Henri Prost and A. Marchiso favoured Art Deco within a severe modernist exterior, but has in part looked back to the Alhambra-inspired school for the restaurant and patio.

The King David's Art Deco style gave life to the interior, as is seen particularly in the lobby.

visitors and those who preferred rail travel and a base on dry land.

Luxor presented an obvious stopping place and site for a new hotel. This materialized in 1877 in the form of the original Luxor Hotel, where trade was stimulated by Thomas Cook's coupon system, whereby travellers using them at approved destinations would 'save the invariably unpleasant business of discussing prices with hotels in the heyday of their season'. Together with a new hotel at Aswan, the Luxor Hotel was 'under the management of Mr Pagnon and the subject of constant supervision and improvement'.[15] Furthermore:

For the general comfort of visitors to Luxor, especially of ladies, Mr Pagnon has appointed Miss Coxon, who has already spent many winters there, to the position of superintendent of the household, assisted by competent English nurses.[16]

The architecture of the hotel was semi-vernacular in style for the ground floor, with upper floors reverting to conventional European design. Demand soon led to the addition of many more rooms and later Moorish arcading probably dates from *c.* 1900. The Winter Palace in Luxor dates from ten years later, opened in 1887 but rebuilt before 1910 with a pleasing neo-Renaissance horseshoe staircase sweeping up to the raised entrance floor in grand style from garden level. The view across the Nile to the Valley of the Kings, and the nearby Temple of Luxor, make a fine, evocative introduction to the scale on which ancient Egypt was built, but a short journey away at Karnak, the size of temple columns 78 feet high is nearly double the size at Luxor.

Temples further up the Nile at Kom Ombo, Philae and Abu Simbel could be reached from Aswan, where a Grand Hotel was, during the 1890s, proving inadequate. Thomas Cook in 1899 therefore 'arranged for the erection of a large new establishment to be called "The Cataract Hotel"'. It had been designed

by an English architect long resident in Egypt, who knows the style of building affording the greatest comfort, and, so far as the expenditure of money and the taking of the best advice go, nothing has been spared on our [Cook's] part to ensure 'The Cataract Hotel' being made a high class house.[17]

Descriptions of the fine, dry but dust-free site, the sanitary arrangements (submitted for Government approval), the filtered water supply, electricity, and English housekeeper, doctor and clergyman – all were intended to encourage the timid. By this time Pagnon was in charge as lessee of two Luxor and two Aswan hotels and F. H. Cook, son of Thomas, personally managed the whole of their 1899–1900 season. In the 1920s the Art Deco style was introduced into the

Cataract and a new dining-room sited in a mosque-like garden pavilion. An isolated Art Deco example also appeared in Morocco – the Hotel la Mamounia of 1925 by Henri Prost and A. Marchiso.

The small country of Palestine, lying close to Egypt at the eastern end of the Mediterranean had, for much of recorded history, been troubled by religious dissent, with Jerusalem as its point of focus. Half a century ago the King David Hotel there, from being simply the only modern hotel in Jerusalem, hit the headlines when Irgun Zionists blew up its southwest wing killing 41 Arabs, 28 Britons, 17 Jews and 5 others in violent pursuit of an independent Jewish state of Israel. Palestine was then ruled under British Mandate, which had a further uncomfortable two years to run, until May 1948. Subsequent history is outside our present scope but the genesis of the hotel was related quite closely to Shepheard's and other hotels in Egypt. The influential Egyptian Jewish family, the Mosseris, had banking interests in Cairo and Alexandria that controlled the Egyptian Hotels Ltd company. In addition to Shepheard's, the Continental Savoy in Cairo and the Mena House at Giza belonged to the group, and the idea of a first-class Jewish hotel in Jerusalem took shape as the post-Great War proposals for a Jewish state followed on the Palestine Mandate after the Balfour Declaration of 1917. Infrastructure was badly needed to compensate for neglect under the Ottoman empire and to support the new administration. Once more, political and social changes generated a grand hotel project. Established names were obtained and Palestine Hotels Ltd was registered in Jerusalem in 1929. Senator and Minister of Finance Joseph Cattawi Bey, Sir Victor Harari Pasha and his son Colonel Ralph Harari and Barons Felix and Alfred Manasca of Alexandria were all registered shareholders. American interest took the form of the Palestine Economic Corporation of New York, founded by Judge Brandeis, Felix Warburg and similar sympathizers. Baron Edmond de Rothschild used the Palestine Jewish Colonization Association to purchase shares, and Lord Melchett with Baron Edmond's son James were other contributors who helped to extend the list until enough capital was raised.

Few sites can have had a higher historical pedigree than the four and a half acres (18 dunans) purchased from the Greek Orthodox Church for the new hotel. The frontage was on Julian's Way, taking its name from the anti-Christian pro-pagan Roman Emperor of the fourth century. At the back of the site to the east and only 500 metres away, the Old City walls rose above the small valley of Ben-Hinnon, from where Titus launched an assault on the walls in AD 70.

This first modern hotel in Palestine was built very much

in the accepted European tradition, its only predecessor of status in Jerusalem being the Grand New Hotel of the 1890s near the Jaffa Gate, used by Thomas Cook. The Swiss architect from Lucerne, Emil Vogt, whose earlier work has already been noted, prepared the design. A plain rectangular exterior having a central entrance and two pavilioned wings bears very little ornament and derives its character and presence from the golden Jerusalem sandstone, rusticated in courses to give a warm textured effect. The name of King David refers back 3,000 years into history, and the interior of the six-storey hotel with 200 bedrooms and 60 bathrooms drew on ancient cultures of the Middle East, using Egyptian, Assyrian, Hittite, Phoenician and Greek-Syrian motifs. Current Hebrew emblems of David and Solomon and ever-popular vine or pomegranate patterns expressed continuity, but plasterwork, lighting fittings, metalwork, textiles and furnishings took on the Art Deco language of the time with great vigour. The setting-up of the hotel was entrusted to Charles Baehler, the experienced Swiss manager of Shepheard's, and the King David provided an excellent example of stylish presentation extending also to staff uniforms – white *galabiyas* and gloves, with red sashes and fezzes for waiters; white with dark-green and gold-braided jackets and waistcoats for pages. Fresh food came from Cairo by overnight train, no doubt a benefit of the business relationship with Cairo hotels and their purchasing contracts. Fruit, vegetables, milk and eggs, meat, poultry and fish arrived each

day for the largely Italian kitchen staff to prepare for varying dietary demands, but after the opening in January 1931 trade was slow and for the summer months the hotel closed down entirely.

The economic depression persisted and tensions between Jew and Arab deterred tourism. The first year the hotel went into profit was 1933 and this was followed by its increased use as a base for Governmental activities. These were, under the Mandate, in British hands, but interest extended internationally with much coverage by foreign press. The Peel Royal Commission on Palestine moved in during November 1936, and the British Army used the top floor as emergency headquarters. The Palestine Administration leased the upper floors of the south wing, where it set up its head office. With much of the building acting as the seat of Government, there was still room for other notabilities. The names of three ex-kings appear in the visitors' lists – Alfonso XIII of Spain, Haile Selassie of Abyssinia and, resident during the Second World War, George II of Greece. Lords Allenby and Samuel and Winston Churchill, all involved in the creation of Palestine, made visits in the 1930s and there were many Arabs and Muslims, including members of the Egyptian and Iranian royal families.

The survival of the King David and its reopening in 1948, restored into the hands of Palestine Hotels Ltd, make another story of continued life at the extreme edge of the new Israeli state.

7.

JOURNEYS TO THE EAST

India and Sri Lanka

The growth of British interests in India after the disintegration of the Moghul Empire early in the eighteenth century resulted in the importation of Western styles of building to meet the requirements of the British Raj. When military and administrative needs had been satisfied, provision of more accommodation for commerce and its management followed. Calcutta in the north was an obvious centre for new development and by the beginning of the nineteenth century Chowringhee Road, which bordered the open space behind Fort William, was described as an 'entire village of palaces'. The palaces were mostly built as two- or three-storey square and rectangular blocks of Italianate design with pedimented windows and balustraded roof parapets. Their frontages were linked by colonnades, arcades or substantial railings and gateways, and the view across the Esplanade open space took in Government House to the right and the Hooghly river ahead to the west. The site of one of these mansions had been won in a lottery by Colonel Grand, who proceeded to build himself a Sussex-inspired version of the English country house.

By the time Mrs Annie Monk arrived to seek her fortune in Calcutta in the 1870s the property, no. 13 Chowringhee, which she acquired for use as a boarding-house, was well past its best days and the interior was described as very ill-kempt with cracked crockery and glass, cobwebs everywhere and an almost non-existent routine of cleaning. Wine glasses had to be stood upside down as their stems were broken. Nevertheless, her establishment seemed to succeed and Mrs Monk took up four other properties, to include no. 17, before, to-

wards the end of the century, she returned with her profits to retirement in Ireland. No. 16 was in use as the Theatre Royal and in 1894 a young Armenian with training as a jeweller made it his first acquisition of many in what was to become a property empire. He was Arathoon Stephen (1861–1927), and he continued to maintain the theatre and rent it out. Presumably it was profitable, though it had been structurally insecure enough for a horse on one occasion to crash through the decaying stage. No tears were shed when it burned down in 1911 except by the Humphrey-Bishop touring dramatic company, who were then playing in the theatre and lost all their uninsured costumes, scenery and scripts. To Stephen it gave opportunity for a fresh beginning towards realizing his hotel ambitions, which would take him into a different world. He bought all the Monk estate and gradually redeveloped the site as his carefully guarded finances allowed.

There were much older hotels in Calcutta, for example Spence's Hotel owned by John Spence and built before 1830, and the Great Eastern Hotel with 100 rooms, built in 1841 by David Wilson, claiming to be the oldest in the British Empire and referred to by Rudyard Kipling who had stayed there in the 1890s as 'refreshing and humming with polyglot life'. Stephen's Grand had higher aspirations and was designed on a fourteen-acre site around a great garden courtyard to take advantage of air currents without assistance from punkah-wallahs. It may have been designed by Stephen Wilkinson, an English architect who later was responsible for the Mount Everest Hotel, Darjeeling, for Arathoon Stephen, although the respective styles are quite different. The Calcutta Grand fits into the neo-classical pattern with baroque touches – rusticated quoins and pediments broken at lintel level to accommodate heavy keystones in a manner exploited a little earlier in London when Regent Street and Oxford Circus were redeveloped. Sections of three-storey building went up along the Chowringhee frontage and by 1918 a further storey was added with heavily corbelled bal-

OPPOSITE Surabaya, Indonesia, Hotel Majapahit, 1910. Opened in 1910, this was one of a number of ventures by the Armenian Sarkies brothers, leading hoteliers in South-East Asia.

cony and a wide front verandah at pavement level, which gave shade for the ground-floor shops. It was a popular viewing platform for the hotel users on the first floor despite reservations about its stability voiced by the Calcutta Corporation's Chief Engineer, W. B. MacCabe.

One of the many extravagant entertainments that took place under Stephen's régime was the New Year party, with expensive gifts of perfume, porcelain, silver and even gold as part of the festive table settings. Iced champagne on the tables added to the wildness of pursuit when twelve piglets were released into the ballroom to be caught and kept by each successful chaser as the old year ran out. So the Grand Hotel went on into the 1930s, providing food, drink and dancing as required by the frequenters of the Empire Theatre, one of Stephen's other properties and so near that interval drinks could be served from the Grand's bar. Arathoon Martin, another member of the family, managed another nearby theatre, the Globe, where boxing and wrestling supplied the entertainment, helping to maintain the family's fortunes. Electricity was installed in the Grand Hotel in 1914 – fifteen years after its first use in Calcutta. No money-saving or profit-making ideas were neglected in managing the hotel without sacrificing its image, but with the death of its creator and moving spirit in 1927, its best days seemed over. A few years later typhoid and enteric fever struck, resulting in the loss of six lives and severe illness among the family and household. The hotel drainage system was suspect and in 1937 the gates were closed and the 500 rooms left empty.

At such a stage in the life of an ageing grand hotel the future was extremely dubious. Land in the city centre had increased enormously in value and rival entrepreneurs would be weighing up the prospects. Demolition and complete redevelopment as offices would be the most likely outcome in this situation, although occasionally civic authorities might step in with prestigious municipal building projects. The remaining alternative might be the appearance at the right moment of a devotee of luxury hotels having the imagination to transform a neglected shell into a new sparkling palace, and the confidence in being able to raise the money to do so. Such a person was Mohan Singh Oberoi, already risen from his first job in Simla as a clerk at the Cecil Hotel to the rank of manager, then lessee of the Carlton Hotel, later renamed Clarke's, also in Simla. By chance he had heard of the state of the Grand in Calcutta and was able to negotiate a lease with the Mercantile Bank, which was acting as liquidator to the estate of Arathoon Stephen. This was in 1938 when the asking price was 10,000 rupees per month, but the final rate was modified in Oberoi's favour. The bank insisted on a European manager as a condition. Oberoi offered this post

to D. W. Grove, who had given him his first job in 1922. With Grove as manager and managing director and himself as chairman, Oberoi pursued a policy of thorough renewal of plumbing and drainage and a recall of all the experienced staff he could find after their enforced year of absence.

The Second World War affected the Far East after Japan's attack on Pearl Harbour and the Grand was requisitioned for army use, accommodating up to 4,000 soldiers, mainly British and American. Grove and Oberoi continued with the practical management while the war lasted, at the same time as Oberoi was paying off his debts and quietly acquiring the lowly-priced shares of the Associated Hotels of India Company. Re-emergence of the Grand, which he was able to buy in 1943, and the steady growth of the Oberoi group are separate stories but fortunately embody a sympathetic approach in conservation and restoration work, as demonstrated in the Windsor Hotel, Melbourne.

Bombay in the 1860s entered a boom period, benefiting from the blockading of cotton exports from the Southern States during the American Civil War and even more vitally from the opening of the Suez Canal. Both of these were major factors in the expansion of Bombay as a port and a centre of commerce and industry. Hotels to provide comfortable accommodation for the influx of European entrepreneurs and administrators were scarce and much needed. As in the case of South Africa, travellers had become familiar with the standards of life on board the well-run steamships and demanded comparable service. Portuguese, Dutch and French had been early adventurers in India, but the impetus of Victorian British Empire-building had the most widespread effect on urban development.

Architectural styles here as in Calcutta followed colonialism from Europe and were used at the close of the eighteenth century as a pattern for administrative buildings and a symbol of the Raj. This influence continued through the nineteenth century, starting with a classicism which merged gradually into neo-classicism and historicism, without the clear definitions made in Europe by these various movements. Climatic conditions dictated some modifications to deal with great heat and heavy rains but the ancient classical forms still proved serviceable. Covered colonnades and verandahs where air could circulate were features of most new buildings, particularly as an amenity in hotels that served oriental tourism as well as trade. Among the first of these to appear at the beginning of the 1860s was the Great Western in Apollo Street, with a Doric *porte-cochère* at the centre of the twelve-bay street façade. Young army officers or civilian staff working for the East India Company found the Great Western a great improvement on the 'chummeries' or clubs

Grand Hotel, Chowringhee Road, Calcutta.

Calcutta, Grand Hotel, rebuilt on the larger scale shown above under the régime of Arathoon Stephen, after the first hotel burned down in 1911. Its architect is unknown, but the Edwardian-style pediments might provide clues.

Bombay, Taj Mahal Hotel, 1903. Sitaram Khanderao Vaidya and
W. Chambers, architects, successively contributed to the grand
design for the developer Jamshetji Nusserwanji Tata. As a statement
of grandeur in the hotel world it is an obvious leader.

BELOW The aerial view, with the later Gateway of India adding
monumentality, situates it firmly on the original fine site that in
the intervening years has disappeared under the mass of high-rise
buildings.

Fluted Corinthian columns lend dignity to a present-day conference setting.

The founder, J. N. Tata, whose contribution to all aspects of Bombay life cannot be overrated.

An open staircase on ornamental corbelling looks effective, but complicates fire precautions.

in the form of communal bungalows that had previously housed and catered for them. A larger hotel based more on American models was Watson's (1867) on Esplanade Road, the first iron-frame building in Bombay, and it established the screened verandah feature used later at the Bycullah Hotel (1871) and at Green's Hotel (1890), originally mansion flats. Watson's, no longer a hotel, embodied Victorian enthusiasm for ironwork after the French colonial style but may also have been influenced by local Gujarati houses with tiered wooden balconies. A contemporary traveller labelled it 'something like a huge bird-cage'.[1] High Victorian taste was manifested by the Majestic Hotel of the 1890s as an Indo-Saracenic successor to some popular essays in Venetian neo-Gothic. The architect was W. A. Chambers from an English practice working in Bombay.

The most ambitious and dramatic Bombay hotel is without doubt the Taj Mahal, opening on 16 December 1903 and from its inception assuming international stature. It was the achievement of Jamshetji Nusserwanji Tata (1839–1904), pioneer industrialist and philanthropist of Parsi family. It is reported that Tata had been, by the then prevailing custom, denied access to another of Bombay's better hotels used by the British Raj, but whether this motivated the project or not, the Taj has had the reputation of being open to all and being a welcome meeting place between differing cultures. It occupies a fine site on the Apollo Bunder looking over the harbour and well fits the description 'palace hotel'. The six-storey building is dominated by a central dome and cupola, two symmetrical wings terminating in cylindrical corner turrets topped by smaller onion domes. Chambers and Sitaram Khanderao Vaidya were the architects and produced a design on the grand scale incorporating the Indo-Saracenic elements seen in the Majestic, with added Victorian Gothic and Romanesque detail plus the Edwardian touches of repeated small gables at main roof level and on the three-storey bay window projections. Such eclectic details are well brought together within the strong compositional scheme. Monotony, a constant trap for the designer of hotels, has been avoided and the red and white brick and stone is well secured visually under the slightly darker red of the differing roof shapes. Both architects had worked with F. W. Stevens, whose contribution towards the building of Bombay in the nineteenth century was unequalled. One of his major works, the Victoria Terminus (1888), is likely to have influenced the Taj design. The original hotel drawings were signed by D. N. Mirza and Sitaram Khanderao Vaidya, but Vaidya died in 1900 and it was then that Chambers was appointed by Tata as consultant architect.

Original access to the hotel was from Esplanade Road, through a well-planted garden between the side wings which gave some screening and a pleasant outlook for the overlooking rooms. More dramatic views were available from the windows facing the harbour and these also enjoyed light western airs to temper the heat. The 'Gateway of India' designed by George Wittet in 1924 with a blend of Arc de Triomphe and Brighton Pavilion styles was built to commemorate the visit to India by George V and Queen Mary in 1911 and now forms a part of this memorable view. Other alterations, in addition to the Taj tower block of the late twentieth century, were a change of the main entrance location from the rear courtyard to the sea-front in disregard of the growing traffic problem there, and consequent construction of a swimming pool in place of the old carriage drive entrance. This reversal implements the previous myth that the Taj had been built the wrong way round in the first instance, it being also incorrectly said to have therefore caused the architect's suicide.

Tata's vision had incorporated all innovations and conveniences available without regard to cost, which mounted to £500,000. The hotel contained its own steam laundry, aerated bottling plant, electroplating plant and a burnishing machine for table silver, a mechanical dishwasher, telegraph service, post office, Turkish baths, electric lighting and lifts. Both a chemist and resident doctor were available. Unfortunately Tata did not live to see the full grandeur his imagination had conceived but there is no question of his contribution to the history of the grand or palace hotel type and to the stature of Bombay as a city. He has had in both a fine memorial.

The Galle Face Hotel in Colombo, Sri Lanka, must receive mention, being opened in 1864 in a neo-classical bungalow of earlier date, near the old race-course and overlooking the Indian Ocean. As tourism increased in the region, other hotels, the Bristol and the Grand Continental, competed and the Galle Face was largely rebuilt in the 1890s. Claims to fame have been that it was one of the British Empire's most fashionable resorts and that it was the first overseas hotel to be supplied with *Pimms*. The style remains stuccoed neo-classical with major work by Thomas Edward Collcutt (1840–1924) carried out in 1912 at a time when he was doing work for the P. & O. company and also for the Reina Cristina Hotel, Algeciras. Grand interiors survive, the chief being a large two-storey ballroom, arcaded and pilastered and where recent times have seen some grand parties.

South-East Asia

Until 1855 when King Mongut (Rama IV) opened the King-dom of Siam to the rest of the world, Siam had, like much of the Far East, secluded itself from distrusted and therefore potentially disruptive influences. The British were the first to arrive in the Chao Phrya River at Bangkok and to make trade and cultural contacts. An American missionary, a Dr Bradley, recorded the burning down of 'The Oriental' in 1865. Whether this was an old royal palace that the King had designated for housing foreigners is not at all certain but the recognized date for the founding of the hotel of that name is 1876, when two Danish sea-captains, Jarck and Salje, built modest accommodation near the French embassy. It was bought by H. N. Andersen, another seafarer, who commis-sioned a new building in Colonial and Italianate style and opened it in 1887 for tourists as well as traders. With terrace and lawns by the riverside and a relatively simple but well-proportioned exterior it recalled the smaller Renaissance towns of northern Italy and was said to have been the work of Italian architects. Although spiced with Oriental fretwork and flora, it had at the same time a familiarity that Westerners found reassuring. This piquant atmosphere, especially when blended with the smiling and efficient service which so frequently met the traveller, encouraged return visits and helped to build a reputation as one of the handful of out-standing luxury hotels of South-East Asia. Its nineteenth-century building survives in the form of the 'Authors' Residence' at the core of the grand building complex, which won for The Oriental in no less than ten successive recent years the title 'Finest Hotel in the World', awarded by the *Institutional Investor* magazine, with a further dozen awards ranging from sponsors World Travel to Condé Nast, in 1994 and 1995.

Andersen was able to find from the outset a recipe for attracting not only Westerners with the novelty of Eastern food, service and culture but in reverse provided a sophisti-cated degree of luxury for wealthy Siamese, made possible by more advanced technology. King Chulalongkorn (Rama V) was an experienced world traveller who visited the hotel in 1890 and set on it a valuable seal of approval. His own over-seas travels, made with a retinue of considerable size, took him in 1897 to, among other hotels, the Bernerhof in the Swiss capital, a favourite hotel for oriental rulers, and then to the Victoria-Jungfrau, Interlaken, from where he tried a little mountain-climbing at Kleine Scheidegg.[2]

What was to become a literary connection with the Oriental was initiated by Joseph Conrad when the 'Old Ori-ental' was still in existence as a clubroom close to Andersen's

Colombo, Sri Lanka, Galle Face Hotel, founded 1864, was rebuilt in the 1890s and then again when T. E. Collcutt worked on the design in 1912.

Bangkok, Thailand, the Oriental Hotel of 1876, rebuilt in 1887, has attracted a succession of authors in search of local colour and backgrounds.

Some of this still lingers in the old buildings where suites are named after Conrad, Maugham, Michener, Coward and others, but the bulk of the accommodation is now in the new multi-storey building.

Surabaya, Indonesia, Hotel Majapahit, 1910 by architect J. Afprey. When opened by Eugène-Lucas Sarkies under Dutch rule it bore the name Oranje Hotel, and indicated in its curved gables a reference to Netherlands style. Courtyard gardens give welcome shade and privacy.

Penang, Malaysia, the E. & O. Hotel amalgamated the Eastern Hotel (1884) with the Oriental (1885). Both these hotels became Sarkies enterprises, and while the elder brothers occupied themselves with Raffles Hotel, Arshak, the youngest, continued to manage the E. & O. with its colonial style and waterfront site.

Moulded plasterwork and mahogany fittings for a sumptuous bathroom.

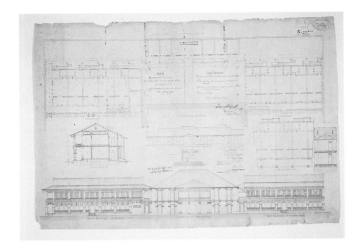

Singapore, Raffles Hotel. In 1887 it was bought by the Sarkies brothers and given the historic name of the founder of Singapore. In 1889 two new wings were built, followed in 1894 by a Palm Court wing and in 1899 the main building was conceived by R. A. J. Bidwell of the established architectural firm of Swan & Maclaren. The different phases of the building programme amalgamated well into a colonial style that has become Raffles' hallmark.

The entrance to the main building looks as appropriate today, after careful restoration, as it did almost a century ago.

A large columned dining room to seat 500 was in full use for the Inaugural Dinner in 1899, being cleared and transformed into a ballroom once the meal was over.

The tiered lobby with its metal balustrades and long glazed roof-light provides a welcoming airy central space.

Bedrooms were planned with a sitting space opening off the interior galleries, leading to the bedroom with its own bathroom, an innovation at the time.

new building. Conrad, a Polish emigrant, was taking over the *Otago*, his first ship as master, and he showed some reluctance to use such luxurious lodging on his meagre salary. Although in 1888 the hotel had already a good name, Andersen knew well the limitations of sailors' pay so kept his charges moderate. Andersen himself founded the successful East Asiatic Company and lived to the age of 85. Contact between the Siamese royal family and the hotel was maintained, even to the extent of rumoured purchase of it in 1892 by Louis T. Leonowens, son of the Anna whose career in the royal household was the subject of the musical *The King and I*.

Somerset Maugham carried on the literary tradition while making a comprehensive tour of the Far East in 1922 after the success of his novel *Of Human Bondage*. After Ceylon and Burma he reached the Oriental, where unfortunately he developed malaria and had to spend some time recuperating. This experience did not deter him from future visits to enjoy the hotel and its riverside terrace, his last being in 1960 when he was able to celebrate there his 86th birthday. Many more recent authors were drawn to look for local colour and found Bangkok and the Oriental an ideal eastern base. They have included Noel Coward, Graham Greene, James Michener, John Le Carré and many more. In appearance the old Oriental, Bangkok, with two storeys and a central feature of freely adapted Renaissance character, seems in its earlier days to have had similarity with Raffles Hotel, Singapore.

The town of Singapore, on a relatively small island at the southern end of the long Malay peninsula, was founded by Stamford Raffles in 1819 as a strategic base for traders on the shipping route to China. His services to the British Empire by way of the East India Company had already been substantial and far-seeing, earning him a knighthood on the personal initiative of the Prince Regent in 1817. On the breakdown of his health and his retirement to England at the age of 43 he was shabbily treated by the Company, after 30 years' service, being refused a pension on unfounded charges of maladministration laid by a British army commander. A quirk of history in the choice of name for a new hotel more than 60 years afterwards spread his fame throughout the world of Eastern travel and went some way towards righting an unjustified slur on his reputation.

The hotel, named Raffles at the sudden inspiration of the Armenian Sarkies brothers who owned it, is now synonymous with oriental glamour and luxury. It originated in an existing house on Beach Road that was in its recent past run as Emmerson's Hotel, Dr Emmerson the lessee having trained as a veterinary surgeon and switched careers to being a hotelier. He had offered, in the years before his death in 1883, such attractions as 'Billiards, Lawn Tennis and Quoits &c'.

In 1887 the four brothers, Martin, Tigran, Aviet and Arshak, took a lease from the owner, Syed Mohamed Alsagoff. Tigran and Martin were already hoteliers in Penang in the north of Malaya and owners there of the Eastern Hotel, George Town, in 1884. Brother Aviet in the following year had joined in with the Oriental, based on an adjacent Penang bungalow of similar Anglo-Indian derivation. This enterprise grew into the 100–bedroom Eastern and Oriental Hotel managed by the youngest brother Arshak, taking on a local variant of neo-classicism expressed in pilasters and overhanging pediments and enjoying pleasantly shaded gardens bordering the sea. Known familiarly as the 'E. & O.' it kept a special place in the affections of Eastern hotel connoisseurs. In the 1920s various additions were built, the 1922 domed Victory Annexe and a large ballroom combining to give a 280-metres-long façade towards the sea. Arshak's further ambitious plans in 1927 led him into financial failure, no doubt accelerated by his easy-going generosity to rubber planters and others who ran out of money in the great depression. It was bought by the owners of the Runnymede Hotel and still exists. Aviet, with a more reserved character, opened the Strand in Rangoon in 1901 in an impressive neo-classical rectangular block suitably columned and pedimented. (The Hotel Majapahit at Surabaya in Indonesia was one of many ventures by the Armenian Sarkies brothers, whose most famous enterprise was Raffles Hotel; designed by J. Afprey, the Majapahit was opened by Eugène-Lucas in 1910.)

The Raffles during the 1890s was extended firstly with two wings of suites facing the sea, each of the 22 suites having a private verandah or sitting space and a bathroom, offering attraction to the business and tourist visitors in the flourishing Singapore background. Opinions from early visitors differed, Rudyard Kipling recommending the food but not the rooms before the extension: 'Feed at the Raffles and sleep at the Europe' was his advice.[3] The Europe had a history dating back to 1839 when it was known as the Hôtel de Londres, which Conrad may have used as a background in *Lord Jim*.

The Sarkies at Raffles, aware of competition, added a Palm Court wing in 1894 with 30 more suites and a new main building of colonial neo-classical style was opened in 1899. This was designed by Regent Alfred John Bidwell, who trained at the Architectural Association in London and was working with the oldest established Singapore firm of Swan & Maclaren. This stage of building crystallized the hotel's image in its central pediment and angled corner pavilions, which are recognized as among the best-known motifs in the hotel world. The three-storey building at the corner of Beach Road and Bras Basah Road, an admirable example of the Colonial style, still retains much of its initial attraction, and

The Sarkies brothers c. 1905; from left: Aviet, Arshak, Martin and Tigran. Between them they transformed hotel standards from Rangoon to Singapore.

Hong Kong, the Peninsula Hotel, 1924–8, by architects Clement Palmer and Arthur Turner. A view of the hotel from the ferry soon after completion.

In its early days the Peninsula dominated its surroundings – when seven-storeyed buildings were looked upon as tall.

great care has been taken to restore original features, such as the decorative cast-iron entrance verandah by Walter Macfarlane's of Glasgow, which had been removed but was remade for the recent reconstruction by an American foundry in Alabama. The bench-mark date for the recent restoration was chosen as 1915, representing the hotel at its peak of condition.[4] Verandahs, curved window heads and red tiled roofs offset the white stucco walls, and the present total of suites is 104, with private verandah, bedroom, dressing-room, bathroom and through ventilation for each one. In 1899 fans and lighting were electrically run from the hotel's generator and the airy fourteen-feet-high rooms with large elegant windows were appreciated by a wide range of travellers. Singapore residents and guests alike were attracted by a French cuisine under a French chef that won good reputation. A favourite anecdote involves the Bar and Billiard Room, a detached structure raised above ground level where the last tiger to be killed in Singapore was cornered and shot in the space beneath. This building was renewed to hold six billiard-tables in 1906, a few years after Swan & Maclaren had constructed another new bedroom wing for Arshak Sarkies, facing Bras Basah Road.

Raffles Hotel Post Office appeared in 1910, adding to the many amenities that inveterate orient-lovers such as Somerset Maugham and Noel Coward were happy to absorb.

The inner covered courtyards carried on the European mid-nineteenth-century glazed winter garden or palm court conception that, a century later, was developed into the double or multiple-storeyed atrium with balconied corridors overlooking interior landscaping. The same basic idea, though uncovered with glazing, comes from as far back as the four cloistered courtyards forming the Hotel Reyes Catolicos, Santiago de Compostela, built in 1499. Swan & Maclaren's practice designed several more Singapore hotels and important buildings for the expanding city in virtually every category of use. The Goodwood Park Hotel (1900) shows features favoured by Bidwell and the firm was responsible also for the Grand Hotel in Still Road (1920), the Railway Station Hotel (1932) and the Great Southern Hotel (1936).

Hong Kong produced the Peninsula Hotel by 1928 after delays due to military occupation. On the doorstep of south China, and without a historic background to compare with the Raffles or the Bangkok Oriental, its name nevertheless took its place in the liturgy of top oriental grand hotels.[5] Hong Kong & Shanghai Hotels Ltd was the company involved in its creation, already with experience of hotels in both places forming its name. Kowloon, where the new hotel was to be sited, had formally become British in 1860 under the Peking Convention, but in the 1920s when the project

The British Army took possession of the new building before the Peninsula could be opened for proper use, necessitating refurbishment to enable it to be used as a hotel.

Decorative plasterwork of the 1920s on the Peninsula's first floor.

developed there were anti-British strikes, and in mainland China before the People's Republic there was much political instability.

Palmer and Turner were the architects for the Peninsula and work had started in 1924 but proceeded slowly, influenced by doubts about the future and beset with foundation problems necessitating 600 supporting piles. Before the neo-classical interior was complete, extra British regiments were drafted to Hong Kong and the Peninsula was used as a temporary billet. By the time it was released, almost a total refit was needed. It was not until 11 December 1928 that the hotel was opened for its proper use and was able to establish the high standards for which it has become so well-known. The exterior has much in common with earlier American designs of Adler and Sullivan, although it is only seven storeys high

The Peninsula's main staircase and lobby today retain decoration of a less exuberant nature.

BELOW The hotel's more recent, high-rise tower reflects Hong Kong's changed scale and immense commercial development.

BELOW Modernity has not extinguished the Peninsula's partiality for vintage Rolls-Royce transport available to guests. This is a Phantom II model of 1934, but the hotel also owns a large fleet of Silver Spur IIIs.

with a dominant projecting wing at each side of the recessed central block. Detail is restrained and takes a colonial flavour from the heavily overhanging bracketed cornice finished with a row of antefixae. Unusually, pediments are absent. Much interior redecoration has taken place, but the Lobby retains its claim as 'the most elegant meeting place in Hong Kong'. Two storeys high, it houses staircase and balconies with much gilded plasterwork on columns and coffered ceilings, recognized classical motifs being applied in a clearly twentieth-century manner with good effect.

The generous access given to all visitors on opening day resulted in wide admiration of the magnificence and laid a foundation for the welcoming atmosphere that was to be one of the keys to its success.

Macau

In the Far Eastern Portuguese territory of Macau, another hotel of some style and *belle époque* proportions was declared open on 1 July 1890. Its site, in some ways similar to that of Reid's in Madeira, was on a promontory, Penha Hill, with commanding sea views, which gave the hotel its name. The owners were William Clarke and his wife, Catherine Hannack, Clarke being a captain on the steamer ferries plying up the Pearl River to Canton and across to Hong Kong. The Boa Vista was sturdily built as a dominant square-looking building three storeys high with chunky Doric columns supporting external arcading to the verandahs. The main façades are vigorously designed apart from the tentative pediments and it has been suggested that the architect may have been British, because of strong similarities with Hong Kong buildings of the same date and less affinity with the building styles in Macau.[6] An internal stairwell formed a central reception area and the room layout proved adaptable to the varied purposes it housed during a very chequered career.

Clarke and his wife were both Britons and his employers were the Hong Kong, Canton and Macao Steamer Company Limited. In the early days of settlement, Macau and Hong Kong had vied for pre-eminence but it was not long before Macau fell behind in the race and drifted away from the lively business culture that was to bring such long-term success to its rival. After the turn of the century the hotel became a pawn in the political game, with rumours of a plot between France and Portugal to exchange the French Congo with Macau and Guinea.

In 1902 there was a suggestion that the French citizens from Indochina might use it as a sanatorium and rest house, but Britain, wary of French ambitions in the region, put pressure on the Portuguese government, who promptly 'confiscated' the hotel. Some sanatorium use was dedicated to the Portuguese, followed by a return to *hôtellerie* for the period 1909–17. First under a Frenchman Auguste Vernon then, during Vernon's serious illness and return to France, it was managed by Albert Watkins until his attempts at making it into a gambling house invited further Government intervention. Transformation into a secondary school, the Liceu de Macau, then took place and lasted for a few years until a new school was built. At this stage it was bought by the Portuguese government and entered a period of alternating hotel use and renting out for other purposes. In 1936 it was used by the British government for service personnel.

Occasionally there would be a burst of activity, such as catering for part of an influx of 800 passengers from three American ships, but competition from the newer Presidente Hotel (1928) had eroded the old hotel's trade, although the Presidente never completely eclipsed the more spectacular presence of the Boa Vista in spite of its 80 rooms, 10 salons and the first lift in Macau. Refugees came and went while, in 1936, the name changed to Bela Vista – 'beautiful' instead of 'good'. Decline and decay beset Macau and the Bela Vista during the Sino-Japanese War, the Second World War and the Cultural Revolution in China, which made its influence felt when refugees doubled the population. While the Bela Vista in the 1930s accepted the role of refuge, the Presidente Grand Hotel and the Riviera (demolished 1971) were run profitably, taking advantage of a vogue for jazz bands and *thés dansants*.

Portuguese management under Adrião Pinto Marques for twenty years until his death in 1985 arrested the Bela Vista's decline. He had an eccentric obsession with Napoleon, by which name he was familiarly tagged, and left an uncertain management inheritance to his son Adriano. Revival of interest in historic hotels brought rescue through the participation of Excelsior Hotels and Investments taking a 25-year renewable lease from the Portuguese government to renovate and operate the hotel as a five-star establishment. Mandarin Oriental Hong Kong Ltd contracted for the management and the local architectural firm of Irene O and Bruno Soares took charge of a sensitively handled transformation in 1990–92. Reduction of the number of rooms to an unbelievable six would seem to leave a large question mark over financial viability.

China

Shanghai developed as a port of entry into China towards the end of the nineteenth century, with France and Britain pre-

Shanghai, China, the Palace Hotel, 1906, and (*right*) the Cathay, 1931, were both designed by the Shanghai office of Palmer and Turner and merged in 1949 as the Peace Hotel.

dominating among the Western nations anxious to increase their trade. Influence in the 1920s and 1930s gave Shanghai the title 'Paris of the East'. Night life and the latest European fashions were quick to establish themselves and a taste for jazz bands escaped even the Cultural Revolution.

When Palmer and Turner had considered setting up a Shanghai architects' office they were uncertain of the prospects there for Western-style building.[7] Their practice in Hong Kong had been inherited from the oldest practice, W. Wilson and W. Salway, founded in 1868, but when

Clement Palmer (1857–1952) with his engineer partner Arthur Turner established the new base they looked for wider opportunities. In the event, the gamble was successful and from 1911 to the outbreak of the Second World War in 1939 most of their efforts were directed to development of the Shanghai Bund waterfront. Their style had moved on from neo-classical to a more modernist approach for the many commercial buildings they designed, and from their Palace Hotel, Shanghai, of 1906 they left neo-Renaissance dressings behind for the cleaner lines of the 1931 thirteen-storey

ABOVE & LEFT Macau, Hotel Bela Vista, 1890. In spite of its small number of rooms, it possesses strong architectural character expressed by its unknown architect in vigorous exterior and interior arcading.

Cathay Hotel, Shanghai, 1931. Some good Art Deco interiors remain from the period when it attracted international café society to its restaurant and jazz band entertainments on the rooftop.

Cathay Hotel. Initially it was called 'The New Sassoon House', presumably with a different usage in mind, but the demand for hotel accommodation from foreign interests became obvious. The fitting-out was to best Western standards and the rooftop dance floor and restaurant, with the addition of a Big Band, achieved fame far beyond Shanghai.

Decoration of the exterior was limited to carved stonework at cornice and plinth levels, with other elaboration in excellent quality bronze work at windows and doors. The corner tower with its campanile roof profile is emphasized by a stylized shield with supporters and still remains a landmark on the Huangpu riverside. With the formation of the People's Republic of China in 1949, both the Palace and the Cathay were taken over by the new Communist régime and managed jointly as the Peace Hotel, now in the Jin Jiang Group. Art Deco interiors have been retained and restored with the eloquent names of Crane Longevity Hall, Lounge of Ninth Heaven Hall, Peace Hall and Peace Grill. Early twentieth-century tradition is upheld by 'the famous Peace Senior Jazz Band', which plays every night in the Jazz Bar.

Japan

Japan at the end of 200 years of isolation and threatened by the persistent American naval presence of Commodore Perry's ships in the 1850s had either 'to respond to the Western challenge on her own terms or to become a meaty bone gnawed upon by various European powers'.[8] Japanese signing of the subsequent treaties permitted access to specified ports and the formation of restricted foreign settlements. Yokohama, Nagasaki, Kobe, Niigata and Hakodate were the original treaty ports and acted as channels for the influx of information on the ways of the outer world. Social and industrial revolution commenced and every effort was made to catch up on Western technology and the attendant changes of lifestyles it was bringing.

Yokohama with its Grand Hotel of 1873 seems to have won the race to be first. It faced the sea, had 30 rooms on two floors, with a restaurant and a library. It was destroyed entirely by the 1923 earthquake but rebuilt to Jin Watanabe's larger-scale plans with 94 rooms and an impressive Western-style staircase hall with wooden columns and Italian marble facings. As the New Grand it opened in 1927 and enjoyed the years before 1940 as an international fashionable favourite with strong American links but also acting as the social centre of Yokohama's foreign community. There was also an Oriental Palace Hotel, French managed, and a Club Hotel patronized by Canadians, Australians and Britons. The New Grand in twelve years of military occupation, first by the Japanese and then by the Americans, was left badly in need of rescue but old staff still survive, as does the hotel.

The Fujiya Hotel in Myanoshita was built more in the traditional architectural language of Japan, although its hotelier, Sennosuke Yamaguchi, had spent three years in the United States crystallizing his ideas. He then presented his completed, Westernized hotel and management system to the public in 1878. Twice rebuilt, in 1884 and in 1924 after the earthquake, it attracted the Japanese Imperial Family, not least Emperor Hirohito, who discovered the mysteries of golf there before he acceded to the throne in 1921. European royalties and statesmen from America were hotel guests at the time of the funeral of Emperor Meiji in 1912.

Kobe as a port had the Oriental, British run, and the Tor with a Swiss manager. The Tor had cylindrical turrets, a dome and red tiled roofs. It was set in extensive gardens. Perhaps the most beautiful of all hotels is the Nara (1909) designed by Kingo Tatsumi and Yasu Katao at Nara, the ancient capital of Japan. It can hardly be thought of as a railway hotel, but was built under the supervision of the National Company of Japanese Railways after the end of the Russo-Japanese War as a prestige building, costing seven times the original estimate. The low building was designed with heavily overhanging roofs and extensive use of timber framing, part traditional imperial palace and part European chalet style. Meticulous interiors epitomize the qualities in Japanese art that had inspired the European reaction against nineteenth-century heaviness and elaboration. Park-like gardens contain sacred deer – to be echoed by the elegant gazelles fed by guests at the Mena House near Cairo in the 1920s and 1930s. The art and craftsmanship put into the Nara Hotel are outstanding.

Although Tokyo's Imperial Hotel lives no more in either of its historic forms, it cannot be left out of a grand hotel history. Japan's struggle for recognition by the Western world of its national and international status continued, and as a part of this exercise the Imperial Hotel project materialized. The grand hotel as an element of civilized social life had been assimilated in the 1870s and 1880s, and a short list of world class hotels to which the first version of the Imperial had added its presence in 1890 was:

> Grand Hotel, Paris, 1850
> Hôtel du Louvre, Paris, 1855
> Kaiserhof, Berlin, 1874
> Frankfurterhof, Frankfurt, 1876
> Grand Hotel National, Lucerne, 1870

Kobe, Japan, Oriental Hotel, founded in 1882 and British run. Rudyard Kipling in *From Sea To Sea*, 1899, extolled the culinary finesse under the proprietor M. Begaux, comparing it favourably with the Oriental in Penang, the Victoria in Hong Kong and the Raffles in Singapore.

Nara, Japan, Nara Hotel, 1909, designed by architects King, Tatsumi and Yasu Katao for the National Company of Japanese Railways, but achieving excellence based on traditional forms.

A bedroom in the Nara's 'Imperial Suite', with space and detail carefully balanced.

The Nara's main lounge in 1930s Art Deco style, completed in a manner more subtle than most similar European examples.

Tokyo, Japan, the Imperial, first version of 1890, designed by Yuzuru Watanabe in a Western five-part formula with classical detail.

View of Tokio.　　　東京景色　　　Imp: No. 102.

Savoy Hotel, London, 1889
Waldorf-Astoria, New York, 1893
Hôtel Ritz, Paris, 1897
Carlton Hotel, London 1899.[9]

Direct adoption of the accepted European style was made, to indicate the country's capabilities and equality in the provision of luxurious standards. *The Tokyo Nichinichi Shimbun* of 9 November 1890 assured its readers, in writing of the first Imperial, that

In the decoration of its rooms it bears comparison with the better class of European hotel. Now at last Tokyo is prepared to provide a hostelry about which visiting gentlemen will find nothing amiss.[10]

Sited near the Tokyo–Kyoto railway terminus it was close to the Imperial Palace and all Governmental activities. These included foreign embassies and made convenient provision for the suitable staging of international meetings on a scale that at last did justice to Japan's long sought-after diplomatic dignity. Westernization had been the aim of Marquis Kaoru Inoue (1835–1915), whose youthful experience in England soon after the Great Exhibition of 1851 had opened his eyes to the technical achievements beyond Japan. As foreign minister he was able to influence his contemporaries in the financial and business fields, Shibusawa and Okura, in the founding of the Tokyo Hotel Company. A four-storey north German design had been prepared *c.* 1886 by Heinrich Mänz in the Berlin office of Ende & Böckmann, but this was superseded by Yuzuru Watanabe's more practical and lower-built three-storey arcaded neo-classical conception with mansard roof and end pavilions. Attention was paid to the possibility of earthquakes and although some brickwork was used, the structural frame was of timber 'stuccoed to give the appearance of a stone structure'. Interiors retained Japanese taste and 60 guest rooms were provided, including ten suites. In addition to a main dining-room, a dining- or meeting-room, a ballroom, reading-, drawing-, music-, smoking- and pool-rooms were provided. For a short time the hotel became a social centre where expensive parties and weddings were held, although a fire in the Upper House of the Diet in 1891 led to the use of the ballroom as the Upper Chamber for two months. After this interlude the first Imperial Hotel fulfilled its role for over 30 years, developing with the times and adding prestige to the capital city. Freedom of travel for foreigners within Japan was not permitted until 1899 and made little immediate impact until victory in the Russo-Japanese War suddenly generated an invasion of travellers by 1906. The hotel industry then felt the need to organize itself, and at the Imperial, changes of personnel from European to Japanese occurred.

Appointment of Aisaku Hayashi as general manager in succession to the previous Swiss, Hans Moser, was eventually achieved, although this took some persuasion and gave Hayashi extensive powers, which he was certainly to need during the rebuilding of the hotel. Hayashi's own words summarized his position:

In 1909 I returned to Japan from New York to spend some time at Yamanaka [Shokai] in Osaka. At that time Kishichiro Okura, Denzaburo Fujita of Osaka, and Jutaro Matsumoto spoke with me in person and by letter, repeatedly, to say that the Imperial Hotel had done away with its foreign manager but was finding it difficult to locate a suitable Japanese manager and they wanted me to take the job.

I had been at Yamanaka Shokai [an art and antiques company] for a long time, had well established business ties abroad, and was used to life in New York. I had doubts about moving to the hotel business and declined the offer. I felt that introducing Japanese art abroad was my mission.[11]

Once persuaded to the contrary, he assumed management of the hotel and managing directorship of the company, full of ideas for stimulating a tired organization that a recent merger

with the Hotel Metropole had failed to revivify. Suggestions for a completely new hotel had already been under discussion and were translated into firm policy at the same time that Hayashi was renovating and improving the existing buildings. The tourist trade had its usual fluctuations but the Imperial performed well and accommodated the businessmen, diplomats and tourists who arrived in increased numbers via the Trans-Siberian Railway, from Australia and the United States.

The welcome revival vindicated the choice of Hayashi as manager, but the real celebrity of the Imperial was through its next manifestation as one of the most remarkable works of the American architect Frank Lloyd Wright (1869–1959). A long and tortuous story unfolded in the creation of the new hotel, starting with the acquisition of the additional land adjacent to the original site. Negotiations between the Imperial Household, the 'Home' Ministry whose official residence occupied the proposed site, and the hotel company, whose chief shareholder was the Imperial Household, were protracted and lasted from 1906 until 1920 when the official lease was granted. Already by then, building had begun after some dispute involving the Japanese architect Kikutaro Shimoda, who claimed, perhaps on the basis of a sketch scheme, to have been commissioned for the job. In fact a definite agreement on terms of employment was signed by Aisaku Hayashi and Frank Lloyd Wright on 17 March 1916 in the following terms:

MEMORANDUM

The architect Frank Lloyd Wright of Chicago and Aisaku Hayashi, manager and managing director of the Imperial Hotel, Tokyo, Japan have agreed to the following terms: Frank Lloyd Wright shall produce plans and specifications for a new hotel for the Imperial Hotel, Inc, of Tokyo, Japan and will oversee its construction. The Imperial Hotel Inc. shall pay Frank Lloyd Wright, as remuneration for his work, a sum equal to 5% of the total costs upon completion of the structure and all facilities. All aspects of the work shall be carried out by specialists. The sum of 5% of the cost of the structure and all outbuildings and facilities shall be paid in the following proportions: For the preliminary rough plans: 1.5%. Additionally, for the final plans: 2%. Additionally, for supervising construction: 1.5%. The cost of the architect's round trips to Japan and those of three assistants shall be borne by the owners, who will insofar as it is possible provide them with room and board while they are in Japan and employed on this project. The architect will make available enough of his time to assure the completion of the plans, specifications, and construction. The architect agrees to give satisfaction to the owners in his efforts to advance the construction. The hotel

The ruins of the old main building after the fire of April 1922.

Ground floor plan of the new Frank Lloyd Wright building, 1916–23, with central axis of foyers, inner hall and auditorium. This was nearing completion at the time the first Imperial was burnt down.

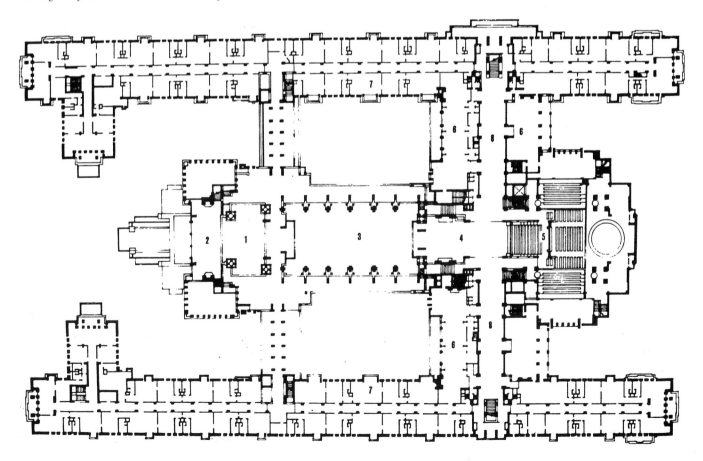

A perspective of the new Imperial, incorporating minor variations.

agrees not to make changes in the design or layout without discussing them with the architect and receiving his approval. Signed in Chicago this seventeenth day of March 1916, by

Aisaku Hayashi   Frank Lloyd Wright[12]

The budget was then 1.5 million yen and the contract period two years. A run-in period of three and a half years elapsed before the main works began in September 1919 and three months later the annexe to the original hotel was burnt out, fortunately without loss of life. Here was major extra work for Wright in designing a replacement to make good the loss of 42 much needed guest rooms.

An issue of prime importance to the architect was the selection of materials. The Oya volcanic tuff, resembling a soft, slightly green-tinted travertine, was selected for facing and carving on exterior and interior surfaces, being used as permanent formwork with a backing of concrete. According to Wright, he

liked this material for its character but soon found that the building committee … considered it sacrilege to use a material so cheap and common for so dignified a purpose. But finally the building committee gave in and we bought our own quarries … We used Oya (the lava) throughout the work, combining it with

concrete walls cast in layers within thin wall shells of slender bricks.[13]

He commended the tireless stonemasons, 600 of whom were continually employed for four years, and welcomed their 'warmth of interest and depth of appreciation' as the overall design began to emerge.

Much has been written about his 'lily-pad' conception of the foundations to overcome the near-impossible conditions of a landfill site eight feet thick over a 60-foot sub-stratum of mud. Earthquakes had to be taken into consideration and, with Paul Mueller, an engineer who had worked also with Chicago architect Louis Sullivan and with Wright previously, a scheme of short concrete piles two feet apart was devised. Footings were laid over each group of piles and these sections linked to each other by flexible movement joints. Wright had 'carried the floor and roof loads as a waiter carries his tray on his upraised arm and fingers'.[14] His theories were put to the test in the 1923 earthquake: the building stood when many others collapsed. Such an exceptional undertaking inevitably generated tensions, not least in respect of time and money, both of which increased far beyond estimates. Correspondence between Hayashi and Wright became acerbic and a financial crisis was aggravated by a fire in April 1922 that left the nearby first Imperial Hotel as a

Main dining-room set against a background of brick and Oya stone.

charred site with only its brick chimneys standing. The company directors resigned, Shozo Yamaguchi replaced Aisaku Hayashi as managing director, and Wright was at this juncture back in the United States. An opening day of 1 July 1922 was set for the new hotel but only the north wing and the central dining-hall were in use and the Wright building was not finally completed until September 1923 at a building cost of 6 million yen.

For 45 years it remained in use, without a doubt fulfilling its purpose of lending prestige to the capital and making a reputation as an 'outstanding work from the historical and architectural points of view' with 'unique and ultimate significance in the field of architecture'.[15] In practical terms it had serious limitations. Firstly, unequal subsidence had been occurring from the outset and eventually reached dangerous proportions. Uneven floors, tilting doors and defective rainwater disposal were the result. Externally the Oya tuff did not stand up satisfactorily to the high rainfall and heavy frosts in Tokyo and continual repairs were needed. War damage in 1945 from incendiary bombing affected nearly half the building, including the Peacock banqueting-room, and temporary repairs estimated for ten to fifteen years life were made under

the United States forces then occupying Japan.

The idea of an all-electric hotel had also been let down in 1923 by inadequate local technology, with all heating being converted to traditional coal and gas-fired methods within a year of opening. Water service pipes and electric wiring all deteriorated and were affected by the subsidence. 'The hotel's fire policy was one of prayer.'[16] In all, by the 1960s efforts at preservation failed in spite of much international support and activity on the part of the Imperial Hotel Preservation Committee, and in December 1967 demolition works began as planned, but not before the building had been fully documented.[17] Some of the building was saved for re-erection at Meiji Mura outdoor museum, though this again had been complicated as their collection officially covered only the years 1868–1912. The entrance and lobby resurrection in the museum took seventeen years to accomplish, but it can now be seen as a remembrance of a great hotel, flawed but magnificent.

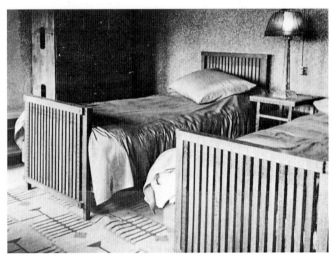

Guest room of the 1920s, its furniture and furnishings integrated in design.

The United States

As in the earlier years of hotel development already surveyed, the United States pursued an independent course, tending to concentrate on capacity and innovation rather than style or service. Across the whole country many large city hotels competed with each other for size, with every extra foot in length or height being carefully recorded. A formula, evolved by the mid-nineteenth century, of six storeys topped with a heavily bracketed cornice, large dining-rooms convertible into ballrooms and accommodation for about 1,000 people in rooms and suites, was widely used. The architect of the Lindell Hotel in St Louis, Thomas Walsh, writing in *The Builder* refers unconvincingly to its 'cut stone window trimmings', although contemporary illustrations give little impression of character in most of these solid utilitarian blocks.[1] The enlightened patronage of William Cornelius Van Horne resulted in the achievement of a house style for the Canadian Pacific Railway Hotels, where design was always considered as an ingredient of much value, but no comparable influence operated in the United States although some excellent architects became specialists in hotel design.

Henry J. Hardenbergh (1847–1918) was one of those working at the turn of the century, having studied for five years with Detlef Lienau before setting up his own New York practice in 1870. His hotels, including the Martinique in New York (1897), the Willard in Washington (1901) and the much talked of Plaza in New York (1907) brought fresh ideas and a sophisticated approach to design in the skyscraper age.

The first Willard Hotel in Washington, D.C., developed out of an earlier hotel, Tennison's, which had been in use since 1818 on the site. In 1842 it had become Fuller's City Hotel and Charles Dickens stayed there on his first visit to Washington. Henry Willard, who had been managing the hotel, and his brother Edwin bought, enlarged and renovated it in 1850 and renamed it the Willard. Enough reputation had developed by 1861 for Abraham Lincoln to stay there as President-elect before taking the oath of office. The words of the *Battle Hymn of the Republic* were written in the hotel by Julia Ward Howe while she was staying in the hotel in the same year. American Presidents, virtually without exception, used the hotel in succeeding years, as did royalties and statesmen.[2]

At the end of the century a completely new building was required, and Henry Willard's nephew Joseph chose Hardenbergh as an architect capable of producing the quality of design needed to make it the leading hotel in America's capital. He had already gained experience with his design for the Dakota Apartments in New York in 1884, inspired by French Gothic influence and pre-dating the first Canadian Pacific château-style hotel at Banff Springs (1886) designed by another New York architect, Bruce Price. It was in the 1880s that 'skyscrapers' had become practicable to build through the use of steel-framed structure, and both Price and Hardenbergh adopted high-rise city centre building methods. For the Willard, on its important corner in Pennsylvania Avenue, a style known as 'French Second Empire Beaux-Arts' was used by Hardenbergh. Classical, Renaissance and baroque features are present, but the twelve- and thirteen-storey elevations, with extravagant crested bull's-eye dormers in the mansard roof, are held together satisfactorily by Beaux-Arts formality. Indiana limestone faced the four-storey plinth, with light brick and terracotta above. Interiors were lavish, with inlaid marble floors, columns, decorative plasterwork and painted ceilings making an impressive background for the opening ceremony. For the first half of the twentieth century it continued to flourish, but by the time the Second World War was coming to an end it was beginning to decline. At this stage it was sold by the Willard family but was allowed to deteriorate steadily both before a sale in

OPPOSITE Paris, the Crillon, which opened in 1909 behind A. J. Gabriel's mid-18th-century façade.

Washington, D.C., the Willard Hotel, 1901, is a good representative of Henry Janeway Hardenbergh's hotel designs. It derives from his Beaux-Arts background and replaced an earlier Willard Hotel, quickly establishing the lead amongst Washington's favourite meeting places.

1968 and afterwards while standing empty for sixteen years. Meticulous restoration allied to imaginative redevelopment of part of the site under the auspices of the Pennsylvania Avenue Development Corporation brought about a new lease of life in 1986 as the Willard Inter-Continental. Long delays in approvals and changes of financing policies had fortuitously contributed to the rescue, owing to the long interim period during which conservation gained public support and enabled the 1901 building to be appreciated and preserved.

William Waldorf Astor had grown up in a family atmosphere of feud and rivalry which came second only to extreme worship of wealth. On the death of his father, John Jacob III, he proceeded with plans for a large new hotel on the site of John Jacob's Fifth Avenue house and next to that of his Aunt Caroline, who was understandably enraged by the dirt, noise and obstruction that ensued. She was, as wife of William Backhouse Astor, queen of New York's hierarchical society and responded by building a new château-style mansion at 840 Fifth Avenue and 65th Street at a construction cost of $2,000,000, the marvels of which were put on display for the populace to see before she occupied it in 1896. In the meantime her husband had died of a heart attack in Europe, leaving his son John Jacob Astor IV in charge of a great fortune. The cousins Jack and William had no liking for each other, nor had they any public popularity, but a suggested idea of

LEFT & ABOVE As a focus for all the capital's eminent visitors, the Willard bred an atmosphere of quality and stability that has been restored after a long state of eclipse from 1968 to 1986. The Main Lobby and Crystal Room have now recaptured their original opulence.

Washington's Carlton Hotel is of later date, 1926, than the Willard. A 'hands-on' building developer, Harry Wardman from Yorkshire, England, was responsible for some thousands of houses, hundreds of apartment buildings and several hotels, including the Carlton.

Mihran Mesrobian, a Turkish architect trained on Beaux-Arts principles in Istanbul, followed Italian Renaissance models, particularly in the lavish interiors.

New York, the Waldorf-Astoria, 1897, was a composite property of William Waldorf Astor and John Jacob Astor IV. Designed by Hardenbergh, it was considered the marvel of the age for a relatively short life-span until it was demolished by a subsequent owner to make way for the Empire State Building.

reinforced by the increasing transatlantic interchanges. Under the lessee George Boldt, it was strictly conducted and staff had to comply with rules designed to encourage high standards of manners and style. Waiters were to command French and German in addition to English and, more controversially, were to be clean shaven. Social life reached its heights at the Bradley Martin Ball, given in 1897 as a fancy dress occasion on the theme of Louis XV at Versailles. New ground was broken in a social world that had previously done most of its entertaining in its own mansions, but the Waldorf-Astoria's combination of size and grandeur, together with the Astor imprint, made it into the first hotel to form the focus of New York's highly organized social world. A further innovation allowing women to patronize its restaurant at any time of the day was introduced in 1907, and gradually similar easing of discrimination against their use

New York's St Regis, refurbished in the 1930s by Serge Obolensky.

building a second Astor hotel linked to the first Waldorf appeared to be in their common interest, and so the Waldorf-Astoria came into being in 1897.[3] Joint resources made possible every magnificence, and Hardenbergh as architect realized the project in a manner that left even New York open-mouthed at the achievement. It was 214 feet high with 1,000 rooms and 750 bathrooms, 300 feet run of wide marble ground-floor corridor, a ballroom 93 × 96 × 50 feet high, a Palm Garden Dining Room beneath a glazed dome and moulded plasterwork ceiling – all executed and furnished to the most luxurious of standards and accessible to anyone able to pay the cost. The corridor, known as Peacock Alley, was said to accommodate 25,000 people a day as they either displayed their fashions or formed an audience to watch the social parade.[4]

Sophistication permeated management and clientèle,

OPPOSITE The St Regis, built in the early years of the twentieth century, was an Astor property designed by Trowbridge and Livingston.

New York, the Plaza Hotel, 1907, is perhaps H. J. Hardenbergh's most important hotel. It radiates glamour and excitement to New Yorkers and visitors alike.

of public rooms spread through the Plaza and other leading hotels. Its dominance of the hotel and social scene lasted only into the 1920s, when real estate values triumphed over tradition and the home of so much social history was reduced to a building site for the Empire State Building.

A new Waldorf-Astoria unrelated to the Astor family was built on Park Avenue in the 1930s, designed by Schultze and Weaver, according to report, over a Thursday to Monday weekend in 1929. Its 42 storeys contributed to the New York skyline with twin towers more than twice the height of the earlier version. This was the pattern in New York City, where Art Deco was in fashion for interiors, and the main lobby of the Waldorf-Astoria was based on gold-veined black marble

clad square columns in the new smooth and glossy manner. Modern murals, probably painted in France, are attributed to Louis Pierre Rigal.

The old 1888 brownstone Plaza Hotel on Fifth Avenue and Central Park South was designed by George W. de Cunha but demolished by developers and replaced in 1907 by the offspring of a leading New York hotelier, Fred Sterry, in collaboration with financier Bernhard Beinecke and the building contractor Harry S. Black at the head of Fuller Construction Company. The handsome design by H. J. Hardenbergh spared no expense and gave rise immediately to a new set of traditions in New York's mercurial life. The architect doubled the number of rooms to 800 and provided 500 private bathrooms. In addition there were 14–17 apartments, the variation being according to the flexible planning that permitted rooms to be linked together into larger units. Two floors of public rooms, ten elevators, five marble staircases and a two-storey ballroom completed the 'greatest hotel in the world'. It was imposing, elegant and opulent for the fashionable and affluent clientèle. For the ballroom a Second Empire style was selected, similar in some respects to the Grand, Stockholm, incorporating a stage and proscenium with added bow-fronted and draped boxes. All such white and gold decoration schemes claim some kinship with Versailles and the *œils-de-bœuf* of the Galerie des Glaces, but in the Plaza, decorative details extend into the Louis XV and XVI styles. Here classic influence predominates, whereas the Stockholm Grand and the Montreux Palace in Switzerland, which bear comparison, lighten the effect in their ballrooms with rococo plasterwork. The Plaza's initial cost was $12 million.

A commemorative plaque erected for the New York Community Trust refers to the architect, to the French Renaissance style and to members of the Gould, Harriman and Vanderbilt families being among the original residents in the hotel. Today's handout literature may sound exaggerated but typifies the character the Plaza has acquired:

The crown jewel of Manhattan's fabled Fifth Avenue, it presides with the grace and glamour that has impressed visitors from the four corners of the globe. … The Plaza is in a class by itself.

So it remains, having achieved a presence rare among outsized hotels and preserving its own distinctive integrity, outstanding even against the increased bulk of newer larger neighbours. Its quality was recognized by New York City as a Landmark in 1969 and as a National Historic Landmark in 1986.

In 1891 the architect John A. Wood from New York, to whom earlier work at the Grand Union Hotel, Saratoga Springs, is attributed, created a most remarkable building on Florida's Gulf coast for the railroad developer and entrepreneur Henry B. Plant. This was to be a really grand hotel, abandoning the accepted classical styles, and the Tampa Bay Hotel arose to much surprise as a Moorish extravaganza. The Alhambra, Granada, once again is quoted as an obvious source, but Brighton Pavilion and Venetian-inspired Victorian civic palaces and railway stations must have encouraged some of its oriental tendencies. A fine domed Grand Salon was furnished with some of the valuable European antiques collected by Plant and his wife on their travels. Many had been historic royal property – cabinets and chairs belonging to Ferdinand and Isabella of Spain, Mary, Queen of Scots, Louis Philippe and Marie Antoinette, and these are now in the local museum. Eccentricity of design in the hotel was coupled with sophisticated equipment. A casino with indoor swimming pool beneath its movable floor, billiard

and shuffle-board rooms, mineral water baths, a café and a concert organ from Europe catered for leisure and entertainment. The 500 rooms had electricity and telephones and almost all had private baths. Mrs Plant's collector's taste resulted also in *objets d'art*, pictures and smaller furniture being assembled to give individual character to the rooms.

A memoir by Alexander Browning, who acted as Wood's site architect during construction, gives a lively picture of the sometimes primitive methods used.[5] Where possible, materials were obtained locally, Browning himself prospecting for suitable building sand that could be transported to the site by means of a short spur specially built from the railroad line. Wood started a brickfield at Campville, making sand lime bricks that continued in production for many years. Oyster shells and broken brick substituted for gravel as aggregates for concrete, but good natural cement had to be brought from Brooklyn on the Hudson river. For a light-coloured mortar, German or Belgian Portland-type cement was shipped across the Atlantic.

As the brick work was going on at the end of the 1200 foot building, the footings were being put in at the other end; all the concrete was mixed by hand, on the sweat board, there was no concrete mixers then, only the stoutest men could do this heavy work, and extra pay was allowed them, the same pay as the mortar mixers. $1.75 a day, while common labor was paid $1.25 for ten hours.

The thirteen silver minarets that lend the building so much of its character were covered by a new product, American-made tin – 'Taylors Old Style Pointiminster'. Reinforcement for structural concrete incorporated old sub-marine telegraph cable from the Key West and West India links. According to Browning, 'Whenever wanted, a piece the length required was sawn off, and unwound, the copper cable in the center, was saved, and almost paid for the freight of bringing it on the job.' Old cable-car wire succeeded the telegraph cable and this had a rope centre that was 'cut up and used as hair in the inside plastering'. Outside labour came 'from different parts of the country, snow birds mainly, some mighty good tradesmen amongst them'. When the hotel was finished, a two-storey servants' quarters and a substantial 'power house' with bedrooms over it were built in keeping with the hotel.

The Tampa Bay, now housing the University of Tampa, survived as a hotel for a few years after Plant's death in 1899 but then entered an uncertain life as a property of the city, run by a succession of managers until transferred to the field of education in 1933. Plant had built the Belleview in Belleair/Clearwater on Florida's Gulf coast in 1897 as a vernacular

Tampa, Florida, Tampa Bay Hotel, 1891, designed by New York architect John A. Wood for the wealthy entrepreneur Henry B. Plant in a full-blooded Moorish style incorporating thirteen silver spires. It is now in use by the University of Florida.

Moorishness pervaded the interiors as well as the exterior, concealing the elevator's modernity behind Arabic design.

St Augustine, Florida, Ponce de Leon Hotel, 1888, was an enterprise of Henry M. Flagler, whose enthusiasm for hotels on Florida's Atlantic coast rivalled those of Plant further west. His architects were John Carrère and Thomas Hastings, whose Beaux-Arts training is evident in the symmetrical layout of the hotel, which nevertheless has a certain Spanish air about it.

The interior also drew inspiration from classical motifs very freely interpreted.

palace in timber and it survived without a fatal fire, being now protected by aluminium siding in imitation of the timber. Since 1919 it has been called the Belleview Biltmore.

A tolerant rivalry existed between Henry Plant and Henry M. Flagler, who operated on the west and east Florida coasts respectively, both having seen the possibilities of development in the Sunshine State. Flagler's first interests were in oil and railroads, the former yielding more than enough wealth to indulge his hotel-building. He had taken up residence in St Augustine on the East coast in 1885 and started his first grand hotel there, named after the Spanish explorer Ponce de Leon. Two young Beaux-Arts trained architects, Thomas Hastings (1860–1929) and John M. Carrère (1858–1911), were fortunate in getting the commission that launched their partnership on its road to distinction.[6] A Spanish Mission style suggested itself, characterized externally with use of traditional bell-towers and tiled roofs symmetrically placed. Interiors incorporated columns, cornices and a large dome, but burst out into eclectic exoticism with complicated caryatid figures, mosaics, vaulted ceilings, frescoes, Tiffany glass and European furnishings. This was opened in 1888 and is now home to Flagler College. Flagler then built the Alcazar and the Royal Poinciana, Palm Beach (1893–4), which could sleep 1,750, but was demolished in 1934. The Breakers, Palm Beach, was another Flagler venture but it succumbed to fires in 1903 and 1925, although the third majestic hotel of this name remains.

When Elisha Babcock and H. L. Story bought the Coro-

nado peninsula near San Diego, California, for $110,000 in 1885, its value had increased more than one hundredfold in the preceding 39 years. Babcock asked the Mid-Western railroad architects James, Merritt and Watson Reid to design a resort hotel 'that people will like to come to long after we are gone – I have no time, it's all up to you'. After discussion, James Reid dictated the following note to clarify what he understood he had received in the way of a brief from his client:

It would be built round a court … a garden of tropical trees, shrubs and flowers, with pleasant paths … balconies should look down on this court from every story. From the south end, the foyer should open to Glorietta Bay with verandahs for rest and promenade. On the ocean corner there should be a pavilion tower, and northward along the ocean, a colonnade, terraced in grass to the beach. The dining wing should project at an angle from the southeast corner of the court and be almost detached to give full value to the view of the ocean, bay and city.[7]

Little time for preparation was given as trade was booming and the developers were in a hurry. The architects had no

San Diego, California, the Hotel del Coronado, 1888, was the creation of the three Reid brothers, James, Merritt and Watson, who had a joint architectural practice.

established suppliers to draw on and no sources of building materials to hand. Workshops, a brick kiln, a foundry, a metal shop and a timber mill had first to be built, and rights to the total output of the Dolbeer & Carson Lumber Company of San Francisco were secured for Douglas fir, sugar pine and redwood. A good labour force was hard to find and unskilled Chinese were brought by boat from San Francisco to form a substantial contingent: about the 2,000 workmen required. During the course of the work, manpower was gradually increased to work both day and night shifts. Design drawings were barely ahead of the workers and yet within eleven months the complex building was opened, on 19 February 1888. For this, 324 trained hotel staff had to be brought from the East coast.

Reid Brothers' interpretation of Babcock's instructions was unusual but effective, executed in a Victorian timber style with the corner tower and ballroom rotunda placed almost on the edge of the Pacific Ocean and dining- and breakfast-rooms with adjacent kitchen in the corresponding corner overlooking Glorietta Bay. An innovation introduced by Reid and among the first in the world was an oil furnace for heating. There were 750 rooms on the five floors, 300 with private baths, and steam central heating reached the public rooms, the private sitting-rooms and 185 bedrooms. Fireplaces heated all other rooms. Further attractions were the 'Beautiful 18-hole Golf Course', the finest climate in the world and the finest fishing and hunting on the Pacific coast. The gardens came up to Babcock's requirements, with pomegranates, guavas, loquats, lemons, limes, oranges, bananas and 'other tropical plants and flowers' listed for the open courtyard. Fan palms and grass plots were terraced towards the sea. The Hotel del Coronado, as it had been called, was open all the year round, and twelve American Presidents have enjoyed its hospitality. It has been able to keep up to date with technical advance while continuing to furnish the 'pleasure, elegance and refinement' referred to in a brochure of 1889. An extensive rejuvenation scheme for owner John Alessio was carried out by a Hollywood scene designer, Al Goodwin, in 1960.

In San Francisco, the Palace Hotel, built for William C. Ralston in 1875, had an even grander seven-storey atrium than Denver's Brown Palace was to get, and was clad in neo-classical style, reminiscences of which appear in the Garden

The style in this instance expressed a vernacular approach using timber inside and out, particularly in the dominant Crown Room where a curved ribbed ceiling seems to emulate an upturned boat. Proximity to the ocean and Mediterranean vegetation make major contributions to the overall effect.

San Francisco, the Palace Hotel, built for William C. Ralston in 1875, had a seven-storey atrium clad in neo-classical style. This building was opened in 1909, designed by Trowbridge and Livingston to replace Ralston's hotel which was destroyed by fire in the 1906 earthquake.

The exterior is of simpler design than that of its bay-windowed predecessor, but is ornamented by a grand entrance in keeping with the more baroque elements of the public rooms.

Court of the present Sheraton Palace Hotel. This building, which opened in 1909, was designed by Trowbridge and Livingston to replace Ralston's Palace, which was destroyed by fire in the earthquake of 1906. The exterior is of simpler design than was its bay-windowed predecessor, but is ornamented by a grand entrance in keeping with the more baroque elements of the public rooms.

Also in California a wild exercise in fantasy grew out of

the Mission Inn, Riverside, dating originally from a very modest start in 1876 when C. C. Miller, an engineer, and his family began to offer board and lodging. The replacement of their property in 1902 by a new hotel fulfilled a long-held ambition. It was designed with courtyard layout in Mission Revival style and enabled Frank Miller to form an astonishing collection of furniture, art and other artefacts from America, the East and Europe. When space was cramped, a new wing was built, and this process came to be repeated in successively varying styles, although a touch of Spanish historicism could usually be identified. A virtual museum gradually resulted, and, although now a separate enterprise, it was then run in tandem with the hotel. One wonders whether this extraordinary agglomeration could perhaps be seen as the forerunner of the Disney ventures.

Denver, Colorado, acquired a grand hotel in 1892 that had the uncommon advantage of adequate time spent on careful planning, to the extent that two tons of drawing paper were said to have been consumed by the architects in preparation of the design. Denver was a thriving city even then, well placed for communications and with reported access to over 100 railroad lines.[8] A year before the hotel was built, its architect, Frank E. Edbrooke from Chicago, had built a smaller hotel in the town, the Oxford, which is close to Union Station. In this building a plain exterior concealed rich decoration of marble, murals and silver chandeliers beneath a glass roof, exciting forerunners of the quality that would be a part of the Brown Palace. The Oxford retains considerable atmosphere in spite of some alteration, and a 1930s Art Deco bar scheme to resemble in part the interior of the liner *Queen Mary* is a notable survival.

When Edbrooke started to build a palace for the entrepreneur and builder Henry C. Brown, his painstaking preparatory work had made the most of the triangular site at the junction of 17th Street and Broadway. The plan forms a thin wedge with rounded tip, and the plain exterior of the building gains its character mainly from the quality of the facing materials – pink-tinted granite for the three-storey plinth section and a warm sandstone from Arizona for the upper floors. Two 700-feet-deep artesian wells were drilled for the water supply, and electrical, heating and plumbing services were of the most advanced types available. Building costs were $1.6 million with addition of a further $400,000 for furnishings, and room prices per night ranged from $1 to $4.50. Financial difficulties were caused by panic in the silver market in 1893, but Brown managed to survive his losses and remain as part owner until his death in 1906 at the age of 86.

The fame of the Brown Palace rests to quite an extent on the dramatic effect conceived by Edbrooke of the seven-

Denver, Colorado, the Brown Palace Hotel, 1892, designed on a narrow triangular site by Civil War veteran Frank E. Edbrooke, who, with his brother, 'envisaged a building in the Italian Renaissance style to be created in Colorado red granite and Arizona sandstone' for Henry Cordes Brown, contractor and developer.

The famous seven-storey atrium with metal balustrades, columns and glazed roof contains (at the bottom right of the picture) a marble fire surround so large that the fireplace itself could accommodate a shop doorway.

storey atrium. This gives access to the perimeter rooms from six upper tiers of cast-iron galleries that themselves are supported on iron columns. The iron balustrading takes the form of light lacework patterns, often an approved feature in late nineteenth-century architecture, while Mexican onyx clads the robust structural features in the lobby, introducing a rich quality to the decoration scheme. Even richer is a very large-scale fireplace flanked by neo-Renaissance columns in solid onyx, supporting the mantel above the central opening. No fire grate occupies the opening now but its size accommodates instead the access to a shop. High above the lobby, stained glass of similar design to the original filters in the necessary light, and a number of lighting fittings within the arches of the lobby are said to survive from the days before the 1930s, when the hotel generated its own electricity. Public rooms, though now on the two lowest floors, were originally split up, the ballroom, a men's club and the ladies' 'ordinary' or sitting-room being on the top floor. This arrangement was more common in the United States than in most other countries. Throughout its life the Brown Palace has benefited from owners and managements who collected antiques of various kinds. English Georgian silver and Sheffield plate were acquired by C. K. Boettcher, a previous hotel owner. Prize among his collection is a 1763 Chinoiserie silver épergne made in London but finding its way west via Christie's auction rooms. Relics of the Napoleonic Wars have also been added to the historic background of the 'Palace Arms', while seafaring souvenirs and model clipper ships decorate the 'Ship Tavern'.

Eminent visitors to Denver have usually patronized the Brown Palace, and these have included a good score of Presidents, from Teddy Roosevelt to Dwight D. Eisenhower. Under many changes of ownership it has consistently maintained its national status.

A small Colorado hotel in Georgetown, only 46 miles from Denver, is worth mentioning here, for it gives an indication of unexpected cultural flowering among the mine-workings and Rocky Mountains in the area. The hotel represented a Frenchman's personal tribute to the cuisine and hotelkeeping of his own country after many years in America.[9] Built in a straightforward classical style with two storeys of pedimented windows and a crested cornice it was christened 'Hôtel de Paris' by its owner, designer and builder, known in Georgetown as Louis Dupuy but born in Alençon, northern France, as Adolphe François Gerard. He was a man of many talents, and since these included that of master chef, on opening the hotel in 1875 he quickly established it as a place for fine wines and excellent food. Isabella Bird during her intrepid travels appears to have referred to it as 'a good

hotel declivitously situated', and Dupuy's ambition to create a stylish and luxurious hotel as a 'little souvenir of Alençon' seems to have been fulfilled. Since 1954 a comprehensive programme of conservation has been carried out under the ownership of the Colonial Dames of America.

Chicago, after its disastrous fire of 1871, developed as a centre of architectural innovation and excellence. Louis H. Sullivan (1856–1924) was prominent in this movement and created his first great work, the Auditorium Building (1887–9), as a focus of business and social activities. This incorporated, together with the extensive office accommodation, an opera house and a hotel, setting standards and introducing new ideas well outside the well-worn neo-classicism of the time. This seminal building is still in existence but no longer houses either an opera or a hotel. It was listed as a Historic Place in 1981. At a later date, although still drawing on inspiration from the Auditorium, Ben Marshall (1874–1944) of the Marshall and Fox architectural partnership designed the Drake Hotel on a fine site with views of Lake Michigan. The Drake opened in 1920 and remains a highly-regarded landmark with external reminders of the Sullivan tradition. Necessary renovation had become feasible after Hilton International acquired a lease in 1979, and much of the original neo-Renaissance interior style was retained under the direction of designer David T. Williams and the management of Victor T. Burt. Most notable among the grand public spaces are the lobbies and the Italianate, lavishly-gilded Gold Coast Room. This style of décor is similar to that in a number of important American city hotels where large public functions required space and grandeur.

Europe

Substantial parts of Europe and North America had been transformed by industrialization into urban cultures in the nineteenth century but the year 1900, when it came, made no neat watershed between old and new, leaving established ways of life to continue in their own directions until the momentous upheaval of the Great War.

Historically each century acquires its own classification, and although for Britain the term 'Victorian' ceased literally with the death of the Queen in 1901 after 63 years on the throne, the Edwardian social inheritance showed few signs of the revolution to come. The great days of British railway hotels had reached a peak in the 1860s boom and had been closely followed by the Swiss achievements examined in chapter Four. Rudyard Kipling's remark that 'The Swiss are the only people who have taken the trouble to master the art

Chicago, Drake Hotel, 1920, designed by Ben Marshall,
drew inspiration from Louis Sullivan's architectural style.

ABOVE & LEFT Marshall's interiors incorporated Italian
Renaissance features, to be seen in the Lobby and Palm Court,
but embodying his flamboyance most emphatically in the Gold
Coast Room.

of hotel-keeping' contains a great deal of truth. The 1880s and 1890s had shown steady increase in other European countries, and Canada experienced an exceptional burst of railroad hotel development that began in the 1880s. The pattern in the United States was more irregular and had at first lagged behind Canada but moved rapidly after the techniques of skyscraper building were mastered. South-east Asia and other far-flung places where trade and colonization was maturing, or where tourism had reason to be established, had also come late into the scene but were able to use the inventions of the twentieth century in accomplishing international standards.

The early twentieth-century hotels we have looked at in territorial outposts generally continued in the traditional architectural dress without attempting 'modernity'. Edwardian lushness, which was, after all, still an indispensable part of the *belle époque*, expressed itself unashamedly in a language close to that of the Second Empire. Competing styles were not often used and some of them stemmed more from Victorian historicism than from the opposing trend of unadorned utility originating in the German Bauhaus movement. Between the two extremes, Art Nouveau and the British Arts & Crafts Movement offered complementary approaches to decorative design. These styles were sometimes accepted as suitable backgrounds to hotel life but never replaced the more familiar grandeur. Even this was close to demise, losing its suitability in the social revolution of war, women's suffrage and the new political theories. The great days of grand hotels sparkled again spasmodically until the Second World War, sustained by industrial wealth and the café society that could use cars or aeroplanes as well as private yachts to reach the latest centres of fashion. Exclusivity, which had been such an important factor in the development of the European grand hotel, diminished as this mobility increased and as previously strict social restraints were relaxed. The greater part that women began to play in the conduct of affairs had been accelerated during the Great War as active and professional fields were opened to them.

Bearing in mind that many hotel projects coming to fruition in the new century had been conceived before widespread social changes, it is not surprising to find both old and new ideas of design in this period of transition.

Britain: London Enterprises

Britain's first new grand hotel of the twentieth century was in fact originally a railway hotel and has been discussed as such in an earlier chapter. This is the Midland Hotel, Man-

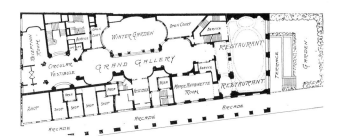

London, Ritz Hotel, 1906, by Charles Mewès and Arthur Davis remains one of their best known designs, a skilful use of interrelated spaces producing interior vistas that enhance the apparent size of the public rooms.

A Beaux-Arts exterior with Parisian-style arcade and mansard roof adorns the south side of Piccadilly.

chester, which with the Caledonian, Edinburgh, was opened in 1903. Both had long periods of gestation and belonged essentially to the mainstream of nineteenth-century railway culture. Rebuilding the Adelphi, Liverpool (1914), has also been mentioned, and the Queen's, Leeds (1937), was altogether more up-to-date in amenities but is uninspiring as architecture and beyond our time-span.

In Edwardian London, the site of much building in the first years of the century, several new hotels came to life. The Savoy was being extended in 1904 by T. E. Collcutt and continued to hold its foremost position among the stylish younger generation that still drew its clientèle from the world of theatre and from across the Atlantic. Times were indeed changing – not only could unescorted women eat in public restaurants, they could also smoke in them. Compton Mackenzie maintained that 'it was the bicycle that gave women their liberty by giving them mobility', and at this

The restaurant, looking over Green Park, maintains a Parisian atmosphere. For the interior décor of the Ritz's ground-floor rooms the architects received a fee of 5 per cent of the cost of the work, twice the rate payable on the overall building cost.

A sitting-room in one of the suites, perpetuating the Louis XVI style that César and Marie-Louise Ritz had made a hallmark of their earlier hotels.

stage in women's liberation London preceded New York.

Another new London hotel competing in the fashionable stakes was the Ritz in Piccadilly, completed on 15 May 1906 on the site of the previous Walsingham House and Bath Hotels. Ritz himself had been closely involved with the creation of the Hôtel Ritz in Paris a few years before, but his London interests at the Savoy and the Carlton had more recently been difficult and exhausting. The further shock of postponement (through peritonitis) of Edward VII's coronation two days before the planned date affected Ritz, who was deeply concerned in organizing the celebrations at the Carlton that had to be cancelled. He collapsed into a breakdown that marked the effective end of his active life.

The project for the new hotel nevertheless proceeded, with financial backing from Alfred Beit and other subscribers to the hotel company, and was still to bear the name Ritz. Charles Mewès (1858–1914) was the architect, in partnership with Arthur J. Davis (1878–1951), a brilliant École des Beaux-Arts student who had recently worked with Mewès on the Paris Ritz. Parisian influences from the Louvre, the Place Vendôme and the Rue de Rivoli therefore were paramount in a unified neo-Louis XVI style reflecting 'the general desire which arose in his [Mewès'] day for comfort and good cuisine amid well-planned and tasteful surroundings with a background for historical interest'.[10] The Palm Court and the Restaurant overlooking Green Park are splendid apartments furnished with plasterwork, marble, bronze statuary and fittings, and accomplished mural painting. A circular vestibule at the eastern end near the Arlington Street entrance is ingeniously planned to link up with the Piccadilly entrance and also give access to the Palm Court or Winter Garden and the Restaurant. From its inception, the Ritz emanated its own atmosphere and caught the approval of a rich established society connected with royalty and the Court without neglecting changing manners and tastes. Comfort and decoration observed hygienic principles laid down by Ritz, with absence of heavy fabrics and designs, often just a simple white décor enriched with gold-leaf mouldings. The 150 bedrooms and 75 bathrooms were arranged on six floors as suites, each with its separate lobby, lavatory and sitting-room.

As the first large steel-framed building in London it made history. Its granite facing at ground-floor arcade level, its Portland stonework to the upper floors and the green patina of its mansard roof proclaimed it a London landmark, unchanged externally for 90 years. To comply with the London Building Act (1894), the District Surveyor insisted on the traditional materials being capable in themselves of carrying the necessary loads, and therefore the steel frame designed by Sven Bylander was duplicated by an entirely unnecessary loadbearing 'cladding' system.[11] American and German expertise assisted in the mechanical as well as structural engineering and much care was taken to reduce noise transmission and provide (short-lived) air conditioning. The Waring White Building Co. Ltd were general contractors, working to the quantity surveyors' estimate of £347,000. Waring and Gillow's £102,000 for furnishing was contained in this figure, Mewès and Davis having researched into Louis XVI furniture designs that were accurately reproduced from the architects' drawings by Waring and Gillow. Bronze figures after Clodion and the Parisian Neptune and Nereid showpiece on the buffet enhance the Restaurant although the latter has now been gilded. Consistency of style and quality suffered damage over the years but was substantially restored in a 1980s refit. The basement Ballroom is now separated from the hotel as the Casino after a chequered experience as the Grill Room in 1930s International Modern style. Present décor, reverting to Louis Seize, is the work of Richmond Design Group.

Not far from the Ritz, the Piccadilly Hotel (1908), now under change of name to Le Meridien, has occupied a site related to the redevelopment of the Quadrant section of Regent Street near Piccadilly Circus. Part of a grand colonnaded south façade to the design of Richard Norman Shaw (1831–1912) had to be sacrificed to the requirements of another lessee, but the major section still screens an open air Tea Terrace at second-floor level. The north side, in Regent Street, took its part in the overall design of the Quadrant, leaving problems for the hotel company's architect, William Woodward (1846–1927), in reconciling detailed planning of the hotel with the overriding exterior design. Demolition of St James's Hall, which previously occupied the site, revealed foundations 40 feet below the street, allowing satisfactory construction of three extra floors 'of great practical utility', as a prospectus stated. The 'practical utility' encompassed grill-room and kitchen, Turkish and swimming baths, cellars and other offices, two billiard-rooms, lavatories and lifts. Above ground, the entrance foyer from Piccadilly, the rotunda adjoining the Quadrant entrance and the grand lounge between the two made an impressive introduction to the restaurants and other public rooms. Interior design and decoration were allocated to three different specialist contractors. Goodalls of Manchester dealt with the grill-room, ground, first and second floors in which French neo-classicism was favoured. Floors three to five went to Liberty of London, floors six to nine being shared between two Norwich firms, Chamberlin and Bunting. 'Old English, Adam, Chippendale, Sheraton, Empire, or the more modern

The Ritz became fashionable as soon as it opened, and this artist's view expresses its lively Edwardian atmosphere.

London, Piccadilly Hotel, 1908. Richard Norman Shaw had designed the Regent Street Quadrant, and the Piccadilly (now Meridien) Hotel was fitted by William Woodward into the space behind the imposing façades. Unlike the unified interior style of the Ritz, the Piccadilly appointed three different furnishing firms to produce a variety of period rooms.

school of English design' were all on offer, and the last-mentioned included 'Fitment rooms' with 'extensive wardrobe space and various conveniences cunningly arranged by devices rarely found even in the best private houses'.[12]

The general contractor for the building was Perry & Co., who completed the work in about eighteen months. Quantities of materials used included 6½ million bricks and 104,000 cubic feet of Portland stone, 11,000 square yards of wall tiling, 200 miles of piping for light and heating, 16,000 electric lamps and 8 passenger lifts plus luggage lifts. Expenditure must have outrun practical finance, and in another eighteen months the enterprise had failed but was bought by R. E. Jones of Cardiff and revived through vigorous advertising campaigns aimed at Cunard and Norddeutscherlloyd steamship passengers as well as readers of the *Gentlewoman's Court Journal*. Also built by the contractors Waring White, who were responsible for the Ritz, is the Waldorf Hotel, designed in early twentieth-century classical style by A. M. and A. G. R. Mackenzie, father and son, who had studied under René Sergent in Paris.

Entirely different design characterized two large new hotels on the Bedford Estate in Bloomsbury that were designed by Charles FitzRoy Doll (1850–1929). The Russell, opened in 1900, is an eight-storey pile in brick and terracotta, termed 'super-François-Premier-château' by Pevsner, but although acknowledged to have been inspired by an engraving of the Parisian Château de Madrid that stood in the Bois de Boulogne until 1785, it seems more of an undisciplined amalgam of arcading, bays, corner turrets, Dutch gables and a campanile-style tower at the south-east corner. Before Woburn Place and Southampton Row were turned into a traffic artery, the hotel was linked visually to the gardens of Russell Square. A wealth of detail, both outside and internally, make it into a memorable but overpowering structure.[13] Two large salons, one a space for banqueting or receptions and the other a ballroom sunk between this and the entrance hall, allowed by way of the changes of level the opportunity for dramatic entrances to display feminine finery. Marble pilasters are surmounted by broken pediments and wild baroque caryatids that would have competed with any but the most opulent Edwardian beauties. Marble from many sources decorates the main entrance foyer and staircase with balustrading derived from strapwork and terminating at second-floor level with a lively winged dragon in bronze. An inlaid marble zodiac pattern at the foot of the main stair is badly worn and now covered with carpet. Frederick Hotels Limited owned the lease and Maples, with close connection to the hotels chain, furnished and decorated the whole.

Doll, as surveyor to the Bedford Estate, then designed the Imperial Hotel nearby in a similar ebullient manner, but this time attracting the Pevsnerism 'equally colossal but a much more vicious mixture of Art Nouveau Gothic and Art Nouveau Tudor'.[14] This hotel was demolished in the 1960s for replacement by a modern version, only a few royal stone statues being saved and repositioned as mementoes of what went before.

A contemporary advertisement for the Hotel Russell states 'Prices same as at the popular and famous Hotel Great Central', and draws our attention to the successful career as hotelier of Frederick Gordon. The Great Central (1899)

London, Waldorf Hotel, 1908 by A. M. and A. G. R. Mackenzie. Flanked by two theatres, the Waldorf occupies a northern block of the Aldwych. India House now occupies the site in the foreground.

A Palm Court occupies pride of place as the centre of the Waldorf's raised ground-floor area.

with eight storeys containing 700 bedrooms and brick with terracotta exterior pre-dated the Russell by a year, but the two bear close resemblance. The design by Edis for the Great Central preserves more classical detail well-integrated into disciplined proportions, but the similarity surely owes something to the preferences of the developer.

Frederick Gordon (*c.* 1840–1904) started his career as a solicitor practising in Holborn and living in Chigwell, Essex. The death of his wife in 1869 plunged him into City politics as a distraction. This completely changed the course of his working life after his election to the City of London Common Council one year later. With his brother-in-law Horatio Davies he took interests in businessmen's restaurants, starting with the London Tavern and Pimm's. Crosby Hall and the Holborn Restaurant followed with growing success until he instigated a new hotel for the middle and business classes on a site in Trafalgar Square. The 1870s slump had followed the 1860s boom in the Victorian hotel-building world, but the newly converted hotelier took the risk of financial recovery being imminent and began to build the Grand in 1878–9, having obtained young and vigorous support from among his City contacts. The architects were F. and H. Francis (1818–96 and 1821–94 respectively), whose City style at 33–5 Cornhill (1857) and 39 Lombard Street (1868) incorporated rich ornament on a background of classicism. Such sculptural decoration of the Grand Hotel had existed but was evidently chiselled away when it went out of fashion. Multi-coloured marble and mosaics, an 'arched roof of stained glass' over the dining-room and a 'spectacle almost distressing in its magnificence' greeted the Lord Mayor when he opened the hotel in May 1881.[15] The 1880s saw two more hotels, the First Avenue in Holborn and the Metropole in Northumberland Avenue, being added to Gordon's chain, and success on this scale raised his sights to focus on an international enterprise. In England the classical Burlington at Eastbourne, and the Metropole, Brighton (1888), were acquired in addition to the Royal Pier Hotel, named for its connection with Queen Victoria, on the Isle of Wight. Overseas, the Metropole, Cannes, had just been built above the town, with wonderful views, tennis courts and well-designed subtropical gardens. Along the coast, the Metropole (1889) in Monte Carlo was designed by Hans-Georg Tersling (1857–1920) as his first independent major work. It pays restrained tribute to the high style of Charles Garnier's Monte Carlo Casino built ten years previously, and is still in use. Both these Riviera Metropoles were part of Gordon's empire. Building in Monte Carlo was frenetic and, although international society was sensitive to every vagary of politics and fashion, before the end of the century as many as 50 first-class hotels

London, Hotel Russell, 1900, by Charles FitzRoy Doll for Frederick Hotels Limited, a profusion of features and detail which leaves no architectural stone unturned.

were competing for the winter season visitors. Gordon Hotels by the 1930s was finding the Cannes property unprofitable and sold it for use as a seminary, but the gamblers in Monte Carlo continued to patronize their Metropole to a satisfactory extent.

Collaboration with Maple & Co. of Tottenham Court Road, London, for fitting out Gordon Hotels helped to consolidate Maples as one of the leading furnishers and decorators in the generation following its formation as a private limited company in 1891. Already John Blundell Maple, an MP since 1887, had looked to royalty and the British Empire for his company's trade, offering an extraordinarily wide scope of contracts, from supplying 'Artistic Cosy Corners' for well-to-do domestic customers to making fine quality furniture for the Viceregal Palace in Simla. His company may have provided limited risks for investors but was carefully structured to give 'the Governor' control of management and appointment of directors. A Paris branch of Maples handled the redecoration and furnishing of the Elysée Palace Hotel, and Maples in 1894 was one of three contractors for the interior work at the vast new 800-room Cecil Hotel on London's Thames Embankment, now replaced by Shell-Mex House, which could seat 1,000 for a banquet and possessed its own masonic temple. An immense 'Empire' chimneypiece designed by Maples for the Drawing Room was almost a temple in itself.[16] Walls panelled in green silk, soft colours for silk-covered furniture and tapestry woven curtains seemed to have been popular lines in the 1890s. The other two firms who contributed to the interiors for the Cecil were Shoolbreds and S. J. Waring & Co., the latter evolving into Waring & Gillow through the amalgamation of Lancashire furnishers and furniture makers of distinction.

With Frederick Gordon and Sir John Blundell Maple as directors on each other's company boards, Maple emphasized that Maple & Co. had no financial interest in either Gordon Hotels Ltd or the Henry Fredericks Syndicate. The furnishing work would be 'carried out on the same terms as the work which we did for all the Gordon Hotels'. These pronouncements were presumably aimed at reassuring public and shareholders that fair contracts were being made. Maples obviously concentrated on hotel furnishing, as a random sample from their 1898 customers' list shows, the following being included in their total of about 40 hotel names:

Royal Station Hotel, Hull (for NER)
Grand Hotel, Brighton (new bedroom wing)
Charing Cross Hotel, new wing (50 bedrooms)
Grand Atlantic Hotel, Weston-super-Mare
Coburg (later Connaught) Hotel
Savoy, Victoria Embankment
Royal Station Hotel, York
Hotel Carol Ire, Kustendjie, Roumania
Avenida Palace Hotel, Lisbon.[17]

The length of list clearly indicates the boom conditions in the hotel world and a spread of demand that was not as exclusive as it had been.

The Great Central Hotel at Marylebone Station gave mutual aid to its close associate, stating 'Decoration and Furnishing by Maple' in its advertising material. A brief survey of the Great Central's life this century is worth following to encourage optimism towards other equally unlikely candidates for rescue and conservation. In its first state, the hotel suffered requisitioning by the War Office during the Great War, and was then released for hotel use until 1939, when a new war forced the government to take it over once more. Nationalization led to its conversion into the headquarters of the British Railways Board until 1989, after which a Japanese corporation restored it to the original conception with added state-of-the-art technology and a spectacular and wholly successful late twentieth-century covered atrium that also made increased floor areas possible. In this form and with active marketing it appears to have flourished, first as the Regent and presently as the Landmark.

British Modern Movement buildings of any kind were comparatively rare, even in the 1920s and 1930s, and the

London, Hotel Cecil, 1896, by architects Perry and Reed, now demolished, was the largest hotel in Europe when built. Its drawing-room fire surround by Maples was probably the largest in Europe, too.

style, descended from Bauhaus ideals, never became widely popular. Cinemas, seaside pavilions (such as at Bexhill) and specially-commissioned house or apartment schemes comprised the main body of work built, and these have since dwindled in number although a single Art Deco hotel has managed to survive: the Midland Grand Hotel, Morecambe (1932–3). Convincingly designed by Oliver Hill for the LMS Railway Hotels, the sweeping lines of the undecorated cement-rendered exterior are crescent-shaped in form with concrete balconies integrated as part of the design. A rotunda café and bar at one end takes full advantage of the site on the shoreline, and the seaward view across Morecambe Bay to the Lake District fells would alone justify a visit. Internally, work was commissioned from distinguished artists – Eric Ravilious and Eric Gill – who contributed mural decoration as part of the Jazz Moderne décor, although the Gill relief was unfortunately removed some years ago. Recently, after

long neglect, the Midland has found a sympathetic owner
with enthusiasm for the style and willingness to restore it to
its original state.

London, Strand Palace Hotel, 1925–30, by F. J. Willis contained
extensive Art Deco interiors by Oliver Bernard. Most of these have
disappeared, although the basement has escaped destruction and
restoration is being considered. Various items in glass and chrome
removed from the hotel and now held in the Victoria & Albert
Museum's reserve collection might then reappear.

Morecambe, Midland Grand Hotel, 1933, by Oliver Hill.
A railway poster showing the circular café.

The Midland Grand was a railway hotel, but is now endeavouring
to survive under private ownership.

A section of the repainted Eric Ravilious murals in the café.

An Eric Gill mural in the form of a map, with transport motifs headed by *The Royal Scot*.

Portugal

The Iberian peninsula, aside from the European mainstream in the nineteenth century, featured little in the culture of wealth, fashion and business that generated the grand hotels. The present successful state sponsoring of *paradores* and *pousadas* in Spain and Portugal respectively does not come within our scope here, being concentrated on the conversion of historic buildings created for other uses and on purpose-built hotels of recent date outside our time span.

One that fulfils all our criteria is the Palace Hotel at Bussaco, Portugal. It was built for another purpose, but like the Imperial in Vienna was almost immediately used as a hotel without major adaptation. Reminiscent of the follies Ludwig II had been building in Bavaria from 1870 onwards as summer palaces, this was intended as a royal hunting lodge for King Carlos I and had its beginnings in previous ideas of Luis I that had not come to fruition. On this occasion the Minister of Public Works, Emidio Navarro, backed the project. The concept of creating a large hotel seems to have arisen as part of the same scheme, with the royal apartments visualized as occupying only a private section of the whole building.[18] The site is a historic one, passing through monastic orders from the Augustinian canons of Coimbra to a Carmelite order who built on it in the early seventeenth century a large monastery, enclosed behind walls as required by the monks' way of life with enough cleared forest to give room for cultivating their own sustenance. Apart from these needs they planted trees, forming the nucleus of a now famous arboretum that is still maintained and now contains 400 native and 300 exotic species. Cedar, cypress, gingko, sequoia, araucaria and palm have grown into exceptionally fine specimens, many obtained from Mexico, Lebanon, India and Africa by Portuguese navigators. Numerous chapels and other retreats were built by the monks, as were basins and fountainheads, scattered along the forest paths and culminating in the Fonte Fria cascade with 144 water steps flowing down to a large basin. A papal decree of 1643 prohibited felling or the damaging of trees.

A later brush with history was during the Peninsular War, and one of the trees is labelled 'Wellington's olive tree' in commemoration of the battle of Bussaco (1810). Wellington occupied the monastery and defended the ridge, to be attacked from the rear by seasoned Napoleonic troops who fought a bitter battle against British and Portuguese reserves and went on, under Massena, to take Coimbra. Soon afterwards, at Torres Vedras, fortunes were reversed as Napoleon's third attempt at seizing Portugal failed. Religious houses in Portugal were secularized in 1834 and became

Bussaco, Portugal, the Palace Hotel, opened in 1911, by Italian architect Luigi Manini, who proved a very skilful interpreter of the historic Portuguese Manueline style.

The Palace's covered open-air restaurant area looks out over formal gardens and towards what was originally the royal wing.

On the upper section of the Palace's grand staircase wall an attractive *trompe-l'œil* panel breaks a large flat surface into further apparent vaulting and balustrades.

Coimbra, Portugal, Hotel Astoria, 1926, by Adães Bermudes shows French influence coupled with individuality of detail, especially as seen in the crown of the cupola.

Goanese furniture in the Palace's entrance hall recalls Portuguese overseas ventures and blends well with the intricate neo-Manueline decoration of the building.

the property of the crown, but at Bussaco the surviving Carmelites were allowed to remain in occupation. As the century progressed, state interest in the property revived and the building scheme gradually took shape. Little remained of the monastery, although coloured stone mosaics in black, white, red and ochre still ornament an entrance screen, probably the work of the last monks, and the small church still stands. The architect selected for the new building was Luigi Manini, an Italian with experience as a stage designer. In this there was another parallel with Ludwig's Bavarian palace at Linderhof, where the interiors had been designed by Franz von Seitz (1817–83), director and stage designer at the Munich State Theatre. Manini started the work at Bussaco c. 1888 and it continued until 1907. The style of the building attracted very mixed opinions, but Manini's dedication to his neo-Manueline invention is obvious. Externally the building appears as a square castle-like block with a corner tower and spire on which the Portuguese heraldic armillary sphere is mounted, a reminder of Portugal's one-time domination in the age of great discoveries. Twelve-arched Manueline arcading on two sides provides access to an inconspicuous entrance, every arch encrusted with carving. This prepares the eye for interior door frames, colonnettes, vaulting ribs and window tracery carved to simulate ropework. Leaves, flowers, gargoyles and armillary spheres decorate pierced balustrades and friezes and the local limestone, finely tooled by Portuguese craftsmen, even on undecorated surfaces. The extent and complication of the work explain in part the length of time needed for completion. Freely adapted Italian Renaissance motifs dominate the two large sitting-rooms and play strange tricks of scale, with short fat columns supporting the dividing archway and oversized urns flanking an undersized but elegant lute-player sculpted by Costa Mola on a heavy chimneypiece. Hexagonal coffering of natural redwood for the ceiling of the large dining-room recalls the Alhambra or the Doge's Palace, Venice, or both, while in the same room and on the vast staircase, over-scaled windows sit uncomfortably with the highly detailed decoration. A delightful stone-vaulted rotunda leads out of the dining-room with pointed gothic openings permitting open-air dining. The main staircase is far more robust, with its *azulejo* tiled panels from Caldas da Rainha depicting historic occasions and the great tinted window distributing light to the highly decorated inner hall below, where Batalha-inspired motifs run riot in door surrounds and vaulted ceiling. On the upper level of the staircase a frescoed panel of *trompe-l'œil* illusion repeats the reality of the adjacent balustrade, columns and vault.

Furnishings for some public spaces depart from the prac-

Curia, Portugal, Curia Palace Hotel, 1926. Described as 'one of Europe's last Art Nouveau palaces' and designed by M. J. Norte júnior, the Curia Palace has a main façade with later additions in a formal garden setting. It is under the same Almeida management, and its vineyards contribute grapes to the exclusive Bussaco wines. Ironwork and decorative woodwork characterize the interior.

tice of using local materials and craftsmanship and represent instead Portugal's oriental interests. The furniture in the ground-floor inner hall is Goanese Indian, and on the first floor is Macau Chinese, native Portuguese pieces reappearing on the second floor. The Bussaco Palace Hotel is full of contradictions, and in the context of a large and seemingly overpowering building, bedrooms are light, airy and well-furnished with Portuguese reproductions of Louis XVI and English Edwardian periods. Bathrooms en suite were provided from the date of opening as a hotel in 1911. The Palace never had the opportunity of housing Carlos I, who was assassinated in Lisbon in 1908. His young son reigned as Manuel II long enough to enjoy its royal apartments in one summer only before going into exile when Portugal was declared a republic in 1910.

Management was let out to the hotelier Alexandre de Almeida from three years earlier, and his grandson and namesake is now in charge of the same company, still in possession of the lease. The first Alexandre entered the wine-making business to supply local wine to the hotel restaurant. The exclusivity of his wines, only available in the group's small number of hotels and not on the retail market, attracted attention and stimulated custom. Its growing reputation owes much to the Palace manager, Jose Rodrigues dos Santos, who, starting as bellboy in 1934, added this unusual extra to his duties. The hotel's own cellars house the fermenting and ageing processes in vats made from home-grown oak. Sixty thousand bottles constitute the stock of white and red wines made from local grapes, some from Curia where

Madrid, Spain, Ritz Hotel, 1910, by Charles Mewès and Don Luis de Landecho, who followed the principles of Cèsar Ritz, balancing quality and luxury with good taste rather than excess. It now belongs to Trusthouse Forte.

In the main and lower halls ornament is elegant and unobtrusive.

another Almeida hotel, the Curia Palace, is of some interest. It was opened in 1926, a work by architect Manuel Joachim Norte júnior (1878–1962) who was Beaux-Arts trained in Lisbon and Paris and also architect for the Portuguese Royal Palace. The main entrance is placed centrally and surmounted by a tall baroque screen embodying typical Portuguese elements. Art Nouveau ironwork, woodwork and glass attract attention in the entrance hall.

The Hotel Astoria, Coimbra, is in the same hotel group and was opened in the same year as the Curia Palace, but its designer was Adães Bermudes (1864–1948). He was another Beaux-Arts student, more at home in a classical vocabulary and incorporating the familiar domed corner-turret motif. A respectfully designed modern wing was added in 1947.

Spain

Developments in continental Europe had already satisfied most demands during the nineteenth century, and the hotels of the next decade usually answered some specific needs of politics and fashion. National prestige came into play when international standards of accommodation could not be met for travelling statesmen and celebrities. This awareness, traced in preceding pages, almost always found entrepreneurs with enthusiasm and enough financial backing to solve the problem. Grand hotels with every available comfort and with first-class cuisine provided the practical answer.

Madrid had remained provincial in atmosphere and did not until the beginning of the twentieth century explore the benefits of modernization as a city. During the first quarter of the new century rapid advances were made, and two luxury hotels in the heart of the capital were established as of world class, a position that both still justify. In October 1910 under the patronage of Alfonso XIII, grandfather of the present monarch, Juan Carlos, the Ritz Hotel in the Plaza de la Lealtad was opened and a few months later the King laid the foundation stone for the Palace Hotel on the opposite side of the plaza. Both instances arose from the difficulties he had experienced in obtaining suitable lodging for guests at his own wedding, to an English granddaughter of Queen Victoria to be known as Queen Ena, in 1906. The Ritz was financed by a hotel company, the Sociedad Hôtel Ritz, created to develop just such accommodation. The scheme received the approval of César Ritz by employing as architects Charles Mewès and Don Luis de Landecho. Landecho was to deal with the building process on the ground in accordance with Mewès's detailed design, which in its turn satisfied all the standards of a Ritz hotel. Mewès, born in Strasbourg, had

the authentic Parisian Beaux-Arts training and the achievements of a distinguished career behind him, including the Hôtel Ritz in Paris (1898), which combined fastidious neoclassicism with the elegance of Louis XVI interiors. The Madrid site required his architectural finesse in handling a concave entrance façade and, with a circular corner turret surmounted by a cupola, he seemed to dismiss the difficulties with an apparently easy solution. Art and artifice skilfully applied have produced an impression of symmetry and balance that extends also to the interior disposition of public rooms and salons on the ground floor. Interior finishes, true to Ritz's principles, are light in colour, with the emphasis on the quality not the quantity of decoration. Works of renovation have largely kept the original style, and carpets which were beyond repair were rewoven (at £300 per square metre in the 1980s) by hand at the Royal Factory in Madrid. Many of those needing repair were worked on in situ. In the restaurant, two skilled workers could work only in the clear times between meals.[19] Carefully chosen antique furniture and works of art punctuate the public rooms, the sculpture of *Diana the Huntress* acting as a focal point in the lower hall. Fresh flower arrangements follow Ritzian principles.

Things became different during the Second World War, a sensitive period for Spain since it was, in spite of the Franco régime, pursuing a delicate course of neutrality after emerging from its Civil War. Secret agents of the various combatant nations watched each other carefully on the neutral territory of the hotels but violence stayed away from the Ritz, which lived to see another day.

The Madrid Palace Hotel, not more than a stone's throw away, presents a contrast in style and approach. The two hotels have much in common and both received royal interest and approval under the grand improvement plans that aimed to make Madrid a worthy capital city for the twentieth century. Both occupy prominent corner sites and are rooted in the classical elements so widely adopted in grand hotel design. Their façades are divided vertically into the usual zones of rusticated plinth, then a mid-zone for several floors of bedrooms where pilasters or similar vertical features take the place of columns in the classical vocabulary. A horizontal decorated band and balustrade represent the frieze and cornice above, with a final and variable treatment of roof and attics according to the needs for space and architectural emphasis. The design for the Palace, as for the Ritz, came under strong French influence but looked less towards Beaux-Arts principles and derived freer inspiration from neo-baroque and Art Nouveau sources. Belgian architect Edouard-Jean Niermans (1859–1928) with previous hotel building experience worked on it in conjunction with Edu-

Madrid, Palace Hotel, 1909, by Edouard-Jean Niermans, assisted by
Eduardo Ferrès Puig, adopted a neo-classical style similar to that of
the Ritz in the same city. The two hotels are in close proximity, on
opposite sides of the Plaza de la Lealtad.

ardo Ferrès Puig (1873–1928) from Vilassar del Mar, responsible also for the Ritz, Barcelona (1920), and the Grand Hotel, Lisbon.

Where the Ritz, with less than 200 rooms and suites, was catering for an exclusive and often royal clientèle, the Palace offered more than twice the accommodation and filled a central role in *madrileño* social life. Practical technology was innovative, using structural reinforced concrete for the first time in the capital. The luxury of a private bathroom to every bedroom was also looked on as extravagant – even the new Ritz had only half that ratio. Grandeur in the arrangement of public rooms is given full consideration without being overpowering. From a marble-floored low level porch and vestibule decorated in *trompe-l'œil*, the main floor is reached, with access to the winter garden roofed with a fine stained-glass dome, a favourite treatment of Niermans harking back to the glass structures of London's Crystal Palace or Kew Gardens. The dome is designed to imitate a circular tent, showing the painted rings and ropes by which it is 'secured' and ornamented with stylized painted red rose garlands. Carpets from the Royal Factory provide an important element, being made in geometric and arabesque patterns to suit each individual salon or public space. Salons, restaurant and shopping arcades are accessible from the circular central hall, which forms an ideal social rendezvous. A fine chandelier with lustre drops to emulate palm fronds hangs centrally within the dome.

The island site that the Palace possesses has solved the question of planning for adequate daylight in all rooms, it being built in an irregular trapezoid form around a central patio. An extensive basement provided space for heating and lighting equipment and plant for water purification and refrigeration. The latter cooled the air for the winter garden when required and made ice for a skating rink opposite the hotel, in the Calle del Duque de Medinaceli. Stores for wine, food, silver and linen, a coffee-roasting machine and a large coal store with its own miniature wagon system for distribution took up more space, but enough was left for carpentry, plumbing, painting and upholstery workshops, furniture and other storage rooms, lockers for staff use and the house laundry. The kitchen on the main floor could distribute to three service pantries on each of the upper floors and the topmost level housed any servants travelling with their employers.

In 1925 an addition of bar and billiard-room was carried out by the architect Martin Dominguez, and during the Civil War the hotel was used as a hospital and as the Soviet Embassy. After this, part of the frontage to Plaza de Canovas was let off as commercial premises. Fortunately a 1973 scheme

Madrid, Palace Hotel. Niermans was an experienced hotel architect, and comparison between the grand salons in the Palace and in the Negresco, Nice, of three years later (*see pages 285–6*), shows substantial similarity.

OPPOSITE ABOVE Nice, Hotel Negresco, 1910–13, one of E.-J. Niermans's period rooms.

ABOVE & OPPOSITE BELOW Glimpses of the interiors to be found in Niermans's Palace Hotel in Madrid.

A *trompe-l'œil* mural in the Madrid Palace's lower entrance hall dwarfs the reception staff.

was abandoned, saving the hotel for the current revival of interest in conservation and preservation of the *belle époque* interiors. Close proximity of the *Cortes* or parliament building encouraged politicians and journalists, but guest lists also covered the usual wide range of actors, artists, singers and writers.

Ferrès Puig's Hôtel Ritz, Barcelona (1919), is a pleasing symmetrical neo-classical façade now cleaned of thick paint-work to reveal the real stone facing. Reinforced by Puig's inspection of Ritz's other hotels from a functional point of view but in architectural origin clearly bred in Madrid, the three-bay corner entrance is placed between five-bay wings. The two convex linking sections bear not cupolas but Edwardian-type curved pediments, columns, cartouches and stone balconies, each flanked by a pair of putti and cornucopia sculptured groups. Internally there are axial approaches to eight different salons via a lobby with an impressive horseshoe staircase and some likeness to Niermans's work. The original interior design was by Santiago Marco, later recognized for his work in the fine arts by a royal decoration, the Cross of Alfonso X. The architect at present dealing with the interior design is José Canals. Marble floors, crystal chandeliers and some fine carpets establish the good pedigree of the building, and in the Salon Jardin a marble fountain with Neptune-head spouting into the basin is pleasantly framed by long-established planting. The 155 rooms and 6 suites all with telephones and bathrooms offered space and unaccustomed luxury, but a strike sabotaged the opening ceremony. Four months passed before the unhappy start could be overcome on 20 January 1920 and a proper hotel service provided. Political unrest continued and trade was slow, enlivened by the visit in 1922 of Alfonso XIII and Queen Ena to inspect work in progress on the Royal Palace of Pedralbes. For the inauguration festivities of the Royal Palace two years later, the Barcelona Ritz handled all the services and accommodated the Italian royal family, including supplying and servicing on board the Italian naval flagship *Dante Alighieri* the farewell banquet given by the King and Queen of Italy.

In Seville, where Moorish architecture from the Middle Ages still contributes vitally to the special character of the city, another hotel of the twentieth century was built to serve national prestige on the occasion of the Ibero-American Exhibition. Royal support was once more given, the King having presented the site of the hotel to the city. He was also involved with the hotel's inauguration, allowing it to bear his name and performing the opening ceremony on 28 April 1928. An architectural competition had been held in connection with the exhibition, and the winners of the close-run con-

Barcelona, Hôtel Ritz, 1919, carried out by Ferrès Puig, clearly under the influence of both the Ritz and the Palace in Madrid.

San Sebastian, Hotel Maria Cristina, 1912, by Charles Mewès and Francesco Urcola Lazcanotegui.

test were José Espiau y Muñoz (1879–1938) in collaboration with Francisco Urcola Lazcanotegui, who had experience of hotel planning. Espiau, with many of his contemporaries in Seville, had been searching for a new architectural style to supplant that of the nineteenth century, which they considered to be outworn. They were not, of course, alone in this, and the work of the Viennese Secession movement, particularly of Josef Hoffmann, made a strong impression on Espiau, with its geometric interpretations of Art Nouveau motifs. Their winning hotel design was of very individual style, with a bias towards experiments in Andalucian structural and decorative traditions that had not escaped the influence of William Morris. Espiau concentrated on finding an *estilo sevillano* that would reflect historic influences in eclecticism.[20] He combined neo-Renaissance and baroque with neo-Mudéjar form and, mainly for the interior, a riot of polychrome *azulejo* set into marble and rich ivory coloured backgrounds. Architectural good manners were observed in the hotel's relationship to nearby buildings, one of which was the vast tobacco factory, now put to university use, celebrated in the opening scene of Bizet's *Carmen*. The burst of decoration inside the entrance hall and the successive elaborate interior

San Sebastian, Hotel Maria Cristina. With its neo-classical façades, domed corner tower and *belle époque* interiors, it clearly stemmed from the same Beaux-Arts influences as the Madrid and Barcelona grand hotels, and after refurbishment in 1986 it was mentioned as the best hotel in Spain.

Seville, the Hotel Alfonso XIII, 1928. José Espiau y Muñoz was the winner of the architectural competition for a hotel to serve the Ibero-American Exhibition, and sought for a modern *estilo sevillano* of which the city would be proud. Espiau worked in collaboration with Urcola Lazcanotegui, whose hotel experience was very valuable.

I. Salón Real
II. Salón la Cartuja
III. Salón Hispalis
IV. Salón Andalucía
V. Salón Triana
VI. Salón Betis

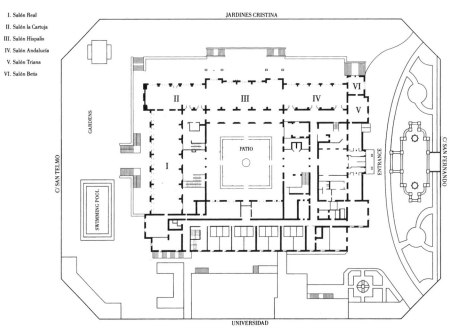

Arabic influence, including the traditional arrangement of enclosed patio, fostered richness of decoration restrained within a symmetrical arrangement at the Hotel Alfonso XIII.

The patio has changed very little since the Alfonso XIII was first
built, although its centrepiece has become more prominent, with
a raised fountain and basin.

Colour, in a disciplined range of blues and ochres, brown and black,
is used for tiling and ceramics, wrought metal and woodwork, within
a relatively sober exterior.

spaces recall Islamic traditions of creating a secluded inward-looking territory, a system of design that adapts itself well to the conception of the grand hotel as a self-contained world.

The construction process was fraught with delays, many occurring through the experimental nature of the design and through practical shortcomings. It took nearly ten years to complete the building, with ever-mounting costs. Fortunately it had the constant support of the committee for the Exhibition under the presidency of the Count of Urbina, which organization took occupation of part of the building as its own offices. At the final reckoning of 6,800,000 pesetas, after more millions had been spent on hot and cold water and telephone installations, air conditioning, decoration and furnishing, Seville was proud to possess a unique building and one of the greatest hotels of the world.

Russia: Moscow

The Hotel Metropol, Moscow, in Sverdlov (previously Theatre) Square was constructed between 1899 and 1903 to the designs of William Walcot (1874–1943), whose mother was Russian and whose father English. Its main five-storey façade is symmetrical in a version of the familiar five-part subdivision. The 23 bays contain a central crocketed and bay-windowed focal point flanked by a wing and pavilion treatment at each side. Large windows at ground-floor level carry arched heads in deference to the original 1820s classical design for the whole square. The most memorable highlight of the building, in the *style moderne* that Walcot used, is the ceramic facing of the two top floors. The fourth floor takes on the character of a bas-relief frieze by N. A. Andreev with a continuous composition of figures, drapery and plant forms, while the fifth floor supports coloured painted ceramic panels. Most notable of these is the central one above the main entrance entitled *The Princess of Dreams* from an original oil painting by Mikhail Vrubel after Rostand's play *La Princesse Lointaine*.

Such interest in art stemmed from the financier Savva Mamontov, whose family had bought themselves out of serfdom only 40 years before he was born and then had proceeded to make a fortune out of cotton textiles. Savva had created the Mamontov Art Workshop at Abramtsevo for the encouragement of art and artists. Vrubel was one of these; others were the Vasnetsov brothers, Elena Polenova and Nikolai Andreev. When a fire in Theatre Square left the present Metropol site open, an architectural competition was held for a new hotel and cultural centre. Walcot was not the winner of the competition, but his Art Nouveau design, to Mamontov's taste, won him the job. Walcot's other buildings in Moscow were houses in N. A. Ostrovsky Lane, Okhotny Row and Myashitsky Proezd, and also a hostel in Spiridonsevsky Lane. In 1906 he went to live in England on account of his wife's health and there became an eminent watercolour and perspective artist working on architectural subjects both antique and projected. His training at St Petersburg Imperial Academy of Art under Louis Benois and at the Beaux-Arts and Atelier Rodin in Paris stood him in good stead. Mamontov's part in the hotel enterprise came to an abrupt end, with charges of financial fraud being tried in 1900. Surprisingly, sources differ on the verdict given, but agree on the cessation of his involvement with the hotel. Work did proceed with Golovin, Chekonin and others, perhaps including Walcot himself, providing designs for ceramic panels to be made in the Abramtsevo workshop. A disastrous fire took place in the nearly finished building in December 1901, and *The Moscow Information* newspaper noted:

Fourteen fire brigades and six steam engines took part in putting out the fire. In spite of the enormous efforts of the fire brigades, all the four top floors, the huge sumptuous concert hall and the building in the courtyard were all completely gutted; the roof fell down and the ceilings caved in one after the other.

Over a foot of ice in Theatre Street and Neglinny Proezd was left by the fire-fighting appliances. Fortunately, the decorative ceramic work was saved but another three years of work was needed before the hotel could be opened in February 1905. Nearly seven years and seven million roubles had been invested in it, but this included the cultural cen-

Moscow, Hotel Metropol, 1903. William Walcot, half-Russian, half-English, designed a *style moderne* hotel for financier Savva Mamontov, who encouraged the new ideas in architecture. The ceramic frieze is of particular interest.

ABOVE & LEFT The lobby and restaurant have been refurbished, the latter with distinctly Russian treatment of the wall and dome surfaces.

tre, shops and offices, which made it a thriving centre. Culture included an impromptu rendering, in October 1905, of *Duninushku* by the great bass Fyodor Chaliapin, standing on a table in the domed restaurant.

During the October Revolution in 1917, the Metropol was defended by the Junkers but taken by the Red Guards after much shelling. It then housed new Soviet institutions, chiefly the All Russian Central Executive Committee under its Chairman Sverdlov, who virtually lived in the building. Reinstated as a nationalized hotel in the late 1920s, it was visited by Sergei Prokofiev in 1927 and George Bernard Shaw for his 75th birthday in 1931. Many other interested visitors went to see the Soviet Union and stayed at the Metropol, which remained largely unchanged but unkempt for half a century. Extensive renovation followed structural repairs in 1986 and a policy of modernizing to current international standards while conserving all historic items had produced a five-star result. The present 403 guest-rooms are a reduction of approximately 100 on the original number, to allow space for the necessary ratio of bathrooms. The usual requirements of swimming pool, health centre, conference facilities and auditorium have been added, but the Art Nouveau glass and bronze work of the lift shaft, the coloured glazed roof, marble columns, sculptures and fittings of the Metropol Restaurant and many other decorative details have been restored to their pre-Revolution state. Many of these were sent to the Hermitage Museum in St Petersburg for expert attention. Today it is managed by the Inter-Continental Hotels Group, although Intourist remains the owner.

Poland: Warsaw

It is unlikely that any other grand hotel at the end of the nineteenth century could have claimed as founder such a romantic figure as did the Hotel Bristol, Warsaw. Ignacy Jan Paderewski was then widely known as a pianist and composer and who, in the future, was to acquire political fame as Prime Minister and patriot. Before this happened he and his financial representative, Stanislaw Roskowski, had joined forces with Edmund Zaremba to buy a seventeenth-century Baroque palace in Warsaw, owned successively by noble families, including the Tarnowskis, from whom it acquired its name. This small group in 1898 made an unsuccessful attempt at running a panorama show on part of the Tarnowski site and Zaremba then left the consortium. Roszkowski considered that a luxury hotel was needed in Warsaw and should prove a good investment, so with Paderewski he formed a company and embarked upon the venture,

Paderewski making over his previous interest in the property to the company but still remaining the chief shareholder.

Dismemberment between Greater Russia, Germany and the Austro-Hungarian Empire had left Poland in the nineteenth century without a political identity, but Warsaw as a city had preserved an individual historic existence. With a general climate of technical advance and a rising inclination towards nationalism, development in Warsaw took place at the end of the century. In these circumstances the idea of an architectural competition for the design of a new city centre hotel caught much public and professional attention. When the competition took place, the winners were Tadeusz Stryjeński and Franciszek Maczyński, architects from Cracow whose design embodied the then modern Art Nouveau style. Reluctance in accepting such innovation brought into action a time-honoured sequence of post-competition events. Another more conservative architect was consulted for the modification of the design, Wladyslaw, son of Henryk Marconi, whose nearby Italian Renaissance-inspired Europejski Hotel of 1877 had been the first substantial hotel in Warsaw. Wladyslaw Marconi created neo-classical façades for the hotel on its corner site, eight storeys high, with decorative detail and a circular belvedere of slightly uncertain scale dominating the exterior. Many new amenities were incorporated in the hotel which was named 'Bristol' to give an aura of noble respectability rather than to celebrate any actual connection with the eighteenth-century Earl-Bishop. Structural fire precautions, built-in vacuum cleaning, central heating, refrigeration, no fewer than six telephone lines and a lift containing armchairs for the passengers were among the most admired features. Eighty suites were included in the 200 bedrooms, but only twenty bathrooms seem to have been considered necessary. Service shops were given space on the ground floor, and the usual public rooms had benefited greatly from the appointment of Otto Wagner the younger, who was responsible for an excellent interior design scheme in the Viennese Secession manner. Wagner's Art Nouveau décor for the favourite Apartment no. 109, carried out in 1902, was considered to be one of his masterpieces.

The opening festivities took place in 1901, making a joint celebration with the city's new Philharmonic Hall. Warsaw was a strange territory to many of the eminent visitors and this occasioned embarrassment for one elderly composer, whose acceptance telegram read 'Coming. Please find me a room without bed bugs. Grieg.' On being installed at the smart Hotel Bristol by Aleksander Rajchman, Director of the Philharmonic Hall, Edvard Grieg was mortified at his own inappropriate words.

Warsaw, Hotel Bristol, a *belle époque* design with characteristic neo-classical treatment and circular turret over the corner entrance, brought into current use under the auspices of Forte Hotels' extensive renovation.

Management of the hotel, which started under a Swiss, Herr Helbling, soon devolved upon Tadeusz Jentys, successor to Roszkowski, who with Jan Golkowski, ran it as joint Directors. Instability in Russia affected business after a few years, but matters improved and the hotel flourished as a social and cultural centre until the Great War, when German requisitioning interrupted expansion towards profitability. It was in January 1919, when Poland sought to regain independence and unity, that Paderewski, still chief shareholder and proprietor, was persuaded to serve his country by becoming its Prime Minister and Foreign Minister. The Hotel Bristol for a short time was the seat of government until the Royal Castle could be adapted for use. Within the remainder of the year, alternative pressures at home and abroad at the Peace Conference became irreconcilable and he relinquished first his political status and then his Polish properties, to reside in Switzerland and resume a musical career. Josef Pilsudski, soldier hero and Head of State at the time of Paderewski's government, remained at the centre of affairs until he, too, retired from public life in 1923. The banquet given in his honour was inevitably at the Hotel Bristol, in the *Sala Malinowa* with its customary stylish background, but his speech made no attempt to disguise deep disillusionment with the world of politics.

Like all other Warsaw luxury hotels except the Europejski, the Bristol was once again running at a deficit. The *Sala Malinowa* restaurant was able to maintain its reputation under separate management, providing for all important national, civic and cultural occasions as well as keeping public popularity. Bank ownership rescued finances in 1928 when a profitable year was once again achieved. Under the management of Marian Szaniawski, interior modernization was instigated, designed by architect Antoni Jawornicki but not completed until 1931. The fine Art Nouveau interiors had gone out of fashion and were destroyed and replaced by the modern equipment and amenities that were required to attract essential custom. The pace of hotel life had speeded up, punctuated by the occasional near-orgy, such as one recorded through the eyes of Artur Rubinstein after a Chaliapin concert, when the dinner party at the Bristol exploded under pressure of vodka mixed with charming dancers from the Warsaw Opera.

Dancing, here as elsewhere, became a great attraction in the inter-war years, with singers and jazz bands giving regular entertainment in the *Sala Dansingowa*. These were the years of the Great Depression, with only tight financial control making survival possible. At all times the hotel staff seem to have been treated well, in return giving their loyalty and good service. High standards were encouraged by the formation of a national hotel organization whose president was the Bristol's director, Szaniawski, a participant also in the International Society of Hoteliers' conferences. High fashion and enjoyment went on, following the pattern of the best European grand hotels of the 1930s once economic revival was fully established.

September 1939 changed everything, the German invasion of Poland initiating the Second World War and the Bristol being centrally placed in the hopeless defence of Warsaw. From the east, Russia also had invaded and the hotel faced years under German control during which it endeavoured to supply what assistance could be secretly given to the Polish resistance. Damage to the hotel in 1939 was limited, but when the uprising of 1944 occurred, Warsaw became a wasteland in which, through good fortune, the Bristol remained standing.

Communism triumphed in Poland after the Yalta and Potsdam summit meetings, but somehow the Bristol survived as the most prestigious hotel for foreigners under the management of the Orbis state tourist agency. The Chopin Piano Competitions and a visit to his homeland by the tenor Jan Kiepura were cultural events of note, and a link with the past was retained by the arts patron Dr Bronislaw Krystall, whose first visit to the hotel had been in 1914. He had commissioned works in the 1920s and 1930s from the composer Szymanowski and the painter Kossak, both of whom had lived in the hotel between the wars. Many of Wojciech Kossak's canvases, some received in lieu of payment for board, were preserved throughout the Second World War, rolled up and hidden in boxes of sand. Dr Krystall, by some special arrangement, was able to resume residence in the hotel, even to the extent of having the same room, 116, which he had occupied in 1914 on his first visit. His art collection had survived and he revived patronage towards the National Museum on a regular basis, which involved selling a picture to pay his hotel bill, then matching each sale with the gift of another painting to the Museum.

In 1980, because the Bristol was about to close on account of deterioration, Krystall had moved to the Europejski opposite, also run by Orbis. The latter days of the Bristol's first incarnation ended in the following year, 80 years after its opening, and has been described in its 'sublime seediness' by an English journalist. Timothy Garton-Ash, on assignment to cover the Gdansk shipyard strike, wrote 'My room had three illuminated call-buttons: porter, waitress, shoe boy. I pressed them each in turn. Nobody came. A scraggy cat stalked through the french windows in the dining room. There were cockroaches in the bath.'[21] The Bristol mouldered further after its closure, but eventually Forte Hotels negotiated a major interest with Orbis, covering execution of the restoration and building work and a subsequent management contract. Reconstruction of the 1901 ambience was

decided on, and a seventh storey, together with all necessary present-day technical installations, was required. Austrian contractors and the architect Ivan Zelenka from Vienna were employed, with Polish conservationists Maria Brukalska, Ewa Pustoła-Kosłowska and Marek Kwiakowski. Zelenka took inspiration from Gustav Klimt in designing the frieze and ceiling decoration of the central hall, and the Paderewski Suite has been restored in French neo-classical elegance. Re-entry of the revivified Hotel Bristol into the world of market economies was suitably marked by Lady Thatcher, who re-opened it officially on 17 April 1993.

Hungary

Bishop St Gellért, born in Venice c. 980, entered the monastery on the Isola di S Giorgio and, by some unknown sequence of events, found his way to Hungary and the Court of King Stephen with the rank of Bishop. In defending the inheritance of Stephen's pro-Christian policies, Bishop Gellért was martyred by a violent partisan mob in Buda at the foot of what is now known as Gellért Hill. Both he and Stephen were canonized in 1083, and Gellért's relics were eventually returned to the abbey of S Giorgio in Venice, where they remain.

Thermal springs were present near the site of his martyrdom on the banks of the Danube, and records from nearly a century later indicate the presence there of a hospital or hospitals founded by the Order of St John and St Elizabeth. Subsequent references to curative baths are scarce, but they are mentioned in the sixteenth and seventeenth centuries, the latter when under Turkish rule. After Habsburg repossession in 1686, a chequered career for the springs continued until in 1832 Szilárd Koischer, a lawyer, and his wife Zsófia Sagits purchased additional land, creating a substantial hotel and baths with delightful views, two restaurants and at least 16 baths and 21 rooms. Gardens and a promenade enhanced the establishment. 'Muddy Baths' with excellent quality mud were advertised in 1866 and the number of visitors rose to 80,000 or 90,000 a year. Success did not ensure long-term security as the building of the Franz Josef (now Liberty) Bridge across the river in 1894 involved demolition of the whole development. The benefit of the springs was not entirely lost, as their outflow had been protected in a subterranean chamber under the new road. Negotiations by the city in June 1901 to purchase springs and land from the Crown Treasury proceeded with the intention of building medicinal baths and a hotel. The finalizing of the proposals took more than eight years, the joint work of three architects,

Artur Sebestyén, Isidor Sterk and Ármin Hegedüs.[22] During this period the sinuous forms of the Art Nouveau style in France and The Netherlands were being tempered by a variant that reacted against academicism, the Viennese Secession movement. This undoubtedly had an influence in Budapest on the design of the new 176-room hotel, which dispensed with the normal classical design treatment and found its own individual architectural language. The designs of Josef Hoffmann and J. M. Olbrich were exploring similar means of expression. The earlier Secession-style (Steigenberger) hotel in Bad Neuenahr, near Bonn in Germany (1897) is now a listed building, and its central domed tower bears strong likeness to the Gellért, which it could have influenced.

Building work on the Gellért began in 1911 and at the outbreak of the Great War had reached no further than being a bare shell. Work slowed even more in the wartime circumstances, but with much effort and improvisation, completion of the Saint Gellért Medicinal Baths and Hotel was finally achieved in September 1918. The main façade faces Gellért Square, while the Baths entrance is in Kelenhegyi Street at a right-angle to the front. Axes from the two doorways intersect in a monumental baths hall giving access to the Venus room, named after an appropriate sculpture. From the Venus room smaller thermal baths for men and women separately are reached. Because of the rising ground towards the back of the building, connection between the hotel and baths areas is at mezzanine level in the hotel. Outside, pools and terraces provided focal points for exercise, food and drink and *thés dansants*, which were popular social occasions.

Much of the exterior is stone-faced and incorporates very distinctive features. Though the Gellért Square façade is symmetrical, the side view with baths entrance is eccentrically crowned with different sized and variously shaped cupolas. Parapets to roof and balconies also take on varying unorthodox profiles, mixing ironwork and carved stone reliefs. Those surrounding the large doorway symbolize healing and are by József Rona. A team of decorative artists headed by Ferenc Szabja executed many designs for the interior features. Faience and ceramic mosaics decorated walls and floors in the bath areas, and tiling from the Zsolnay Factory has been used more recently to maintain the overall style and harmonize with the products used when the building was new. Turquoise is the most important colour in the tile decoration, with ochre for patterned cladding on the columns and pale grey for floors. A modelled figure by Miklós Ligeti of a nude girl playing with ducks adorned the old winter garden, and Ligeti also made groups of putti in faience decoration for the entrance to the thermal baths. Stained glass for the Venus room came from the workshop of Manó Róth.

Budapest, Gellért Hotel, 1918, by architects Artur Sebestyén, Isidor Sterk and Ármin Hegedüs. Classicism had been shed under the joint pressure of Art Nouveau and the Vienna Secession in favour of a new vocabulary.

Assorted sizes and shapes of domes, curving cornices, parapets, and balconies all combine in a unique building.

The Thermal Baths survived wartime onslaughts in 1945, when much damage was done to the Gellért's interiors. Mosaics, tiles and ceramic sculptures were renewed where necessary and the old spa atmosphere lives on.

Even after the opening of the baths and hotel in 1918, revolution further delayed its proper functioning as a hotel. It was put to military and administrative uses for a limited period but failed to succeed after being opened again to the public. Management and staff formed a committee early in 1921 and submitted a development scheme to the Mayor for extension and improvement of the hotel section. In conjunction with building the Artificial Wave Pool with 286 dressing cubicles and 164 clothing lockers, just under 60 new bedrooms were added, bringing the total to 234 and increasing the number of bathrooms to 70. Artur Sebestyén, one of the original architects, designed and carried out the work, which came into use in August 1927. The next and last major scheme six years later involved the creation of an indoor winter swimming pool in place of the winter garden, enlivened by the injection of compressed air from below to attract new custom to the 'Bubble Baths'.

Severe damage to the hotel was suffered during the Second World War when the Franz Josef Bridge was destroyed by retreating German troops. Lajos Mencseli, the business manager, wrote of his inspection on 20 February 1945:

only the walls were left standing, the roof and dome were lost and even the ceiling collapsed ... I found a dreadful sight as I entered the building through the main entrance. Everything was burnt ... the walls and columns were black with soot. The paving of the gallery in the foyer had sunk. Everything was destroyed.[23]

This part of the interior was completely redesigned in the 1950s after short-term repairs made it possible to reopen the hotel with 50 rooms in little more than a month. The baths and medical department escaped serious harm and have been restored much to their original state in a continuing programme of conservation, by which it attracts those celebrities who visit Budapest to enjoy its historic atmosphere. It has also played a leading part in training hotel and catering staff in Hungary to the standards necessary for keeping international status.

Germany: Berlin and Hamburg

Berlin before the Great War could boast two hotels of almost equal status that competed against each other and remained in fashion until the Second World War. Of the two, the Adlon (1907) probably exceeded the Esplanade (1908) in style and fame. Two architects with hotel-building experience elsewhere in Berlin collaborated on the Adlon, large in size by European standards, with 305 bedrooms and 140 private bathrooms: Carl Gause, also designer of the Bristol, and Robert Leibnitz with the Hotel Cumberland to his credit, made use of the Schinkel neo-classical tradition and created a well-articulated building faced with substantial stonework and built around an attractive courtyard lightened by decorative carving. Art Nouveau-cum-Secession content wedded to neo-baroque inclinations resulted in some heavy but convincing interiors, recalled now only through photographs.

The Esplanade by Boswau and Hermann Knauer was smaller but was enlarged in 1912 to take 400 guests, who were then provided with 102 bathrooms. Schinkel's fine brand of classicism still had some influence, but the sumptuous interior included neo-rococo, Louis Seize and Art Nouveau among its extravagant styles. Boswau and Knauer formed part of the building consortium that created the Atlantic Hotel on the Alster in Hamburg (1909), which still exists. Modernization has altered its traditional neo-classical appearance, but the ballroom and the Ionic front portico recall the grand hotel quality of the early part of the century. The original interiors were executed by the Bauer Brothers of Berlin in the large dining-hall, winter garden and vestibule; Schneider, Hanau & Company of Frankfurt in the large and small banqueting halls and reception rooms; M. Ballin of Munich created the Moorish smoking saloon and the court furnisher Anton Pössenbacher took charge of the smaller clubrooms. The Atlantic was well supplied with the latest technical equipment, the Otto Meyer engineering company being responsible for heating and ventilation; electrical plant came from Hanseatischen Siemens Schubert in Hamburg and a diesel power plant from Friedrich Krupp A-G of Kiel-Gaarden. Sanitary installations from Thiergärtner, Voltz & Wittmer of Berlin, and full kitchen planning and equipment from Hildesheimer Sparherdfabrik A. Senking, Hildesheim, completed the components needed to underpin the first-class hotels in the 1900s.[24]

Business conferences were mentioned in hotel literature even at that time, with a dictating room available as a forerunner of our electronic age. The comfort of visitors in the 250 bedrooms was not ignored and 100 private bathrooms were a generous provision.

The trading port of Hamburg has been well-served by another famous hotel, the Vier Jahreszeiten, developed from humble beginnings and eleven rooms by Friedrich Haerlin, who gained a good reputation and eminent clientèle through the exceptional service he provided. Neo-Jacobean or Renaissance plasterwork and panelling, touches of Art Nouveau and an Art Deco bar of the 1920s all within a plain neo-classical envelope did not add up to architectural distinction, but the Vier Jahreszeiten's presence in more than one 'Top Ten in the World' list speaks for the comfort and atmosphere instead. Every refinement of service has been consistently practised and an indexed file of guests' preferences – and special quirks – is meticulously kept. Few hotels could compete with its great range of delights on offer, from the 200 vases of flowers filled daily to the 42 types of praline created by the *pralinier*.

Italy, 1900–1930

Italian hotel development in this period was chiefly in towns or cities needing accommodation for commercial interests, although our first example, the Hotel Excelsior in Rome, was still conceived as desirable to support the prestige of the capital. Cast very much in the same mould as the Madrid Ritz or the Negresco in Nice, it is much larger than either, with more than 300 rooms. Built in 1907, it enjoyed a few successful years before the vicissitudes of the Great War. Revival came in the 1920s when Rome was beginning to acquire a twentieth-century outlook and hotels benefited accordingly. The Holy Year of 1925 made consequent demands on accommodation, and the Excelsior's reputation for service appealed to Italian aristocracy and café society alike. Foreign notabilities and diplomats frequented it, and the Shah of Persia, Reza Pahlevi, first saw there his future queen, Soraya, daughter of Persia's Ambassador to Berlin. Life, *la dolce vita*, seemed to be lived at high speed in Rome, and the hotel was one of its focal points. Development of the Italian film industry added to the excitement, with personal dramas occasionally overflowing from the screen into the Via Vittorio Veneto.

An Excelsior in Naples was built in the same year, a square neo-classical block by the waterside. It is attributed to Emil Vogt, the Lucerne architect, who may have received the commission by way of Baron Pfyffer of the Grand Hotel National, Lucerne.

The third Excelsior, also 1907 vintage, makes an entirely different subject on its site on the Venice Lido, but first the Hôtel des Bains, also on the long sand-bar and dunes that protect the Venetian lagoon, must be examined. This site

Berlin, Adlon Hotel, 1907. A legend in its time in fashionable society, the Adlon, designed by Carl Gause and Robert Leibnitz, was regarded by Robert Ludy when it was twenty years old as 'a very modern and gorgeous hotel' with luxurious interiors. It was totally destroyed in World War II.

Hamburg, Atlantic (Kempinski) Hotel, 1909; Boswau and Knauer were architects who had designed the lavish Esplanade in Berlin and then formed part of the building team for the Atlantic in Hamburg. Their classical leanings paid respect to Schinkel, and the two illustrations show their original façade with its pilasters, urns and sash windows in contrast with the pared-down effect that is now preferred.

had attracted by its wildness Goethe, Byron and other Romantic poets, and the fascination it held inspired succeeding writers and artists, retaining a dream-like quality even when developed as the Venice Lido. Those who have seen the drifting frieze of *belle époque* travellers in Visconti's film of Thomas Mann's novella *Death in Venice* will retain an atmospheric impression of the Hôtel des Bains there. It opened in 1900, an embodiment of the spirit of the age, and since the shooting of the film its identity as a hotel has been restored. Aschenbach and Tàdzio, created by Mann after a visit in 1911, could still be weaving in and out of their strange tentative relationship, which inspired Benjamin Britten's last opera. Here in 1929 Diaghilev met a quiet death in a misty August dawn, weeping, according to Serge Lifar, a single diamond-like tear.

The symmetrical neo-classical façade looking out over the Adriatic sea belies the Liberty style romance generated within, but elegance pervades both. A Pompeian atrium adds to the mixture of styles, and Art Deco also insinuated its presence later. Addition of a grand *salone* followed a destructive fire in the north wing during the Great War and the opportunity was then taken to increase the capacity to 305 rooms. Fatal damage was done to historical documentation in the floods of 1966, but more recent comment on the nature and Secessionist tendency of the rebuilding and extension pointed out that

at the same time it inclines towards decorative modules 'alla Mackintosh'. It is a style in which the flowing suppleness of Guimard or Horta is replaced by an almost neo-gothic stiffness. Only in certain exquisite 'nuggets' such as the wrought iron intertwinings of the balustrade do the authentic tones of the golden age of Liberty-style come through. But the Lido always aimed at reconciling Art Nouveau with the taste for lacy florid-gothic which underlies the architecture of Venice.[25]

The acceptance of sunbathing as a pastime and the presence of a sandy beach had made a success of the Hôtel des Bains, so another hotel project was launched. The Excelsior, built on a spacious site to the east, had similar advantages of location to the Hôtel des Bains, but was designed and presented with great flamboyance. Awareness of the Lido's possibilities had arisen about 40 years before, when a chalet and bathing place had been used privately by Margharita di Savoia and by Vittorio Emmanuele as a child. Nicolò Spada played the part of entrepreneur for the enterprise, overcoming repeated civic resistance, managing to raise the necessary capital and obtaining a lifting of military restrictions, which had been in operation. The first development of a bathing beach, the Società Bagni, was taken over by the

Rome, Hotel Excelsior, 1907. With its 300 rooms it was larger than most of its contemporary European counterparts, but features familiar rusticated plinths and a domed corner feature. The Excelsior was for long the centre of high fashion in Rome.

Empire period furniture and generously draped curtaining are matched by inlaid doors, all in accordance with the original style.

Venice Lido, Grand Hôtel des Bains, 1900. The neo-classical exterior (*above*) gave way to an interior that adopted the *stile floreale* or Liberty style, more suited to the idle holiday life of the Lido.

Venice Lido, Excelsior, 1907, by the architect Giovanni Sardi.
Called initially the Excelsior Palace, it was the setting for one
of Venice's great parties (21 July 1907), providing a suitably
extravagant Moorish background.

Venice Lido, Excelsior. The recent revival
of interest in grand hotels has resulted in
extensive planting, a fountain in the *cortile*
and appropriate redecoration elsewhere.

Salsomaggiore Terme, near Parma, the
Grand Hôtel des Thermes, 1901, now the
Palazzo dei Congressi. It was designed by
Luigi Broggi of Milan, but extended in 1926
by architect Ugo Giusti with decoration by
Galileo Chini. The most spectacular of the
interiors still remaining in use is the Moorish
salon.

This elaborate decoration would not have
met with approval from César Ritz, who had
earlier managed and partly held an interest
in the hotel.

Giusti and Chini produced a decorative masterpiece in the later addition based on the Liberty style, but freely introducing a wide variety of motifs.

Compagnia Italiana Grandi Alberghi (CIGA) in 1906. Spada and his partner Giuseppe Volpi, both involved with CIGA, foresaw the potential for sunbathing and swimming as popular recreation and made bathing chalets with coloured awnings a feature of the hotels.

Choice of a Moorish style of building for the Excelsior was in tune with a fashion in the later nineteenth century for exoticism. In Venice, traditional trader with the East, Arabic culture was far less strange than in Florida, where the Tampa Bay Hotel had created endless wonder. The basic inspirations for 'Moorishness' were the Alhambra in Granada and the Great Mosque in Cordoba, but in the Excelsior the architect, Giovanni Sardi (1863–1913), mixed together coffered ceilings, Venetian Gothic windows and Byzantine columns with horseshoe arches, squat domes and minarets. It being Venice, rows of traditional stone merlons give a battlemented finish to the walls. Land reclamation and bathing facilities drew investment separate from the finance for the main building project, but all was soon merged and supported by the Banca Commerciale manager, Giuseppe Toeplitz. At its inauguration on 21 July 1907, the building was named the Excelsior Palace, and it was in this capacity, not primarily as a hotel, that the vast entertainment party took place. Thirty thousand Venetians watched as 3,000 eminent guests assembled, all no doubt in carnival mood, for one giant banquet served in four locations – the ground and first floor salons, the Dutch garden and the sea terrace. Lanterns, garlands, spotlights and a lighthouse beam helped the musicians, the waiters and the festivities, and everyone – Venetians and guests – was reported to have been fed. Completion of the hotel took place under CIGA administration in the following year.

After the Great War, echoes of the *belle époque* still vibrated and the old pattern of celebrities was restored. Wealthy Americans, Hollywood stars and Belgian royalty came. Italian society and the Duke and Duchess of Windsor stayed, while after the Second World War Winston Churchill used to make daily visits from the Volpi palace on the Grand Canal. During recent renovation the neglected *cortile* has been given renewed importance, with Alhambra style fountains and formal planting. Both the Hôtel des Bains and the Excelsior, aware of the climatic limitations, open only from April to October.

Moorish flamboyance may have caught the spirit of Venice, but the most remarkable flowering of early twentieth-century styles had no such historic background at Salsomaggiore Terme, a small spa in the foothills of the Ligurian Apennines near Parma. The spa building itself dominates the town centre, 'a cathedral among bathing houses which rose on the site of the old salt-works and absorbed the earlier neo-classical building'.[26] It was built in the years 1914–23 under direction of architects Bernardini and Giusti, and has probably never been surpassed as an example of decoration, inside and out, eloquent of Art Nouveau, Vienna Secession and oriental inheritance. Before this gem of the period, the exploitation of the waters as a means of survival for the town after the salt extraction had declined was accompanied by the erection of the Grand Hôtel des Thermes. This opened in 1901 and introduced the Liberty style, the Italian version of Art Nouveau, a year before it generally became known through the Exposition of Decorative Arts in Turin. Luigi Broggi was commissioned as architect by the Società Magnaghi and was at the same time working on various Milanese buildings, including the new Milan Stock Exchange. A clientèle from nearby Tabiano and Salsomaggiore itself existed for the summer season and interest was stimulated more widely when César Ritz was consulted about hotel details and management, and then, with Baron Pfyffer, acquired it in 1910. Three-hundred rooms were to be fitted out, four storeys high and arranged as three sides of a courtyard. The outstanding decorative metalworker Alessandro Mazzucotelli was employed on the entrance marquee, railings and other fittings, while the painter Gottardo Valentini was experimenting with the new *stile floreale* for the interior. The Great War ended the patronage by royal and foreign clientèle and the hotel was sold to the Salsomaggiore company, the Società Anonima Grandi Alberghi, also owners of the nearby Grand Hôtel de Milan (1882) and the Hôtel Centrale Bagni (1902). The company, looking for fresh attractions and more interest from within Italy, turned towards greater extravagance of background for the 1920s and added, with the loggia and Red Tavern, the Moorish Salon. Ugo Giusti (1880–1928) was by this time the chief architect for the Tèrme Berzieri spa building, supported by the gifted decorator, designer, painter, potter and long-time friend Galileo Chini (1873–1956). Their joint achievement at the hotel, now part of the Palazzo dei Congressi, satisfied all that could have been asked in the way of a splendid setting. The Alhambra again provided the source of inspiration as Nouveau blossomed into Deco style.

Disciplined but intricate geometric architectural elements were interspersed with Chini's swirls and currents, plants, flowers and swooping birds. Celebration of the hotel's new approach took musical form, and the opening entertainment in 1926 was a spectacular performance of *Turandot* prepared by Giuseppe Adami in sets by Galileo Chini and costumes by Luigi Caramba, staged as a gala tribute to Giacomo Puccini. Toscanini was in the audience and, from

Palermo, Sicily, Grand Hotel Villa Igeia, inspired by the Florio family, was begun in 1908 under Ernesto Basile, the foremost Liberty style architect.

Milan, Excelsior Gallia Hotel, 1905–15. The central entrance with Baroque touches and large hotel sign above the cornice is typical of many Italian grand hotels.

Milan, Hotel Principe e Savoia, 1927. Designed by C. Tenca, it features a variation on the Gallia frontage.

Milan, La Scala's *corps de ballet* took part. The first performance of the opera had been given at La Scala in April of the same year, also in sets created by Chini.

The team of artists and craftsmen that produced, in a relatively short time, high levels of artistic achievement deserved great credit. Painted glass came from the factory in Borgo San Lorenzo and, for the central skylight, from the workshop of Antonio Veronesi. Furniture was made by Franco Spicciani in Lucca and models for the stucco work were made by the sculptor Salvatore Aloisi. Symbolism without pedantry was woven into much of the decoration, and the whole design scheme gives a sense of pleasure.

For a successor in the Liberty style to the first version of the Grand Hôtel des Thermes one can look south to Sicily, where a vigorous European society maintained Palermo as a cultural and artistic centre. The Grand Hotel Villa Igeia was based on a *quattrocento* inspired villa belonging to an Englishman, Downville, but was enlarged and transformed at the instigation of the Florio family into a grand hotel. Ernesto Basile (1857–1932), pre-eminent architect of the style, designed furniture and buildings, using an individual fusion of occasional sturdiness with the more familiar whiplash lines. His furniture designs were almost always executed by Ducrot in Palermo, and at the Villa Igeia the 1908 Salone Basile is decorated with a large fresco by Ettore Maria Bergler to complete a fine room.

A major work by the well-known Milanese architect Giuseppe Sommaruga (1867–1917), another enthusiast for the *stile Liberty*, was the Tre Croci (1909–12) near Varese, on the massif of Campo dei Fiori. The local Società Grand Alberghi commissioned from Sommaruga a complex of Grand Hotel Campo dei Fiori and Restaurant Belvedere together with the cable-car Station Terminal, a brief to be compared with the Dolder group of buildings above Zürich. Sommaruga designed in grand style and the buildings were constructed in the years 1908–12 for the encouragement of tourism in the Varese area, where they were once important representatives of the Liberty style and of the work of a distinguished architect. Much of the auxiliary building has been allowed to decay and the future of any survival seems doubtful, as its presence seems scarcely to be remembered in the area.

France: Paris and the coasts

Monumental street architecture, which shaped much of the centre of Paris in the late seventeenth and early eighteenth centuries, consisted of exercises in urban design aimed at creating palatial grandeur and scale. This satisfied the ambitions of both patron and architect and prevailed in France to an extent far greater than in Britain or Italy, where in each instance society was organized on less centralized or codified principles. In Paris, formal arcaded and pedimented street façades were frequently backed by buildings of differing sizes and uses. 'Hôtels' in the meaning of substantial townhouses, mansions or palaces tended to predominate, but property could be bought more or less by the metre of frontage or, where the continuous arcaded street fronts were a requirement, by the number of arches considered necessary for the chosen development. Commercial enterprises sought premises close to good residential areas, easily accessible to the affluent and influential.

When César Ritz after nine years at the Savoy in London was seeking to crown his career with a new hotel of his own in Paris, his searches settled on a modest-sized property behind Jules Hardouin-Mansart's façades in the Place Vendôme. The Place had been designed in 1685 as a complete conception, classically treated in the Renaissance manner on an arcaded base of 210 arches arranged in a rectangle with splayed corners. The equestrian statue of Louis XIV made by Girardon for its centre was destroyed in the Revolution, to be replaced in 1810 by the present column. This column was to celebrate Napoleon and his campaigns and was made from the bronze of cannon captured at the Battle of Austerlitz in 1805. It was, in its turn, damaged by royalists and then Communards, who managed to pull it down. Restoration took place and a new Roman effigy of Napoleon was once more erected in 1875.

Ritz was confident that the long and narrow site of no. 15 Place Vendôme he had in mind could house the ideal luxury hotel that had long been his ambition, grand without resorting to excessive size. Financiers he approached for initial backing were less enthusiastic, but a friend whom he had helped in the past, Marnier Lapostolle, maker of Grand Marnier liqueur, the name of which Ritz had suggested to Lapostolle, advanced the payment for an option. The Place and the Rue de la Paix were already becoming centres of fashion and exclusivity capable of helping to attract 'his' sort of clientèle. Stimulated by Ritz's conviction, enough shares in The Ritz Hotel Syndicate Ltd were taken up, and the property, previously occupied by the Crédit Mobilier bank, was acquired in 1896. The names Neumann, de Gunzbourg, Crawshay and Hirsch joined Calouste Gulbenkian and Alfred Beit as principal shareholders. Ritz's own Savoy staff team of Escoffier, Echenard, Agostini, Baumgartner and Collins were involved, as were his constant friends and patrons Earl de Grey, Harry Higgins and Arthur Brand, who became directors. The ideas of hygiene and nutrition that he and Escoffier had developed during their long association, together remained cornerstones of management and catering. Style, elegance and quality were to be paramount in all aspects of luxurious comfort and cuisine. His chosen architect to achieve such 'infinite riches in a little room' was Charles Mewès, whose Beaux-Arts background inevitably triumphed over the more modern approach that Ritz had been considering. Application of classical skills to the manipulation of space had the advantage, and Mewès's interior design was based on successive French historical styles from late Louis XIV to the First Empire. Furniture was accurately copied from Louis XV and Louis XVI pieces, and chairs were painted to blend with colour schemes. Mme Ritz cooperated closely with Mewès in the choosing of furnishings. Plain walls and light colours offset works of art, and, particularly in the fine sweeping staircase, bronze and ironwork made a light, effective contribution. Plasterwork in Mewès's recognizable style was kept to a minimum where space was limited, and the possibility of dullness was overcome by finely designed door furniture and other functional items, such as electric light switches, all giving the impression of high quality. Ritz had upheld his principles of hygiene and efficiency while his architect achieved style without excess.

Though Ritz's active career had not much longer to run, the achievement embodied in the Hôtel Ritz came remarkably near to perfection and continued as a fitting tribute in the sad years when his legendary capabilities were there no longer. Success in Paris had come through the personnel of hotel and construction teams knowing, under Ritz, the aims he wished to realize and giving dedicated service accordingly. Mewès had devised backgrounds completely suited to the rich Parisian society of the *belle époque*, and the unobtrusive efficiency of the hotel machine was managed by Henry Elles from the London Savoy, assisted by Victor Rey, a Swiss who had been at the Baur au Lac in Zürich and the Trianon Palace, Versailles,[27] and, as *maître d'hôtel*, Olivier Dabescat, a Basque whose half century and more in the restaurant at the Hôtel Ritz brought him considerable fame. Marcel Proust found inspiration in Olivier for the comparable character in his fictional 'Balbec' grand hotel, an establishment that owed much of its character to the real-life Grand Hotel in Cabourg on the Channel coast.

European royalty was still active in high society and lent distinction by its presence, while transatlantic magnates may have been more welcome for their copious spending. International circles in the 1890s contained well-known leaders of style, such as the English Lady de Grey and the French Count Boni de Castellane, who were both strong supporters of Ritz for much of his career. Winter and summer, these

Paris, Hôtel Ritz, 1898, designed by Charles Mewès. In the urban centre of Paris, shaped by Haussmann, façades were predetermined to an approved pattern and design skills had to centre on the interior of a building.

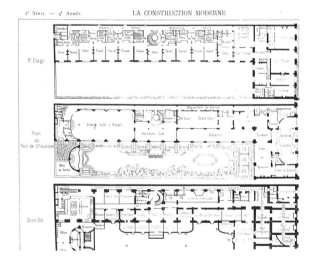

The planning of the ground floor for the Ritz was a feat of ingenuity in wasting not a square centimetre and yet giving an impression of grandeur and space.

Paris, Hôtel Ritz. Marie-Louise Ritz took part in choosing much of the furniture and furnishings for this unique hotel, where she lived for many years after the death of César.

circles migrated according to the seasons: Naples, the Riviera and capital cities – for opera, ballet and drama – all offered winter attractions, while mountains and the coasts provided places at which to stay cool in the hottest months. The 'season' from early summer consisted of important art exhibitions, dress shows, balls, horse racing and a widening field of other entertainments and sports to fill the social calendars. An occasion such as the 'incognito' visit to Paris in 1907 made by Edward VII and Queen Alexandra, when they held a lunch at the Ritz for the Marquis de Breteuil and his Marquise, is a reminder of how strong was the British social element present on the Continent at the time.

Shortly before the Great War erupted, the Hôtel Ritz, then under the supervision of Marie-Louise Ritz, who had been born into *hôtellerie* herself, was extended into no. 17 Place Vendôme and at the back into a house in Rue Cambon. War turned this house and one of the main hotel floors into a hospital, and great care was needed in managing the separation of the two functions and their attendant odours. Air raids took place, watched from a balcony by Marcel Proust,

Cabourg, Normandy, the Grand Hôtel. Under the ownership of Charles Bertrand, a new Grand Hôtel took the place in 1908 of the existing hotel of that name and, with the Casino and Baths, attracted more visitors to the seaside resort.

Marcel Proust, having known the preceding Grand Hôtel since childhood, became a more frequent guest, staying annually in the summer from 1907 to 1914 for about a fortnight.

Cabourg became 'Balbec' in *A la recherche du temps perdu*, and Proust's descriptions include a vivid vignette of sitting and gazing out of the large windows of the dining-room.

an habitué for whom a room was always available, but no serious damage was done. Winston Churchill and Lady Violet Bonham-Carter were wartime visitors to the hotel, as were Nancy Astor and Edith Wharton, although the latter was never an admirer of Ritz. Throughout the hostilities Marie-Louise Ritz was in charge of a restricted hotel service and for a period of eight months even this ceased. For her, 1918 brought the death of her younger son René at the age of 21, and in October, only a few weeks before the armistice, César died after years of a twilight life in his Swiss retreat near Lucerne.

Life none the less was revived in the Hôtel Ritz after the armistice, and the 1920s generation set about enjoying itself. Victor Rey succeeded as managing director and carried on its traditions. Proust and Cocteau sparred with each other. Proust impressed the British Ambassador, Lord Derby, as 'the first chap we'd ever seen dining in a fur coat'.[28] The list of celebrated names became longer and the American presence increased, particularly in the Cambon Bar, still restricted to men only, where Cole Porter, Ernest Hemingway and Scott Fitzgerald were regulars and the cocktail was a favourite drink. Gulbenkian, Hutton and Vanderbilt stayed for weeks or months, representing riches at the highest level until the financial bubble burst in 1929.

Claude Auzello, a Frenchman from Nice, followed Rey as manager then as managing director in difficult economic conditions, and in the 1930s the elder son Charles Ritz was persuaded back from America to take part in management. During the Second World War when the Germans occupied Paris, Hermann Goering could be found at the Ritz in the Imperial Suite. Hans Elmiger, the grandson of the Swiss Colonel Maximilian Pfyffer, and César Ritz's first patron, was as a German speaker invaluable as resident manager. On the advice of the French Minister of the Interior, Georges Mandel, who had been living in the Ritz, Elmiger managed to tread a difficult path in maintaining the hotel's survival. Auzello and Marie-Louise Ritz continued in office as directors and after liberation in 1944 gradually restored proper standards. It was another nine years before Marie-Louise – at the age of 85 – handed over chairmanship of the board to her son Charles. The following years were troublesome, with Auzello and Charles Ritz holding widely differing views. Auzello's problems included a seriously ill wife, and he tragically ended his own life after having first shot her dead. Charles carried on, until his death in 1976, without the investment needed to maintain the building or to keep abreast of the times. His much younger Swiss wife Monique, whom he married late in life, was left to preside over a liability for which a good sale was the only solution. To general surprise

this occurred in 1979, when it was bought by the three Egyptian brothers, Mohamed, Salah and Ali Al Fayed. They had no previous experience in *hôtellerie* but possessed obvious entrepreneurial skills, enabling them to embark on a project that would cost them $130 million, only $30 million of which represented the purchase price. Their respect for history and the creation of a well-equipped, technically modern hotel has proved an entirely successful blend. Tradition is incorporated in the person of the president of the hotel company, Frank Klein, with a background of experience at the Savoy and Berkeley in London, the Madrid Ritz and the Zürich Baur au Lac. He was sixth in the line of general managers after Henry Elles, Victor Rey, Claude Auzello, Janus Zembrzuski and Bernard Penché, and has made an important contribution to the revival of César Ritz's dream in terms of the Al Fayeds' devotion to his original ideas.

The Elysée Palace, built for the 1900 Exposition, opened in the same year as the Ritz. It was designed by Georges Chédanne (1861–1940), one of the foremost hotel architects at the turn of the century, whose grand rococo style was still in fashion. It is no longer a hotel, being occupied by the bank Crédit-Commercial de France. Chédanne's 1897 Riviera Palace Hotel at Beausoleil, Monaco, is now converted into apartments, as are many similar buildings on the Riviera.

Augustin Meurice, who gave his name to one of the best hotels in Paris, was born in the Pas-de-Calais in 1738 and became a postmaster on the Paris–Calais route. Venturing into the hotel business with English travellers in mind, he prospered in Calais and then in Paris as well by endeavouring to meet all their discriminating standards, and 'would probably make special prices for single people or families whether resident by the day or by the month, whether taking *table d'hôte* or having meals in their apartments, wine and all inclusive except for firewood which clients may buy'.[29] Meurice's direct descendants ran the flourishing business for most of the nineteenth century, satisfying royalty and nobility and catering for a substantial proportion who wished to take apartments for extended periods of time. A move from the first site of his inn in the Rue St Honoré to one in the Rue de Rivoli maintained the exclusive clientèle, but the ownership of the hotel passed to a company that acquired adjacent buildings so that more space would allow for a third version of the Meurice, still in existence. The new hotelier, Arthur Millon, had reached his position of authority up the familiar ladder of experience from café waiter to *maître d'hôtel* to entrepreneur and was fully prepared to take on competition with the Hôtel Ritz. The work of renovation and rebuilding to take in the larger site was carried out under the architect

Henri-Paul Nénot (1853–1934). During it, *Le Figaro* noted that 'nothing was being kept of the old hotel except the façade, uniquely placed; as for the rest, it appears to be splendour itself with comfort and luxury such as one has never seen'. The work was completed in 1907 to similar enthusiastic notices on all sides and with demands for accommodation once more from their faithful clientèle.

One great change was the relocation of the public rooms on the ground floor, not the first floor as previously, and the incorporation of the adjacent hotel, the Metropole, gave longer frontage towards the Rue de Castiglione and a new entrance from the Rue du Mont-Thabor. Reinforced concrete was used structurally and solid 140–150mm thick partition walls reduced the transmission of sound between rooms. Floor construction using heavy reinforced concrete beams had ceramic tile floor finishes for bathrooms and a layer of cork beneath the carpets for rooms and salons. Nénot, a brilliant young architect and holder of the *grand prix de Rome*, had recently made similar rearrangements of rooms at the Grand Hotel.

Millon's appointment of Frédéric Schwenter as director or general manager was fortunate. He proved to be an ambitious and devoted servant of the Meurice, an exceptional hotelier virtually in the Ritz class. Experience in Germany, Austria, Italy and England had set the young Swiss on the right road to reach the top. A management position at the Savoy in London and directorship at the Prince de Galles, Paris, had already matured his abilities and he, together with his wife, had strong views on hygiene and dispensed with heavy dust-collecting furnishings. Even the lace curtains in the post room had to be starched every day. Schwenter – who during a French postal strike in 1909 sent a daily courier to London to post letters to other countries – was a genius at work in the job he fulfilled in front of *le tout-Paris* for 40 years. In the 1920s new ideas supplanted old and an openair Roof Garden restaurant became the place to be seen. Writers, artists and distinguished foreign visitors augmented the royal element among the residents. Alfonso XIII, who had inherited the Spanish throne at birth, spent some of his exile during the Spanish Civil War at the Meurice with his family *and* his own royal furniture from Madrid. The Prince of Wales (later Edward VIII) and his brother the Duke of York (later George VI) were both welcomed, as had Edward VII before them, earning the tag *palais royal* for the hotel. Coco Chanel, Picasso, Cocteau and Diaghilev, Franklin Roosevelt, Anthony Eden and Gabriele d'Annunzio all enjoyed its hospitality, and, with less joy, Von Choltitz had signed the German surrender of Paris in the grand salon. Salvador Dalí in most years after the Second World War

occupied the royal suite for a month at a time, his eccentricities no doubt testing the patience of the staff but winning plenty of notice from the press.

Like the Meurice and the Ritz, as a *luxe* hotel within a pre-existing framework, the Hôtel de Crillon obtained a ready-made exterior that exceeded both and might be acknowledged as the best architecture belonging to any grand hotel. It originated in part of the twin palaces built in 1755 on the north side of the imposing new *place* for Louis XV by the architect Ange-Jacques Gabriel (1698–1782). Between the two palaces the Rue Royale leads north to the church of the Madeleine, and the mid-eighteenth-century palace façades in the best classical style of the period were then at the very edge of the city of Paris. The space that is now, after several changes, called the Place de la Concorde extended southwards to the Seine, not bridged there until Louis XVI's reign. The western end of the Gabriel buildings forms the frontage of the Hôtel de Crillon. Louis François Trouard (1729–94) took a lease on this property and enlarged it along the Rue Boissy d'Anglas. The Duc d'Aumont, a collector and patron of art, undertook to finish the building and its interior, which he did on a lavish scale, but he died a few years later, in 1782, and the Trouards agreed to cancel the lease and resume ownership. After short occupation by the Spanish Ambassador, a descendant of the *Brave Crillon*, friend of Henry IV, took up the lease. François Félix Dorothée Berton de Balbes, Comte de Crillon, had a distinguished military career himself, and his family, after temporary retirement into Spain during the Revolution, returned to occupy the inherited property until 1907. This was the point at which the building entered *hôtellerie*, being purchased by the Société des Grands Magazins et des Hôtels du Louvre for transformation into a modern luxury hotel. Further property in the Rue Boissy d'Anglas was acquired and Walter Destailleur, who had taken over his father's architectural practice, received instructions to carry out the work. Gabriel's magnificent façades form an integral part of the Place de la Concorde and contribute substantially to an image of Paris as, above all things, a city of style. Gaining historic monument classification, it received protection against alteration that extended to Trouard's eighteenth-century interiors as preserved and embellished by Destailleur in 1909. These consist chiefly of the staircase and three first-floor salons with balconies overlooking the Place. Original sculptures have in some cases found their way into museum collections, but have mostly been replaced by good copies, as in the Salon now named after Marie-Antoinette, used occasionally as a royal diningroom when first built. The Salon des Aigles, with stucco work and military trophies, has been the scene of many historic

Paris, Hôtel de Crillon. The Salon des Aigles and the Salon Marie-Antoinette (*above and top right*) convey an elegance in keeping with the nature of the building.

BELOW The fine eighteenth-century decorative stonework above the balconies.

ABOVE Designed by Walter Destailleurs, the Crillon opened as a hotel in 1909 behind the 1755 façade of Ange-Jacques Gabriel's two palaces.

OPPOSITE The Crillon's Restaurant Les Ambassadeurs, with its delightful *putti* frieze just showing at the top of the picture.

meetings, of which the 1919 Peace Conference Commission for the founding of the League of Nations is commemorated by a marble plaque. At the corner of the building, the Salon des Batailles no longer possesses the two large battle paintings that occasioned the name. These are said to have been given, unaccountably, to the King of Morocco, who had expressed admiration for them. Much repair and regilding of the public rooms formed an important part of Destailleur's work, which succeeded in balancing splendour with style. An especially enjoyable application of wit and humour is the frieze in the restaurant painted by Gustave Moreau, showing working parties of putti employed on all aspects of building construction against backgrounds illustrating Paris's landmarks – the dome of the Invalides, Sacré Coeur church, and the Luxor obelisk that stands in the centre of the Place de la Concorde. Indeed, when this obelisk was erected on 24 October 1833, Louis-Philippe and his family watched the operation from the balcony of the Ministère de la Marine, twin palace with the Hôtel de Crillon.

Chronologically, the Lutétia (1910–12) by Louis Boileau and Henri Tauzin represented new ideas for a Parisian hotel on the Left Bank, contributing vigorous and unorthodox design, both interior and exterior, paying more tribute to the decorative value of the vine rather than to Art Nouveau or Art Deco, to which successive styles it may technically belong. A contemporary, in Versailles, was the Trianon Palace, traditional in design and important in hotel history for the clientèle it acquired. The Société du Trianon Palace Hôtel financed the project and bought a small park of three hectares near the Trianons. The site was cleared, and René Sergent was commissioned to design a new palace hotel. He embarked on the familiar five-part formula with mansard roof and dominating end pavilions, the innovation being that the careful and pleasing Louis XVI classical stone exterior concealed a steel-framed structure, a system then by no means widely used in France. Wrought iron, carved stone, ornamental urns and garlands give clean lines, offset by black and white paving. The 300-square-metres dining-room accommodated a banquet for 300 given by Gabriele d'Annunzio in 1911, and the same room, to be called Salon Clemenceau, was used for the preparation of the Treaty of Versailles in 1919. During the Great War, Allied military commanders used the Trianon Palace as their permanent committee headquarters, while parts were run as an auxiliary hospital. Social life revived after the war and a private bus service to the Place de la Concorde ran three times daily. In the 1920s it became such a popular fashionable haunt that the dozens of private car chauffeurs had to be called by means of loudhailers. Sarah Bernhardt, André Citroën and Jean Borotra with his tennis four training for the Davis Cup were all habitués. American serious money came, then war and the German occupation. The Swiss hotelier family Rey, involved with the Paris Hôtel Ritz and more recently with the Baur au Lac, Zürich, had connections with the Trianon Palace through three generations.

The Plaza-Athénée in the Avenue Montaigne and the Bristol at 112 Rue du Faubourg-Saint-Honoré both arose from previous establishments and were developed as luxury hotels when, early in the twentieth century, Paris was in need of such accommodation. Emile Armbruster, with interest in building up a 'Plaza' group of hotels, had bought the Grand Hôtel de l'Athénée in Rue Scribe in 1900, but by 1911–13 built a grand hotel of lavish classical style in the exclusive centre of fashion near the Champs-Elysées and planned around a central courtyard adorned with fountains, flowers and greenery. Designed by Jules Lefèvre, it established an international reputation, although the fact that it was the home in 1916–17 of the beautiful Mata Hari, who was subsequently shot as a German spy, seems unjustly to have eclipsed its true merits.

The Bristol's claims to fame rested more securely on standards of traditional service laid down by Hippolyte Jammet. He had acquired an eighteenth-century townhouse by way of a profitable property deal that gave him the necessary capital. A father who was a restaurateur in Paris, then a hotelier in Dublin, was part of his background, and Hippolyte had clear ideas of his own ambitions in the hotel world. To provide the best possible level of service, every detail of his clients' preferences was carefully recorded and all wants were supplied in a manner that justified the description 'guests'. He wished to generate an air of comfortable ease not always found in Paris hotels and was pleased to encourage international statesmen and diplomats for whom his hotel and its garden formed an oasis scarcely expected in the diplomatic quarter. Major works were embarked on in 1924–5 under the direction of Gustave Umbdenstock (1866–1940) with recognizably 'modern' flavour. The eighteenth-century townhouse atmosphere was not destroyed, and the winter garden dining-room, based on an original small oval theatre, is one of the most attractive in Paris. Antique furniture, old *boiseries* and an Art Nouveau panel of the Four Seasons by Gustave-Louis Jaulmes make an acceptable mixture of décor, and at the time of the refurbishment of the hotel Jammet took the opportunity to rename it the 'Bristol', a title that had recently vanished from the Paris hotel lists. Although his own reign has ended, Jammet's ideals have remained valid, proved by continued loyalty among the Bristol's 'guests'.

Last in line of the grand Parisian hotels of the period 1830–1930 were the Georges-V (1928) by Lefranc and Wibo

Versailles, Trianon Palace Hôtel, 1910, by René Sergent. During the Great War it served as a hospital for British troops and housed the Allied War Council; later the Peace Treaty conditions were handed over here by Clemenceau.

VERSAILLES — Trianon-Palace
Dans cet hôtel a eu lieu la remise du Traité de paix aux plénipotentiaires allemands

Ch. Macé, Versailles

Social life soon recovered and the Trianon Palace once more entertained the eminent and powerful. Its classical façades remain unchanged in their convenient but rural setting within ten miles of Paris and provide a sharp contrast to life in the city centre.

Paris, Hôtel Prince de Galles, 1929, designed by André Arfvidson,
contained much marble and mosaic as part of its Art Deco style, but
taste in respect of interiors was changing in favour of the traditional
historic style.

and the Prince de Galles (1929) by André Arfvidson, both in the Avenue George-V near the Champs-Elysées. The George-V was built as three sides of a long rectangle, its exterior repeating some simplified neo-classical motifs allied to a modern 1920s background; neo-classicism with definite Art Deco overtones could describe the interiors of this very stylish Parisian hotel which consistently maintains its eminent position. An inter-war committee on the regulation of war reparations and a period after the Liberation of Paris in the Second World War when it was General Eisenhower's headquarters, before he transferred to the Trianon Palace Hotel at Versailles, kept it in the public eye. So, also, did many stars and magnates of the film world, Cecil B. De Mille, Greta Garbo and Sophia Loren among them, all enjoying its high-priced hospitality and an opulent atmosphere of antique rugs and furniture with a fine art collection on its walls.

Regular guests of the Hôtel Prince de Galles similarly included artistes of screen and stage, statesmen and princes of industry. Here there is more positive Art Deco interior design in the form of sculpted keystones, marble work and mosaics mingling with Louis XV and XVI styles. These two examples indicate that, even at this late date, grand hotel building still took much of its stimulus from traditional models with innovative design and decoration generally failing to dominate.

The work of Edouard-Jean Niermans (1859–1928), a prolific architect from The Netherlands, spanned the *belle époque* years, winning praise particularly for hotels. He specialized in building for leisure activities mainly in France before the Great War. Making an auspicious start with the Netherlands Pavilion in the Exposition Universelle of 1889, he progressed with commissions for brasseries and restaurants to theatres, music-halls and casinos, then adding palace hotels to his list of works. The Royal Palace Hotel in Ostend (1900), since demolished, with an outer entrance worthy of the Gateway of India, displayed the traditional classical pavilioned form interpreted from a 'modern' viewpoint, incorporating more glass than wall for the hotel's central block.

Rebuilding the Hôtel du Palais, Biarritz, after a fire in 1903 presented the exceptional opportunity of giving new life to the remains of the Villa Eugénie, originally the favourite home of Napoleon III's Empress. It had been converted into a hotel about twenty years previously but the hotel owners, Gabriel Lévy and M. Pattard, wished to enlarge its capacity and amenities, giving 300 rooms, 20 apartments, several salons and a large restaurant. The external walls were to be repaired and their original character restored, the south wing extended and a large fan-shaped bay facing the sea was to accommodate a splendid new restaurant. Two to three additional storeys altered the scale and modified the character of the palace, but Niermans assisted by Dourgnon produced the desired space for the entertainments that were still indulged in by the royalty that frequented the Palais. Some with recollections of the Imperial villa would continue to regard the new hotel in a similar light, but they could enjoy in it even larger salons and a *salle des fêtes* perpetuating an atmosphere of Second Empire taste. White and gold decoration, crystal and polished brass chandeliers still catch the eye, although the architects had employed twentieth-century methods of concrete construction and large windows flanking the main entrance. The rebuilding was completed in 1905.

Between 1908 and 1913 Niermans was fully occupied in the transformation of the Hôtel de Paris, Monte Carlo (1908–10), the building of the Palace Hotel, Madrid (1910–12), and the Hôtel Negresco, Nice (1910–13), which remains one of his best-known buildings. The Henri Negresco of its title was a Romanian with ambition who travelled around Europe and obtained a foothold as manager in the well-esteemed Municipal Casino restaurant in Nice. He established his own clientèle, pleasing those of royal eminence and substantial wealth. Rockefeller, Vanderbilt and Singer were among the transatlantic patrons, but it was the automobile manufacturer Alexandre Darracq who provided financial backing for a new hotel of the highest possible standard. Negresco had met Niermans in 1904 when he was redesigning accommodation for the Cercle Privé du Casino Municipal and, with Niermans's successful record of hotel building, he was an obvious choice as architect. The first proposals were drafted in 1906, but official approval to proceed was not obtained until January 1911. Work started five months later, taking the short time of fifteen months to see the hotel completed. It is sited close to the sea, on the Promenade des Anglais, which had been built as a promenade at the suggestion of the English colony in Nice to provide local employment after failure of the orange crop following a great frost affecting the Mediterranean in 1822.

Many of the features in the Madrid Palace and its contemporary, the Negresco, are similar, and it would be difficult to assign seniority between the two. A corner entrance rotunda and dome, Art Nouveau-modelled friezes below the main cornice and the main interior feature of a great winter garden or royal salon forming the central public space are common to both designs. Paired classical columns, stuccoed and gilded, support a large glazed dome, the metal framing designed by Gustave Eiffel for the Negresco and painted with lively putti, urns and neo-Renaissance architectural

Nice, the Hotel Negresco, 1910–13. Edouard Niermans produced yet another fine design with an oval domed foyer which is to be compared with a similar space in the Palace Hotel, Madrid (*see page 252*). Other interiors in the Negresco are decorated in varying period styles, notably an Empire salon and a Louis XIV room on the ground floor.

RIGHT Biarritz, the Hôtel du Palais was rebuilt in 1905 after a fire destroyed much of the previous hotel, which had made use of the Villa Eugénie. The present building represents one of Edouard Nierman's substantial works.

scenes all draped with flowery garlands and painted ribbons. This salon acquired National Monument status in 1974 and the exterior of the Negresco was similarly protected in 1975. By good fortune the salon's memorable carpet, the chandelier and glazed dome above, all remained intact. The Savonnerie carpet was specially woven – the largest ever to be produced by the Royal Factory founded in 1615 by Marie de' Medici. It is principally red with an ochre and beige central medallion, and one-tenth of the whole building cost was spent on it. Hung from the centre of the ceiling is an enormous crystal chandelier, a ton in weight and one of a magnificent pair made by Baccarat, the other being for the Czar of Russia and still hanging in the Great Hall of St Catherine in the Kremlin, Moscow. The Salon Massena used for banquets remains unaltered, with Empire-style decoration that includes 24-carat gilding and typical Fontainebleau star and bee motifs in woven silk wall-hangings. There are frescoes of Venice by P. Gervais and a pastoral scene by H. Lucas dating from 1912, and many antique pieces contribute to the interior decoration. The Louis XIV reception salon and most of the upper floor redecorations scheme representing different historical periods have been the work of Madame Jeanne Augier since she and her husband bought the hotel in 1957.

Henry Negresco did not receive due rewards for his enterprise, for war intervened in 1914, the year following the grand opening of his hotel. When it was temporarily turned into a wartime hospital the clientèle he had so carefully built up dissolved, leaving him financially ruined, and he died in Paris at the age of 52 in 1920. Under the subsequent ownership of a Belgian company there were decades of decline until new spirit entered the hotel with the Augier purchase. Niermans's legacy, in Monte Carlo, Biarritz, Nice and Madrid, of four of the best European hotel interiors of their time, summarizes the splendour that was the ideal of all promoters in the palace or grand hotel business.

9.
REALITY AND ILLUSION

Preceding chapters have indicated some of the techno-logical and social factors fertilizing the growth of the palace or grand hotel and its existence as a separate building type over a hundred-year period from the 1830s. The subject defies neat summaries but evolved a hotel culture with well-defined international standards playing a vital part. The terms 'reality' and 'illusion' identify the contrasting aspects of this culture, ingredients which need careful blending to produce the desired smoothness of texture. Both were essential to the realization of personal ambitions, but often the illusion was not underpinned by enough realism, and many hotel ventures failed. Good fortune was another requisite in a field with so many prospective hazards, with politics, economics, fashion and fire posing exceptional risks. The consistent need was a capacity for complete dedication and hard work. Husband and wife teams have widely succeeded throughout hotel history, and frequently both sides of the partnership have come from hotelier families. Marie-Louise Ritz had a hotel family background and was invaluable to the Ritz Development Company in the years of César's failing health. Gottlieb and Thérèse Lang sustained the Richemond in Geneva over a gap in the Armleder dynasty after the early death of the first Victor, and a younger Armleder wife, Ivane, played an active part in their hotel's twentieth-century alter-ation and refurbishment programme. Richard D'Oyly Carte was greatly assisted by his wife Helen at the Savoy, and there are many more joint managements and ownerships that have already been noticed.

The complexities of running a world-class hotel, for this was the aim of most hoteliers at the height of their achieve-ments, have been touched on, but a further look at the end-less daily decisions to be taken and tasks to be completed is not out of place. However good the management systems,

improvization can repeatedly be called on at the daily meet-ings to give instant solutions to problems which have arisen. A list of the qualities looked for in selecting a manager was formulated by Magoichiro Yokoyama, business manager of the old Imperial Hotel, Tokyo, at the beginning of this cen-tury, and it remains largely valid, although aesthetic con-siderations would not always be considered of prime concern in the Western world and knowledge of business practices would need to be expanded:

The heart of a hotel is its manager … on whose skills rest its success or failure. In general, its standards for selecting such a manager are as follows:
1. Artistic turn of mind
The first thing a guest notices is the decor; the facilities must stir an aesthetic response.
2. Scientific training
The food requires great care, and scientific and hygienic con-siderations and flavor must be harmonised.
3. General knowledge
The manager must be capable of conversing with guests of all types – entrepreneurs, politicians, military men, literati – and meeting their demands.
4. Legal knowledge
The manager must be able to advise foreigners succinctly on legal matters such as answering questions on current law con-cerning contracts to rent land.
5. Skill in managing others
The manager must lead and oversee the employees justly and kindly, without being either too strict or too lax.
6. Physical health
The manager must be in good physical health, to withstand early rising and late nights and maintain a pleasant manner and fresh complexion for contact with guests.
The above are requirements for hotel managers.[1]

The managerial hierarchy would normally be divided, below the general manager's immediate assistants, into sections

OPPOSITE Service with a smile at the Savoy in London on Valentine's Day.

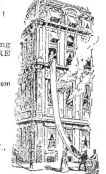
Merryweathers' formerly supplied a 'Kit-Bag' fire escape, 'As supplied to H. H. the Khedive of Egypt'.

dealing with the front office, restaurant and kitchen, bars, accounts and administration, housekeeping and maintenance. According to the size of hotel there would be floor assistants below the head housekeeper, a linen keeper and her staff and usually, in the most luxurious hotels, a florist. Chambermaids, cleaners, porters and valets and cloakroom attendants come in contact with guests, and room-service waiters might operate from a pantry on each floor linked to the kitchens by a hoist or lift. Laundries would originally have been on the premises, but as floor space became valuable in city centres they would be moved to other locations. Butchering and baking were also carried out within the confines of older hotels, but purchasing in the markets became usual and good chefs and hoteliers would have their own specialized suppliers for all sections of their menus. And, of course, the wine was to be bought and properly treated. Pâtisseries and other forms of baking still have their place in hotel kitchens, where the most modern tendency in our own time is for all chefs to be equipped with individual ovens, grills, cool storage, refrigerators and other appliances according to their special activities. The restaurant and kitchen constitute domains within the hotel, with key personnel in positions of vital importance controlling their own territories.

Fine cuisine, a whole subject in itself, was vital to the success of every good hotel and by the end of the nineteenth century had reached high levels of sophistication. From the assemblage of numerous dishes all available at once as the *table d'hôte*, a meal had been transformed into a series of successive courses served *à la Russe*. Attention was paid to the balance of flavours and to the quality and finesse of the china, glass and silver as a designed setting for the food rather than the actual modelling of the food into works of art, which the Carême school in France had developed in the eighteenth and nineteenth centuries. This had subordinated taste and temperature to the visual presentation of food designed as miniature architecture. Simplified table dressings relying on quality and function evolved from the discussions of Ritz and Escoffier. The latter, whose experiments and practical knowledge in the preservation of foods had opened up new areas of choice, by no means excluded illusion in the serving of food, as the deceptive title for frogs' legs as *cuisses de nymphes à l'Aurore* when set before the Prince of Wales confirmed. His imaginative cookery skills were great and his personal interests lay in the theatre and the opera house, hence the dishes of his devising:

pêche Melba, toast Melba, filets de sole Coquelin, salade Réjane, mignonettes de caille Rachel, poularde Adelina Patti and *consommé Sarah Bernhardt.*[2]

Staff accommodation has to be considered and provision was usually made in the attics or in adjacent properties for this. When hotels were seasonal, this arrangement was more common than it is today when year-round opening has reduced the need for so many of the staff to migrate regularly from winter-only hotels to summer resorts. Medical care for staff is provided at the Suvretta House, St Moritz, with a sickbay and resident nurse benefiting staff and management. A house doctor is generally on call for emergencies, made many times more frequent in the mountains by the advent of winter sports but also having been a requisite in the earlier days of travel up the Nile. Spa facilities, never as popular in Switzerland as in France, Germany or Italy, continue to offer the usual combinations of rest and exercise, diet and mineral waters.

The training, organizing and direction of some hundreds of staff might suggest a military style of operation, but, paradoxically, success depends on a far more relaxed approach, with a large element of theatre in which staff and guests can interact. Without strictly observed discipline no grand hotel would survive, but without willingness to serve, ability to extemporize and deep reserves of goodwill, the daily round would collapse. The show must go on, the guests must be welcomed, fed and cossetted in accordance with their preferences, if already known. This sense of performance permeates the 'front of house' sections of the grand hotel, beginning with the doormen and uniformed staff. Guests may arrive in a historic car elegantly coach-painted with the hotel name, or in one of a fleet of Rolls-Royces, having been met at the main travel terminus. Notes of greeting, flowers, bowls of fruit, chocolates and mineral waters in one's room are quite modern inventions, but before the advent of César Ritz the use of flowers anywhere in a hotel was scarcely known and greenery in the public rooms or winter gardens was most likely to be confined to potted palms, ferns and aspidistras. On arrival, luggage would disappear into the system, sometimes a surviving one of rails and trollies in the basement and connected with the service lifts. In past times, the quantities of baggage could be considerable, as Marie Louise Ritz described:

Twice a day … the corridors of the Rigi-Kulm Hotel, almost at the summit of the mountain, were stacked with luggage – Saratoga trunks from New York; smart calfskin and cloth valises from Drew's in Piccadilly Circus, band-boxes from Vuitton's in Paris and, in 1874 at least, bags of every description from Berlin.[3]

Those who came as accepted patrons were treated as honoured guests, and the welcome they received would give the right atmosphere for the whole of their visit. Many of the top hotels maintained, as they still do, an index of the tastes and peculiarities possessed by regular visitors, and a good concierge would retain the names and characteristics in his mind for year after year, creating a familiar and favourable reception from the first instant of arrival. Addressing guests by title or name wins considerable bonuses, tips as well perhaps, provided that *faux pas* are invariably avoided. On the other side of the coin, Herr Badrutt's black books at the Palace in St Moritz recorded not just peculiar tastes but distinct failings expressed in such spicy terms as 'distinguée, mais ne peut pas payer', or 'Est allé au Grand Hotel avec sa maîtresse?' and 'Petit Americain, sans argent, grands prétentions'.[4]

To the hotelier families living in the great hotels, and whose lives are dedicated to their successful operation, the proprietorial attitude of 'guests' presents both a compliment and a conflict. Having made reservations, visitors expropriate for the length of their stay the private territory of their rooms. They also take a share in the public rooms and the services provided, which are made as attractive and efficient as possible. For all of these they pay substantial sums, but the last, invisible and most precious ingredients for the devotees are the responsibility they do not have and the freedom thus given. Grand hotels are often described as the second homes of the wealthy, and most regular visitors regard them as such. In the United States, permanent retention of suites by the richest families is not uncommon. On the basis of a home from home attitude to their accommodation, the slightest suggestion of institutionalizing would give offence and destroy the whole illusion. A special temperament combining patience, optimism and unlimited energy is needed in all sections of management to balance the practicalities of running the establishment and controlling its fine details, against the public face of deferring to all requests. Here the element of fantasy may sometimes operate, with difficulties being smoothed and impossibilities achieved as if by magic. Superexcellence in such magic was practised by César Ritz and his carefully assembled staffs, often by way of arduous but concealed operations calling on unlikely sources, as when Olivier at the Paris Ritz bought, to satisfy an outlandish restaurant order for cooked elephant's feet, a suitable beast from the Jardin des Plantes. Hospitality reached remarkable levels as competition for the luxury trade increased and technical improvements simplified many practical processes.

The 'Golden Books' of the top hotels before the Great War record an

endless line of great names and noble titles where Bourbon and Habsburg, Hohenzollern and Schouvaloff visited; majesties and highnesses, imperials and royals, archdukes and duchesses, barons and baronesses, counts and countesses; maharajahs and pashas. They are the mirror of a European aristocracy which, after the setbacks of the 1848 revolutions still enjoyed golden days, and of an overseas society in which the powerful rulers had yet no fear of displaying their great riches.[5]

Noble visitors with large retinues provided a special form of street entertainment, and in such cases as the arrival of the Dowager Empress Frédérique-Louise-Charlotte-Wilhelmine of Russia at the Hôtel de Trois Rois, Basle, in June 1857 with eighteen carriages drawn by a total of 86 horses, crowds assembled to watch. Tsar Nicholas I took the entire Hôtel des Trois Couronnes at Vevey, amounting to 60 rooms on four floors, in October 1859 when he was arriving for the whole winter. Russian royalty felt safer living in European hotels after the assassination of Tsar Alexander II, but Grand-Dukes, arriving in a special train from St Petersburg to stay at the Montreux Palace with an escort of armed bearded Cossacks, still took things seriously.

A further bizarre episode relates to a vizir's staff at the Hotel Euler, Basle, who were seen, robed and scimitared, in full cry after a sheep that had escaped from ritual slaughter in their private apartments.[6]

The staging of balls and banquets had always been within the regular schedules of most grand hotels, and treaty signings or the surrender of armies brought history into their most impressive apartments. Fancy-dress balls were the most obvious manifestations of illusion, the Bradley Martin ball setting the pace in New York at the Waldorf-Astoria in 1897 with a Louis XV reception at Versailles as the theme. According to *Town Topics*,

Incredible as it may seem confidential applications were made to Mr Boldt [the manager] by several well-known men and women who had not been invited, to be allowed to disguise themselves as waiters, ladies' maids and even chamber maids, so that they could see the show.[7]

American champagne millionaire and financier George A. Kessler was a great party-giver, and at the Savoy in London made history for the hotel in 1905 with a Venetian Gondola dinner to celebrate his birthday. George Reeves-Smith and Thouraud were in charge, with no price limit to restrict their planning. The old forecourt of the hotel was flooded and a large silk-lined gondola to seat the 24 guests was set in the water. Backcloths of San Marco and the Doge's Palace were painted, 400 Venetian lamps installed, 12,000 carnations and as many roses arranged, and 100 white doves were part of the cast. Ice sculptures of the Lion of San Marco cooled the dessert fruits at the end of the meal, prepared by fifteen cooks. The only failed effect was the attendance of live swans in the water – these had been poisoned by the blue dye intended to colour the 'lagoon', and were sorrowfully removed. A five-feet-high candle-lit cake was carried across the gangplank on the back of a baby elephant, and Gaiety Girls *en bloc* joined in the toast to Kessler with glasses of Moët & Chandon 1898. The last *coup* was a contrived moonlit scene, curtains parting to reveal Enrico Caruso, who crowned the proceedings with an operatic ending.[8]

The most imaginative party – one never surpassed – took place at the Grand Hotel National, Lucerne, in 1885. An interesting Neapolitan royal connection came through Colonel Pfyffer, César Ritz's patron, and the grandest of parties was ordered in honour of the betrothal of Count Trapani's daughter, Princess Caroline de Bourbon, to Polish Count Zamoyski. At short notice, just two days, there was to be dinner, dancing, entertainment and a surprise climax. Money was not in question and Ritz was in his element. It was a warm summer evening at the hotel and a faultless dinner was succeeded by the enjoyable *cotillon*. After midnight the guests moved outside onto the terrace and promenade to see the lake shore alight with coloured fountains and on the water a fleet of sailing boats firing Roman candles and Bengal lights. Music ensued, *O Sole Mio*, to general delight but there was more to come. A red light showed on the summit of Mount Pilatus across the lake, turning into a blazing beacon erected by hard manual labour with none of today's hi-tech laser ignition devices. One by one the Rigi, then the Urirotstock mountain peaks and finally the Stansterhorn completed the circle of fire conjured from the fertile imagination of Ritz the impresario.[9]

Grand hotel party-giving is not extinct; there was recently one at the Galle Face Hotel, Colombo, Sri Lanka; nor is the grand hotel any longer an endangered species. At one time, after the Second World War, this seemed a serious probability, but awareness of the practical and historical value of these buildings and their adaptability to current use has steadily grown. Affection too has been generated, and even vital financial interest came to the rescue of many, without the expectation of large profits. The quality of much conservation work is heartening, although this is frequently paid for by income from the tower blocks that are permitted to be built on part of the hotel sites, but interest in the older buildings and their corresponding lifestyles flourishes in a young generation of enthusiasts and business people who enjoy the revived and technically equipped hotels as they approach the millennium.

Hotel Records, as well as various brochures, leaflets, advertising, etc., are signalled as 'HR' in the references that follow.

CHAPTER 1. INTRODUCTION AND ORIGINS

1. *The Travels of Marco Polo*, a modern translation by Teresa Waugh (London, 1984).
2. A. E. Richardson, *The Old Inns of England*, 5th edn (London, 1948), quoting the Torrington Diaries for 1789, p. 73.
3. Nikolaus Pevsner, *A History of Building Types* (London, 1976), p. 170. The whole of chapter Eleven is recommended.
4. William S. Childe-Pemberton, *The Earl Bishop: The Life of Frederick Hervey, Bishop of Derry, Earl of Bristol*, 2 vols (London, 1924).
5. Iris Leveson Gower, *The Face Without a Frown: Georgiana, Duchess of Devonshire* (London, 1944), p. 175.
6. See *The Shorter Oxford English Dictionary* (Oxford, 1978).
7. HR. The gala opening was on 28 October 1829.
8. Sources for the Queen's Hotel are the HR and Cheltenham Public Library.

CHAPTER 2. SIZE AND GRANDEUR IN THE UNITED STATES

1. Charles Dickens, *American Notes* [1842] (Harmondsworth, 1972), p. 184.
2. *Ibid.*, p. 110.
3. HR and extracts from John McCabe, assisted by David de Giustino, *Grand Hotel* (Mackinac, 1987).
4. Quoted by Joseph Wechsberg, *The Lost World of The Great Spas* (New York, 1979).
5. *Ibid.*, p. 205.

CHAPTER 3. EUROPE BURGEONING

1. Harry Hearder, *Europe in the 19th Century, 1830–80* (Harlow, 1988).
2. Nikolaus Pevsner, *North Somerset and Bristol* (Harmondsworth, 1958), p. 436.
3. HR, Midland Hotel, Derby.
4. Oliver Carter, *An Illustrated History of British Railway Hotels, 1838–1983* (St Michael's, Lancs, 1990), p. 62.
5. *Ibid.*, p. 11.

6. Derek Taylor and David Bush, *The Golden Age of British Hotels* (London, 1974), pp. 47–50.
7. HR, Randolph Hotel, Oxford.
8. HR, Great Eastern Hotel, Liverpool Street.
9. Taylor and Bush, *Golden Age*, p. 122.
10. Gordon Mackenzie, *Marylebone* (London, 1972).
11. Tom Steel, *The Langham, Opened 1865 – Re-opened 1991: A History* (London, 1990).
12. Details supplied by architects for the 1991 renovation works, The Halpern Partnership, London.
13. Pascal Boissel, *Le Grand Hôtel Inter-Continental, Paris, 1862–1992, 130 ans*, hotel booklet (n.d.).
14. *The Life and Adventures of George Augustus Sala* (London, 1895), II, pp. 226–7.
15. Quotation from a leaflet distributed at the opening of the Grand Hotel Terminus-Saint Lazare (1889).
16. Willi Frischauer, *An Hotel is like a Woman* (London, 1965).
17. HR, Badischer Hof, Baden-Baden.
18. HR, Frankfurterhof, Frankfurt.
19. HR, Grand Hotel Villa Serbelloni, Bellagio.
20. HR, Royal Hotel, Sanremo.
21. Sarah Gainham, *The Habsburg Twilight: Tales from Vienna* (London, 1979).
22. Olga Wallenberg, *Grand Hotel, Stockholm* (Stockholm, 1988).

CHAPTER 4. THE SWISS GENIUS

1. B. Laederer, ed., *Histoire Illustrée des Bergues 1834–1984 Pionnier de l'hôtellerie suisse* (Geneva, 1984).
2. Thierry Ott, *Palaces, Une histoire de la grande hôtellerie suisse* (Morges, 1990), the source for much of the material in this chapter.
3. Edward Whymper, *Scrambles Amongst the Alps in the Years 1860–69*, 2nd edn (London, 1871), p. 139.
4. *Ibid.*, p. 24.
5. Raymond Flower, *The Palace, A Profile of St Moritz* (London, 1982), pp. 19–20.
6. *Ibid.*, p. 24.
7. Ott, *Palaces*, p. 26.
8. G. Armleder and P. Bertrand, eds, *The Armleder Saga, Le Livre du Richemond*, hotel book (Geneva, 1982).
9. Marie Louise Ritz, *César Ritz, Host to the World* (London, 1938), an extensive source.
10. *Ibid.*, pp. 21–2.

11. *Ibid.*, pp. 34–5.
12. Ott, *Palaces*, p. 39.
13. Ritz, *César Ritz*, pp. 59–60.
14. *Ibid.*, p. 66.
15. Isabelle Rucki, *Das Hotel in den Alpen* (Zürich, 1989), pp. 58–9.
16. Ott, *Palaces*, p. 57 (trans. author): 'In case of bad weather, vast rooms, entrance halls with verandahs and terraces allow visitors to take exercise almost as though they were out of doors'; publicity for Johannes Badrutt's Engadiner Kulm Hotel, St Moritz.
17. Rucki, *Das Hotel in den Alpen*, p. 169, a reference to an article in *Bündner Zeitung* (10 July 1982), p. 8.
18. *Historismus 'Nostalgie des 19. Jahrhunderts?' Die Architekturentwürfe von Jacques Gros*, exhibition booklet (Zürich, 1979); also HR, Dolder Grand Hotel, Zürich.
19. Ott, *Palaces*, p. 47.

CHAPTER 5. FIN DE SIÈCLE

1. Leo A. van Heijningen, *Gasten te boek / Guests Registered* (Scheveningen, 1989); also HR, Kurhaus Hotel, Scheveningen.
2. Jo Gerard, *Hôtel Metropole: 100 Years at the Heart of Europe* (Brussels, 1994); also HR, Hotel Metropole, Brussels.
3. Gerard, *Hotel Metropole*, p. 59.
4. Compton Mackenzie, *The Savoy of London* (London, 1953), p. 15.
5. *Ibid.*, p. 32.
6. Stanley Jackson, *The Savoy, A Century of Taste* (London, 1989), an extensive source.
7. Ritz, *César Ritz*, pp. 135–6.
8. HR, Hyde Park Hotel, London.
9. Andrew Saint, 'The Growth of a Hotel: Claridge's, London – 1', *Country Life* (25 June 1981), p. 1798.
10. HR, Connaught Hotel, London.
11. Bohumír Mráz, *Karlovy Vary (Carlsbad) & Grandhotel Pupp* (Karlovy Vary, 1991), an extensive source.

CHAPTER 6. FOUNDED IN EMPIRES

1. E. J. Hart, *The Selling of Canada: The CPR and the Beginnings of Canadian Tourism* (Banff, 1983), pp. 16–17, an extensive source.
2. HR, Banff Springs Hotel; also Bart Robinson, *Banff Springs: The Story of a Hotel* (Banff, 1988).
3. France Gagnon Pratte and Eric Petter, *Le Château Frontenac, Cent ans de vie de Château*, hotel book (Quebec, 1993), an extensive source.
4. *Ibid.*, p. 9.
5. Hart, *The Selling of Canada*, p. 86.
6. Chrystopher J. Spicer, *Duchess: The Story of the Windsor Hotel* (Melbourne, 1993), an extensive source.
7. HR and booklet by Elaine Hurford, *The Mount Nelson, in the Grand Tradition* (Cape Town, 1992).
8. Linda Duminy, *The Royal Hotel: History in the Making, 1845–1995*, hotel book (Durban, 1995), p. 41.
9. *Ibid.*, p. 66.
10. H. J. Weaver, *Reid's Hotel, Jewel of the Atlantic 1891–1991* (London, 1991), p. 14.

11. *Ibid.*, p. 35.
12. *Ibid.*, p. 69.
13. Martin Meade, Joseph Fitchett and Anthony Lawrence, *Grand Oriental Hotels* (London, 1987), p. 101.
14. *Ibid.*, p. 25.
15. *Cook's Excursionist and Tourist Advertiser*, an article for 12 August 1899.
16. As above, but dated 9 December 1899.
17. There seems just a possibility that this 'English architect' might have been G. Somers Clarke junior on the grounds of hotel-design experience.

CHAPTER 7. JOURNEYS TO THE EAST

1. Sharada Dwivedi and Rahul Mehrotra, *Bombay: The Cities Within* (Bombay, 1995), p. 145, quoting the traveller James Douglas on Watson's Esplanade Hotel.
2. Ott, *Palaces*, p. 94.
3. Rudyard Kipling, *From Sea to Sea* (London, 1900), I, p. 251.
4. Gretchen Liu, *Raffles Hotel Singapore* (1992), hotel book, an extensive source.
5. HR, Peninsula Hotel, Hong Kong.
6. Luís Andrade de Sà, *Hotel Bela Vista*, hotel book (Macau, 1994), p. 67.
7. Malcolm Purvis, *Tall Storeys, The First 100 Years* (Hong Kong, 1985).
8. Ichiro Inumaru, *The Imperial, The First 100 Years*, hotel book (Tokyo, 1990), p. 21.
9. *Ibid.*, p. 27.
10. *Ibid.*, p. 26.
11. *Ibid.*, p. 73.
12. *Ibid.*, p. 96.
13. *Ibid.*, p. 99.
14. *Ibid.*, p. 101.
15. Nikolaus Pevsner, article in *The Architecture Magazine*, 989 (1967).
16. Inumaru, *The Imperial*, p. 228.
17. Documentation of the building was carried out by the Department of Architecture of Waseda University.

CHAPTER 8. INTO THE TWENTIETH CENTURY AND TIMES OF CHANGE

1. *The Builder*, XXI (1863), p. 92 *et seq.*, quoted by Pevsner, *Building Types*, n. 78.
2. HR, Willard Hotel, Washington, D.C.
3. Virginia Cowles, *The Astors* (New York, 1979), pp. 127–30.
4. Catherine Donzel, Alexis Gregory and Marc Walter, *Grand American Hotels* (New York, 1989), p. 51 (illustration).
5. *Memories by Alex. Browning, Sarasota, Florida* (Tampa Bay Hotel Co., 1888–1891), a typescript kindly made available, together with a booklet on the history of the Tampa Bay Hotel, by Art Bagley in charge of Special Collections, Merl Kelce Library, University of Tampa, Florida.
6. Donzel, Gregory and Walter, *Grand American Hotels*, pp. 23–4.
7. HR and 'The Lady Who Lives by the Sea', *The Journal of San Diego History*, XII/1 (January 1966). Hotel del Coronado, San Diego, California.

8. HR, Brown Palace Hotel, Denver, Colorado, and a booklet by Corinne Hunt, *100 Years of Memories, 1892–1992, The Brown Palace Story*.

9. Information on Hôtel de Paris, Georgetown, Colorado, supplied by Mavis Bimson.

10. Hugh Montgomery-Massingberd and David Watkin, *The London Ritz* (London, 1989), p. 32.

11. Information supplied by A. F. Knight, Managing Director of engineers Bylander Waddell Partnership Ltd.

12. HR, Piccadilly Hotel, London.

13. Nikolaus Pevsner, *London except the Cities of London & Westminster*, The Buildings of England (Harmondsworth, 1952), p. 217.

14. Ibid., p. 217.

15. Taylor and Bush, *Golden Age*, p. 87.

16. Hugh Barty-King, *Maples, Fine Furnishers: A Household Name for 150 Years* (London, 1992), p. 58 (illustration).

17. Ibid., p. 70.

18. HR and Bussaco booklet (Lisbon, 1972), Palace Hotel, Bussaco.

19. Clive Aslet, 'The Ritz Hotel Madrid', *Country Life* (29 May 1986).

20. HR, Hotel Alfonso XIII, Seville and A. V. Movellàn, *Arte hispalense, Arquitecto Espiau (1879–1938)* (Seville, 1985).

21. Timothy Garton-Ash, *The Polish Revolution, Solidarity, 1980–1982* (London, 1983), cited in Mary Pininska and Joanna Puchalska, *Hotel Bristol* (Forte Hotel Bristol, 1994), p. 86.

22. Dr András Rubovsky, *Hotel Gellért* (Budapest, 1988), p. 15.

23. Ibid., p. 31.

24. HR, Atlantic Hotel Kempinski, Hamburg.

25. HR, Hôtel des Bains, Venice Lido, extract from Paolo Rizzi, 'Romanticism at the Venice Lido', *CIGA Hotels Magazine*, no. 30.

26. Valerio Riva, ed., *Salsomaggiore Art Deco Termale* (Milan, 1989), p. 52.

27. The following extract from a letter written to the author by Michel Rey, General Manager of the Baur au Lac, Zürich, indicates the contribution of the Rey family to European hôtellerie:
'Mr Victor Rey … who was living and working at the Ritz, Paris, last as a General Manager, was my great uncle, respectively my father's uncle. I have recently been at his tomb, located in Sion (Valais). On his tombstone is a plaque which was a gift to his widow, Mrs Victor Rey, from the staff of the Ritz in 1937 praising his leadership and honouring his management from 1917 to 1937.
Mr Eugène Rey and his wife Mrs Jeanne Rey were at the time the main shareholders of the Trianon Palace in Versailles and were the first great cousins of Victor Rey. My father lost his parents very early. Therefore he was brought up by Mr Eugène Rey in Versailles, where he stayed up to the age of 19. They were for my father like his own parents. Mr Eugène Rey passed away at the age of 53. Mrs Jeanne Rey who was for me like a Grandmother continued very successfully conducting the Trianon Palace after the death of her husband (later with her own son). She sold the hotel in 1961. During the Second World War the property was chosen by Grosfield Grossfeld-Marschall Milch and by General Eisenhower! as their general headquarters. My father as well as myself had a very intensive

relationship with Tante Jeanne until her death in 1987. She was an extraordinary lady of great discipline, intelligence, empathy and will-power. She reached the great age of 94 in a very good state of health.
My father was born at the Hôtel Victoria, Monte-Carlo which was at that time owned and managed by his father, Jules Rey, who was also co-owner of the Hôtel Prince de Galles. He furthermore managed for many years during the summer seasons the Hôtel Normandy in Deauville. Unfortunately he passed away much too young at the age of 36 in 1916. In his career, being cousin to the great César Ritz, he worked as a Maitre d'hôtel at the famous Savoy Hotel in London.' Zürich, 10 August 1995.

28. Mark Boxer, ed., *The Paris Ritz* (London, 1991), p. 78.

29. Bernard Etienne and Marc Gaillard, *Palaces et Grands Hôtels* (Paris, 1992), p. 114, quoted from a tourist brochure discovered by Pascal Boissel, hotel historian (trans. author).

CHAPTER 9. REALITY AND ILLUSION

1. Inumaru, *The Imperial*, p. 65.

2. Ritz, *César Ritz*, p. 149. Professor Linstrum writes, as a parallel of today, 'A Sydney hotel in which Dame Joan Sutherland's son works has a dessert named after "La Stupenda", devised for the dinner after her farewell in the Opera House.'

3. Ibid., p. 55.

4. Flower, *The Palace: A Profile of St Moritz*, p. 52.

5. Ott, *Palaces*, p. 16 (trans. author).

6. Ibid., p. 19.

7. Cowles, *The Astors*, p. 130.

8. Jackson, *The Savoy*, pp. 44–5.

9. Ritz, *César Ritz*, pp. 82–5.

Anderson, Janice and Swinglehurst, Edmund, *The Victorian and Edwardian Seaside*, London, 1978

Arnold, Wendy and Morrison, Robin (photographer), *The Historic Hotels of London: A Select Guide*, London, 1990

——, *The Historic Hotels of Paris: A Select Guide*, London, 1990

Bacchini, Maurizia Bonatti and others, *Salsomaggiore, Art Deco Termale* (Italian and English texts), Milan, 1989

Barty-King, Hugh, *Maples, Fine Furnishers: A Household Name for 150 Years*, London, 1981

Baum, Vicki, *Grand Hotel*, London, 1930

Bennett, Arnold, *Grand Babylon Hotel*, London, 1902

——, *Imperial Palace*, London, 1930/1969

——, *Journals*, Harmondsworth, 1971

Berghaus, Erwin (trans.), *The History of Railways*, London, 1960

Bierman, John, *Napoleon III and his Carnival Empire*, London, 1989

Bird, Isabella L., *A Lady's Life in the Rocky Mountains*, London, 1880

Bonavia, Michael R., *Historic Railway Sites in Britain*, London, 1987

Boniface, Priscilla, *Hotels and Restaurants, 1830 to the Present Day*, London, 1981

Borer, Mary Cathcart, *The British Hotel through the Ages*, London, 1972

Boxer, Mark (ed.), *The Paris Ritz*, London, 1991

Branson, Joan and Lennox, Margaret, *Hotel Housekeeping*, London, 1965

Calman, Harold D., *The Railway Hotels and the Development of the Château Style in Canada*, Canada, 1968

Carter, Oliver, *An Illustrated History of British Railways Hotels*, Garstang, 1990

Casson, Lionel, *Travel in the Ancient World*, London, 1974

Childe-Pemberton, William S., *The Earl Bishop: The Life of Frederick Hervey, Bishop of Derry, Earl of Bristol* (2 vols), London, 1924

Cook's Tourist's Handbook, Egypt, the Nile and Desert, London, 1876

Cooper, Brian, *A Century of Trains*, London, 1989

Cowles, Virginia, *The Astors*, New York, 1979

D'Ormesson, Jean (intro.), Watkin, D. and others, *Grand Hotel: The Golden Age of Palace Hotels*, London, 1984

Damase, Jacques (trans. William Mitchell), *Carriages*, London, 1968

Davies, Philip, *Splendours of the Raj: British Architecture in India (1660–1947)*, London, 1985

Denbigh, Kathleen, *A Hundred British Spas*, London, 1981

Dickens, Charles, *American Notes and Pictures from Italy*, London, 1842

——, *American Notes and Pictures from Italy*, Harmondsworth, 1972

Dixon, Roger and Muthesius, Stefan, *Victorian Architecture*, London, 1978

Donzel, Catherine, Gregory, Alexis and Walter, Marc, *Grand American Hotels*, New York, 1989

Drabble, Margaret, *Arnold Bennett*, London, 1974

Duff, David, *Victoria Travels*, London, 1970

Duminy, Linda, *The Royal Hotel: History in the Making*, Durban, 1995

Dwivedi, Sharada and Mehrotra, Rahul, *Bombay: The Cities Within*, Bombay, 1995

Etienne, Bernard and Gaillard, Marc, *Palaces et Grands Hôtels*, Paris, 1992

Fawcett, Jane and Hobhouse, H. (ed.), *Seven Victorian Architects*, London, 1976

Fermor-Hesketh, Robert, *Architecture of the British Empire*, London, 1986

Flower, Raymond, *The Palace: A Profile of St Moritz*, London, 1982

Fothergill, Brian, *The Mitred Earl – An Eighteenth-Century Eccentric*, London, 1974

Frischauer, Willi, *An Hotel is like a Woman: The Grand Hotels of Europe*, London, 1965

Gerard, Jo, *Hôtel Metropole: 100 Years at the Heart of Europe*, Brussels, 1994

Girouard, Mark, *Cities and People*, New Haven and London, 1985

Gray, A. Stuart, *Edwardian Architecture, A Biographical Dictionary*, London, 1985

Hailey, Arthur, *Hotel*, London, 1965

Harvey, Dorothy, *The Land of England*, London, 1979

Hearder, Harry, *Europe in the Nineteenth Century*, Harlow, 1988

Hibbert, Christopher, *The Grand Tour*, London, 1987

Hitchcock, Henry-Russell, *Architecture: Nineteenth and Twentieth Centuries*, Middlesex, 1958

Hurford, Elaine, *The Mount Nelson, in the Grand Tradition*, Cape Town, 1992

Jackson, Stanley, *The Savoy, A Century of Taste*, London, 1964

Karkaria, Bachi J., *To a Grand Design*, Calcutta, 1988

Kipling, Rudyard, *From Sea to Sea*, London, 1900

Kramer, J. J., *The Last of the Grand Hotels*, New York, 1978

Latham, Jean, *The Pleasure of your Company: A History of Manners and Meals*, London, 1972

Limerick, J., Ferguson, N. and Oliver, R., *America's Grand Resort Hotels*, New York, 1979

Linstrum, Derek, *Scarborough in Fact and Fiction*, unpublished papers, 1984–5

——, *Scarborough and the Grand Hotel*, unpublished papers, 1984–5

Liu, Gretchen, *Raffles Hotel, Singapore*, 1992

Ludy, Robert B., *Historic Hotels of the World*, Philadelphia, 1927

Mackenzie, Gordon, *Marylebone*, London, 1972

Matthew, Christopher, *A Different World: Stories of Great Hotels*, New York and London, 1976

Mavor, Elizabeth, ed., *The Grand Tours of Katherine Wilmot (France 1801–3 and Russia 1805–7)*, London, 1992

McKay, A. G., *Houses, Villas and Palaces in the Roman World*, London, 1975

McNeil, William H., *A World History*, Oxford, 1979

Meade, Martin, Fitchett, J. and Lawrence, A., *Grand Oriental Hotels from Cairo to Tokyo 1800–1939*, London, 1987

Medlik, S., *The Business of Hotels*, London, 1980

Mesuret, Geneviève and Culot, Maurice, *Architectures de Biarritz et de La Cote Basque*, Brussels, 1990

Monkhouse, Christopher P., *The Station Hotel in Nineteenth-Century England* (MA thesis report), London, 1970

Montgomery-Massingberd, H. and Watkin, D., *The London Ritz*, London, 1989

Moritz, Carl Philip (trans. and ed. Reginald Nettel), *Journeys of a German in England in 1782*, London, 1965

Movellán, Alberto Villar, *Arte Hispalense, Arquitecto Espiau 1879–1938* (Spanish text), Seville, 1985

Naudin, Jean-Bernard and others, *Dining with Proust*, London, 1992

Nelson, Nina, *The Mena House: A Short History of a Remarkable Hotel*, Egypt, 1988

Newton, A. P. and others, *Travel and Travellers of the Middle Ages*, London and New York, 1926

Orbach, Julian, *Victorian Architecture in Britain* (Blue Guide), London, 1987

Ott, Thierry, *Palaces: Une histoire de la grand hôtellerie suisse*, Yens/Morges, 1990

Pergamon, *Annals of Tourism Research*, periodical, vol. 18, no. 1, 1991

Pevsner, Nikolaus, *A History of Building Types*, London, 1976

——, *The Buildings of England*, Harmondsworth, various dates

Pininska, Mary and Puchalska, Joanna, *Hotel Bristol* (English text), Warsaw, 1994

Polo, Marco (trans. Teresa Waugh), *The Travels of Marco Polo*, London, 1984

Purvis, Malcolm, *Tall Storeys: the First 100 Years of Palmer & Turner*, Hong Kong, 1985

Rahola, Agustín Gomez, *Palace Hotel* (Spanish text), Madrid, 1987

Richardson, A. E., *The English Inn, Past and Present*, London, 1934

Ritz, Marie Louise, *César Ritz, Host to the World*, London, 1938

Rogers, Michael, *The Spread of Islam*, Oxford, 1976

Rucki, Isabelle, *Das Hotel in den Alpen: The History of Oberengadine Hotel Architecture 1860–1914* (German text), Zürich, 1988

Sà, Luís Andrade de (trans. Marie Macleod), *Hotel Bela Vista*, Macau, 1994

Sévigné, Madame de, *Lettres*, Paris, 1806

Sala, George Augustus, *The Life and Adventures of*, London, 1938

Schmitt, Michael, *Palast Hotels, Architektur und Anspruch eines Bautypus 1870–1920*, Berlin, 1982

Senarchens, Jean de, van Berchen, Nathalie and Marquis, Jean M., *L'Hôtellerie Genevoise*, Geneva, 1993

Sharp, Ilsa, *There is only one Raffles: The Story of a Grand Hotel*, London, 1981

Shaw, Timothy, *The World of Escoffier*, London, 1994

Sparkes, Ivan, *Stagecoaches and Carriages: An Illustrated History of Coaches and Coaching*, Buckinghamshire, 1975

Spencer, Raine and John, *The Spencers on Spas*, London, 1983

Spicer, Chrystopher J., *Duchess: The Story of the Windsor Hotel*, Melbourne, 1993

Stamp, Gavin and Amery, Colin, *Victorian Buildings of London 1837–87*, London, 1980

Steel, Tom, *The Langham, A History*, London, 1990

Steve, Michel, *Hans-Georg Tersling, Architecte de la Côte d'Azur* (French text), Menton, 1990

Tackach, James, *Great American Hotels*, New York, 1991

Taylor, Derek and Bush, David, *The Golden Age of British Hotels*, London, 1974

Taylor, Derek, *Fortune, Fame and Folly: British Hotels and Catering from 1878 to 1978*, London, 1977

Trevelyan, G. M., *English Social History*, London, 1944

Watkin, David and Mellinghoff, T., *German Architects and the Classical Ideal 1740–1840*, London, 1987

Wechsberg, Joseph, *The Lost World of the Great Spas*, New York, 1979

Wharton, Edith, *The House of Mirth*, New York, 1905

——, *The Custom of the Country*, New York, 1913

——, *The Glimpses of the Moon*, New York, 1922

White, Arthur, *Palaces of the People*, London, 1968

Wild, August, *Mixed Grill in Cairo – Experiences of an International Hotelier*, privately printed, 1952

Young, Fay, ed., *Edinburgh, Balmoral Hotel, Souvenir of Opening*, the 1902 'souvenir' with an added chapter, Edinburgh, 1991

As *hotels* and their *architects* form the basis of this book, these two subjects have been indexed under separate sub-headings, hotels being found under the names of the cities or towns where they are, or were, located. For the sake of brevity, the word 'hotel' has been omitted from their titles except where, in a few instances, it forms an integral part of the name. The grouping of hotels on modern lines has largely been ignored in this Index, as little occurred before 1930. More recently, changes of ownership and management have multiplied, and any record soon becomes out-dated. The term 'hotelier' as used here covers a wide field, from director or manager to entrepreneur, usually with the indication of pecuniary interest in the business.

Page numbers in *italics* indicate illustrations and/or their captions.